Author Fern Buzinski has be
speaker for the most of her ad
insight gained through the many years of her life's experiences. In her
third book *As Sure as the Dawn,* she offers us truth, communicated
through a daily thought, prayer and scripture. You will find her words
clear and uncomplicated. As you launch into this deep well of wisdom,
the dawn of each new day will unfold like a nugget of pure gold. Fern
has tapped into heaven's throne room and has come away with the
mind of Christ, relating to where we live right now in today's world.
This daily devotional will take you on a year's journey like no other.
Be ready to let hope arise. The transformation you have been praying
for will surprise you with each new day.

Fern counseled and facilitated healing Bible studies for over 20 years
at her local Pregnancy Resource center. Her compassion and love for
hurting women is evident in all she undertakes. She is honored as a
spiritual mother to many precious women and hopes to leave a legacy
of spiritual wisdom and pure devotion for the Lord Jesus Christ.

Other books by Fern Buzinski:

Portraits; Unveiled Freedom, a Bible study for healing after abortion.
Refuge, My Safe Place, a grief recovery Bible study.

Books available at Pregnancy and Parenting Center, Canton Ohio
330-455-7500, or on Amazon.com

Fern also recommends:

Unbound: Heal, Reclaim, Unleash
by Stefanie Libertore

Waiting Well, Caring for Your Heart While You Wait
by Lonette M. Baity

Living Prime in Every Season: Emerging Hope Through Shattered Dreams
by Laura Strabley

Cathy Griffith, editing.

Shawn Wood, Studio 7 Photography.

As Sure as the Dawn

A Women's Devotional

Fern Buzinski

[signature: fern buzinski]

WESTBOW
PRESS®
A DIVISION OF THOMAS NELSON
& ZONDERVAN

WestBow Press books may be ordered through booksellers or by contacting:

WestBow Press
A Division of Thomas Nelson & Zondervan
1663 Liberty Drive
Bloomington, IN 47403
www.westbowpress.com
844-714-3454

ISBN: 978-1-6642-7302-3 (sc)
ISBN: 978-1-6642-7303-0 (hc)
ISBN: 978-1-6642-7301-6 (e)

Library of Congress Control Number: 2022913190

Print information available on the last page.

WestBow Press rev. date: 7/29/2022

As Sure as the Dawn

Beginning the day with Jesus.
Discovering God through devotion, prayer and scripture.

A Woman's Devotional
by
Fern Buzinski

Let us know; let us press on to know the Lord; His
going out is sure as the dawn; He will come to us as
showers, as the spring rains that water the earth
(Hosea 6:3; ESV)

As Sure as the Dawn

God remains as faithful as the sunrise every morning;
His love is as sure as the dawn.

If ever we need quality quiet time in prayer and the study of God's Word, it is in our generation. With the world being turned upside down and inside out, we need a place where we can anchor our soul; a place of stability, peace and hope. Jesus is all of that and so much more. In Isaiah 33:6, speaking of the promised Messiah, Isaiah says, *"He will be a sure foundation for your times, a rich store of salvation and wisdom and knowledge; the fear of the Lord is the key to this treasure."* As we live in this time of shaking, peril and testing, we also live in the earnest expectation of Jesus' return. We can face each new day with hope and courage knowing that the Lord has provided all we need to live godly lives in an ungodly world.

Who am I and what has inspired me to write a devotional that daily puts the spotlight on Jesus and his eternal Word? I am not a theologian. I am an expert on nothing. I am a sinner saved by his amazing grace. But this I know, the God who saved me has called me to share some valuable truths that I have mostly learned the hard way. This devotional has been simmering on my heart for many years. I have by no means arrived spiritually, but my desire to see women set free and growing in the love and knowledge of Jesus Christ burns in me and hopefully through me.

My prayer is that each day the Lord will speak to your heart in very personal ways. My hope is that you will make each prayer your own as you open your heart to the One who holds your life in his hand.

It is with great love and respect I dedicate this book to my friend Patty Davis. If not for her persistent diligence and sweet encouragement this book would not exist.

To God be the glory for all He has done

January 1

Today's Thought

In all of history, there has never been a day when the sun did not rise in the east. There may have been mornings when we could not see the sun because of cloud covering, but we can be sure the sun was there. God's Word likens his faithfulness to the rising of the sun. In Hosea 6, Israel had been unfaithful to God. Hosea the prophet entreats the people to return to the Lord. If they return, God will heal them, revive them, restore them, and bind up their wounds. Hosea says if the people will press on to know the Lord, he will respond to them, as surely as the sun rises, as sure as the dawn. I don't know what your need is as you begin this yearlong devotional, but God does. Maybe you need healing or revival or restoration. Perhaps you have been neglectful of your time with the Lord, or you simply desire to go deeper. Whatever your need, I trust that God will meet you every day as you press on to know him. He will respond to you in his faithfulness, as surely as the sun rises.

Today's Prayer

Father God, we cannot even begin to fathom how great your faithfulness is. You have betrothed us to yourself in love forever. There is nowhere we can go that you will not find us. There is no pit too low where you cannot reach us. How you long for us to know you. How you yearn for us to come to you in anticipation that you will meet us in our searching. As you lead us through this year, I pray you speak tenderly to us and restore us. I pray you bring healing, revival, direction, guidance, and hope. Fill our hearts with the knowledge of you. We thank you now for all the ways you will respond to us. In the name of our faithful God. Amen.

Today's Scriptures

Psalm 89:1–2; Lamentations 3:22–25; Hosea 2:19–20; Hosea 6:3

January 2

Today's Thought

As we launch into a new year, Philippians 3 holds a wealth of wisdom for us. Let's camp on it today as Paul gives us a biblical perspective on how to move forward. In verse 12 he confesses that he is not perfect, but presses on to obtain the goal. He forgets what was behind and strains toward what lies ahead. What does that mean to us? God does not intend for us to strive for perfection. He does want spiritual progress to be evident in our lives. So, ultimately, it's not about perfection; it's about making progress. If we are standing still, we will begin to move backward. God requires maturity in us, and that's the work of the Holy Spirit as we yield to him and God's Word. Paul is giving us the picture of an athlete approaching the finish line. As he sees the goal, he pushes and strains to reach it. In order to reach his goal, he must forget the mistakes and those things in the past that have hindered him. His focus must be on the road ahead, and his goal is to gain the prize. As together we face a brand new year and new beginnings, as we let go of the past and move with confidence and trust into the future, may we run a race that is pleasing to the Lord.

Today's Prayer

Father God, you are our finish line, Jesus is our race, and the Holy Spirit is our coach and trainer. As we face a new year, we have another opportunity to grow up into Christ. We can strain into the maturity you desire; we can stay right where we are, or we can move ahead to all you have waiting for us. I pray we choose the highest goal and the worthiest race. I pray our spirits reach out toward that finish line of faith. In the name of our forerunner, Jesus. Amen.

Today's Scriptures

1 Corinthians 9:24–27; Galatians 5:7–8; Philippians 3:12–14; Hebrews 12:1

January 3

Today's Thought

The year 2020 ushered in a new way of life. COVID-19 kept us locked down, shut in, and living behind masks. I like to make comparisons and explore analogies. How many of us were already wearing masks before the pandemic hit? For whatever reason, all of us at one time or another, put on those invisible masks. Some of us hide our insecurities behind a facade of bravado. We don't want others to see how fearful we are of being rejected or left behind. Other masks hide our hurt and the emotional pain of abuse and loss. So many ways we cover up our true selves and our humanity. We hold our breath, hoping not to be found out. Our vision and perception are fogged as we labor to keep the mask in place. How does that happen? Expectations are thrust upon us by a myriad of well-meaning people. When we cannot live up to their demands, or our own, we put on our masks and pretend to be something we are not. We were not born wearing masks; it is a learned behavior. Just as we learn to wear masks, God can help us to remove them. As we allow him to heal those deep places in our souls, the masks begin to slip, and sooner or later they can be removed completely as we accept our true selves and allow them to shine through.

Today's Prayer

Father God, you made each of us according to your unique design. The bruises of life mar the image in which we were created. Lord, we need restored hearts and minds. I pray that you expose the masks we have been wearing and, by your grace, help us to let them go and permit our true selves to shine through. We are your image bearers. I pray we walk that out with honor in our lives. In Jesus' name. Amen.

Today's Scriptures

Genesis 1:27; Genesis 3:8–10; Colossians 3:9–10; 1 Thessalonians 5:23–24

Today's Thought

Oh my, how we needed to be rescued! We humans scuttled around on planet earth searching and seeking the truth that would lead to peace and serenity. We needed a way to reach God, to find forgiveness and salvation. We tried it all—every book, every religion, every good idea presented to us. Then something amazing happened. God raised up godly men who were able to hear his voice and record every word that proceeded from his mouth. God knew all along that we could never find truth apart from him. In his kindness and mercy, he sent us the Word made flesh, his own Son. In God's Word, we find a blueprint for living. We find him and we find the path of righteousness he has ordained for us. A divine book that journeyed through time and space. A love so great he could not hold anything back from us. Think of the miracle of it! What we do with this miracle book is up to each of us.

Today's Prayer

Father God, today and every day we say amen to your truth. I pray that we live by every word that proceeds from your mouth. I pray that we embrace your Word as our daily nourishment that feeds our spirits and our faith. Cause us to allow your Word to dwell in us richly that we may know your good, acceptable, and perfect will. We thank you, Father, for revealing to us your timeless truth, and I pray the spiritual soil of our hearts be good ground that soaks up your Word like rain. You took utmost care in every word, every passage, and every story so that we might have all we need to live a life that pleases you. Your Word is the answer to our every need. In Jesus, the Word made flesh, we pray. Amen.

Today's Scriptures

Matthew 4:4, Luke 8:5–8; John 1:14; Colossians 3:16

January 5

Today's Thought

Once upon a time, a frog fell into a deep hole. His frog friends were sitting around the rim, peering down at him and shouting discouraging words. The frog began to jump as high as he could, even as the other frogs told him to give up. They told the poor frog to stop trying; it's no use; he would never get out. The frog in the hole jumped higher each time they screamed. Finally, the frog used all his might and jumped high enough to reach the top and hop out. Amazed, his friends asked him why he kept trying, why didn't he give up. The frog explained, *"Each time you yelled down to me, I thought you were cheering me on. I was so encouraged; I kept trying harder and harder until I succeeded."* We all need encouragers who will help us stay in the game, even when all the odds seem to be against us.

Today's Prayer

Father God, when your servant Job lost everything, he lifted his hands toward heaven and declared by faith, *"The Lord gave and the Lord has taken away; may the name of the Lord be praised."* The Bible goes on, *"In all this Job did not sin by charging God with wrongdoing"* (Job 1:21– 22). As we face these challenging times, help us follow Job's example by giving honor to you and trusting that you do all things well. God, I pray today that you give us a profound understanding of these times in which we live, and show us, Father, how you would have us respond in all situations. May we spread hope and not fear; may we encourage and not discourage others who struggle. God, I pray we build each other up and not tear each other down. I pray we speak words of truth and life, that we be shining lights in these uncertain times. In Jesus' name, our Great Encourager. Amen.

Today's Scriptures

1 Chronicles 12:32; Job 1:20–22; Philippians 2:14–16; Hebrews 10:23–25

Today's Thought

I love chocolate. I can't help but think of those hollow, empty chocolate bunnies I sometimes got in my basket on Easter morning. Did you ever get one? It looks so solid and delicious on the outside, but when bitten into, it crumbles into tiny bits of cheap chocolate. Sometimes the world can leave us feeling like that, hollow and empty. When we set our sights on the vain things of the world, hoping they can bring fulfillment and satisfaction we can be deeply disappointed. Paul gives us a rock-solid word in 1 Timothy 6:6 as he points us to that which will leave us feeling full and satisfied. *"But godliness with contentment is great gain."* For me, this verse is the trustworthy anchor I need in navigating through a world that promises so much and delivers so little. When we learn true contentment, our lives become filled with every good and perfect gift from above.

Today's Prayer

Father God, we thank you for a new day, a fresh start, a clean slate. We are ready to hear from you and we want to respond to your Word. Lord Jesus, as we launch into this day, I pray you take the truth of 1 Timothy 6:6 deeper into our hearts. Lord, you alone can bring us the satisfaction our souls long for. This world cannot provide the fulfillment that you alone can give. Help us to fully know that you are our contentment, you are our portion, and our reward in this world. Help us live godly lives that promise us blessed contentment. May we seek after you and pursue what pleases you. In the name of the One who satisfies. Amen.

Today's Scriptures

Psalm 73:25–26; Ecclesiastes 2:1–11; 1 Timothy 6:6–8; 1 John 2:15–17

Today's Thought

I once sat with a friend who was reading a portion of a magazine article to me. The writer was offering some advice on how to gain the attention of others. When she finished, I looked up and said, *"What did you say?"* There are times in life when we feel no one hear us. Our prayers seem to bounce off the heavens and return to us void. As Jesus was praying, he said, *"So they took away the stone. Then Jesus looked up and said, 'Father, I thank you that you have heard me.'"* John 11:41. What a beautiful proclamation of faith. An account in Genesis assures us that God sees us. Hagar was alone and scared in the desert and God showed up to give her specific comfort and direction. In her aloneness she declared, *"You are the God who sees me ..."* (Genesis 16:13). Since God never changes, we can be certain that he always sees us and always hears us. We never go unnoticed by God.

Today's Prayer

Almighty God, we praise you today because you are a God who is near to us. You are intimate. You are personal. Father you never distance yourself from us; but as we draw near to you, you draw near to us. You are not withdrawn and aloof, you are as close as our next heartbeat. Lord in these uncertain times we can feel alone and isolated from those we love, but we can never be separated from your love. God, I pray that we choose intimacy with you today. I pray we choose patience and grace toward others. May we allow you access to every part of our lives. We are grateful that we do not have to strive for your attention. Your loving eyes are always on us and your ears are always attentive to our voices. In the name of the God who sees. Amen.

Today's Scriptures

Genesis 16:13; Psalm 35:15; Psalm 73:28; John 11:41–42

January 8

Today's Thought

During the days of the COVID-19 pandemic, we saw things in our community we never thought we'd see. At my local grocery store I saw cashiers behind plastic shields meant to be protection from people who could possibly pass on the virus. We wore masks and gloves when we went out. It was a strange time of questions, fears, daily stats, and a lot of uncertainty. Even as we tried to be careful, sadly, some folks still contracted the virus. One attribute that God ascribes to himself is that of a shield. We are not immune to sickness and disasters. As long as we live in this world there will be illness, trouble and tragedy. Sometimes we will be touched by adversity, but take heart, dear child of God, do not fear. In the midst of it all, he is with us, and he will be a shield round about us. In sickness and in health, we are never left alone.

Today's Prayer

Father God, you surround us as a shield. We rejoice today that you have not given us a spirit of fear. You have given us reasonable minds. The Bible tells us that you prepare a table of love and blessing in the midst of trouble. Lord Jesus, when the storms come, in you we are always safe. God, I pray that we will not fall prey to the lies and fear surrounding us, but that we wholly lean on the One who loves us and on the truth in your Word. We are not in the camp of fearful hearts. We are of the fellowship of faith; we are in Christ and our lives are hidden in him. We are the children of eternal hope, both in this life and the one to come. What have we to fear, what have we to dread? O death, where is your sting? O grave, where is your victory? In the name of Christ, our Sun and Shield. Amen.

Today's Scriptures

Psalm 23:4–5; Psalm 28:7; Colossians 3:3; Revelation 12:11

January 9

Today's Thought

I once heard an old Chinese proverb that painted a picture of the whole world taking their problems and burdens, putting them in a sack and laying them all together in a huge pile. Each person could go to the pile and select any sack other than his own, and claim it as his. By and by, as each person examined the sacks of others, each decided to go away with his own. What a godly truth we see here. Our burdens and sorrows are the ones God entrusted to us. He alone knows us and he never gives us more than we are able to bear. Even more so, he promises to daily carry those sorrows and burdens with us and for us. Every challenge in life is customed-designed by the One who knows us completely. His intentions toward us are always good.

Today's Prayer

Lord God, you assure us in your Word that you are our Burden-Bearer. How comforting to know that we do not bear the weight of life on our own. We do not carry the concern of our lost loved ones alone. We do not struggle with sin on our own. We do not suffer through sickness and disease alone. We do not carry grief on our own. We do nothing apart from you. It pleases you to be our Burden-Bearer. I pray it pleases us to allow you to take up those burdens and concerns that we have tried to carry on our own. Father, I pray that we cease from attempting to carry life on our own shoulders. I pray for the grace to lay down the weight of doing it ourselves. Help us to remember that you are big enough and strong enough to carry not only our lives, but you easily carry the weight of the whole world. In the name of God, our Burden-Bearer. Amen.

Today's Scriptures

Psalm 55:22; Psalm 68:19; Matthew 11:28–30; 1 Corinthians 10:13

January 10

Today's Thought

There have been many debates over when the rapture of the church will take place. As Christians, we ought not to allow these differing opinions to divide us. Scripture assures us that he will come in the clouds, the same way he left earth after his resurrection (Acts 1:11). Perhaps some of us may yet be alive when the rapture occurs. Nonetheless, whether we are taken up alive or we are among the dead who rise first, we need to give earnest thought as to how we fill our time till Jesus comes. We are to *occupy* as we await that glorious day. The essence of *"occupy"* is from a Greek word that means, *busy oneself, conduct business*. While we wait for his return, we are to be about kingdom business. For each of us this will look different; but the truth of filling our time well is indeed for each of us who believe. We ought to give earnest thought as to how the Lord would have us live out our days on earth.

Today's Prayer

God of Glory, with longing hearts we await Jesus' return. He will descend from heaven with a shout. In a moment, in the twinkling of an eye the trumpet will sound, and we will be raised imperishable. One day these earthly bodies will put on the imperishable and the immortal. Death will be swallowed up in victory. Father, in the light of these truths I pray we always stand immovable, strong in faith, steadfast, always abounding in the work of the Lord. Father, may we occupy till our Redeemer returns for us. We know that our labor is not in vain; we will be rewarded. In the name of our soon and coming King Jesus. Amen.

Today's Scriptures

Acts 1:9–11; 1 Corinthians 15:51–58; 1 Thessalonians 4:16–18; Hebrews 6:10

Today's Thought

During the COVID-19 pandemic we were advised to "shelter-in-place." We all knew what that meant, whether we liked it or not. It was for the good of all that we listened. Often, I am impatient and fail to shelter in place with God. When I feel the absence of God's leading, I know I have not waited on him. When life gets topsy-turvy for me, it could be because I have run ahead of him. When every day seems to be the same mundane experience, I know I need to continue in the waiting. God is an encourager and I am learning to be thankful for quiet days, for seemingly uneventful days. These are the times when he wants me to himself, when he wants me to altogether enjoy his company. It is during these times that I remember the fruit that came forth in past seasons of waiting. No day is just an ordinary day. Some days are simply quieter days; these are days to be treasured. These are the seasons when we learn to trust him more.

Today's Prayer

Our God who waits with us, we remember today that waiting is never wasted. Father, even when we do not see your hand at work, you are working. Even when we do not hear your voice, you are speaking. Even when we do not sense your guidance, you are leading. Even when we do not feel your love, it never fails. When we do not sense your presence, you are with us always. Lord Jesus, I pray today that we trust that you are ever present in our existing circumstances and you are working on our behalf to bring about your perfect will. Lord, be glorified in our waiting. You are the one who remains with us in the waiting. In Christ, our Shelter. Amen.

Today's Scriptures

Psalm 27:14; Proverbs 3:5–6; Matthew 11:28–30; John 15:4–5

Today's Thought

Humanity has always struggled in understanding the doctrine of the Holy Trinity. In Deuteronomy 6:4, Moses declares, *"Hear O Israel: The Lord our God, the Lord is One."* At the same time, throughout scripture we see God as three distinct persons: Father, Son and Holy Spirit. In a sense, our finite brains will never truly grasp the richness and comprehensiveness of a God who is One and at the same time three. However, there is an illustration that helps me grasp the reality of the Trinity, and it is as simple as water. Water's makeup is H_2O. If I hold a glass of water, it is H_2O. If I freeze that glass of water, it is still H_2O. If I boil that same water, the escaping steam is H_2O. The same compound in three different forms: liquid; ice; and steam. This simple illustration is indeed finite. The truth is, God never changes. He is always, at all times, all three persons of the Godhead. What a miracle! What a mystery!

Today's Prayer

Father, Son and Holy Spirit, Lord you are One just as you have declared. The Godhead works together harmoniously with one heart and one mind. At the same time, you knew we would need you in three persons, a Father who rules heaven, a Savior who came to seek and save the lost, and a Holy Spirit to comfort, counsel and dwell within us as we journey toward home. Each person of the Trinity has his role in God's redemptive plan. May we trust you, God, as our loving Father. I pray we embrace Jesus as the One who became one of us. I ask that we appreciate the role of the Holy Spirit in our lives; our Comforter and Divine Helper as we walk out our days on earth. In the name of Father, Son and Holy Spirit. Amen.

Today's Scriptures

Deuteronomy 6:4; Luke 1:35; 2 Corinthians 13:14; Colossians 2:9

January 13

Today's Thought

Some of us spend our whole lives looking for love in all the wrong places. I played that losing game for 35 years. In each relationship I thought for sure that he was the "one." Somewhere down the road, the love offered me proved to be flawed and unfulfilling. Soon I realized that the love I offered others was faulty as well. After much disappointment and thought I concluded that in this life, in our humanity, none of us are capable of perfectly loving another and yet that is exactly what we all long for ... perfect love. God in his wisdom designed us to desire perfect love, then he fashioned our hearts in such a way that only his absolute and complete love would fulfill that longing. Armed with this truth, I am able to lay down all the hopes of being loved flawlessly by another. Even the best human love cannot begin to compare with the love God has for me. Dear one, we are the object of his highest love and affection.

Today's Prayer

Father of perfect love, in your wisdom you created us for love. We are so grateful for those you have given us, those who love us as best they can. We know that they will never fulfill every need we have, but you will. Jesus, your desire for us is so great; you died to win our love. I pray we are able, by the Holy Spirit, to understand more fully a love so deep and wide and indescribable ... the love of God. I pray our souls be bathed in this great love. I pray that we more fully know the depths and heights and width and breath of the love that passes all understanding. Your love created us and your love sustains us. We affirm today that we are loved beyond measure. In the name of the One who loves us perfectly. Amen.

Today's Scriptures

Hosea 2:19–20; Ephesians 3:14–19; 1 John 3:1; 1 John 4:9–10

Today's Thought

When Jesus allowed himself to be nailed to the cross, He had forgiveness on his mind. We see that by the words He spoke, *"Father, forgive them, for they do not know what they are doing"* (Luke 23:34). Stephen followed Jesus' example. As he was being stoned to death, he fell to his knees and cried out, *"Lord, do not hold this sin against them"* (Acts 7:60). With these extraordinary models in mind, it is possible for us to forgive even the most horrendous offense. When we refuse to forgive another for unkind words, physical and emotional damage, betrayal and any other form of abuse, we in effect nail ourselves to that experience. Another consequence of unforgiveness is the power it gives the offender over us. If God has forgiven us our many transgressions, so we ought to be forgiving in return. The price of unforgiveness is far too high a price for any of us to pay. The benefits of forgiveness are priceless.

Today's Prayer

Father God, one of our greatest needs is forgiveness. Jesus met that need on the cross. When we carefully examine your Word, it is clear to us that forgiveness is of great importance. You count it so crucial that you took the initiative and first offered it to us. We receive that forgiveness with boundless joy. Now I pray that we offer it to those who have hurt us. Lord, show us any unforgiveness we may be harboring in our hearts. As you do so, you will also extend the grace we need to release the offender. Help us to understand that being a forgiving person is one of the most important virtues we can pursue as Christians. In the name of the great Forgiver. Amen.

Today's Scriptures

Matthew 6:14–15; Luke 23:34; Acts 7:59–60; Colossians 3:13

Today's Thought

How aware are we of the pain of others? They sit in church with us. They go to school with us. They are our neighbors and even family members. Can we be so absorbed by our own miseries that we miss the crying hearts all around us? Without any doubt the Lord cares deeply about our personal sorrows and heartache, but what would he want us to do while we wait for our own consolation? He calls us to reach out to those around us, which will prove to be significant in our own recovery. We are created for relationship. Involving ourselves in the pain of others makes for the richest of connection. Jesus modeled this perfectly when he became one of us. Jesus is our Great High Priest who is touched by all that touches us.

Today's Prayer

Father of all comfort, you conceived such a perfect plan for the comfort of humanity. You sent Jesus so that we could know how much you care about our lives and the pain that we often experience. He became one of us and suffered even more than we can imagine. This truth gives us the hope and assurance we need when we suffer. Jesus understands rejection, because he was rejected. He understands loss and grief because he lost so much. He felt excruciating pain and in shame he hung naked on the cross. Jesus alone is qualified to be our Great High Priest who stands before God on our behalf. I pray, Lord, that we would submit to your Word that persuades us to extend to the hurting that same comfort we have received from you. You are the God of *all* comfort who is able to comfort us in *all* our distress. In the name of the God of *all* Comfort. Amen.

Today's Scriptures

Isaiah 53:3; John 1:10–1; 2 Corinthians 1:3–4; Hebrews 4:14–16

Today's Thought

We can be certain that difficult and trying times will come. How we respond in these unexpected times is of utmost importance. God is never taken by surprise as we sometimes are. From his vantage point he sees past, present and future all at once. He knows the exact circumstances that will befall us, and as always, he has a plan. What is it God wants to accomplish in us? I can't answer for you, but I am certain that he wants my responses to line up with his Word and his character. In Psalm 131 the writer compares a calm soul to a weaned child in his mother's arms. What a beautiful picture of the child of God resting in his love. Then he goes on to talk about hope. *"Israel, put your hope in the Lord, both now and forevermore"* (Psalm 131:3). We are loved by a God who cares enough to test and stretch us through the circumstances that come our way. Jesus is our living hope. Let us ever hope in his goodness.

Today's Prayer

Lord God, we are grateful beyond measure that when we cry out to you, we are heard. God, you have been our Helper in all generations, and you never change. Your steadfast love is sweeter than any other love we could know. Your love pulls us through every crisis. Father, I ask today that by Your Spirit we are calmed and made still, like a little child in his mother's arms. When chaos swirls around us, we will not be swept away; your peace will reign in our hearts. We rest today in the shadow of your wings; we sing for joy because we know our God, and we know we are loved. We will be still in the peace of your presence. In the name of Jesus, our Prince of Peace. Amen.

Today's Scripture

Psalm 63:3–8; Psalm 89:1–2; Psalm 131; Hebrews 13:6 =

Today's Thought

Where did God come from? If you are a parent or Sunday School teacher you have probably been asked this thought-worthy question. It makes my brain hurt when I try to think about a God who had no beginning and will have no end; a God who always existed. How do we answer such a weighty question? Truly, we cannot give an adequate answer because God is beyond. He is beyond anything and everything our finite brains can think or imagine. And though he is beyond our understanding, God's Word reveals to us all we need to know about him. He has equipped us with enough truth so that we can know how he wants us to live now. He has revealed his plan of salvation in such a simple and clear way that even a child can understand.

Today's Prayer

Infinite Father, what an awesome truth that you had no beginning. You always were, and you will always be. This is so beyond our comprehension as we think within our time-bound dimension. We can, however, believe that just as you have no end, neither will we. We are children of the eternal Father. Father, today I pray that we learn to live in the life beyond ... the eternal ... even as we finish out our days on earth. I pray we learn to rise above our circumstances, move beyond our failures, pray through our weaknesses and live even beyond our finite selves. Lord, may we push through our self-imposed limitations and move into the living and infinite power of the beyond, in the power and presence of Christ. May we always come to you in the simplicity and humility of little children. In the name of the One who was, who is and is to come. Amen.

Today's Scriptures

Psalm 90:1–2; John 3:16; 2 Peter 1:3; Revelation 1:8

Today's Thought

In the Genesis 1 account God created the heavens and the earth. Darkness covered the face of the earth. Then a remarkable thing happened. The Spirit of God moved upon the face of the earth and God spoke for the first recorded time. *"And God said, 'Let there be light,' and there was light. God saw that the light was good, and he separated the light from the darkness"* (Genesis 1:3–4). Isn't this a beautiful picture of what God does spiritually in every salvation experience? Light breaks forth into our hearts; we believe, and suddenly we see the truth. The darkness is scattered. When I do laundry, I separate my darks from my lights. I do this because if I mix them the darks will taint the lights. So it is in our lives. We must remain in the light and not allow any darkness to invade our minds and hearts and so pollute the light that is in us.

Today's Prayer

Father of light and truth, we see in your Word that you are Light and in you there is no darkness at all. What a reassuring truth! You can never lie or do evil. You are light and you produce light in us through Christ. Lord, as we walk in the light, I pray you light our paths so we can see clearly in this world. Protect us from those who love the darkness of evil. The wicked hate the light because it exposes their sin. Jesus, your light sets us free. Father, by your Spirit I pray you shine the light of truth on any area of darkness in us. Expose any lies we believe and uncover any deception that ensnares us. Help us today to walk in the pure light of truth. We know that one glorious day the darkness will be abolished forever as we abide with you in heaven. In Jesus, the One who lights our paths. Amen.

Today's Scriptures

Genesis 1:1–5; John 3:19–21; Ephesians 5:8–14; 1 John 1:5–7

Today's Thought

In ancient Jewish culture, when a man and woman were engaged, the future husband spent the engagement period preparing a home for his bride. Many times that home was an extension of his father's house or even a room inside the father's house. That's the picture Jesus painted for us in John 14:2. He assured them, *"In my Father's house are many rooms; if it were not so, I would have told you, I am going there to prepare a place for you."* As the bride waited for the day that her groom would come for her, she was also preparing. She made ready a bride's trousseau which included an array of beautiful garments she would wear for her beloved. In scripture, garments represent attitude, character and personal integrity. As a bride who waits for her groom, we ought to be putting on the garments of a pure bride, a wardrobe that pleases the One who loves us with an everlasting love.

Today's Prayer

Father God, you choose us to be your Son's beloved bride. We know that Jesus is preparing a place for us. We live in this world awaiting his imminent return. We have been lifted above these trying times and we are seated with Christ in heavenly places. You carry us on the wings of security and love. Lord as you continue to make ready our forever home, I pray that we live in this world as the bride of Christ, as one who anticipates his soon return. May we be found faithful. Father, give us a renewed determination to cleave to Jesus. Help us to overcome our doubts, to forget our past, to forsake our sin and to be all that a beautiful bride is called to be. In the name of our faithful and soon coming Bridegroom. Amen.

Today's Scriptures

Isaiah 61:10; Jeremiah 31:3; John 14:1–3; Revelation 3:4–6

Today's Thought

In John 11 we have an account of a family's tragedy. Two sisters and a brother live in small town outside Jerusalem. The brother died, and the sisters were inconsolable. When Jesus showed up, they spoke their mind. Both sisters accused Jesus, *"If you had been here my brother would not have died"* (John 11:21, 32). We are not always wise in our words when we are hurting. The important thing is what Jesus said to them, *"I am the resurrection and the life. He who believes in me will live, even though he dies"* (John 11:25). Jesus did not come to merely point us to the resurrection or hold a seminar on the value of resurrection. We must not miss this. He *is* the resurrection and the life. Immerse yourself in that truth. He is resurrection personified, resurrection appearing in the flesh. He then went on to demonstrate that by raising Lazarus from the dead. Jesus did not do funerals; he raised the dead!

Today' Prayer

Jesus, you are the Resurrection and eternal life. What a blessing to realize we will not live with sin forever. Now we are clean through the blood of Jesus and the washing of your Word. One glorious day we will be perfect and holy as you are perfect and holy. Now we struggle; then, we cease from struggling. One of the greatest joys of heaven will be final freedom from our sinful hearts. Lord, I pray that we live in the light of resurrection; raised incorruptible. Lord, I pray that we live now as ones who have a sinless forever home with the sinless One. In the name of Jesus, our Resurrection and our Life. Amen.

Today's Scriptures

John 11:17–26; 1 Corinthians 15:42–44; 1 Peter 1:3–4; Revelation 1:4–5

Today's Thought

If you were like me, a child growing up in a relatively normal home, you went to bed without any concerns about provision for the next day. We woke up to food in the fridge, clothes in the closet, shoes ready to be worn, as well as so many other essentials and non-essentials. Why was that? For me it was because my parents who loved me and made provision for all those things even before I was born. As each day came and went, they continued to provide for my daily needs and my future needs as well. They did all the work, all the planning; I simply trusted, even before I knew what trusting meant. If our human parents were so attentive in fulfilling our needs, how much more will our divine Parent fulfill our needs. Perhaps we need to return to that same childlike trust when we lay our heads on our pillows at night. Let's begin to make it a habit to thank God in advance for all he has prepared for us in advance.

Today's Prayer

Father, you call us your beloved children. You knew us before we were conceived; before our parents knew us. You carved out a unique plan for each of our lives. Lord, we trust your plan because we believe in your steadfast love and faithfulness. We rest in this truth thus allowing us to enjoy every moment, free of fear and worry over our future. We purpose to keep our eyes on you and on heaven. For the present you give us everything we need. You are everything we need for this present day and every future day. Lord, we desire to return to the trust we knew as children. Thank you in advance for every future provision. In the name of our faithful Provider. Amen.

Today's Scriptures

Psalm 139:14–16; Jeremiah 29:11; Matthew 6:25–34; Matthew 7:9–11

Today's Thought

Have you ever experienced a natural disaster? Tornados? Hurricanes? Floods? They are all a frightening reality of the times we live in. We can be certain that these catastrophes will continue. There is something else we can be absolutely sure of. Our God is not moved or shaken by the events taking place on planet earth. God is greater than any calamity that can come our way. He is unmovable and unshakable. At the same time, he cares deeply about everything that touches us. He uses these adversities to test us. Will we trust him? Will we pray for those affected by tragedy? Will we take action to help victims of disasters? Will we honor God in the midst of events we do not understand? We should not fear as God shakes the world, because he has seated us in heavenly places with Christ. Our future is secure. Though the earth be moved, God will not change.

Today's Prayer

Great and awesome God, you never change; this is our blessed assurance. Even though the earth be removed and the mountains quake, you remain unmoved and unshakeable. When all around me is ever changing, I can trust that my life is held securely in your hands. You, O Lord, are bigger than life; you exist outside of time and history, and you are not touched by uncertainty. You remain constant; my rock and my sure foundation. Lord, I stand on that truth today and every day. This world constantly evolves and changes, but I remain safe in Christ. My world will not be rocked as this world passes away. I pray we hold firm and steadfast while you shake the heavens and the earth accomplishing your eternal purposes. In Jesus' name, the same yesterday, today and forever. Amen.

Today's Scriptures

Psalm 46:1–3; Psalm 102:25–27; Hebrews 12:26–29; Hebrews 13:8

January 23

Today's Thought

I need a Shepherd. You need a Shepherd too. Certain verses in scripture liken us to sheep. My understanding of sheep is not a flattering one. Sheep can be stubborn, lazy, and in need of constant attention and care. Please don't be offended, but let's be real. At times we can exhibit any one of those sheep-like traits. If the shepherd is not watching the sheep 24/7, they manage to get themselves into the worst of predicaments. If sheep have a good shepherd, they are blessed sheep indeed. We are assured by the gospels that we have a Good Shepherd who cares for us just as he cares for his own life ... so much so that he laid down his life for his sheep (John 10:11). That's us! Call me a sheep any day. With Jesus my Good Shepherd leading me I will follow him anywhere; I will always be safe with him.

Today's Prayer

Jesus, you are the Shepherd of our souls. We want for no good thing. You guide our steps in righteous paths. You uphold your reputation as the Good Shepherd with the tender care you show us. From your vantage point you know when we are in trouble and you rush to our sides to help. So often we go astray, but your goodness and mercy chase after us and your love always brings us back. When we are weary you revive us with the living water of your Holy Spirit. You feed us with your Word and our souls are nourished. When the world seems to be closing in around us, you are the glory and lifter of our heads. God, I pray that we learn to listen to our Shepherd. I pray we are sensitive to his discipline and correction. All the Shepherd does is for our good and his glory. In the name of Jesus, our Good Shepherd. Amen.

Today's Scripture

Psalm 23; John 4:14; John 10:11–15; Hebrews 12:6–11

Today's Thought

I was always the smallest in the group when I was a child. I remember childhood games when teams were selected. I was almost always the last chosen. Sometimes I was not chosen at all and had to sit on the sidelines. I was the littlest one and had no athletic ability. That reality did not ease the rejection and hurt I felt. The mentality of not being enough pursued me into adulthood and even into my Christian faith; always afraid I would be last with God. It took diligent scripture searching and understanding to come out of those lies. Nowhere in scripture does God show favoritism. Yes, there are certain people that God selects for a specific assignment at a specific time, but that does not constitute favoritism. Because we are all unique, God will show his love to each of us in different ways.

Today's Prayer

Father God, in you there is no partiality or favoritism. Sometimes we can feel that others are extra special and favored by you. Lord, help us to see that this is sinful thinking. You tell us clearly in your Word that we are all equally loved and cherished by you. Each one of us is your favorite chosen child. In your sovereignty you alone are able to possess that level of equality. Lord, I pray we never feel unloved by you, rejected by you, or feel left on the sidelines. I pray we are always able to rejoice with others as you bless them, heal them and grant them favor. We know that you do the same for us. You are a just and loving Father who knows what we need and when we need it. May each of us today acknowledge that we are your favored child; because we all have that honor. In the name of the God who shows no partiality. Amen.

Today's Scriptures

Psalm 5:12; Acts 10:34–35; Romans 2:11; James 2:1

January 25

Today's Thought

If you are human, you struggle. I struggle, a lot. Just when I think I have conquered a bad habit, another one hits me. Always a new set of challenges. When I feel as if I will never move past that thing that keeps tripping me up, I go down memory lane with the Lord and he shows me all that I have overcome. He shows me all the sinful habits that no longer have control over me. It is then that I realize that I prayed over those sinful behaviors, sometimes for a very long time. But by and by, I overcame. That really gives me hope when I come up against another defect that has been exposed. I can be sure that as I pray about it and give it to the Lord; he will help me to overcome once again. I don't despair because I know this will be a lifelong process. My God who helped me before will help me again.

Today's Prayer

Holy Father, as we come before you today, we want to thank you for all you have brought us through. We are not what we use to be, nor are we yet all we will be. As you work in our lives, perfecting holiness in us, we determine not to be discouraged. Why? Because we will always be a work in progress. We will always have challenges in righteousness, but at the same time, you already see us as righteous in Christ Jesus. You declare us to be no longer slaves to sin. We cling to that truth as we hold up to you the sins and failures with which we struggle. We know with certainty that as long as we struggle, we are in a good place. Lord, help us to never give up on the battle for holiness. You enter the struggle with us and assure us victory. I pray that we see ourselves more and more as overcomers. In Jesus, who has made us more than conquerors. Amen.

Today's Scriptures

Psalm 139:23–24; Romans 6:17–18; Romans 8:36–37; 1 John 5:3–5

January 26

Today's Thought

Did you have a toy box as a child? The wonderful thing about a toy box is that it conformed to your wishes. You could fill it anyway you liked. Your toy box was your domain and you were the head honcho. I had a toy box as a child, but I also had one as an adult. Let me explain. One day the Lord exposed my adult toy box. In my mind's eye, I opened the lid and looked inside. When I did, I had a visual of multiple "people molds." There was a mold for my mother and one for my father. My husband's mold was in there along with my children and several of my friends. Point is, I wanted to mold the people in my life into what I wanted them to be. I had my own idea of who they should be, how they should act and how they should treat me. It was no wonder I was so miserable in my relationships. No one was living up to my expectations. One by one I took each out of the box and gave them up to him. With tears of repentance streaming down my face I surrendered my desire to control those I loved most.

Today's Prayer

Father God, you created each of us to be who we are. We are grateful that you are not finished molding and shaping us and those we love. Lord, forgive us for wanting others to be who we think they should be. Forgive us for trying to be in control of others' lives. Help us to accept others for who they are right now, trusting that you are at work in them just as you are in us. When we see things in others that are not right, may we be in prayer for them. Lord, help us to accept others as you do. Grow us up into the image of Christ who accepts all without demands. In the name of the One who accepts us. Amen.

Today's Scriptures

Romans 12:3; 1 Corinthians 13:11; Philippians 1:6; Colossians 3:12–15

Today's Thought

Our words are powerful weapons. James goes as far as to say our tongues can set a world on fire (James 3:6). Wow, what do we do with all that power? An elder from church demonstrated to me how important words are. When he would be in the pulpit it seemed as if he would take forever to get his words out. For a while it frustrated me, then one day I saw the wisdom God had given him. Ben was carefully weighing his words. I am convinced that Ben had little to regret over the use of his words; he influenced me in many ways. I asked the Lord to help me carefully weigh my words before they came out of my mouth. God has brought me a long way. I still have a long way to go. Scripture has much to say about the power of the tongue and I repeatedly go over those verses. Will you join me in the quest for the expression of life-giving words?

Today's Prayer

Father of life-giving words, we thank you for the many words of encouragement you give us every day You always know exactly what we need to hear. You speak to us through your Word, the Holy Spirit, and through the words of others. May we understand more fully the power of our words. I pray that you show us any speech or actions that are life- draining. I pray we promote healing and not wounding. May we think carefully before we speak, weighing our words and our responses. May we never abuse the power of our words. I pray we remember Proverbs 16:24, *"Pleasant words are a honeycomb, sweet to the soul and healing to the bones."* We pray for the sweetness of Jesus on our tongues. In the name of the One who created the tongue to speak life. Amen.

Today's Scripture

Proverbs 18:21; Colossians 4:5–6; James 1:19–20; James 3:5–10

January 28

Today's Thought

I have been faced with many choices in life. In my pre-Christ years, most of those decisions were not good. Consequently, I had to live with some dire results of my actions. In some respects, I still live with the aftermath of poor choices. The good news is that I can bear them because God in his mercy pours out his grace as I live out those consequences. Even as a Christian my poor choices have affected my life and the lives of others. Somewhere along the way I learned to pray over my choices every morning. Just this morning I affirmed to God and to myself that I choose joy, I choose peace, I choose righteousness, I choose to love. You get the picture. In verbalizing good choices, I am empowered to live out those choices with God's grace and help. Sometimes for different results we need to make different choices.

Today's Prayer

Father God, you give us the ability to choose; we are blessed with minds that are able to reason. You have given us freedom in our choices. I pray that we take that responsibility seriously. You will not violate our free will, but you have given us guidelines so that we can choose wisely. Your Word is full of examples of men and women who made good choices, and also of those who made bad ones. Lord, may we learn from their stories. May we learn that there is a high cost to ungodly and unwise choices. Oh, but how blessed we will be when we choose the way of the Spirit; when we choose the higher ground; when we choose the better way. Father, you have shown us clearly that our future hinges on the choices we make today. In the name of Jesus, our wise Counselor. Amen.

Today's Scriptures

Deuteronomy 30:19–20; Joshua 24:14–15; Psalm 25:8–9; Proverbs 16:17

Today's Thought

I am a wall builder; and, I am good at it. You hurt me once; I won't let you do it again. Does this sound familiar? In actuality, we all know how to erect walls around our hearts. Those walls can become fortresses in no time at all. We dread further damage that infects the existing wounds. Each brick has a name: fear; insecurity; rejection; abuse; grief; you name it. Your bricks are different than mine, but they all do their damage. They are barriers that hinder the flow of love and authenticity. They enable us to hold God and others at a distance. They have been in place for so long that we don't even recognize their existence. Walls are not built in a day and they do not come down in a day. But, they can be demolished. We call them what they are, a stronghold; then, we go to the only One who can bring them down. If God can bring down the walls of Jericho, he can unburden our hearts brick by brick.

Today's Prayer

Father God, we praise you today for all the tender loving care you extend to us. Life can leave us badly bruised and wounded. It's good to know that you see it all and that you care so deeply. Lord, often when we are hurting, we build walls around our hearts to protect ourselves. Jesus, today I pray over those walls that we put up to keep others out. You alone are able to dismantle those walls, brick by brick. Show us how we imprison ourselves and shut out those who love us. God help us to take off the masks that hide the true self. I pray you heal us and help us to be as authentic as we can be. Reveal to each of us the personal hurts we carry, and cause your love to bring them down. In the name of Jesus, our Stronghold. Amen.

Today's Scriptures

Joshua 6:20; Psalm 18:4–19; Psalm 147:3; Jeremiah 17:14

January 30

Today's Thought

What Jesus knew about her mattered more than what others thought of her. Who is she? In John Chapter 4 we are introduced to a woman who had a lot to hide. There are so many rich truths in this story, but I want to zero in on one statement she made; *"Come see a man who told me everything I ever did. Could this be the Christ?"* (John 4:29). Through this encounter with Jesus at Jacob's well in Samaria, this dear woman endured the Lord revealing all her past and current sin. Rather than deny and run, she realized this man was not like any man she had ever known. He knew her fully and completely. In spite of her lifestyle, I have to believe that what kept her riveted to the spot was his look of love and compassion. It's both scary and wonderful that God knows everything we ever did. What freedom there is in being fully known and fully loved by the One who created us. Take note that Jesus did not embarrass her by publically calling out her sin. She was the one who ran into town to tell everyone who would listen to come see the man who knew everything she ever did.

Today's Prayer

Father God, as our creator nothing is hidden from you. You indeed know everything we ever did. There is not one word, one action, one thought you do not know. And yet, you do not condemn or shame us. Yes, you call us to repentance and change, but you remember that we are dust. You knew all we would do before we did it, and you died for us while we were yet steeped in our sin. You made for us a way to come out of the darkness of immorality. We are grateful that we cannot hide from you. In the name of the One who fully knows us. Amen.

Today's Scriptures

Psalm 103:8–14; John 4:28–29; Romans 5:8; Hebrews 4:13

Today's Thought

Today has been a difficult day for me. The Lord revealed something in my heart that is not pleasing him. Ouch! It's been an issue that he has been putting his finger on, but I am really good at ignoring what I don't want to see. I know through scripture that there will always be struggles with the old nature, but knowing that doesn't make it any easier. I cried in the shower for a while, humbled before the Lord. After I dried off, I threw on my white robe. As I lay across my bed in anguish, I reminded myself that in spite of my faults, I do not have to despair. I am already righteous before him. I am dressed in the white robe of the righteousness of Christ. No sin or struggle can ever take that from me. Yes, I will have to wrestle with this latest revelation; but even as the Lord and I work it out, he will always see me through the righteousness of Christ.

Today's Prayer

Merciful Father, we are in need of your mercy every day. We are rebellious at heart. We thank you that you are persistent in forming us into the character of Christ. We are also grateful that while that transformation is taking place within us, you see Christ in us, the hope of glory. Lord, as long as we struggle with sin, we know it confirms that we are indeed in the faith. Saints of all the ages struggled with sin, and we are no exception. We see accounts of those in the Bible who were not perfect, but you continued to love and use them. The acknowledgement of our sin is the beginning of freedom. Help us to remember that, even as we struggle, we are beautiful and loved through the eyes of grace. In the name of Jesus Christ, our Righteousness. Amen.

Today's Scriptures

2 Corinthians 5:21; Philippians 3:7–9; Colossians 1:27; 1 John 1:8–9

Today's Thought

What is your greatest need today? Do you know that Jesus stands before you waiting to fulfill those needs? All we have to do is ask. In Mark chapter 10 a blind man was sitting by the roadside begging. When he perceived that Jesus was passing by, he cried out, *"Jesus, Son of David, have mercy on me"* (Mark 10:47). Jesus had his disciples bring the blind man to him. As Bartimaeus stood before him, Jesus asked, *"What do you want me to do for you?"* (John 10:51). I am sure that Jesus already knew the specific need, but he wanted the man to voice his desire. *"Rabbi, I want to see!"* (John 10:51). It was done. The man saw. Jesus opened the eyes of the blind. All Bartimaeus had to do was ask. Jesus is always standing by, ready to meet our needs. My challenge today is that as we pray, we be specific in what it is we want Jesus to do for us. He loves to hear our voices calling out to him. Every day, the Lord Jesus is asking, *"What do you want me to do for you?"*

Today's Prayer

Father God, we praise you today because you are worthy of all praise and honor. You give us everything we need; you are all we need today. As we face new challenges, I pray we embrace you as the One who fulfills every void in our lives. Whatever the need, you will meet it. All we have to do is ask. To the widow you will be a Husband. To the orphan you will be a Father. To the grieving you will be our Comforter. To the lost and confused you will be Clarity and Truth. To the sick you are Healer. To the blind you are Sight. Your love never fails, your faithfulness is sure, and your grace is sufficient. All we need is found in you. In the name of Jesus, who meets our deepest needs. Amen.

Today's Scriptures

Psalm 68:4–5; Mark 10:46–52; Romans 8:32; Philippians 4:19

February 2

Today's Thought

Down through the ages, false religions erected temples and shrines to their various gods. These places of worship were on the hills, the high places. Even now people groups travel great distances to worship at the shrine of their chosen god. Usually, these treks take them up great mountains and over vast hills. The Psalmist David had that picture in mind when he wrote these words, *"I lift up my eyes to the hills; where does my help come from?"* (Psalm 121:1). Then he renounced all the false worship of his day and stated, *"My help comes from the Lord, the Maker of heaven and earth"* (Psalm 121:2). David looked beyond the hills, beyond the false gods, beyond man- made shrines, beyond human help. He looked to the One who created the hills. He looked to the One who delivered him from the claws of the bear and the mouth of the lion. He looked to the One who gave him victory time and time again. David looked beyond the giants in his life.

Today's Prayer

Father of heaven and earth, we worship you and you alone. We are grateful that you have revealed yourself as the one true God. We do not have to travel to a remote hillside to be in your presence. We do not have to bow down at a shrine on the high places. You came down to us and now you dwell in us by your Spirit. I pray that we always look beyond the hills, beyond the giants, beyond the circumstances, and beyond our own humanness. Where does our help come from? Our help comes from the Lord, the Maker of heaven and earth. You do not slumber or sleep. You are ever aware of every situation in our lives. In the name of the One who we look to for our help. Amen.

Today's Scriptures

1 Samuel 17:37; 1 Samuel 17:45–47; Psalm 28:6–7; Psalm 121:1–4

Today's Thought

In December of 1964 the doctor confirmed my suspicions, *"Yes, you are pregnant."* My firstborn was due in July 1965. That left me with seven months of expectant waiting. I knew it would be important how I spent those months. It didn't take me long to get busy. I started collecting basic items for my baby: diapers; bottles; bibs; and onesies. As time went on, I moved on to purchasing larger items: crib; changing table; and rocking chair. I dreamed up boy names and girl names. I never doubted that the baby would come. As I waited, I prepared as if he or she was already here. When we are waiting for God to move in a situation, we should be waiting expectantly. My friend Renee recently shared these words from a song, *"I don't mind waiting, I don't mind waiting, I don't mind waiting on the Lord."* Those precious words changed the way I think about waiting on God. As we wait, we usually get more than that for which we are waiting.

Today's Prayer

Father God, we have been expectantly waiting. Sometimes the waiting seems so long; we have lost our sense of hope. We know from past experiences that you work in your own time and in your own way. You're never too early and never too late. Father, in your wisdom you are always right on time. Those prayers we prayed 20 or 30 years ago are still before you, you have not forgotten. Waiting on you is not a burden; it is an honor. Lord, teach us to wait as children who trust you completely. Teach us to honor you in the waiting by thanking you before we see any tangible results. Like the expectant birth of a baby, our time will come. We don't mind waiting on you Lord because while we wait, you work. Amen.

Today's Scriptures

Psalm 130:5–6; Romans 5:4; Romans 8:24–25; Hebrews 11:1

February 4

Today's Thought

In Psalm 32:9 God warns us, *"Do not be like the horse or the mule."* I have been both. Often, I run ahead of the Lord like the horse runs ahead of its trainer. Then there are times when I play the mule, stubbornly lagging behind in obedience. I always lose out when I run ahead; and, I usually miss out on a blessing when I lag behind. So, what is the Lord asking of us? In the same Psalm the Lord says," I *will instruct you and teach you in the way you should go. I will counsel you and watch over you"* (Psalm 32:8). God wants to be in the lead and as the follower we are to stay in step waiting patiently for his guidance and direction, only moving ahead at his prompting. Is God asking something of you in this season of your life? Have you been stalled in following through? Do you need to slow down and wait for his instruction before you move ahead? Stay close to Jesus and in step with his plans, and you will discover the sweet place of his pleasure.

Today's Prayer

Father, your plans for us are all good. You do not leave us in the dark. You clearly give direction and guidance. You say you will instruct us in the way we should go and watch over us. God, help us to be tranquil when you call us to be still. Help us to move ahead when that is what we need to do. You tell us that our steps are ordered by you. Help us to recognize your still small voice at any given time. Lord, we don't want to miss you by not keeping in step with you. I pray that each day we will seek you for our daily instruction. We thank you that you have marked out our steps and where you call us to, your grace is there. In the name of the One who guides us. Amen.

Today's Scriptures

Psalm 32:8–9; Psalm 37:23–24; Proverbs 16:3; Proverbs 16:9

Today's Thought

Have you ever loved someone so deeply you could never let them go? Now add to that the reality that that person had been unfaithful to you, over and over again. That's was the situation between God and Israel. After all God had done in preserving them, Israel had shamelessly left the God who loved and provided for them to chase after foreign idols and armies. They thought their foreign lovers were the ones who provided their food, clothing and housing. They trusted in the militia of Syria, Egypt and other ungodly nations for their safety and security. It was the God of Israel who protected them all along. And yet, after all their unfaithfulness, God cried out to them, *"How can I give you up … how can I hand you over?* (Hosea 11:8). He loved Israel so much that it pained him to even think of letting them go. Isn't that the same love and compassion God has for us; even as we turn from him to go our own way? When we chase after that which can never protect or satisfy, God's heart never turns away from us. He never lets go of you. His mercies are new every morning, his compassions never fail.

Today's Prayer

Father God, what a faithful God you are. When we are faithless, you remain faithful. When we stray, you seek us out. When we turn to other things for fulfillment, you wait patiently for us to come to our senses. You have promised us mercy and compassion when we deserve otherwise. Lord, help us to walk in such a way that we stay close to you in love and obedience. May we always know that all we have comes from your loving heart and hand. Amen.

Today's Scriptures

Jeremiah 31:3; Lamentations 3:22–24; Hosea 11:8–9; 2 Timothy 2:13

February 6

Today's Thought

How much are you worth? How do you measure that? Do you assess your worth by what others think and say about you? Do you calculate your value by how you look or how much wealth you have? There are many standards we can use to determine our worth. People flatter and mirrors can deceive. Actually, in a worldly sense there is not much by which we can accurately evaluate ourselves. So how can we know our value? The masterpiece that you are can only be defined by the One who created you. God placed a value on you. He said that all the gold and silver in the world would not have been enough to purchase you. There was only one price high and worthy enough. *"For you know that it was not with perishable things such as silver and gold that you were redeemed from the empty way of life handed down to you, but with the precious blood of Christ, a lamb without blemish or defect"* (1 Peter 1:18–19). You have been bought back by God with a price tag so high that only One in all of eternity could ransom you.

Today's Prayer

Father Redeemer, we could never have redeemed ourselves, not with all the gold in the world. All our good intentions and good deeds could not have made us right with you. Our fame or position in life means nothing in light of what our sin cost us and others. While we were yet sinners, Jesus paid the price for our eternal souls. You looked at our hopeless condition and, in your mercy, you ransomed us from the grave. Father, I pray that we lay hold of the immense truth of the value you place on us and the price you paid. I pray we never lose sight of the true treasures we are. May we always look to Jesus' finished work on the cross to gain a proper perspective of our worth. Now, Jesus, we cling to you as our greatest treasure. In the name of our Holy Redeemer. Amen.

Today's Scripture

Isaiah 43:1–4; Romans 5:5–8; 1 Corinthians 6:19–20; 1 Peter 1:18–19

Today's Thought

I grew up with a special needs child. My brother was blind and mentally challenged from birth. I was often a caregiver to him, dressing and feeding him. Rege was pretty much helpless without the family looking after his wellbeing 24/7. I enjoyed being a teacher to him. I would attempt to teach him to count and recite the alphabet. After my parents passed, I became his legal guardian. We have had many visits throughout the years and I always love my time with this sweet man. In truth, I learned more from him than he ever learned from me. I remember one morning when Rege and I were sitting in my living room. I watched him rock in his chair and I thought about how blessed I was to have my sight and a strong mind. That was when the Lord impressed me with a precious truth. We are all his special needs children.

Today's Prayer

Father, we are so needy. I know we like to think we are all grown up and self-sufficient. Thank you for the reminders that we are ever dependent on you no matter how grown we think we are. Lord Jesus, I pray that we live as ones who need a Father at all times; One who will lovingly correct us when needed; One who will comfort us when we hurt. Physically we may be strong in mind and body, but your Word tells us that the flesh is weak. We don't like to think about how fragile we truly are. You knew we would need constant care and you provided yourself as our caregiver. Lord, we all have our special needs. Help us to remember that reality when we are ready to judge another. You are the Father of all and your love for us transcends our imperfections. In the name of our faithful caregiver. Amen.

Today's Scripture

Psalm 33:18; Matthew 18:2–4; Romans 14:10–13; 1 Peter 5:6–7

February 8

Today's Thought

When John the Baptist announced in John 3:30, *"He must become greater, I must become less"* he was not talking about his body mass. On a diet of locusts and wild honey, I am sure weight was not his problem. He did however have a dilemma. It was the weight of his popularity that was increasing among the Jews. Some went so far as to ask him if he was the long-awaited Messiah. John knew his place. No super saint, just human like you and me. It could not have been easy for John to shun all the accolades coming his way. Who doesn't like to be praised and applauded? John continually pointed to Jesus. He went so far as to say he was not even worthy to strap on Jesus' sandals. That's awesome humility. John knew that life was a stage for the greatest story ever told. God, as the producer; the Holy Spirit as the director; and Jesus the star. John was content to be a bit player. It's crucial that we know our place on the stage of God's grand story; that we not attempt to assume the role of another.

Today's Prayer

Father of our Lord Jesus Christ, you are telling a grand story and we are honored to have a part to play. When good things happen, help us remember that ultimately it does not matter who gets the credit as long as you get the glory. Like John, may we always know our place in the kingdom. You are not asking us to think less of ourselves but to think of ourselves less. We are all part of the history of mankind, we are all created to bring glory to you, just as Jesus lived to bring you glory. We will ever live in your glorious heaven giving you the honor and glory you are worthy of. In the name of the eternal Glorified One. Amen.

Today's Scripture

John 3:29–30; John 17:24; Romans 12:3; Revelation 5:11–13

Today's Thought

How many mirrors do you have? How many times a day do you gaze into one? We feel compelled to check ourselves out in a mirror several times a day. I imagine this can be a good thing. Now here is the rub, how critical are you when you see yourself in the mirror; and what do you do about it? God's Word is also a mirror? As we gaze into his Word, we are to critique ourselves according to what we read there. Are we loving our neighbor? When the Word commands us to forgive, do we? When we are told not to worry about tomorrow, do we still worry? James 1:22–24 says it like this, *"Do not merely listen to the Word, and so deceive yourselves. Do what is says. Anyone who listens to the Word but does not do what it says is like a man who looks at his face in a mirror, and after looking at himself, goes away and immediately forgets what he looks like."* When the mirror tells us that our hair needs groomed, we groom it. So, it should be with the things that God's Word reflects back to us. James 1:25 goes on to say, *"But the man who looks intently into the perfect law that gives freedom, and continues to do this, not forgetting what he has heard, but doing it, he will be blessed in what he does."*

Today's Prayer

Father God, your Word is intended to give us freedom from sin, selfishness and unnecessary pain. As we hear and do your Word, blessings await us. Lord, we want to live a life that pleases you. I pray that as we continue in your Word, we use it as a spiritual mirror, reflecting back to us the right path, the good choices and the better way to live. You heart is for us, not against us. May we take heed to all you ask of us. In the name of Jesus, the One we want to reflect. Amen.

Today's Scripture

Psalm 119:9–11; Matthew 7:24–27; 2 Timothy 3:16–17; James 1:22–25

Today's Thought

I did not think of her as a gift. She continually rubbed me the wrong way, usually contradicting what I said; a real know it all. Sound familiar? Perhaps there is someone in your life who is a thorn in your side, but the circumstances do not allow you to just walk away? These hard-to-love folks can be a gift from God. It's a matter of perspective. I began to pray earnestly every time I was obligated to be in her presence. I prayed for a change of heart and a love for her that in my humanness I was not able to give. I had to do this time and time again. One day it dawned on me, my feelings for her were changing. Even more amazing, she was beginning to treat me differently. With all honesty, I can tell you, after many years of pursuing God for a change of heart, she is now one of my favorite friends.

Today's Prayer

Father God, it is possible to thank you for the difficult people you bring into our lives. You have allowed these relationships for important reasons. We trust that there are good things you want to bring about in us through the ones who bring more hurt than joy. Sometimes we are the ones in need of change. As we pray over these relational situations, help us to pray with the mind of Christ. Help us to see the lessons you want to teach. You know what we are up against with difficult people, and we thank you that you see and care. As challenging as it may be, I pray that we begin to see these ones as the gift you intend them to be. A gift, when managed in a godly fashion, can benefit everyone involved. We thank you for your Spirit who empowers us to love the most unlovely. In the name of the One who changes hearts. Amen.

Today's Scriptures

Matthew 5:43–48; Romans 8:28; Ephesians 4:31–32; 1 Peter 1:6–7

February 11

Today's Thought

In the last few chapters of the book of Daniel, Daniel was given a vision of end-time events. Daniel wrote down all that he saw. When the vision was complete Daniel was told to close up and seal the words of the scroll. In Daniel 12:8 he asked, *"My Lord, what will the outcome of all this be?"* He was told, *"Go your way Daniel, because the words are closed up and sealed until the time of the end"* (Daniel 12:9). What a mystery! What were the final words written on that scroll, and why were they hidden? Recently in my reading of the book of Revelation I came across these words written by John, *"I wept and wept because no one was found to be worthy to open the scroll or look inside"* (Revelation 5:4). Could this be the same scroll Daniel was told to seal until the end? John wept and wept, then the elder spoke these words: *"Do not weep, see, the Lion of the tribe of Judah, the Root of David, has triumphed. He is able to open the scroll and its seven seals"* (Revelation 5:5).

Today's Prayer

Father of our Lord Jesus Christ, we may not understand all that will happen in the end times, but we know the outcome. Our Lord Jesus will triumph. Jesus leads us in victory. The book of revelation reveals to us what is to come as Jesus opens the scroll. Father, we thank you that we do not have to fear the things coming on earth. You will make all things right as you judge with equity. We know that now is the time. Today is the day of salvation. I pray that we are bold in sharing the good news with those who do not yet know you. I pray you give us many opportunities to pray with those whose hearts are failing them from fear. In the name of the One who is worthy to open the scroll. Amen.

Today's Scriptures

Daniel 12:5–13; 2 Corinthians 6:1–2; 2 Timothy 4:1–2; Revelation 5:1–5

February 12

Today's Thought

Comparison! What a trap. Just when we think we are on top, someone or something comes along and knocks us off our flimsy pedestal. We are each of a unique design. God makes no mistakes. If he wanted me to be like you, I would be. If he wanted you to be like that one you envy, you would be. When we feel inferior to another, we have given ourselves permission to do so. There will always be someone who does something better than you; and you will always have gifts and talents that rise above the norm. Comparison is a losing battle. Paul said it like this, *"When they measure themselves by themselves and compare themselves among themselves, they are not wise"* (2 Corinthians 10:12). God made everything to compliment the other. I believe that's how we need to look at ourselves. We are a compliment to those who lack, and they complement us in our insufficiency. We honor God most by accepting the unique person he created us to be. You are special, and no one in all of eternity could be you with all your unique traits and personality. Now, dear one, that is something to celebrate.

Today's Prayer

Father Creator, we are most happy when we accept ourselves as your unique child. You made us exactly as you intended. In our humanness we do compare, almost as if it's built into us. From the time we first noticed someone had something we wanted, we began the comparison game. Lord, I pray that you show us how we compare ourselves to others and how futile that is. God, I pray you make us aware and break this persistent habit in our lives so we can be free in who we are. In the name of the One who created us perfectly for himself. Amen.

Today's Scriptures

Isaiah 45:9; Isaiah 64:8; 2 Corinthians 10:12; Ephesians 4:16

February 13

Today's Thought

As I write today, we are coming up on a presidential election. You will probably go to the polls to vote or cast an absentee ballot. This can be an exciting time. We can experience elation or feel deflated when the results come in. Regardless of our political persuasion, we take the responsibility to vote seriously. It can be quite daunting to sort through all the political material sent to us. The TV campaign ads inundate us day after day until we just don't know what to believe. One thing I do know, we can believe that the day is coming when God will rule all the world. We can depend on the promise of Isaiah 9, *"For to us a child is born, to us a Son is given, and the government will be on His shoulders ... of the increase of his government and peace there will be no end ..."* (Isaiah 9:6–7). When Jesus finally rules all the nations, elections will cease because his rule will be forever. Praise his wonderful name!

Today's Prayer

Father God, thank you for sending us your Son. He came as a suffering Messiah, a servant to the needy. He is coming again as King and Ruler over all. As we wait for this blessed time, I pray we are wise in choosing our governing officials. Your Word compels us to honor those in authority. We may not always agree with them, but we honor them as men and women you have set up to govern. We know they are not perfect, but give us wisdom to choose rightly. Some you use to bless and protect us, and some you use to discipline and correct us. We look to the glorious day when our Lord Jesus will rule with justice and righteousness. His throne is forever and his kingdom will be one of everlasting love, joy and peace. Amen.

Today's Scriptures

Psalm 2:1–6; Isaiah 9:6–7; 1 Peter 2:13–14; Revelation 11:15–17

February 14

Today's Thought

When I look into the mirror, I see the years taking their toll. When did this happen? I still like to think of myself of a kinder age. It helps a lot to take my glasses off before I look in the mirror. I never got the memo that said beehives were out of style. I now realize the older I get the better I use to be. Seriously, I would not trade all the youthful looks in the world for all that the years have taught me. I desire to be a godly mature woman of rare beauty. Our world needs more of her kind and less of the artificially put- together divas. God's Word in 2 Corinthians 4:16 seals the aging dilemma for me. *"Therefore, we do not lose heart. Though outwardly we are wasting away, yet inwardly we are being renewed day-by-day."* What an outstanding truth! We are not growing older; in Christ we are growing younger day-by-day. Hopefully we are growing wiser as well. It will be our choice how we age; grudgingly or gracefully.

Today's Prayer

Father of the ages, we are grateful that these human bodies were not designed to live forever. Your Word tells us that you are preparing for us a new body; a body just like our glorified Savior's body. And even as Jesus enjoys his glorified body, so shall we. That process is silently at work in us now as we are renewed day-by-day. Lord, help us to embrace the aging process as a gift that stretches us and grows the beautiful inner women you created us to be. Rather than looking in the rear-view mirror longing for bygone days, I pray we look ahead to the wonderful renewed life waiting for us. In the name of our ageless God, Amen.

Today's Scriptures

Isaiah 46:4; Corinthians 15:42–44; 2 Corinthians 4:16; Philippians 3:20–21

February 15

Today's Thought

Sometimes I would rather go home to be with the Lord than face my issues. Have you ever been there, crying out, *"Lord, just take me now"*! Life can be so hard at times that we want to curl up in a fetal position and sleep our way into eternity. Paul felt this way many times. On one occasion he despaired of life itself. Paul talks about beatings, arrests, shipwrecks, dangers of all kinds, persecution and hunger. He said he was torn between the two; wanting to be with the Lord, and at the same time knowing he was needed here to do the work God assigned him. He concludes, *"For our light and momentary troubles are achieving for us an eternal glory that far outweighs them all"* (2 Corinthians 4:17). Did you know that your earthly troubles are accomplishing heavenly rewards? The key is how we respond to these situations that threaten to drown us. Paul always kept the heavenly perspective and so must we.

Today's Prayer

Father God, it is reassuring that you see our troubles and that you care deeply. You understand our tendency to want to escape these struggles that sometimes seem unbearable. Realistically we know that we will not leave this planet until your ordained time set for us. While we wait, Lord, I pray we remember that even in the darkest times, your grace is sufficient. I pray that we consider your promise that these challenging times are temporary and they are working blessings for us, both now and in the life to come. When we feel we are going to drown in our sorrow, I pray you be the glory and lifter of our hearts and minds. In the name of the One who understands and upholds us. Amen.

Today's Scriptures

Job 23:10; 2 Corinthians 1:8; 2 Corinthians 4:17–18; Philippians 1:21–24

February 16

Today's Thought

There was a time, a time before Christ invaded our world, a time when performance was everything. Before Jesus, people had to get it right. There were laws upon laws, regulations upon regulations. Animals had to be sacrificed day after day, year after year. The blood shed was horrendous! It was never enough, never good enough. Always questioning, *"When will it be enough."* I can only imagine the frustration of it all. So much of what we read in the Bible pertains to Israel's rise and fall, upsurge and downfall, all because they strived in their own strength to be right with God. This is meant to be an example to us that we can never make ourselves right with God by our works and performance. Jesus did that for us. At just the right time Christ died for the ungodly. Now it is by grace we are saved and not of ourselves. We are ever grateful that we live in the amazing age of grace. We are set free from the law because Jesus fulfilled the law for us.

Today's Prayer

Father of heaven, today we lift our praises together in gratitude that you choose a wooden cross stained with the blood of the Darling of heaven, your Son Jesus. The cross is foolishness to those who will not believe, but the cross is the wisdom of God to we who believe. Father, your Word tells us that you were pleased to save those who believe Jesus is the only way to you. Today I ask that we never look back on that old life. I pray that we never attempt to live by the law, rules and regulations. May we always live by the power and by the wisdom of the cross. We thank you for the new covenant, the better way, which comes by Jesus Christ and him alone. May we cast off anything that hinders us from fully living the new way of the Spirit. In Jesus our Savior we pray. Amen.

Today's Scriptures

John 14:6; Romans 6:14; Romans 7:6; 1 Corinthians. 1:18

Today's Thought

If I were to title this day's devotion, I would call it, *"Deadly Raisins and Other Tall Tales."* As a child I was visiting a friend's home for dinner. The vegetable dish included raisins, which I despised. When my friend's mom asked me why I was picking out the raisins, without hesitation I told her I was allergic to raisins. *"Oh my, she asked, what happens when you eat raisins?"* Again, without a second thought I told her that if I ate a raisin I would die. We are born with lies on our tongue. It's our native language. But we were created for truth. God esteems us worthy of truth. That is why every word that proceeds from the mouth of God is trustworthy. As children of the Most High God, our words should be truthful as well. The Word has a lot to say about the lying tongue and we should fear the disastrous consequences of lies. Exaggerating a truth is lying and minimizing the truth is lying. We are good at both. As new creations in Christ our lying tongues need to be sanctified by the Word of God. Being truthful may hurt at the moment, but lies hurt everyone they touch for a long, long time.

Today's Prayer

Father God, thank you that we can absolutely trust every word you speak. In you there is no falsehood at all. You are God and you cannot lie. We are so grateful that there is truth in which we can always trust. God, I pray that you expose any lies that we believe, and any lies we are speaking. Help us to understand that when we speak an untruth, we are not loving our neighbor and we devalue ourselves. Lord, cleanse us from our lying tongues. In the name of Jesus, our Truth. Amen.

Today's Scriptures

Psalm 15:1–3; Psalm 51:6; Proverbs 26:28; Colossians 3:9–10

February 18

Today's Thought

God's love is a purifying love. One of God's attributes is that of a Refiner. A refiner sits patiently watching the fiery process of precious metal in the making. God's goal with each of his children is to bring us forth as gold. Being placed in the refiner's fire is not pleasant. Some will lose their trust in God as the flames begin to envelope them. Those who are wise will embrace the eternal perspective as they understand that the fiery trials are God's way of perfecting us. God's refining fire is intended to bring us out of apathy and complacency. It is meant to bring us freedom from that which binds us. Just as Shadrach, Meshach and Abednego were bound with bindings in the fiery furnace and came out free of what constrained them, so shall we (Daniel 3). God's ultimate purpose for us in this life is not about our comfort; it's about being conformed into the character of Christ.

Today's Prayer

Father God, you are a gentle Refiner. Just as the three Hebrews youths knew you would bring them out better than they went in, you have that in mind for us every time we face a fiery trial. Your purposes are not to hurt us, they are to mature and perfect us in our faith. Without trials we remain as infants spiritually. Lord, we want to grow, we want to be stretched, and we want the abundant life Jesus promises. As the Refiner you never leave the furnace, your gaze is fixed upon the flames and upon your children continually. Likewise, as our Father, you walk through the flames with us so we will not be destroyed. Lord, cause us to grow. In the name of our Gentle Refiner. Amen.

Today's Scripture

Job 23:10; Proverbs 17:3; Isaiah 43:1–3; 1 Peter 4:12–13

Today's Thought

The longer I live the more comfortable I become with mystery. The longer I live the more I realize how much I do not know, but the few things I do know, I know for sure. I know that God loves me. I know he is good. I know that he is working all things in my life for my good and his glory. There will always be unanswered questions. Soren Kierkegaard said it like this, *"Life is not a problem to be solved, but a reality to be experienced."* God invites us into our own circumstances to work with him in solving our dilemmas. Our relationship with our Creator is a partnership. As we co-operate with God's plans, life unfolds for us as he intends. Yes, there will always be mysteries in the ways that God works, but the things we know for sure will sustain us through the toughest of times. What are the few things you know for sure?

Today's Prayer

Father God, we know there will always be difficult circumstances. There will always be mysteries. There will always be doubts and questions. Lord, I pray that we cling firmly to those things that you have revealed about yourself. God, we want to know you in such a way that we know for sure that we can always trust you, even when we don't understand. You gave us Jesus as the answer to our every uncertainty. In you there is no indecision or hesitancy. You are always on the throne and in control of all world events and of the intimate details of our lives. Lord, I pray that we will trust you when we don't understand, and that we will continue to love you and serve you in all the unexpected trials. I pray our faith not waver when our world is rocked. In the name of our sovereign God. Amen.

Today's Scripture

Psalm 22:3–5; Proverbs 3:5–6; Jeremiah 9:23–24; Romans 11:33–34

February 20

Today's Thought

Did you ever wish you could have a do-over? That one foolish thing you did that changed everything? Some things can never be reversed, but mistakes can be redeemed. Take Jonah for instance. He made a critical misstep when he decided to run from God and disregard the mission he was called to. Consequently, he found himself swimming around in the belly of a fish. After three days in that condition, morning came. It was a new day and God was ready to redeem Jonah from his watery grave. It took repentance on Jonah's part, then, God did his part and caused the fish to spit out Jonah. After putting the prophet on his feet again, God gave Jonah a second chance to prophecy God's warning to Nineveh. Do you know that it's never too late for God to redeem that thing in your life that tripped you up? He is not only the God of the second chances, He is the God of chance after chance after chance. His mercy is new every morning; great is his faithfulness.

Today's Prayer

Father God, we thank you for another new day; new choices, new chances and new beginnings. You are a God who is able to redeem even our worst day. Lord, how good to know that we can always start anew. What a blessing to know that the slate is clean every morning. We can now write a new story, a better story. You give us renewed strength and vigor to tackle this new day. You never hand us yesterday's leftovers. Your grace is always sufficient and exactly what we need. I pray we live this day in the light of your gracious daily redemption. In the name of the God who every morning gives us a fresh start. Amen.

Today's Scriptures

Lamentations 3:22–24; Jonah 2:1–7; 2 Corinthians 9:8; 2 Corinthians 12:9

February 21

Today's Thought

One lovely day when I had my brother for a visit, God used him in a most unexpected way. My brother is blind and profoundly mentally-challenged. We were sitting together in my living room. I was reading and he was rocking in his favorite chair. Suddenly, seemingly out of nowhere he said, *"You were sick, Fern, and daddy carried you."* I wasn't sure I heard him correctly, then, he repeated the words. At the time, I did not think much of it. Perhaps an old memory was triggered. Rege is a few years older than I, so maybe something like that did happen and he somehow remembered. As the years passed this is what I have come to understand. God wanted me to know that in his love, he has carried me through the dark times of my journey. As I search the scriptures, I see that God does carry us in times of overwhelming burdens. The words my brother spoke that day have been an anchor for me in difficult times. Daddy carries me.

Today's Prayer

Father God, we never outgrow our need for you. In many ways we are all just little children, no matter how old we become. You always see us through the loving eyes of a good Father. When we are vigorous and strong you watch us with delight. When we are weak and feeling helpless, you pick us up and carry us. You said that we could always find shelter under the shadow of your wings. Your promises to always be with us and help us, prove true over and over again. We thank you that we are never apart from your strong and loving arms. I pray that we remember that we abide securely in your everlasting arms. In the name of the Helper of the helpless. Amen.

Today's Scriptures

Deuteronomy 33:27; Psalm 91:4; Isaiah 46:3–4; 2 Corinthians 12:9–10

Today's Thought

In my many years of facilitating Bible studies one statement I heard again and again was, *"God must be so disappointed in me."* I am always taken back by the realization that many of his children believe God has the emotion of disappointment, and more heartbreaking is when she supposes that his disappointment is directed at her. Disappointment is what we experience when we have had expectations or needs that were not met. God has no expectations of us and he certainly has no needs as he is sufficient unto himself. Scripturally, I see God having pity for us in our fallen state. God knows everything we ever did and he knew it long before we did it. No expectations, no disappointment, just a love that beckons us to come into his arms and be restored. He will be there waiting; he will never disappoint us.

Today's Prayer

Father God, you delight in us as your beloved children. Our earthly parents often show disappointment in our choices and behavior. Likewise, we can be frustrated by our own children's actions. Lord, we are so grateful we do not have to perform for you. You know all about us, our weaknesses, our struggles with sin, our broken promises and you love us still. I pray, God, that we will forever put aside the notion that you are disappointed in us. Father, show us how much you delight in us as you watch us grow into maturity. When we slip up and fall short, I pray we come running to you for a new start. Help us to remember that your arms are wide open to receive us at all times. In the name of the God who loves us just as we are. Amen.

Today's Scriptures

Psalm 23:2–3; Psalm 103:13; Isaiah 63:9; Jude 24–25

February 23

Today's Thought

My friend Sue had a dream. She was in a vast ocean and was being swept away by the current. Her husband and two sons were in the water with her and she struggled to reach and save them. She grabbed hold of her husband's wrist but felt the power of the water stealing her grip. She was carried away from her loved ones. Suddenly, a great peace came over her. She felt as if she were drowning in the great and vast love of God. As we talked about the dream, she realized that it was the letting go that gave her the peace. Sometimes when we hold onto something or someone too tightly it can pull us into an ocean of despair and desperation. Great peace can be found in the letting go. As we do, God's love and peace begin to fill our hearts with hope in his competence to move into our situation and do what only he can do.

Today's Prayer

Father of unimaginable love and peace, when we try to conceive the great depths of your love, we find that we cannot. So deep and so high and rich is your love for us it leaves us at a loss for words. Your love is like the depths of the ocean and beyond. We want to plunge ourselves into the full reality of such a love. Father, I pray you sweep us up into your love and overtake us with the peace that passes understanding. Help us to let go of anything that hinders our knowing the reality of your love. Take us where our trust is without borders. Help us to soar above the circumstances that threaten to drown us. Overwhelm us now, Lord, with the sense that your great and awesome love is for each of us. In the name of the One who loves us beyond our wildest dreams. Amen.

Today's Scriptures

Isaiah 43:2–3; Ephesians 3:14–21; 1 John 3:1–3; 1 John 4:10

February 24

Today's Thought

Pencils have erasers for one simple reason, we all make mistakes. And so, it is with life. Sometimes those mistakes are minor and are easily remedied. Often though, our mistakes are more than that. They are sins committed that do much harm to us and to others. God has the only cure for those transgressions against his holiness. David once confessed to God, *"Against you, you only, have I have sinned ..."* (Psalm 52:4). It is true that we hurt others by our sins and asking their forgiveness is something we clearly must to do. But going to God for his forgiveness is not optional. When we genuinely confess our sins and ask forgiveness God goes above and beyond forgiveness, he wipes out the sin as if it never happened. The eraser on our pencil is a great resource to have, but the blood of Jesus that cleanses and covers our sins is the greatest blessing we can know.

Today's Prayer

Father God, we all sin against your holiness in one way or another. We are ever grateful that in your love and mercy you provided a way for us to be forgiven. As your Son hung on the cross, he asked that you forgive those who crucified him. In that request was a treasure for all of us to hold onto. Your forgiveness is enough for each of us, no matter how grave the sin. Sometimes, Lord, we feel we must add to what Jesus did by forgiving ourselves. Father, help us understand that what Jesus did on our behalf was enough. Help us walk in the truth that you alone have the power to forgive sin and it is finished. As we fully receive your pardon, I pray we walk out of the prison of condemnation and the lie that we need to do more. In the name of the One who forgives fully and freely. Amen.

Today's Scriptures

Psalm 103:10–14; Isaiah 1:18; Luke 23:34; 1 John 1:9

February 25

Today's Thought

Are you battle weary? Does it seem as if no one is listening? Nothing can throw us into discouragement and despair as quickly as battle fatigue. The enemy comes upon us most often while we are exhausted and vulnerable. Paul warns us not be ignorant of Satan's schemes. We are urged to encourage ourselves in the Lord during times of stress and disappointment. How do we do that? The scriptures are the place to which we run when we feel threatened. Within God's Word we find that the battle is the Lord's. We discover that we can cast our cares upon the Lord because he cares for us. We find that communion with God can bring peace and refreshing. Whatever you are going through, look up in hope. This difficult time did not come to stay. It came to pass. Encourage yourself in the Lord and he will lift you up.

Today's Prayer

Father God, you are the glory and the lifter of our heads. When we feel we cannot survive another moment, you come to us at just the right time to strengthen and encourage us. While we wait for the times of refreshing, I pray that we learn the wisdom of encouraging ourselves in the Lord. Your Word is more than adequate to bring us up out of any pit. In it we see the stories of so many others who had lost hope and despaired even of life. But at just the right time you rescued them and you do the same for us. When our souls feel barren and thirsty, you provide that living water and you revive us. Father, we praise you that you see us as we struggle with discouragement. You know how we got here and you know how to bring us out triumphant. In the name of our Great Encourager. Amen.

Today's Scriptures

1 Samuel 30:6; Psalm 3:3; Isiah 40:28–31; Isaiah 63:1–3

February 26

Today's Thought

As our thoughts are, so are we. Our thought life will determine where we end up. When our thoughts begin to go down a wrong road, we must intentionally take them captive. Our actions, whether good or bad, begin in our minds. We never just fall into a bad place, it's a process. Negative thoughts will lead us into dark places. Reflecting on God's Word will bring us into the light. The sooner we catch those unruly streams of thought, the less chance they have to take root and bring forth a harvest of grief. Taking control of our thoughts can be a constant battle. Paul gives us an outstanding set of standards. *"Whatever is true, whatever is noble, whatever is right, whatever is pure, whatever is lovely, whatever is admirable, if anything is excellent or praiseworthy, think about such things"* (Philippians 4:8). If we put Paul's admonition into practice, we will yield a harvest of God's peace. The quality of our thoughts will determine who we become.

Today's Prayer

Father God, you have blessed us with brilliant minds. You have also equipped us with the ability to choose how we think. Sometimes we believe that undesirable thoughts just jump on us, but your Word tells us differently. We do choose our thoughts. When we choose to linger on those thoughts that are not pleasing to you, we do harm. When negative and immoral thoughts come, help us to counter them with scripture and truth. Lord Jesus, help us to align our thoughts with yours. You say we have been given the mind of Christ, may we not pollute ourselves with anything that is contrary to the love and purity of the heart and mind of Jesus. In the name of the One who knows all our thoughts. Amen.

Today's Scripture

Psalm 139:1–2; Romans 12:2; 2 Corinthians 10:5; Philippians 4:8–9

February 27

Today's Thought

We will not all earn a PhD, but we can all be wise. Wisdom is the ability to judge and act accordingly. None of us are born with wisdom oozing out of us and age does not guarantee wisdom. So how do we acquire this treasure trove of perception? The book of Proverbs holds many key verses for gaining wisdom. I have found over 120 verses on the theme of wisdom in the book of Proverbs alone. If we are diligent in studying and applying this prized attribute, we can develop a wise heart. The journey to wisdom begins with asking God for it. James tells us that if anyone lacks wisdom, he should ask God who gives generously. Ultimately though, wisdom is learned through living well. Every good choice in accordance with God's will is a stepping stone to a wise heart. Proverbs 9:10 gives us the launching pad to wisdom. *"The fear of the Lord is the beginning of wisdom, and the knowledge of the Holy One is understanding."*

Today's Prayer

Father God, you are the source of all wisdom. The depths of the riches of wisdom you personify are unsearchable. In wisdom you created the world and everything in it. In wisdom you sent your only Son to save us from our sins. In wisdom you give us your Holy Spirit to guide us on this journey. In wisdom you will guide us safely home. Father, how much we need this attribute. Today we ask again that you show us the path to understanding. May we begin with holy fear which leads to obedience. As we obey you one step at a time lead us into wise living; wisdom in our relationships, our finances, our choices and our walk with you. In the name of the only wise God. Amen.

Today's Scriptures

Proverbs 9:10; Proverbs 16:16; Romans 11:33–34; James 1:5–6

Today's Thought

FORGIVEN! The sweetest word we will ever hear. Next to love, forgiveness is what our hearts most long for. God has generously and abundantly provided both the love and forgiveness we so desperately crave. He held nothing back when he secured absolution for our sins. Jesus the Son laid it all down, even his very life so we could experience the Father's mercy and compassion. How do we respond to this extravagant gift? First, we must confess that we are sinners in need of forgiveness. We repent and turn away from sin, as the Holy Spirit empowers us to live with power over sin. What a burden of guilt we carry when we don't believe that we are forgiven. Unfortunately, this is true of many Christians, especially when they feel their sins are "unforgivable." Dear heart, no sin is beyond reach of the Lord's mercy. What Jesus sacrificed on the cross was enough then and it is enough today.

Today's Prayer

Forgiving Father, in your love and mercy you made a way for us. Even while we were yet sinners, Christ died for us. From the beginning of time, you knew that we would sin. Just as our original parents, Adam and Eve, disobeyed you in the garden, we disobey you also. It's our very nature to be rebellious against your holy commands. But praise be to God, we have a way out through repentance and forgiveness. We can always come humbly to you no matter how grievous the sin, and as we ask, you forgive. God, we thank you that we do not have to live in the muck and mire of guilt and condemnation. When you forgive it is full and free. It's a cancelled debt. Amen.

Today's Scriptures

Romans 5:6–11; Romans 8:1; Colossians 1:13–14; 1 John 1:8–9

Today's Thought

Fear is Satan's greatest weapon. 2 Timothy 1 assures us that God has not given us the spirit of fear. He has given us weapons that are greater than any attack that comes against us. He has given us the weapon of praise to call down the awesome presence of God. He has given us the weapon of a righteous life that quiets our enemies. He has given us the weapon of his Word, the sword of the Spirit. Jesus' greatest weapon in the wilderness against Satan was the spoken Word of God. We do not need to fear because no weapon formed against us will prevail. If he is for us, no enemy can be against us. It may feel like an attack, but God's Holy Spirit in us is greater than the evil one who roams the world looking for whom he may devour. God is for us; he is on our side.

Today's Prayer

Father God, you have provided us with everything we need to live a godly, victorious life. We praise you that we do not have to live in fear because Jesus has overcome this evil age. In him and with him we are overcomers. God you are for us, not against us. You are cheering us on as we put on our armor and enter the battle against sin and temptation. We acknowledge that our weapons are not as the world's futile weapons, our weapons are mighty through God and they have your power behind them to pull down strongholds. Father, we thank you that no scheme or plot formed against us will prevail. We take up the high praises of God in our mouth and the sword of the Word in our hands as we defeat the plans of the enemy. In the name of our God, our victory. Amen.

Today's Scriptures

Psalm 149:5–6; Isaiah 54:16–17; Romans 8:31–32; Ephesians 6:10–13

Today's Thought

God knows all of our secrets. I often wonder why we think we can hide them. Sometimes our secrets are so deep we don't even know they are there. Secrets can be like a cancer of the soul, eating away at our sense of well-being. God desires to expose those poisonous deceptions to the light of his truth. When we lay our hearts out before him, he exposes the things we cannot see. All too often we try to "fix" ourselves when we don't know the real source, what secrets our hearts hide. If we truly desire transformation, we must come into God's presence with an openness that permits him to expose to the light those things that are unhealthy. When Adam's sin was exposed in the garden his impulse was to hide from God. If he had gotten away with hiding, where would we be today? God wants those hidden things brought into the light of his healing and restoration. Are you willing to allow God to search out any hidden and secret things in your soul that keep you from experiencing a heart at rest in his presence?

Today's Prayer

Father God, we dread our hearts being exposed, and at the same time we must embrace it. With exposure comes your blessed healing. There are secret places within us that only you know. Hidden things just between you and me. Things that only your eyes see. We acknowledge that they need to come out of the darkness into your glorious penetrating light. We want to stand before you with everything unveiled, nothing hidden, nothing covered. I pray we not fear the revelations of our heart but that we draw near with full assurance of your love that breaks down every deception. In the name of the One we trust with our secrets. Amen.

Today's Scriptures

Psalm 139:23–24; Jeremiah 23:23–24; Hebrews 4:12–13; 1 John 3:19–20

Today's Thought

You are an artist! Every day your life is painting a canvas that others will scrutinize. The paint you use is your words and actions. Your canvas tells your story; who you are, what you believe, and it reveals who your God is and speaks of his character. Paul says it a different way, but the essence is the same. He says we are a living epistle read by all. Our epistle is the message we give out. We are a living letter that is being read every day by those with whom we come in contact. The question I present to myself and to you is this. Does my canvas, my message, line up with what I profess? Do others see an accurate picture of the God I love and worship? Is my canvas in harmony with the truth of God's Word and am I living the truth I claim? The world around us desperately needs to know the one true God and sometimes we will be the only Bible someone will ever read. I challenge us to take a good look at the canvases we are painting and the messages we are giving the folks around us. What, if any, changes need to be made so others will want to know the loving Jesus of the Bible?

Today's Prayer

Father God, when Jesus left us those many years ago, he commissioned us to continue his message here on earth. He has fully equipped us by sending us the Holy Spirit to empower us to live as if we believe what we profess. In us reside the treasures of heaven. In us lives the message of God's love and redemption. Father, help us to reflect you and your Word accurately in our homes, schools, workplaces and in the marketplace. Remind us daily that we are being watched and read. In the name of the One who calls us his ambassadors. Amen.

Today's Scriptures

Matthew 5:14–16; 2 Corinthians 3:2–3; 2 Corinthians 5:20; 1 John 2:6

Today's Thought

The most beautiful women are joy-filled women. How do you define joy? Have you considered that joy is a choice? Every day, regardless of our circumstances, we must choose joy to experience the full abundant life Jesus offers. He has set the ultimate example of choosing joy. Scripture exhorts us to look to Jesus, the author and perfecter of our faith. Then the amazing words, "*...who for the joy set before him, endured the cross ...*" (Hebrews 12:2). The implications of that verse! Have you considered that Jesus counted it all joy as he died on the cross? Dear one, the joy before him was you! He looked down through the ages and saw you bring your broken heart to him. He saw all your tears and disappointments and all the circumstances that would cause you to seek him. He heard you cry out for forgiveness and restoration. That was his joy! He endured it all with joy because he could not bear to live without you.

Today's Prayer

Dearest Lord, thank you for all you endured so you could have us as your own. We cannot imagine the cruelty of the cross that you stained with your own blood on our behalf. As you suffered there, you looked ahead to the joy that would be yours and the joy that would be ours. Amazing love, how can it be! You saw us in the future, choosing you. Father, as we launch into this new day, I pray that we choose joy as Jesus did. When we are hurting, when we suffer, when others let us down, and when we struggle, may we choose joy. We know that life will not always feel good, but in the midst of it all we can choose the deep-down joy in our souls as we fix our eyes on Jesus, the Man of Joy. Amen.

Today's Scriptures

Isaiah 71:10–12; John 15:11; John 17:13; Hebrews 12:1–2

Today's Thought

Life is an obstacle course. Fear. Loss. Divorce. Illness. Debt. Anger. Navigating through these unexpected circumstances can be complex and complicated. Not one of us will escape adversity. I hope you have that one trusted friend who is walking alongside as you struggle through the perils of life. We all need a friend we can depend on when everyone else walks away. Scripture tells us that God calls us his friends. He sticks closer than even the best friend we could ever have. To be called a friend of God implies that we can enjoy continual friendship and fellowship with him. He doesn't look the other way when hardship comes. He sits right with us and holds us close as we weep. While we hide in him, he is already about the business of bringing us through the trial, working on our behalf in the background. What a friend we have in Jesus, all our sins and grief to bear. Yes, beloved of God, he is the friend who sticks closer than any other.

Today's Prayer

Father God, we are so grateful that you call us friend. When hard times come, you never leave us alone; you are the God who stays. As we walk in the midst of this fallen and broken world, even friends with the best intentions will let us down. As we draw near to you in times of trouble you draw ever closer to us. How we need that manner of commitment. We know that life will have its upsets, but your Word confirms that adversity matures our faith. Your Word also assures us that you have purpose in all you allow to touch us. Lord, we determine to embrace you as the friend we need at all times. In the name of Jesus, who sticks closer than a brother. Amen.

Today's Scriptures

Proverbs 18:24; John 15:13–15; James 2:23; 1 Peter 5:6–7

March 6

Today's Thought

"For God so loved …" How many times have we heard, read or vocalized John 3:16? Have you considered that God loves the whole world, representing every human being he ever created? But there is another truth hidden in scripture, a truth that is only for those who trust in Christ for salvation. The world is loved by God, but we are *"beloved"* of God. That makes us something very special in his sight. Loving the world is a broad brush stroke. Being his beloved, places us in a most high place, which is above the world that he loves. The moment any man, woman or child receives God through Jesus Christ, he or she immediately becomes the *"beloved."* Here is what I discovered as I examined the difference in my concordance. Those that are loved by God are loved in a social or moral sense. Those *"beloved"* of God are the ones he delights in, those who are precious to him and the beloved are loved with a burning love. Embrace that truth today, you are not simply loved, you are the *"beloved."*

Today's Prayer

Father God, you have distinguished between those who receive and love your Son and those who do not. You make it clear to us that you love all the world. Jesus came to save all who will believe. You also reveal that we are your *"beloved"* ones as we embrace Christ as our personal Savior. That amazing truth calls us into a very special relationship with you. A bonding that is stronger than any love we can know on earth. Yes, we are your *"beloved"* and you are our *"beloved"*! We are precious to you and you delight in us as we delight in you. In the name of the Beloved One. Amen.

Today's Scriptures

Song of Solomon 2:3–4; Zephaniah 3:17; Ephesians 5:1–2; Colossians 3:12

Today's Thought

Our lives are shaped by the various seasons we live through. How we respond to the changes of life determines who we become in the end. Are you able to clearly identify the season you are in right now? Is it a wilderness, a river of peace, or something else? Recognizing our seasson of life goes a long way in helping us to understand what God may be up to. Just as the physical seasons look so different, so do our spiritual seasons. Each has its own form of beauty and purpose. God nourishes the earth through spring, summer, fall and winter. He nourishes us in our various seasons. Change is necessary for growth, but God never changes. Through it all he remains an anchor where our soul can find security and stability no matter the season. In the dry, rain will come. In the sorrow, joy will come. In the uncertain, clarity will come. Wise Solomon tells us that for every season under heaven, there is a divine purpose.

Today's Prayer

Father God, we thank you that life is not mundane and dull. Life is an exciting adventure with you in our midst. Every season has its own beauty and purpose. Lord, help us not to yearn for the next season, but to embrace the one we are in. Help us to not miss the lessons being taught, the hand of God we need to see, the voice of your Word we need to hear. May we appreciate all you are doing in and through this time. May we celebrate each season as it comes knowing you are taking us from glory to glory, from the shallow to the deep. Underneath the cold winter snow, you are growing a springtime of joy. In the name of our unchanging God, Amen.

Today's Scripture

Psalm 1:1–3; Ecclesiastes 3:1; Acts 1:7; Galatians 6:9

March 8

Today's Thought

The most successful people in life are those who have focus. Where ever our center of attention falls, that will determine our motivation. If my life is dull and unclear, without direction, I am shooting in the dark. If I don't know where I am going, my life becomes haphazard and misplaced. Focus comes by living for God and his eternal purposes. If I make his will and goals my own, my aim is clear; my focus is centered in his Word and will. Paul said it this way in 1 Corinthians, *"Therefore, I do not run like a man running aimlessly; I do not fight like a man beating the air. No, I beat my body and make it my slave so that after I have preached to others, I myself will not be disqualified for the prize."* Paul knew his race was just that, a race against distractions and hindrances. He was reaching for the gold, the prize and crown that will last forever. My challenge for today is for us to evaluate our degree of spiritual focus. What race are we running, where are we headed, and how do we want this to end?

Today's Prayer

Father God, we acknowledge that this life is full of distractions and detours that hinder our spiritual growth. We desire to make your purposes our aim, your will our goal. God, help us to run well, with determination and spiritual grit. You have lovingly provided everything we need to win; we are more than conquerors. Jesus runs with us in every step we take and will bring us through triumphant. Lord, may our focus be a laser beam fixed upon your Word, a spotlight guiding our paths to the finish line. Father, we thank you that you bless our desire to please you. In the name of our Forerunner. Amen.

Today's Scriptures

Ecclesiastes 10:10; 1 Corinthians 9:24–27; Philippians 3:14; Hebrews 12:1–2

Today's Thought

In 1959 a man named Phil Phillips penned a song that was an overnight hit. The song was *Sea of Love*. I was 13-years-old and that song shaped a yeaning in my heart for a love that was as deep as the ocean. In his song Phil entreats his love, *"Come with me, my love, to the sea, the sea of love. I want to tell you how much I love you."* I am not 13-years-old anymore, but I still have a need to be beckoned into that fathomless sea of love. When I was 35 years old, my desire was realized. It was an invitation from the One whose love truly is an ocean. It was Jesus calling me to encounter the deep, deep love of God. If I were to live for a million years and more, I could never exhaust this love so deep, so wide and so limitless. God's love for you is intensely personal. It is a love you can never earn or deserve; his love just is. Are you ready to dive into deeper waters today? I pray God makes his love so real and tangible that you will never be the same.

Today's Prayer

Precious Lord, today you call us to your sea of love. You invite us to cast off anything that would keep us from accepting your personal invitation to deeper depths of knowing you and your love. You have long desired to tell us how much you love us. Lord, give us ears to hear that love when it speaks. Give us eyes to see that love when it appears. Give us a heart to invite that love in when it beckons us. To know you is to love you. To know you is to trust you. Father, we need this love of yours more than we could ever know. May we embrace the true and genuine love you offer us. In the name of the One who is our Sea of Love. Amen.

Today's Scriptures

Jeremiah 31:3; Romans 8:38–39; Ephesians 3:14–19; 1 John 3:1

Today's Thought

What will they say about me after I am gone? That is a question I have often pondered. Will they refer to the degrees I earned? The wealth I accumulated? The illustrious career I accomplished? The beautiful things with which I filled my home? All the places in the world I toured? Since I accomplished none of those, what will they say? I really don't know the answer to; but, this is what I would like them to say. Her life was a life well-lived. She loved God and she loved people. She shared her faith with anyone who would listen. She served selflessly even when she would have rather been served. She lived what she professed and walked what she talked. She was kind to everyone and was not partial to color or culture. She loved God's Word and obeyed the best she knew how. She reflected Jesus in all she did. She did not accomplish any great things; but, her life was a life well-lived. What do you want them to say about you after you are gone?

Today's Prayer

Father God, thank you for the one life you give us. We are on a brief journey. We have this one chance to get it right. Lord, help us to set our life's priorities according to what is important to you. May we know what we have been called to just as Jesus knew his calling. He lived a simple life without degree or wealth; and yet, he turned the world upside down. He paid the price for all sin and he was raised from the dead so we could have the hope of eternal life. It was said of him, *"He did all things well."* Father, I pray that be what is said of us. Help us to live a simple remarkable life after the pattern of your Son's time on earth; a life well-lived. Amen.

Today's Scriptures

Mark 7:37; Acts 10:37–38; 1 Corinthians 1:26–29; 1 Thessalonians 4:11–12

Today's Thought

Charles H. Spurgeon once said, *"I have learned to kiss the waves that throw me up against the Rock of Ages."* I love how this quote fits with what Paul said, *"For our light and momentary troubles are achieving for us an eternal weight of glory that far outweighs them all"* (2 Corinthians 4:17). When we are in the midst of it all, it sure does not feel as if anything good is happening. That's when we have to decide if we believe what God's Word says, or if we believe our feelings. Our emotions are often in conflict with what is true in the spiritual realm. In times of great distress, we must rise above what our feelings tell us and reach for that truth ... God has not forsaken us and he is up to something of eternal value. Perspective is crucial. When we set our sights on being drawn closer to our Rock of Ages, the billows and waves become dear friends that achieve God's desire of knowing and trusting him more. Allow these momentary troubles to throw you right into his arms.

Today's Prayer

Father God, Rock of Ages, your presence is our desire. To know you more and more is our aim. If it takes trials and sorrows to achieve this, then we say, *"Amen."* Lord, we know we can trust you because your desire is for us, not against us. How you long to draw us into the deep hidden places of your heart. We acknowledge and believe that this is often accomplished through pain. When we think of what you suffered, the pain you experienced on our behalf, we can truly see that what we suffer is indeed momentary and of little significance in the light of the eternal rewards. Thank you for the waves that throw us into your loving arms. In the name of our Rock and Refuge. Amen.

Today's Scripture

Exodus 33:18–22; Song of Solomon 2:14; John 14:27; 2 Corinthians 4:16–18

March 12

Today's Thought

Antiques can be costly. Do you know your true worth? I am not calling you an antique, but then again … in a sense we are all old souls simply because the Lord knew us even before we were formed in the womb. Christ knew us as he hung on the cross. The God of creation knew us from the foundation of the world. Yes, dear one, you have always existed … first in God's heart and mind, then in your mother's womb, and now as his precious child. God has great plans for you. He does not want you hidden away in a musty museum. His desire is for you to shine as the diamond that you are in a world that is dark and without hope. He plans to use your life in such remarkable ways that no price could ever be paid. The God of the universe has placed such value on you it cannot be measured. I hope those around you are treating you with the worth and value you deserve.

Today's Prayer

Father God, we praise you for creating us in your image. How priceless we are! Of all you created, we are the ones you crowned with your glory and splendor. You call us your children. Not even the holy angels have that honor. Lord, I pray we understand our great worth and know that nothing we could ever do or not do can devalue us in any way. Father, I pray we do not allow others to devalue us, but that our closest relationships are those with mutual appreciation and respect. I pray you show us any ways in which we devalue ourselves or any ways others cheapen our existence through their words or actions. Help us to address these issues in loving and healthy ways. In the name of the One who created us in his image. Amen.

Today's Scriptures

Proverbs 31:29–31; Isaiah 62:3; Matthew 10:29–31; 1 Peter 2:4

Today's Thought

The first chapter of the Song of Solomon opens in a most intimate way. The lovesick maiden entreats her love, *"Let him kiss me with the kisses of his mouth, for your love is more delightful than wine"* (Song of Solomon 1:2). She longs for one of the most intimate of loves expression, a kiss. Have you noticed how new parents can't stop kissing that sweet-smelling baby; or, how a couple in love steal kisses every chance they get? God wants to kiss you today. You are the darling of his heart. As his beloved child, he can't take his eyes off of you. He aches to kiss you today. Be prepared. His kiss could come in many different ways. It could come in the sunrise, or a bird singing outside your window. It could come in finding that one special thing you have been searching for. It could be those special words spoken by a friend, or a surprise kiss from a loved one. Be on the watch. Please don't miss those kisses the Lord wants to give you all through the day; and not only today, but every day, your whole life long.

Today's Prayer

Father God, you fashioned us in your image, and we like to be kissed. I imagine you love our kisses as well. We kiss you when we worship you and when we study your Word. We kiss you when we walk in obedience and when we love our neighbor. These are spiritual kisses that bless us both. God, I pray that we are aware and sensitive to the many ways you reach out to us in intimacy, making yourself ever so real and personal. Lord, help us not to miss one single kiss you send our way. Help us to see you in the common and ordinary as well as the powerful and profound. Thank you for all the ways you show us your love every day. Amen.

Today's Scriptures

Psalm 2:11–12; Song of Solomon 1:2; 2:3–4; Luke 7:36–38

Today's Thought

Two men, two choices, two destinies. One man hurling insults, the other acknowledging the deity of Christ. One feared God, the other curses Christ. One knows he is deserving of death, the other arrogant and rude. One man condemned to an agonizing death with no hope beyond the grave, one man promised a trip to paradise that very day. Each was at a crossroads, his eternal destiny hanging in the balance. In this event we see both the mercy and the justice of God. Both sinners, both deserving of death, hanging between heaven and earth. Our lives also hang in the balance. We all come to a fork in the road where we choose our eternal destiny. Each man was given an opportunity to claim Christ as his own personal Savior. Jesus came to seek both men, to redeem both men. Only one opened his heart to the love and mercy of God. The greatest question we are faced with in life is this, *"What will you do with Jesus?"* Scorn or embrace? Receive or reject? Accept his grace, or walk away? His arms are open wide.

Today's Prayer

Father God, like sheep we have gone astray. We are like sheep without a shepherd. You sent Jesus as the answer to our dilemma. We could never save ourselves from the empty way of life handed down to us from long ago. Our spiritual well-being hangs in the balance. Lord, I pray for anyone reading these words today who needs you as Savior. I pray that your loving arms reach to the core of her soul with the salvation that gains her a place in heaven with you. I pray for that one who has strayed and needs to find her way back to you, Father. I pray for the one who has lost hope, that you restore her to yourself. In Jesus' name. Amen.

Today's Scriptures

Deuteronomy 30:19–20; Luke 23:39–43; John 1:12–13; Revelation 3:20

Today's Thought

Who was Barabbas? We find mention of him in all four gospels. He is described as a notorious prisoner, a bandit, a rebel, and a murderer. Now it was custom that before the Feast of Passover, a pardon be granted to one Jewish prisoner as an act of goodwill. On this particular day the choice was between two men, a high-profile killer and rebel-rouser named Barabbas or, Jesus, a miracle worker who was clearly innocent of any wrong doing. Shockingly, the crowd chose the guilty Barabbas, while with the same breath they called for Jesus' crucifixion. Which man would you have chosen? Of course, we know the answer, but do we understand that it *had* to be Jesus? Barabbas could not have died for our sins as he was fully steeped in his own. It had to be Jesus. Think of the irony of it all. The guilty set free, the innocent crucified. He who deserved death was given life; he who was the giver of life was condemned to death. Barabbas' story is really our story. Just as he deserved to die for his sin, so do we. Just as he was granted a pardon, so were we. We don't know what Barabbas did with the life that was granted him, but the question remains, what will we do with ours?

Today's Prayer

Father God, you made a great exchange on that historic day. Your Son's life for ours. We know it should have been us on that cross. But your mercy was greater, and Jesus' death canceled our debts. "Paid in Full." We all have to choose what we will do with the grace and mercy you have shown us. Will we walk away from the cross unchanged, or will we allow the cross to change us. Thank you, Jesus. You took what we deserved! Amen.

Today's Scriptures

Isaiah 53:5; Matthew 27:15–23; Romans 6:23; 2 Corinthians 5:21

March 16

Today's Thought

According to the Gospel of Matthew, Pilate washed his hands in front of the crowd and declared, *"... I am innocent of this man's blood ..."* (Matthew 27:24). He told the crowd that the blood of the blameless man was on them. Pilate tried to wash the guilt blood from his hands as he endorsed the crucifixion of an innocent man; but he could not. The guilt followed him right into the act of suicide. Tradition has it that after the crucifixion of Jesus, he continually washed his hands raw, attempting to wash away the guilt. Our sins also demanded Jesus' death. Without his payment on our behalf, we had no hope for salvation. Without the forgiveness of Christ, we try to cover the disgrace of sin that is on us; but, by the blood of Christ, we no longer carry the crimson stain of sin. Praise God, in Christ, we can live guilt free because of God's merciful plan for our redemption.

Today's Prayer

Father God, on that historical day, a man who had great authority buckled under the demands of a crowd that hated Jesus. If only he had known, if only the crowd had known. Lord, now we see the whole story of what happened that day and why it had to happen just as it did. Without the shedding of sinless blood, there is no forgiveness of sin. Pontius Pilot was an instrument in your hand in carrying out your redemptive plan for mankind, your plan for us. We are fully cleansed by the blood of the blameless Lamb, and you do not hold our sins against us. I pray that we each receive this free but costly sacrificial gift of salvation's forgiveness. I pray we ever walk in the freedom of your lavish love and faithfulness. In Jesus' name. Amen.

Today's Scriptures

Psalm 126:2; Proverbs 17:22; Proverbs 31:25; Zephaniah 3:17

Today's Thought

An empty heart, an empty tomb. Mary Magdalene encountered both. When she stood outside the sealed tomb of Jesus she faced the truth of what had happened with an empty heart. She had lost the best thing that ever happened to her. When she later looked inside the empty tomb, her heart was revived with renewed hope. We are born into this world bringing nothing with us. Our lives are an empty page, ready to be filled with various colors of love, acceptance, experiences and relationships. In the rough places of life, we suffer losses, love betrays us and people, places and things do not fulfill as we hoped. As Mary stood outside the tomb we feel her sadness. Her sense of disappointment can be ours as well. If all we do is stand and gaze at the tomb where Jesus lay, we will feel the gaping emptiness. It's wasn't until Mary encountered the empty tomb, the living Christ, that she dared to hope. Her empty heart was filled and overflowed with joy as the realization came. He had risen. The tomb was empty. Her heart exploded with hope.

Today's Prayer

Father God, you did not allow the tomb to remain occupied. You raised Jesus by the power of your Spirit, and we now have hope for our empty hearts. The best part is knowing that because he lives, we will live as well. You raised your Son and you will raise us. The same resurrection power that raised Jesus dwells in us. It's our Resurrection Day, our day to celebrate and praise our Lord Jesus as we sing of his glorious power. Oh death, where is your sting. Oh grave, where is your victory? Thanks be to God! He has given us the victory through his Son Jesus Christ. Amen.

Today's Scriptures

John 11:25–27; John 20:10–18; Romans 8:11; 1 Peter 1:3–5

Today's Thought

My friend has a beautiful autistic son. When she needs to interrupt one of his meltdowns, she often helps him to settle by taking him into her arms, gathering him close and holding him tight. I think there is a spiritual truth here that we need to lay hold of. Often, we think that when we are not at our best God pulls away and waits for us to get it right. Nothing could be further from the truth. He is not a distant God. He is not one who loves us and holds us close only when we are at our best. When we are in a struggle or battle, that is when we need his nearness more than ever. God always comes through for us. He loves the prodigal, he loves the rebellious, and he loves the runaway. His grace covers it all. It's that unchanging love that brings us back to our true selves. I am not advocating sin and rebellion; those behaviors never end well. What I want us to grasp is that God never lets go. His arms are always drawing us into his embrace. That's his grace.

Today's Prayer

Father God, you know that we can be better than our behavior sometimes portrays. Thank you for the love that does not desert us when we need it most. When we struggle, you do not pull away, you draw us closer into your being until we see the truth about ourselves. We are dearly loved and accepted in the Beloved Son, not because of our goodness, but because of Jesus' goodness and mercy. We pray, Father, that when we are not living well, rather than running *from* you, that we run *to* you. Help us to remember that you are always waiting and longing to pull us in close. There is never any distance between us other than the distance we create. In the name of the Father who holds us. Amen.

Today's Scriptures

Psalm 34:18; Psalm 73:21–26; Psalm 139:7–12; Psalm 145:18

Today's Thought

I was once the victim of a stalker. It's frightening. There is another type of stalking that I think we have all experienced in one way or another. Fear. It is the worst of stalkers. It comes up on us so gradually and subtlety that we hardly notice it until we are paralyzed by it. Just as a fog moves in on a misty morning, before we know it, we are blinded. Living with fear takes a lot of energy. The good news is we don't have to live under the shadow of fear. God gives us a way out through Jesus Christ. The answer when fear stalks you is in God's Word. I have listed four scriptures today for you to embed into your heart that can help overcome fear. I know it's not an easy road, but if you persist, with God's help, you can conquer this hideous stalker. The abundant joyful life you desire is on the other side of your fear. I realize that danger is real, but fear is a choice.

Today's Prayer

Father of peace, today we confess that there are times when we allow fear to stalk us and take hold of us in unhealthy ways. Lord, I pray that we come to recognize the ways we harbor this damaging emotion in our hearts. Often we allow fear to terrorize us. That is not the life you promise us. You assure us that fear does not come from you. Jesus came to give us life, and life abundantly. He also said that we could be of good cheer because he has overcome the evils of this world. Fear lies to us and intimidates us so as to hinder us in our spiritual and emotional growth. We thank and praise you that you are able to deliver us from this hideous emotion by your Holy Spirit and your Word. In the name of our Prince of Peace, Amen.

Today's Scriptures

Psalm 46:1–3; Psalm 56:1–4; 2 Timothy 1:7; 1 John 4:14–18

March 20

Today's Thought

I like to imagine myself as a woman of great faith. The sad reality is, I often doubt. There are so many ways we doubt. We question our faith. Is it real? We are uncertain that God hears and will answer our prayers. Does God love me? Is his will for my life going to make me happy? Can he heal me? Thomas doubted, so did John the Baptist. Questioning God and our faith is not unique to any of us; we all doubt at times. When I begin to doubt, I bring that reservation to God. Remember the father of the child who was invaded by a deaf and mute spirit? He came to Jesus and said, *"I believe, help me overcome my unbelief"* (Mark 9:24). I have returned to those brave words again and again. It does take courage to confess to the Lord that we have doubts. He understands our weakness. On the cross Jesus cried out in dismay to his Father, *"My God, why have you forsaken me?"* (Matthew 27:46). He understands our humanness; and he knows our limitations in believing what we cannot see.

Today's Prayer

Father God, how we want to have that great faith that is so precious in your sight. Sadly, we often fail in our belief. You have equipped us with so many biblical examples of both failing faith and great faith. When we begin to doubt you, we frequently bring trouble down on our heads. Lord, help us to avoid these calamities that arise from not trusting you. Help us to cease from leaning on our own human understanding, and may we come to you with the childlike faith that you love and reward. We know we will doubt again, but we ask that you grow us up in our faith, that you take us from unbelief to belief. In Jesus' name. Amen.

Today's Scriptures

Matthew 28:16–7; Mark 9:23–24; John 11:40; John 20:24–29

Today's Thought

We are bombarded every day with the viewpoints of man. These opinions come at us from every direction imaginable; TV, magazines, Hollywood, Washington, social media, newspapers, you name it. Everyone has a personal viewpoint. It is rare to get accuracy from a world that does not seek truth. How can we expect the deceived culture of our day to correctly inform us on the issues of our day? God's Word is the only source of truth that we can trust. The Son was sent to us so we could be certain that truth does exist. How often do you rely on your Bible for wisdom in navigating in this unstable world? How much time do you devote in seeking the answers for today's uncertain times? Dear one, you will not get truth from the world's conversation. I counsel that we set our hearts and minds to the study of God's timeless Word in seeking how we are to live and respond in these troubling times.

Today's Prayer

Father of truth, how desperate we are to know truth and to understand the times in which we live. We thank you that we can turn to a source that is absolutely reliable. Lord, I pray that we turn first to you and your Word so we can discern what we are hearing. May we not be deceived by what the culture dishes out. Your Word must be our anchor in these unstable times. I pray we not neglect this Book that you sent from heaven so we can know and understand the times and know how we are to respond. You have not left us in the dark. You have made yourself and your will abundantly clear. God, I pray your people return to discernment by the reading and hearing of your Word. In the name of Jesus, our one flawless source of truth. Amen.

Today's Scriptures

Proverbs 28:5; John 14:6; 2 Timothy 2:15; 2 Timothy 3:14–17

March 22

Today's Thought

On the day Jesus died, strange things happened. Darkness was over the land. The earth shook; rocks were split in two. Bodies of the saints in graves came out, walked around and were seen by many. The curtain of the temple was torn in two, from top to bottom. Today, I want to look into the tearing of the curtain and the significance it holds for us today. The temple in Jerusalem contained the presence of God. It was in the Holy of Holies where the High Priest interceded on behalf of the people for the forgiveness of their sins. Only the high priest could enter that holy place. When Jesus took all our sins upon himself on the cross, the torn curtain revealed that the way was now open for all to enter the Holy of Holies, the very presence of God. The tearing of the curtain indicated that Christ was making a new and living way. Now, through Christ, we have full access into the presence of God. The writer of Hebrews entreats us to *"Let us then approach the throne of grace with confidence, so that we may receive mercy and find grace to help us in our time of need"* (Hebrews 4:16).

Today's Prayer

Father God, how merciful you are! While we were yet dead in our sins, you sent your Son to die in our place. You have replaced the old covenant of the law with the new covenant, the precious blood of Jesus. We thank you that we now have access to the very throne of heaven. We can come without fear; with full assurance that we are accepted in your beloved Son. What a miracle! The curtain is torn; the door to your presence is wide open. Your arms are ready to receive us, your mercy is complete and we are forgiven. Blessed be our Savior and Lord, Hosanna in the highest! Amen.

Today's Scriptures

Matthew 27:51–53; Hebrews 4:14–16; Hebrews 9:11–14; Hebrews 10:19–22

Today's Thought

It seems as if the battles never end. If I am not in conflict over a relationship, finances, health, or something else, it's a good day. The quiet days are few and far between. I have come to recognize the real battle; the actual fight is the war that is raging for my heart. I am learning that God is relentless in pursuing and exposing the true condition of my heart. Outwardly the struggle is real, but God is more interested in the undercurrent beneath the struggle. He is more concerned about my reactions and responses to the circumstances. He sits as a Refiner desiring to burn away the impurities and bring forth precious gold. The Refiner is also the Father who never leaves his child in the fire of adversity a second too long. He knows exactly when to rescue his child. He is not out to destroy us. His aim is to purify of our hearts. His purpose is to perfect us into the image of his righteous Son.

Today's Prayer

Father God, this life is full of trouble and trials. Often, we want to blame circumstances and situations, we say, *"If only things were different, I could be different."* In your infinite wisdom, you look for the heart to change so the circumstances can begin to change. You are always after our hearts; the purifying of our motives and intentions. Help us to see the great truth in the refining process. Lord, help us to see every situation for what it is. To see the lesson we need to learn or the pride and deceit that lurks there. I pray that in every battle we first look inward and see what it is you want to change in us. We are grateful that you care so much about our hearts. In the name of our Loving Refiner. Amen.

Today's Scriptures

Job 23:10; Hebrews 4:12–13; James 1:2–4; 1 Peter 1:6–7

Today's Thought

Solomon once said, *"Even a fool is thought wise if he keeps silent, and discerning if he holds his tongues"* (Proverbs 17:28). One of my pet peeves is to be held captive by a person who will not stop talking. The Bible has a lot to say in regard to useless chatter. Scriptures goes as far as to say, *"In the multitude of words sin is not lacking"* (Proverbs 10:19; NKJV). The old cliché, *"Silence is Golden"* is biblical. I think it is important for us to examine our speech from time-to-time. People who dominate conversations can be wearisome. Those who monopolize can be mind-numbing. The wise person engages in dialog not monolog. The longer we babble on, the more we lose focus on real issues. Wise people are not always silent, but they know when to be. Perhaps the answer to this matter is learning to be a good listener. Oh my, the world certainly needs more people who have mastered the art of listening. I really want to learn those listening skills. They can be a gift to those who need to be heard. How about you?

Today's Prayer

Father God, we thank you for language, good conversations and those who listen well. Forgive us for the ways we abuse the gift of speech. I pray we research and seek out your Word for appropriate guidelines in regard to how we use this important skill. Show us any ways in which we annoy others with incessant talking. We all need to be better listeners and you have set that example for us. You always listen when we have something to say. You always respond in ways that are succinct and on point. Lord, we want to be your gift to others in our speech and in our listening. In the name of the God of language. Amen.

Today's Scriptures

Psalm 141:3; Proverbs 17:27–28; Matthew 12:36–37; James 1:26

Today's Thought

I cringe when my husband goes grocery shopping on an empty stomach. I know he will be coming home with a lot of junk food. Why is that? When he is full on healthy food, he has less of a tendency to go for the sweet and salty. He will be content with the healthier choices. It's the same for me. When I have been dining on the better things, I am less tempted by the things that do not satisfy. The spiritual application is this; when I am full on God's Word, I am less susceptible to feeding on the junk food of the world. If I am being filled up with the things of God, I more easily turn away from sinful temptations. When my spirit is full with wholesome Christian fellowship, I can avoid the company of those who do not benefit me spiritually. All day long I am given choices. The music I listen to, the books and magazines I read, what I watch and what I listen to. Today will be filled with all sorts of options. What we choose will determine our spiritual fullness.

Today's Prayer

Father God, you have given us so many life illustrations. When it comes to physical nourishment, you provide everything good for our bodies. You have also provided for our spiritual nourishment as we feed upon your Word. Lord, help us to think carefully before we choose. Your Spirit is our wise counselor when choices are set before us. When we are empty and hungry, we often make poor choices. When we are full on your Word and satisfied in you, we put ourselves in the right position to desire that which is best. Holy Spirit, fill us today so that we can taste and see that the Lord is indeed good. Amen.

Today's Scriptures

Deuteronomy 30:19–20; Psalm 34:8; Proverbs 27:7; John 6:49–51

March 26

Today's Thought

At one time I worked at a data center. One thing we operators knew well; the quality of the data that came out was only as good as the data that went in. We had a running joke about bad data, *"garbage in; garbage out."* Our hearts are vessels that accumulate and store everything and anything. What we take in through our eyes and our ears remains with us. When we take in the good, we have good to give. When we take in the worldly and unholy, it comes out as garbage when we least expect it. Course joking and insults come from the heart that received it. Gossip and slander are the result of a heart that accepts them. We are deceived when we believe that participating in unholy talk and behavior will not be toxic to our very soul. We must guard our hearts as we would a precious treasure. The Word tells us that from the heart flow the issues of life. May that which springs from our spirit be edifying and profitable to us and a blessing to others.

Today's Prayer

Father God, Jesus revealed all that was in his heart. It was all good. His heart poured out your love and concern for us. Through his life and heart, we saw you. As we imitate him in our lives, we pray to live in such a way that our character and nature would be wholesome and enriching as we interact with those who need you. I pray those around us are blessed by our words and our actions. We understand it begins with our thoughts which filter down to our hearts, then proceed out of our mouths. Lord, those ungodly things we have absorbed into our being must be cleansed by the blood of Jesus and the washing of your Word. We pray your mercy and help in matters of the heart. In Jesus' name. Amen.

Today's Scriptures

Psalm 19:14; Proverbs 4:23–24; Luke 6:45; Ephesians 4:29

March 27

Today's Thought

We all long for success. The culture around us is obsessed with position and accomplishment. How do we as Christians define success and how do we achieve it? That depends on your definition. God has given us clarification of what success means for the child of God. As we think about our goals in life, we know that achieving those ambitions takes a lot of hard work. In my life I have discovered an important key to success. Consistency. When I set my heart on a goal, I know that I may be in for the long haul. For instance, as I write this devotional, I know that in order to succeed in getting it to print I must sit every day and write. If I begin to slack off and make excuses, it will never get into your hands. I must be consistent in reading God's blueprint for life; then, I must be consistent in living it out in my daily life. The more consistent we are in our pursuits, the sooner we will see our dreams become realities.

Today's Prayer

Father God, you created us for success. You designed us to dream and to realize those dreams. You have given us strength and abilities that match our calling. Our part is the consistent effort we must put forth every day in order to accomplish your purposes in our lives. Father, I pray for those who do not have a dream, who do not know their calling. May you deposit your will into their hearts. Lord, I pray for those who have difficulty being consistent. I ask that as they come to you today and ask for the capacity for consistency that you will accomplish that in their lives. Lord, for all of us, I pray that more than anything we have daily time in the study of your Word. In the name of our constant and consistently faithful God. Amen.

Today's Scriptures

Psalm 37:5; Proverbs 16:3; 1 Corinthians 15:58; Philippians 4:13

Today's Thought

There was a man named Gideon whom God choose to be valiant and victorious in battle. The problem was, Gideon was not courageous. An angel of the Lord came to the trembling Gideon and said, *"The Lord is with you mighty warrior"* (Judges 6:12). Gideon had a great calling on his life, but God had to summon it out or Gideon never would have stepped into it. Every child of God has a call on his or her life. Often the things that have caused us the deepest pain are the very things that God wants to use in our lives to help others. Our greatest fears can be the catalyst for God's desire to pour courage into us. Our unfaithfulness may be just the thing God wants to turn into faithfulness; our weaknesses into our greatest strengths. God loves to take little and make it much. In so doing, he is the one who gets the glory. In my own life, I never would have accomplished the things for God that I have if he had not called it out of me. Do you know the call on your life? If not, why not ask God today to draw out of you those things he can most use in the lives of others.

Today's Prayer

Father God, we are often like Gideon, hiding away somewhere where we feel safe and comfortable. You long to use each of our lives to benefit the kingdom of God. We all have past experiences, certain gifts, personalities and temperaments that are unique to us. Lord, I pray each of us recognize the special call you placed on our lives. For those of us who already know that call, I pray you enhance our particular ministry in extraordinary ways. Lord, it's not that we receive the glory, but that you and your name are exalted in and through us. In the name of the One who calls us. Amen.

Today's Scriptures

1 Corinthians 7:17; Ephesians 4:1; Philippians 3:12; 1 Peter 4:10

Today's Thought

"I wish God were more real to me." I hear it so often. Why is God so real to some and others struggle with the sense of his presence and the reality of him? I really don't have the full answer to that, but I can make a few observations. First and foremost, we are not to judge reality by our feelings. Our relationship with God is a faith-walk. We will not always see, hear or understand how God works in our lives. We can be absolutely sure of this; we are always in the presence of God; every moment is sacred and saturated with his presence. We may not feel him or see him, but the reality of him never changes. Secondly, God is looking for those who will diligently seek his will and his presence. He is not playing hide and seek with us; he wants us to know him and experience his abiding presence. Thirdly, God has chosen to reveal himself to us through his Word. In it we see his nature, his character and his guidelines for living a successful life. As we believe what we discover about God through his Word, the reality of him begins to flood our souls.

Today's Prayer

Father God, how we long to know you and to experience the reality of you. You promise to make yourself known to us if we seek you with all our hearts. We are assured that you have freely revealed your nature and character through the person of your Son Jesus. Help us to believe so we may see your glory and encounter the reality of your presence. You reward faith and diligence. I pray we be more persistent than ever in pursuing you through your Word. Help us to walk by faith and not by our feelings. In the name of the One who pursues us. Amen.

Today's Scriptures

Psalm 105:4; Isaiah 55:6; Jeremiah 29:12–13; Hebrews 11:6

March 30

Today's Thought

We don't hear much about a place called Hell these days. No one wants to "offend." There are many different viewpoints on the theme. Some would argue if God is love why would he pronounce Hell as a judgment? God is holy and sinless. Sin and evil cannot exist in his presence. Since we are sinners at birth, in our fallen state we cannot stand in the presence of God. We certainly have a problem. God in his great love gave us a way out of our dilemma by sending Jesus to pay the debt for our sin, and in turn, he extended his own righteousness to us. The condition is that we must accept this great exchange by accepting Christ and his finished work on the cross. That is the only cure for our sinfulness. The truth is God does not send people to Hell. If one refuses to accept Jesus' ultimate sacrifice, then that refusal is what determines his destiny. God loves us so much he will not violate our freedom to choose. G. K. Chesterton said, *"Hell is God's great compliment to the reality of human freedom and the dignity of human choice."*

Today's Prayer

Father God, we are truly grateful for the freedom of choice you give us. Our choices are not always wise, but in your mercy, you offer forgiveness and healing. We confess that Jesus Christ is the only way to you and the only escape we have from eternal separation from you. You have rescued us by providing your one and only sinless Son to pay our debts. As we accept that truth, we now have access to you and a promise of an eternal home in heaven. Father, you are just and you are merciful. Jesus died that all may receive forgiveness and eternal life. It saddens your heart that all will not accept the great sacrifice made by your Son. Amen.

Today's Scriptures

John 3:16–18; John 3:35–36; John 12:48; Romans 6:23

Today's Thought

Continue. What an interesting word. It means, to *remain, stay, endure, persist, carry forward*. The biblical definition of persistence is, *continued effort to do or achieve something despite difficulties, failure, or opposition*. So many times, in my life I threw in the towel, rather than persevere. I remember all the good things I missed out on in my life simply because I walked away. God's admonition for us to persevere is because he does not want us to miss out on the rewards that come with pressing on. Continuance is a characteristic of those who have courage in the face of obstacles, have passion in their pursuits, and who truly want God's best for their lives. They are the ones who allow the Holy Spirit to develop the fruit of patience in them. People who are diligent in their endeavors are rich with success. When we are ready to give up, the Holy Spirit is always ready to help us continue, no matter how difficult it may be.

Today's Prayer

Father God, we acknowledge that we have lost so much because of the tendency to give up rather than press on. Marriages, relationships, careers and other significant opportunities squandered. Lord, even though we can't get those chances back, in your infinite wisdom and mercy, you cause all things to work together for our good and your glory. God, I pray that beginning today we embrace the valued attribute of perseverance. We thank you that you persisted in your pursuit of our hearts. You never gave up on us and we are grateful. Lord, we want to be like you in every way. Holy Spirit, thank you that you are relentless in developing the fruit of perseverance in us. In the name of our persistent Savior. Amen.

Today's Scripture

Romans 8:28; Galatians 6:9; James 1:12; James 5:10–11

Today's Thought

When my two boys were young, I worried when the house suddenly got too quiet. Usually, they were up to nothing good. Even hearing them argue was better than that dreaded silence. On the other hand, when God seems to be silent, we can be sure he is up to something good. God is always working behind the scenes on our behalf. When it seems as if our prayers are falling on deaf ears, God has indeed heard and he is about the business of orchestrating situations to work in our favor. Psalm 121 assures us that God never slumbers or sleeps. God's silence is not rejection. God's silence is not absence. When God is silent, we must be still. We must hope in the silence, believe in the silence and trust that perhaps God does his best work in the quiet places of the heart. When a holy hush falls upon your life, be hopeful, God is perfecting his child in trust and faith. God has a waiting room, and the most faithful sit quietly and patiently wait on God to open that door. Have you learned to trust God in the silence?

Today's Prayer

Father God, we do not like the silence of waiting. We want instant gratification. We want you to act, and we want it now. Lord, help us to understand the precious virtue of waiting. As we remain in a posture of expectation, I pray we not run out of the waiting room of your love, but that we stay where you have placed us until you beckon us to move. While we take pause, I pray we enter into a deeper level of trust. I pray that in the silence you refresh and encourage us. Thank you that you are always at work on our behalf. In the name of the God who does not forget his waiting child. Amen.

Today's Scriptures

Psalm 27:13–14; Psalm 62:1–2; Psalm 121:3–4; Isiah 30:18

Today's Thought

"When perfectionism is driving us, shame is riding shotgun and fear is that annoying backseat driver." Well spoken words by Brene' Brown. Perfectionists search for acceptance in achieving the perfect. Since what they strive for is unrealistic and unattainable, they are often very unhappy. The desire to be and do perfectly leads to incessant worry, depression and anxiety. Since the fall of mankind, perfection is beyond our reach. God did not create us to do all things perfectly, but rather to do all things well. We each have our own abilities and we all accomplish differently. If we are doing our best, God is pleased. If we are driven by perfectionism, shame and fear, he is grieved. Perfectionist fear disapproval and rejection, so they try even harder, getting themselves into a vicious cycle of striving and failure. Only our perfect God can break this unhealthy bond. If you see yourself caught in this vicious trap, I urge you to get before the Lord and ask him to break the bondage of perfectionism in your life.

Today's Prayer

Father God, you alone are perfect. You alone do all things flawlessly. When we attempt to be or do perfectly, we set ourselves up to be our own god. Father, forgive us for the burdens we place on ourselves with the idealistic thinking that we cling to. Lord, we want to do all things well; we want to strive for maturity in all things. You applaud our efforts; you do not criticize when we fail to reach unrealistic goals. Father, help us give ourselves permission to be human and fallible. One day we will be perfected; until then we thank you that we are called to simply do our best. In the name of the One and Only perfect Lord. Amen.

Today's Scriptures

Psalm 18:30–32; Matthew 11:28–30; 2 Corinthians12:9; Colossians 3:23

April 3

Today's Thought

Have you ever considered that weariness can be a gift? Often, we strive to work through the weariness rather than embrace it. We are often so busy striving, seeking, pushing, accomplishing and doing we end up in a place we never intended. Exhaustion soon becomes our constant companion. Those around us are amazed at how much we accomplish, but they do not know the price we pay for overreaching. Our battered and weary hearts feel emptier and more alone than ever. Perhaps weariness is divinely appointed. Have you considered that God allows us to come to a physical and emotional condition of weariness so he can capture our attention? God wants to enlarge the capacity of our hearts for more of him; invade places only he can fill. Sometimes weariness is required because God can do nothing until we come to the end of ourselves. Perhaps God can do his best work when we are weary and spent, resting in his arms.

Today's Prayer

Father God, you never called us to do it all. Why do we so often feel as if we cannot say "No"? We wear ourselves to a frazzle and wonder why we fall into anxiety and depression, all because we are depleted and weary. Lord, you give us the strength to do what you call us to do; not all we want to do. When we feel overwhelmed and drained, I pray we heed it as a warning from you; that we to evaluate our priorities. Lord, help us to know when to say "Yes" and when to say "No." I pray that daily we are guided by your Holy Spirit in all our activities. Thank you, Lord, that you love us enough to allow us to become so weary it brings us to tears. It is then you hold us and fill us anew. In the name of Jesus, our Sabbath Rest. Amen.

Today's Scriptures

Psalm 73:26; Isaiah 40:28–31; Matthew 11:28–30; 2 Corinthians 12:9–10

Today's Thought

Recently I watched documentaries on cults and the resulting devastation that came to the followers. Warren Jeffs from the FLDS Church is serving a life sentence, yet he continues to control his followers from prison. Jim Jones led over 900 followers, including children, to drinking Flavor-Aide laced with cyanide, killing them all. It gave me pause as I wondered how so many well-meaning people could be so deceived. Only God knows. I see however, through scripture a significant part of the problem. Sin is deceptive. When leaders and followers preach the gospel, yet continue in blatant sin, deception is the result. Not knowing God's Word can also lead to deception. Unless we are able to line up what we hear with God's Word, we will believe anything. Knowing the God of the Bible is our greatest protection. We must know him as he truly is, as he revealed himself through scripture, not as who we want him to be or who others tell us he is. We must know him through a personal relationship and a daily walk, thus protecting us from the dangerous charisma of false Christs and false prophets.

Today's Prayer

Father God, we need protection from false teachers of our day. Lord, you warned us that in the last days they would come to deceive us. Your Word is our only source of absolute truth. God, I pray that we look into your Word as never before so we are armed against the deceivers of our day. I pray we press in to know you and your character. I pray we are drawn to healthy churches where the true gospel of Jesus Christ is preached and where Jesus is exalted as Sovereign Lord. In his name. Amen.

Today's Scriptures

Matthew 24:23–25; Acts 20:28–31; 2 Timothy 4:1–4; 2 Peter 3:17–18

April 5

Today's Thought

Humility is a most elusive virtue. As soon as I think I have it, it's lost; that makes the quest for humility a lifelong pursuit. Humility is the foundation for all other Christian virtues. Humility is not weakness; it is quiet strength. It is the ability to see myself through the lens of scripture and to think correctly about who I am. It is a realistic evaluation of my strengths and my flaws. Jesus set the highest example of humility ever recorded. All through his earthly life he continually had control of his mind, will and emotions, yet always yielding to his Father's plan. He knew who he was and whose he was. God rewarded his humility by exalting his name above every other name. Let us strive for the attitude of heart that puts God first, others second, then ourselves. As we stay close to Jesus and study his life, we come to understand this virtue. We may not recognize humility in ourselves, but God knows and sees it and he is pleased.

Today's Prayer

Father God, we pray for a spirit of humility that begins by doing the right thing, loving mercy and walking with humble hearts before you and before others. Help us to give up our self-sufficiency, pride and arrogance, and learn to lean on you. We are all equal in your sight. I pray we not hold ourselves above anyone else, but simply live the lives and calling to which you appointed us. May we cease from competing within the body of Christ. Lord, we want to bless you and be a blessing to others. Jesus, we thank you for coming to be one of us. Even as you walked in humility all the way to the cross, so may we walk humbly in the paths chosen for us. In the name of our humble and exalted Lord. Amen.

Today's Scriptures

Micah 6:8; Matthew 23:11–12; Philippians 2:3–11; James 4:6

Today's Thought

When Jesus talked about being set free in John 8:36, he was referring to the ability to distinguish truth from lies. When we believe lies, we are enslaved. The Jews he was addressing in this passage were disputing Jesus' words. They claimed that because they had Abraham as their father, they were not slaves. Jesus is quick to let them know that they were indeed slaves to their traditions, sins and false beliefs. He was telling them that only by knowing and accepting the truth about Jesus could they be free. He also spoke of abiding in the Word. Sadly, they were having none of it. Jesus is presenting this truth to us today. He is offering us true freedom. Whatever enslaves us can be broken by the power of knowing and embracing the truth. First, we must recognize lies we are believing, then confess and replace them with truth. We must know with certainty that God does not want us enslaved to deception, sin and religious tradition.

Today's Prayer

Father God, we certainly need to be set free from the lies we believe. We praise and thank you for sending your Son, truth personified, so we could know the truth and be set free. We ask that if we are in any way enslaved to the lies of the enemy that you expose them. I pray we know and cling to your Word as the absolute standard of truth that we are to live by. Jesus, I pray we walk as true disciples, learning from you every day. May we hold fast to your teachings and follow in your footsteps. Break the chains of self-righteousness and religious tradition so we can enter into a heart and soul relationship with you. In the name of the Way, the Truth and the Life. Amen.

Today's Scriptures

John 8:31–36; Romans 6:20–23; Galatians 5:1; Colossians 2:6–8

April 7

Today's Thought

As a little girl I was given to fantasy. My favorite was pretending to be a princess, living in a beautiful castle with servants waiting on me. As I grew up, I had to give up my imaginings and face the reality of who I really was. What a sad life I would be living if I had not abandoned my illusion. In Isaiah 29:13 the Lord is chastising his people because they are practicing religious role playing. He says, *"These people come near to me with their mouth, and honor me with their lips, but their hearts are far from me."* We have an expression for that; we call it *"lip service."* Sadly, this practice is going on among us today ... in the church. Lip service is saying "yes" with your mouth, but saying "no" in your heart. There is only one form of worship that pleases God ... true heartfelt worship. We must examine the genuineness of our faith. It is time for God's people to stop playing church. Those who come to him must come to worship him in spirit and truth. Nothing else is acceptable.

Today's Prayer

Father God, at times we are all guilty. We come to the sanctuary and our minds are anywhere but on you. We mouth the words of worship songs without thinking about the rich meaning. We are distracted by looking around and watching others. We walk out of church on Sunday and don't give you another thought till the next Sunday. We profess to be Christians, but often don't look much different from the world. Lord, we need to repent of paying you lip service, of playing church. God, I pray you wake up your people and send revival that will convict our hearts and turn us back to the heart of true worship. Amen.

Today's Scriptures

Deuteronomy 10:12; Psalm 85:6; Matthew 15:8; John 4:23–24

Today's Thought

We are blessed when we encounter sincerity. Have you ever thought about what it means to be sincere? The dictionary defines sincere as: *free from deceit; pure; genuine, real; not altered or added to as if to deceive.* That's what some of the peddlers of Jesus' day were doing. They would add wax or another foreign substance to their wares and sell them as pure. The honest vendors would advertise their vessels as "sincere," indicating they were pure and not altered in any way. That causes me to think about my faith. Is it sincere? Do I walk purely, according to God's Word? Am I careful not to add any hypocrisy to what I say and do? Have I brought any foreign ideas into my faith that do not line up with the God's Word? Beloved, we can be sure that our faith will be tested for sincerity and genuineness. In the Greek it explains the refining of our faith like this: *"Tested by genuine light; judged by sunlight."*

Today's Prayer

Father God, we don't see much sincerity in our culture today. Everyone has an angle, whatever benefits them at the time. You call us to be different. Lord, sadly, we aren't always different. You send trials and testing so that our faith may come forth as gold, sincere, pure and precious to you. Lord, if there be any ways in us that are not sincere, ways that are not honest, ways that are more for our benefit than that of others, expose all of it to the genuine light of your truth. I pray we learn to reject anything that reeks of insincerity and dishonesty. I pray we value a sincere heart as you do. Lord, if there be any hypocrisy in us, purge us by the fire of your Spirit. In the name of our God who treasures sincerity, Amen.

Today's Scriptures

2 Corinthians 1:12; 2 Corinthians 2:17; James 3:16–17; 1 Peter 2:1–2

April 9

Today's Thought

One must be lost in order to be found. I was lost in my sin and shame, then, the Good Shepherd came to seek and save me. Being lost comes in many forms. We can be lost in a physical sense, like the time I drove over an hour to find an address that was 10 minutes away. One can be lost in uncertainty over the future, lost in the past or lost in a toxic relationship. The very worst is to be spiritually lost. Jesus talks about lost things in Luke 15. He talks about a lost coin, one lost sheep and a lost son. These parables are meant to remind us that nothing is ever lost to God. He knew where the coin was. He knew the lost sheep's whereabouts. And, he knew all about the lost son and how far he had fallen. Each encounter has a happy ending, just like our story. We were lost, but Jesus knew where we were all along. Just in time he came to rescue us. Dear one, you are never lost to God. His watchful eye is always upon you. His saving hand is always reaching out to you.

Today's Prayer

Father God, you sent us a Shepherd to seek us out and save us. We thank you that we were never lost to you. You are the God of all lost people. Those loved ones who are running from you are not lost to you. When we feel lost in doubt and uncertainty, you bring clarity. When we feel we have lost our way, you take our hand and lead us to the light of day. Luke 15 is your trilogy of being found and redeemed. No one is too far gone that you cannot bring him back. You found us in our sin and loved us out of it. In this very moment in time, you see us. We once were lost, but now we are found. Praise God. In your name, Jesus, we thank you. Amen.

Today's Scriptures

Proverbs 5:21; Isaiah 41:10; Luke 15:1–32; Luke 19:10

Today's Thought

I like making up the rules as I go along, or so I have been told. Who doesn't like being in control of the game? Or one's own life? There is a problem with that mentality. If everyone made their own rules and lived by them, can you imagine the chaos? That's why the world is in such disorder now. God gave us guidelines for living. His rules are his Word given by his prophets and Jesus his Son. From the Old Testament to the New, God is abundantly clear about what it means to live godly and what that should look like in our lives. When we attempt to live life by our man-made dictates things go downhill very quickly. When we come to Jesus, we should be seeing life through the lens of his Word and submitting to his ways and his will. Eventually we need to choose. Will it be my way or God's way? My rules or God's law of love? The wise person will always abandon the human way for God's way. There is where we find peace.

Today's Prayer

Father God, we pray for peace in our lives, yet we still try to control outcomes. We want your best, yet we want to call the shots. We acknowledge that your Word is God-breathed, but all too often we stray from the good path. We are rule breakers at heart. Lord, I pray that we have the vision to see, know and believe that your guidelines, your ways, your commands are all for our good. You designed them to protect us and give us needed boundaries. When we stray, we stumble and fall. When we obey, we find the peace and joy you intend for us. Oh God, help us to have the wisdom to understand that your perfect law of liberty is truly what our hearts long for. In the name of our Great Law Giver, Amen.

Today's Scriptures

Psalm 119:30–32; Luke 11:27–28; Galatians 6:7–8; 1 Peter 1:14–16

Today's Thought

I appreciate the high beams on my car. On those very dark nights, on those very dark roads, high beams have saved me a lot of grief. God's Word is our spiritual high beam. When I feel as if I am in the dark, I turn on Psalm 119:105. It is there that I find a clear path for my feet, and a beacon of hope for the future. Let's look at this passage close up. The Psalmist tells us that God's Word is a lamp to our feet. In that day, the night watchman held a lantern down near his feet so he could determine his next step. God's Word leads us to our next step and keeps us safe when we obey. God's specific will comes one step at a time. *A light to my path.* When the watchman held his lantern up and out, it lit up the way before him so he could see any dangers up ahead. Likewise, God's Word gives us light, clarity and direction for what lies before us. God's Word has us covered for our present steps and for our future course.

Today's Prayer

Father God, your Word is indeed a light to our path and a lamp to our feet. We are so grateful that you have brought us out of the kingdom of darkness into your marvelous light. God, I pray you continue to draw us to the light, to the truth and to yourself. We need you, Lord, every moment of the day and all through the night. As we follow you, we are never in the dark. You are the light of the world, Jesus. Bathe our hearts with the glow of your love so we can be a light in this shadowy world. May you be seen clearly in us. Cause us to make a difference in the lives of those around us. When we are confused, fearful or doubtful, remind us to turn on the high beams. In the name of the Light of the World, Jesus. Amen.

Today's Scriptures

Psalm 119:105; Psalm 119:130; John 8:12; Colossians 1:13–14

April 12

Today's Thought

Sadly, there are thoughts among the worldly and Christians alike that are just not biblical. The one I have in mind today is, *"God helps those who help themselves."* The Word tells us just the opposite; God is the helper of the helpless. While we were yet dead in our sins, Jesus died for us, the ungodly. Paul warns us that what God began in us by the Spirit cannot be completed in the flesh. The world inundates us with self-improvement plans and formulas. These efforts profit nothing of eternal value. Only through the work of the Holy Spirit in our lives is there profit. We do not have to overcome our shortcomings and failures by our own strength. Praise be to God; he has not left us as orphans to struggle on our own. Jesus promised to send us a helper, and he did. The Holy Spirit is more than able to work the work of God in us and to continually produce the good fruit that God desires to see in our lives.

Today's Prayer

Father God, what a blessing! We do not have to earn your favor and love. We are not enrolled in a self-improvement course. Your Word is not a do-it-yourself package we order from Amazon. You have not left us here on our own to figure it out. We praise you that Jesus Christ did it all for us through his walk on earth and his sacrifice on the cross. Now we can walk free from condemnation and live by the power of the Holy Spirit within us. We once were dead, now in Christ we are spiritually alive. Lord, we thank you that it is you who will complete the good work you began in us and not we ourselves. Our life in Christ is not laborious or a burden. We are changed by your love and grace. In Jesus' name. Amen.

Today's Scriptures

Psalm 54:4; Romans 5:6–8; Galatians 3:2–3; Philippians 1:6 \

April 13

Today's Thought

Today is Julien calendar day101. That brings Psalm 101 to mind; one of my favorites. David wants to talk to God about his conduct, particularly how he behaves in his own home. He begins by saying, *"I will be careful to live a blameless life ..."* (Psalm 101:2). David was talking about his public life, walking without fault before his people. How difficult is that? David knew it was, but it was in his heart to live blameless before the Lord and others. Then he brings the lens in a bit closer into his private life. In the same verse he says, *"I will walk in my house with a blameless heart."* I learned early on in my walk with the Lord that it was easier to walk as a Christian in a church setting than in my own home. David said, *"I will set before my eyes no vile thing"* (Psalm 101:3). Who are we when no one else sees? How aware are we that God sees it all? What we allow to enter our eyes, ears and heart at home determines how blameless we are able to walk before God and others.

Today's Prayer

Father God, we so want our walk to line up with what we profess. Jesus' life was always in alignment with who he professed to be. Lord, it can be especially challenging to walk blameless within our homes. We are so comfortable with those closest to us; they often see us at our worse. There are so many temptations. When no one is watching, we can easily succumb to engaging in ungodly activities. Those we love the most are watching closely, and those little ones will follow in our footsteps. Help us to closely examine our habits and behaviors as we walk publicly and privately. In the name of our all-seeing God. Amen.

Today's Scriptures

Psalm 101:2–3; 1 Corinthians 6:12; Colossians 1:9–10; 1 John 2:15–17

Today's Thought

Yesterday I experienced a deep hurt by someone I consider a dear friend. I felt my time was not valued when she did not show up for a lunch date we had planned. I was offended and choose not to talk with her about it until I had time to step back and consider my response. This morning as I spent time with God and his Word, he helped me sort through my feelings and come to some healthy conclusions. I needed to be honest and admit that I was hurt and disappointed in my friends' oversight. It's always okay to express our feelings. The second conclusion I made was to forgive her; then, rather than focus on the offense, I choose to focus on the blessing this friend has been to me for over 20 years. As I thought back over our friendship, I could not count all the ways she has valued and blessed me. Later this morning we had a good talk and all was resolved. I can't help but think that this is how God deals with us when we offend him. He knows our shortcomings, but he chooses to remember the big picture of our lives. He chooses to dwell on the best in us, not the worst.

Today's Prayer

Father God, it is good to know that you chose to forgive and also forget. Thank you that you always take the big picture of our lives into account and you do not focus on the mistakes we make. You are on our side and you want us to succeed in every area of our lives. You value us and you are always cheering us on. When we slip up, you do not beat us up with our blunder. Your gentle heart entreats us to come near to you for forgiveness and restoration. We thank you in the name of our Great Grace-Giver. Amen.

Today's Scriptures

Proverbs 19:11; Romans 8:31; Ephesians 4:32; Colossians 3:12–14

Today's Thought

Only 23% of Americans meet the daily requirement for physical exercise. In contrast, only 9% of Americans read their Bible. We need to keep ourselves as physically fit as possible, but most important, we need to continually attend to our spiritual health. Paul said, *"For physical training is of some value, but godliness has value for all things, holding promise for both the present life and the life to come"* (1 Timothy 4:8). We need to exercise our spirit man daily and we do that by feeding on God's Word. We are in training. Our race is not a sprint, it's a marathon. We are in this for the long haul. We are to run in such a way as to be gaining ground continually. Paul says we do this to get a crown that will last forever. God has given us his Holy Spirit as our life coach. He trains us up in spiritual vitality and gives us strength for the journey. Let us purpose to run our course well. The finish line will come and when it does there will be One waiting for us there.

Today's Prayer

Father God, you have given us everything we need to endure this spiritual race. Jesus sets the course and the Holy Spirit sets the pace. In your goodness you never call us to run faster or further than our spiritual muscles have been conditioned. You never judge us by how awkwardly we begin, but you are watching to see how well we finish. Father, help us not compare our race with others. You see each of us as unique children with unique qualities and abilities. Help us avoid trying to compete in the world's race. Those who run with the world run to a different beat, and they seek a worldly crown and recognition. We seek after your heart and your approval. In the name of the Forerunner of our Christian race. Amen.

Today's Scriptures

1 Corinthians 9:24–27; 1 Timothy 4:8; 2 Timothy 4:7–8; Hebrews 5:13–14

April 16

Today's Thought

I have several photo albums of my sons spanning their growing up years. I love going through them every now and then; it brings great joy to my heart. From birth on up, page after page of sweet memories. Taking those first steps, losing those baby teeth, learning to ride a bicycle, first day of school and graduation, and everything in between. I am so glad I did not snap pictures of their toddler tantrums, spitting out their food, spilled milk and poor choices. No, as mom I wanted to preserve and remember all the good times. I would imagine that if God has a photo album of you, his desire is the same. He would review all those wonderful things he loves about you. The way he formed you, the times you gave unselfishly, the Sunday school class you faithfully taught and the times you reached out to the hurting. I don't think our loving Father keeps record of our worse moments. He says, *"I will forgive their wickedness and will remember their sin no more"* (Hebrews 8:12).

Today's Prayer

Father God, you know and remember everything we ever did, and you choose to recollect all the good we have accomplished. You choose to forget our sins. We bring joy to your heart as you watch us with a loving Father's eye. You sing over us with gladness and you cause your face to shine on us. Lord, there are still so many ways in which we need to grow up. In your faithfulness, you will keep us moving ahead into spiritual maturity. You know our weaknesses but you don't place your focus there. You place your confidence in the power of your Holy Spirit to keep us and grow us. In the name of the God who remembers us for good. Amen.

Today's Scriptures

Zephaniah 3:17; Colossians 2:1-3; Hebrews 6:10; Hebrews 8:12

Today's Thought

Expectations. We all have them. We place expectations on those we love, on church people, our neighbors and yes, even on God. Unmet expectations can cause us to take things into our own hands. When the children of Israel's expectations did not materialize, they turned to Aaron to build them a god they could see and control. In our modern world we don't build calves of gold and bow to them; our gods are more subtle. They could include, beauty, youth, position, power, money, addictions, sex, and just about anything we strongly desire. But, just like the children in the wilderness, these foreign gods cannot meet our deepest longings. What is the answer? Put aside the expectations and simply trust the true God to meet your needs. Place no expectations on God. Let God be God and accept that he works in his own way and his own time. Cling to him even when you don't understand.

Today's Prayer

Father God, you call us to hope rather than expectations. Help us to know the difference. Show us any ways in which we substitute the reality of you with people, places and things that will never satisfy. Forgive us our idolatry. Forgive us for turning from you when you do not live up to our plans and demands. Help us to cease from turning to other ways and means that we think will give us control. Help us let go and let you be the God we need, even when we feel let down. Lord, even when we do not understand your ways, help us to keep hope alive in the disappointments of life. In the name of our God, who never disappoints. Amen.

Today's Scriptures

Exodus 32:18; Psalm 62:5–8; Isaiah 55:8–9; 1 John 5:21

April 18

Today's Thought

In these troubling times, we are all looking for answers. Who we run to for those answers is crucial. First, we must go to God and his Word to gain understanding and direction as we move through these troubling waters. Sadly, so many are looking in all the wrong places for the wisdom and discernment needed to navigate these treacherous times. Washington can give us a degree of direction, but ultimately, they will fail us. Hollywood is designed to entertain us, not direct our life's decisions. The Democratic Party can't really help, nor can the Republican Party pull us out of the quicksand our country is sinking into. Where is our hope for the present and the future? Where is the confidence we need to keep moving ahead? It begins with prayer for our nation. It begins with us, the Church of Jesus Christ. We are the ones holding the answers. We know the only cure for the sickness in our nation is Jesus, his truth and righteousness.

Today's Prayer

Father God, if ever we needed you, it is now. If ever we needed to understand the plan you have charted out in your Word, it is now. If ever your Church needs to stand up and shine, it is now. You are giving us every opportunity to be your witnesses, your ambassadors and your Bride. The world needs what we have, because we alone hold the hope for this nation. No other source in this world can offer what we have. I pray we be the light on a hill, the salt, the sweet fragrance of Christ to all who come to us with heavy hearts. This is our time Lord; I pray we do not squander the great treasure we possess. In the name of Jesus Christ, the Hope of the World. Amen.

Today's Scriptures

Matthew 5:13–16; Acts 1:8; 2 Corinthians 2:14–16; 1 Peter 3:15

April 19

Today's Thought

You are affectionately invited to dinner. King Jesus wants to dine with you. You can find your invitation in Revelation 3:20. What an intimate scene. You and Jesus, candlelight, sweet fragrant flowers, soft heavenly music playing in the background. This is what I imagine when I read that verse in Revelation. He takes your hand and looks deeply into your eyes and your heart. It's you he wants; it's you he desires. He is always a gentleman. He gently knocks on the door of our hearts and gives us a promise of intimate fellowship if we open up to his invitation. Jesus entreats us every morning, with each new dawn, to open up to the dreams he has for us, open up to his love and grace, open up to the work of his Spirit in us. In Biblical times dining together was an event. So different from quick fast-food meals we partake of today. Right now, Jesus is calling you to come away with him and dine on the heavenly feast he has prepared for you. How will you respond?

Today's Prayer

Father God, you understand us so well. You know how to stir our inner desires for intimacy. You offer us a love so rich and so deep we cannot begin to comprehend it. You offer us Jesus, the bread of heaven, the One who tenderly invites us to know him in profound ways. We are the ones who hold ourselves back. Oh God, help us to make room and time for Jesus. Help us to answer the call, to open our hearts, to invite him into every nook and cranny of our being. Lord, I pray we unlock the latch that keeps him out and throw open wide the door that you may enter in. In the name of the One who invites us to intimacy with him. Amen.

Today's Scriptures

Psalm 37:4; Psalm 73:25; Song of Solomon 2:10; Revelation 3:20

Today's Thought

Living for the acceptance of others will strangle the joy out of life; when they reject us, another little piece of us dies. Trying to please everyone leaves us drained and depleted of life's vitality. It consumes the best part of us. Some people will never approve of us or like us no matter what we do. People-pleasing is a losing battle and we are the victims of our own crusade for approval and acceptance. People-pleasers are dependent on the validation of others rather than trusting in the approval of God. So, what is the answer, what is the cure for the people pleasing trap? The key to freedom is found in Galatians 1:10, *"Am I now trying to win the approval of men, or of God? Or am I trying to please men? If I were still trying to please men, I would not be a servant of Christ."* When we live our lives with the ambition of pleasing God, we will be set free from the fear of the opinion of man. When we truly understand how accepted and loved we are in Jesus, the love and acceptance of others will be an added bonus.

Today's Prayer

Father God, you did not create us to strive for the acceptance and approval of others. We thank you for those ones we have in our lives who do love and accept us as we are. They are gifts from you. Ultimately though, you are the One we aim to please by our love and lifestyle. Help us to love others without the expectation of receiving acceptance and approval in return. If we are pleasing you, it is enough. We may lose some that we consider friends, but we will gather around us those who love us without expecting us to be what they want us to be. We live to please you alone. In the name of the Beloved One in whom we are accepted. Amen.

Today's Scriptures

John 5:44; Galatians 1:10; Ephesians 6:7–8; 1 Thessalonians 2:4

April 21

Today's Thought

"It was the worst of times and it was the best of times." It's the first line from Charles Dickens classic, *A Tale of Two Cities.* The book highlights the contrast between love and hate, evil and goodness, light and darkness. Sounds a bit like the times we live in. We certainly are experiencing many contrasts in our culture. For those of us who are old enough, we remember kinder times. Crime was rare in my little small-town world. Children obeyed their parents and almost every home was a two-parent home. Elections were civil and we slept unafraid at night with unlocked doors. A man was a man and a woman was a woman. Times have certainly changed and continue to change daily. One could say we are living in the worst of times. Pandemics, rioting, racism, lawlessness and sin abound. For those of us awaiting the return of Jesus our Lord, we know the best is yet to come. Jesus will come and fulfill all things, his love will conquer all evil and darkness. It may be the worst of times culturally, but we know the best is yet to come when he makes all things new.

Today's Prayer

Father God, all of creation groans for the liberty that will come through Christ as he returns to redeem all things. While we wait for that glorious day, we must live out your plans for our lives. It seems as if it is the worst of times, but we who love you know differently. For us it is the best of times as many will turn back to Jesus Christ and the Word of God for answers and hope. Those who are confused, weary and fearful will look to the Church for hope. Lord, let us rise up to be that hope, the ever-shining beacon that points to Jesus and his truth. In his name we pray, Amen.

Today's Scriptures

Romans 8:20–25; Ephesians 5:15–20; 2 Timothy 3:1–5; Revelation 21:5

April 22

Today's Thought

God knows the truth about you. We often believe we know ourselves well. We know our likes and dislikes. We know the kind of people we like to hang out with. Our taste in food is unique. We know our deepest darkest secrets and work hard to keep them hidden. The tricky part is discerning why we do what we do ... what motivates us to action and what cripples us. We run to counselors and self-help books just to get to the root of our obsessions and strongholds. I am not at all against good Christian counseling, pastors with wisdom and insight, or even a godly friend who can help us sort through the struggles. I have, however, concluded in my own life that after all is said and done, no one knows me like Jesus. So many times, he has put his divine finger right square on the problem and led me to the answer. He knows the truth about me, and he knows the truth about you. He alone can uncover the reality of who we are.

Today's Prayer

Father God, your Word assures us that you knew us before we were conceived. All our days were written in your book before we lived even one. You formed every one of our parts and knit us together like fine works of art. All through our lives, you saw every joy, every sorrow, every disappointment and all the consequences of sin that we suffer. You know the whole truth about us. You alone are the One who can sort through life's experiences and help us work it all out. You know our struggles, why we do the things we do and why we think the way we do. We come to you today, Lord, as our Wonderful Counselor, our All-Knowing, All-Seeing, Ever-Present Father. The truth you reveal about us will set us free. Amen.

Today's Scripture

Psalm 139:1–18; Isaiah 9:6; John 8:36; John 10:14

April 23

Today's Thought

Love hurts! It hurt Jesus as he bled and died because he loves us. It pierced the Father's heart of love to watch his darling Son suffer for the sins of the world. Love can be such a beautiful word when it comes easily and does not cost much emotionally. We can easily love the lovable people in our lives. It's not so easy when we are called to love the unlovely, those who don't return our love, and those who abuse our love. How do we do it? First, we have to stop saying, *"I can't, I just can't love him/her."* We pray for God's power of love to flow through us so our own heart can be changed. Then we pray for the ones who must be hurting so badly they have the need to hurt us with their words, attitudes and actions. We have not walked in their shoes; we have not felt their hurts. We can defeat the enemy of love with kindness and compassion. As we pray for them and ourselves, God will give us the strength and endurance to overcome the temptation to withhold our love from those who need it most.

Today's Prayer

Father God, you are a wellspring of love and all the power we need to love others comes from that fountain. Lord, today I pray over that dear one who is struggling with loving someone you have strategically placed in her life. You understand the struggle and temptation to walk away, but that is not your way. Father, help her to know that you will enable her to forgive and love her tormenters. Cause her to see the truth of how prayer changes our hearts. Jesus, be a fountainhead of strength and endurance to that hurting one today. May forgiveness and love spring up and overwhelm her today. In the name of the author and sustainer of love. Amen.

Today's Scriptures

Matthew 5:43–48; Romans 12:9–10; Philippians 4:13; 1 Peter 4:8

April 24

Today's Thought

How do you determine your value? Who defines your worth? Some of us devour fashion magazines and compare ourselves with the made-up faces and superficial bodies plastered on every page. TV commercials promote sexy images as being the means of gaining fulfillment. Hollywood bombards us with its version of beauty and acceptance through movie idols. The world has its own way of defining attractiveness and worth. The standards of the world can leave us feeling inadequate when we place our trust in what the culture defines as significant. It leaves us wondering about our personal worth. Remember, the world's way is not God's way. As we look to God and his Word, we find a whole new set of standards. God should have the final word on what is worthwhile. God leaves us with no doubt of the great value he places on every human life. We belong to the one who formed us, and he makes no mistakes. We are his cherished treasure and nothing can devalue what God values.

Today's Prayer

Father God, when you created man and woman in your image, you declared your handiwork to be very good. You formed us perfectly for your pleasure and enjoyment. Lord, help us to renew our minds in those areas where we have fallen captive to the world's definition of worth and value. Bring us to the reality of your Word and let it be the final and absolute truth about who we are and to whom we belong. Help us to accept ourselves as the masterpieces you created with your own hands. As we gaze into our mirrors every day, may we see Jesus shining though us in glorious loveliness. In the name of the Creator of true beauty. Amen.

Today's Scriptures

Genesis 1:27; Proverbs 31:10; Romans 12:1–2; 1 Peter 3:3–4

April 25

Today's Thought

What are you lacking today? As for me, I had a warm bed to sleep in last night. I had plenty of food to choose from this morning. I had absolutely too many articles of clothing to select from. *(I really am going to go through my closet and thin out the herd this year.)* God promises to provide our every need, not everything we want or think we need, although he does that too. So today, rather than ask for anything, I have decided to be intentional in looking around my home, searching my life, and thanking the Lord for going above and beyond my basic needs. I ask that you join me in blessing the Lord's heart through a concert of thanksgiving. Just imagine how pleased our Lord is as each of us reading this devotion today united our voices in gratitude to the One who does exceedingly abundantly above all we ask or think.

Today's Prayer

Lord Jesus, you are our constant Help and Provision. We lack nothing as you care for us. Just as Abraham found you on Mount Moriah as his Deliverer and Provision, so may we find you today. As we journey this upward road, I pray your Holy Spirit opens our eyes to see you everywhere and in everything. Lord, we trust in you and we are not disappointed. I pray we are intentional in seeing your rich blessings everywhere around us and in us. You have not left us as poor orphans; you know how to care and provide for those who belong to you. We are yours and you meet us in every way. As you sing over us today and shower us with blessings, I pray our love songs of gratitude be a sweet sound to your Father's heart. In the name of Jehovah Jireh, our Provider. Amen.

Today's Scriptures

Genesis 22:13–14; Psalm 103:1–5; Philippians 4:19; Ephesians 3:20–21

Today's Thought

2 Chronicles 20 is a most amazing story and holds a life lesson for us. King Jehoshaphat and his army were up against the wall. A vast army from Edom was coming to make war on Judah. Jehoshaphat cried out to the Lord, confessing that he and his army had no power to face this massive army. Then he confessed these words to the Lord, *"We do not know what to do, but our eyes are on you"* (2 Chronicles 20:12). God's Word soon came to Jehoshaphat by the prophet Jahaziel. He said, *"Do not be afraid or discouraged because of this vast army; for the battle is not yours, but the Lord's"* (2 Chronicles 20:15). Rather than fight, they were told to go out singing praises to God. They went out singing, *"Give thanks to the Lord, for his love endures forever"* (2 Chronicles 20:21). As they began to sing and praise, the Lord delivered Judah from the hands of its enemies. What battle are you facing today? Are you willing to allow the Lord to fight that battle as you go forth today, singing his praises?

Today's Prayer

Father God, you are a mighty warrior who desires to fight our battles. Lord, help us to stand still and watch how you work in our midst. I pray we always launch into our day with praise and thanksgiving, remembering your great love and ability to work in every situation. May we be as Judah, keeping our eyes on you, knowing that we are powerless on our own. The vast army of a godless culture seems to be overwhelming us, but you are greater in us than the enemies of our souls. No weapon formed against us can prosper as you go before us with victory in your hand. In the name of our Warrior God. Amen.

Today's Scriptures

Deuteronomy 20:1–4; 2 Chronicles 20:13–15; Isaiah 54:17; 1 John 4:4

April 27

Today's Thought

Turn on any news report today and you will find occasion to be anxious and fearful. Sadly, too many of God's children are living day-to-day with no joy in their hearts. As long as we live in this world there will be sorrow and tragedy, evil and sinful exploitation. God has given us a cure for the heavy heart. He tells us that, *"A cheerful heart is a good medicine, but a crushed spirit dries up the bones"* (Proverbs 17:22). I don't think King Solomon was unrealistic with his proverb. I believe he wants us to see a profound truth. A joyful heart is a choice. Every day we can choose to succumb to the woes of this world or we can choose joy. Medically it is true that happy, cheerful people are healthier, more at peace and live longer. It's not easy. I know because I live in this sinful fallen world with you. People can be cruel and life can be tough. But we do not have to bow to the god of fear, anxiety and sadness. If we allow the fruit of joy to be nurtured in us, we can be contagious women of joy.

Today's Prayer

Jesus, you are a God of Joy. Your Spirit desires to produce this fruit in our souls where it can live and thrive. We are grateful that in our hearts we have the choice to be cheerful because you have overcome this evil world. You give us victory and you promise peace. We are never alone or forsaken. God, help us to remember that it is well with our souls and we have every reason to be filled with happy hearts. I pray we learn to laugh more, sing more, dance more and be the happy little children you created us to be. I pray that as we grow in joy, our bodies will come into alignment with the health and vitality that your Word promises. Amen.

Today's Scriptures

Proverbs 15:15; Proverbs 17:22; John 16:33; Galatians 5:22–23

April 28

Today's Thought

Scripture tells us to *"guard our heart."* What does that mean, and how do we do that? For the next few days, we will explore this very important mandate from God. When scripture refers to our heart it is not pointing to our physical heart in most cases. Scripturally our "heart" refers to our inmost being; our character, our conscience, who we truly are at the core of our being. The condition of our hearts will be evident in our words, our thoughts and our actions. Our hearts are the spiritual part of us, our true selves. In scripture the heart is also referred to as the wellspring of life. If the well is polluted, then pollution and death spring forth. If the well is clean and pure it brings forth life-giving vitality. Why guard our hearts? Our hearts are priceless and God highly values who we are at our core being; everything in our lives are affected by the condition of our hearts. We have an enemy who is determined to attack our hearts at every level. Let us seriously examine the condition of our hearts.

Today's Prayer

Father God, in your wisdom you have given us a spiritual heart that defines who we are. Often our hearts have been broken into pieces, or turned cold by the injustices of life. Lord, I thank you that no heart is too old or too cold that you cannot change it into a vibrant and life-giving core. As we examine our hearts today help us to be open and honest about who we truly are and how you see our hearts. As we venture into these devotions on guarding our hearts, I pray that each of us become more aware of what we allow into our hearts and honest about what needs to be removed. In the name of the keeper of our hearts. Amen.

Today's Scriptures

1 Samuel 16:7; Psalm 51:6; Proverbs 4:20–23; Proverbs 21:2

April 29

Today's Thought

Much is being said these days about the contamination of planet earth. We should be concerned about our environment and strive to be good stewards of our natural resources. But today we are facing an even greater danger, the contamination of our culture and how it is affecting each of us, especially our hearts. Those of us who belong to Christ have been called out to be separate from a culture that promotes sin and corruption. This does not mean that we withdraw from the world; those around us need to see Christ. We are to be shining lights in the darkness of an ungodly culture. We can only be as effective as our hearts are clean and unpolluted. This is an important reason for guarding our hearts. If we do not guard our hearts we will soon be aligned with our corrupt culture and no longer able to discern right from wrong. In contrast, with clean hearts we can be purifying wellsprings of life-giving truth to those around us who are deceived by the cultural agenda. Let us guard our hearts from taking on the social mindset that says it's okay to think and live any way we want.

Today's Prayer

Father God, your heart is pure and undefiled. You call us to imitate you in our lifestyles. You call us to guard our hearts against the lies and deceptions of the world system. You understand that we are bombarded daily with a cultural mindset that does not know you or your Word. Our minds and hearts so easily absorb the pollutions of ungodliness. Lord, I pray that we recommit to a biblical mindset and a holy lifestyle. I pray that we learn how to guard our hearts against the impurities that contaminate. In the name of the pure One, Jesus Christ. Amen.

Today's Scriptures

Leviticus 18:1–5; 2 Corinthians 7:1; James 1:27; 1 Peter 2:11–12

Today's Thought

It's been said that our eyes are the window to our souls. Jesus said, *"The eye is the lamp of the body. If your eyes are good, your whole body will be full of light. But if your eyes are bad, your whole body will be full of darkness"* (Matthew 6:22–23). Jesus wants us to understand that what we look at, what we allow to enter through our eyes will affect our hearts and our spiritual well-being. If we are taking in images that are not appropriate or wholesome, that brings darkness to our hearts. When we allow the truth of God's Word to settle in our hearts, then our spirits can be full of light and truth. Either way, what we allow into our eyes will undoubtedly affect our hearts. The eye also represents perspective. How do we safeguard our heavenly perspective? We look to God's Word and not to the world's rhetoric. In conclusion, what we gaze upon we soon become. Where we get our perspective on life determines our lifestyle. Let's purpose to gaze at Jesus and study his life for healthy guarded hearts and eyes that are full of light.

Today's Prayer

Father God, you gave us eyes that we might see. You call us to be good stewards of our eyes and to be aware of how they affect our hearts. I pray that we use our eyes to see your holiness, the beauty around us and into the hearts of others. Help us to see the needs all around us and to respond to those needs. I pray we gaze at Jesus first and foremost, then at the lovely, true and pure things that surround us every day. Help us to guard our hearts as we guard our eyes and what they behold. Lord, I pray you show us any ways in which we abuse the gift of sight. In the name of Jesus. Amen.

Today's Scriptures

Psalm 101:2–3; Psalm 119:37; Matthew 5:29; Matthew 6:22–23

May 1

Today's Thought

"Be careful, little ears, what you hear." The words of this song are a warning to children. How appropriate for all of us today, young and old. Why the need to guard our ears? What we listen to goes directly into our inner being. Every word or song we listen to invites a certain spirit. When the words and music we listen to are godly and uplifting, out heart is fed. When what we listen to incites sensuality and ungodly attitudes, we ultimately will act upon those impulses. The words and music we take in through our ears will impact the brain in ways that can promote peace and joy, or chaos and even violence. It's no wonder that we are admonished to hear instruction and gain a heart of wisdom. Jesus tells us in scripture, *"He who has ears to hear, let him hear"* (Matthew 11:15). There is a world of difference between having ears and having ears to hear. When we listen to God's commands and live as he teaches, we truly hear. When we truly hear and obey, we guard and nourish our hearts.

Today's Prayer

Father God, thank you for giving us ears so we can hear and appreciate all the beautiful sounds of life. You have given us stewardship over our hearing and a responsibility to listen responsibly. I ask that you show us how anything that we are listening to may be polluting our hearts. Open our ears that we may truly hear what you are saying to us through your Word, through the music we listen to, and through what others speak to us. Lord, you always hear us, you always respond to our requests. We thank you that you are purifying our ears so that we may have hearts that please you. In the name of the One who formed the ear for hearing. Amen.

Today's Scriptures

Proverbs 15:31; Proverbs 18:15; Mark 4:23–24; 2 Timothy 4:3–4

May 2

Today's Thought

Today we continue looking at why and how we need to guard our hearts. Proverbs tell us that the power of life and death is in the tongue. Guarding our words is probably one of the surest ways to guard our hearts. What comes out of the mouth affects the heart and the heart determines what comes out of the mouth. From the abundance of the heart the mouth speaks. Think of your heart as a well. If the well is polluted, the water that comes out of it is polluted. If the well is pure, you will have a cool refreshing drink of water. So it is with our hearts. When we pollute it with negative and unwholesome talk, out comes nasty stuff. When our mouths speak good and uplifting words, the heart brings forth life. There is a profound connection between the mouth and the heart.

Today's Prayer

Father God, you spoke our world into existence, such is the power of your spoken Word. You have now given us power over our words, power to speak forth life or speak forth death. You see our hearts as a wellspring of life and our words determine what fills that well. Lord, help us to really think before we speak; to weigh our words carefully, remembering that they will affect our hearts, the wellspring of life. When we are tempted to spread gossip or slander, convict our hearts of the danger of passing judgment. We have so many choices about how we use our words every day. Lord, may we make heart-healthy choices that edify others and bless you. May our hearts bless your heart and bring hope and life to a hurting and broken world. In the name of the One who puts his Word in my mouth. Amen.

Today's Scriptures

Psalm 19:14; Proverbs 12:18; Proverbs 18:21; Ephesians 4:29

May 3

Today's Thought

The Word of God has much to say about the way we walk in life. It guides us practically and spiritually as we journey. The path we follow will determine the health of our inner being. Where we go and how we spend our time will either move us ahead in spiritual maturity or hinder us. The Psalmist tells us that the steps of a good man are ordered by the Lord. Likewise, Paul admonishes us to walk vigilantly and not as fools. We must guard our steps, our paths, and our journey on earth as if every step has eternal value. As we make wise decisions with the steps we choose, our hearts remain healthy and in a right position before God. Sometimes we do not know what our next step is to be, but as we seek him and his will, God will surely lead us in the right direction. His Word is a travel map and compass for living a godly life. His Spirit is our travel guide as we journey toward our final destination. We can trust him to guard our hearts as we guard our steps.

Today's Prayer

Father God, you call us to be cautious in our walk on earth. How we walk in this world can make all the difference in our lives and the lives of others. Our influence flows from our inner hearts: our character, our integrity and our lifestyles. We are being watched. We long to leave a mark on the world that makes a difference in the lives of others. We want hearts that are godly and healthy. Help us to guard our steps, where we go, what we do, how we invest our lives. I pray we walk as those who are wise, avoiding foolish behaviors and actions. We want you to be glorified in and through our lives. In the name of the God who directs our steps. Amen.

Today's Scripture

Psalm 37:23–24; Palm 119:133; Ephesians 5:15–17; 1 John 2:5–6

Today's Thought

The animated movie *Inside Out* explored these emotions: joy; sadness; and anger; to name a few. We saw that sadness was an okay emotion, when used for good purposes. This is true about all emotions. They are not bad; they are God-given. It is what we do with them that make a difference. The Bible addresses the emotions we experience, and how to deal with them. The key, I have discovered, is the need to bring our emotions under the control of the Holy Spirit. Left on their own our emotions can control us to the detriment of our Christian witness. When we allow God's Word and the Holy Spirit to guide our emotions, we have a great advantage in regard to guarding our hearts. When our emotions are out of control, we allow darkness to rule in our hearts: fear; anger; anxiety; shame; along with many other emotions. Left unchecked they can bring our hearts into bondage. Allowing the Holy Spirit to have control brings real change. He produces the good fruit in us that overrules unruly emotions. God has provided everything we need to live with healthy emotions and healthy hearts.

Today's Prayer

Father God, thank you for our emotions and the Holy Spirit who comes alongside us to help us control those willful human feelings. You desire for us to live free from the tyranny of fear, anger, anxiety and shame. Left unchecked, these emotions produce bad fruit that invade our hearts and do much damage. God, I pray you set us free from the control of our soulish natures. May we cooperate with you in bringing our emotions to you in prayer. Lord, do for us that which we cannot do for ourselves. In Jesus' name. Amen.

Today's Scriptures

Proverbs 25:28; Proverbs 29:11; 2 Timothy 1:7; James 1:19–20

May 5

Today's Thought

Have you ever gotten lost in your thoughts? We all have at times; we just don't view it as *"being lost."* Our thought-life is our own and we often feel we can go anywhere we want, down any road, for as long as we want. The danger in this kind of thinking is that our thoughts can take us to places we really should not go and keep us there longer than we intended. Our thought-life can eventually act itself out. That's scary if those thoughts are immoral, impure, violent, spiteful, fearful or full of anger. Our thoughts need to be guarded by God's Word and Paul's admonition in Philippians 4:8, *"Finally brothers and sisters, whatever is true, whatever is noble, whatever is right, whatever is pure, whatever is lovely, whatever is admirable, if anything is excellent or praiseworthy, think about such things."* When our thought-life consists of everything Paul says it should, then, those things will be what occupies our hearts and eventually our actions. As a woman thinks, so is she. Think about it!

Today's Prayer

Father God, what marvelous works of art are our minds. We have the ability to think about anything we want, anyway we want. Our thoughts are our own, but you give us the responsibility to sensor our thoughts. Thank you for the guidelines you give that serve to protect us. Thank you that you set the standard by your own thoughts. Your thoughts toward us are always for our good. Your thoughts are lofty, pure and holy. Your thoughts plan good for us and not harm. Lord, I pray that we follow that example and set guards around our thoughts so that the impure, unholy, critical and unbiblical do not get a foothold in us. In Jesus' name. Amen.

Today's Scriptures

Psalm 19:14; Romans 12:2; 2 Corinthians 10:5; Philippians 4:8

May 6

Today's Thought

As we conclude this study on guarding our hearts, I ask, what are we taking away? What I hoped we would see is that from our hearts flows every aspect of our lives. If the well is good, the flow is pure and good; if the well is polluted, the flow is bitter. We must not think that our body parts are our own and we can use them anyway we like. That is simply not true. We have been bought with a price, the precious blood of Christ, and we are not our own. Our hearts belong to God and we are to yield all our members to the righteousness of Christ. Our eyes, our ears, our tongues, our emotions and our thoughts. As we bring all of who we are under the control of the Holy Spirit, our hearts begins to change into pure, clean, refreshing wells of goodness and godly influence. I want that and I think you want that too. It is not impossible; with God all things are possible. When we ask, he hears and responds to our requests. The Lord is our ever-present help and when we diligently seek him, he rewards us.

Today's Prayer

Father God, we are yours … all we are and all we have is yours. Your Son Jesus gave his all so that we could be saved and transformed into children of God who please you. We thank you that you love us just as we are, but you love us too much to leave us unfinished. You long to see maturity in us and we desire it as well. Thank you that you are the maker, the keeper and the redeemer of our hearts. Lord, help us to allow you to examine our hearts daily and expose any areas that need attention. May we learn to guard the treasure you have given us … our hearts. In the name of the One who has bought us with a great price. Amen.

Today's Scriptures

Psalm 100:3; Romans 6:11–14; 1 Corinthians 6:19–20; 1 Thessalonians 5:23

126   *Fern Buzinski*

May 7

Today's Thought

Recently, someone began to bombard me with news about all the terrible things going on in the world. On and on it went; I felt like a huge pile of garbage had been dumped on my soul. It wasn't anyone's fault but my own; I let it happen. It got me thinking about joy. Joy is a gift from God, a fruit the Spirit produces and nurtures in us. As with any treasure, it must be valued and protected. Someone will always want to rain on our parade and steal our joy. We must determine that the joy God has given us in our salvation must be guarded diligently. What and who we listen to on a regular basis will lift us up or tear us down. Things we tell ourselves about ourselves will build us up or leave us feeling deflated and defeated. I love being around people who make me smile and laugh. I want to do the same for them. Life is not easy and of course we need to be realistic about the world and its condition; but, the joy God has given us should not be easily shaken or taken. It's our responsibility to hold fast to joy at all times.

Today's Prayer

Father God, thank you for the joy you have lavished on us. Your Spirit gives us good gifts and we treasure every one. Joy is the gift that gets us through tough and difficult times. It's the gift we can give to others and the blessing they give in return. Lord, help us to find ways to enter into the joy of the Lord when we need that. Help us to protect the joy we have and to keep adding to it. I pray we learn to choose joy every day, even in the midst of those times when joy is hard to find. May we dig deep every day to bring forth the sweet fruit of joy. In the name of the Man of Joy, Jesus. Amen.

Today's Scriptures

Nehemiah 8:10; Psalm 16:11; John 15:11; Romans 15:13

Today's Thought

As I was writing this morning, an ad popped up on my screen, cute little tops and shorts. Even thought I was on my way to researching scriptures for this devotion, I clicked on the ad and looked at several garments before I came to my senses. It was quite a surprise to me that I could be so easily distracted from my mission. Martha, the sister in Luke 10 knew all about distractions There she was, Jesus, her Lord and Messiah right in front of her and she is so preoccupied with impressing her guests that she missed the most important thing. We can't judge Martha. After all, to some degree we are all like her. What is the mission God has entrusted to you and what distracts you? When we are not centered in Christ and what he calls us to, we end up all over the place. The Lord does not lay any burden on us that he himself will not help us carry. He does ask that we stay focused and fixed on our calling. We must weed out the things that so easily hinder us and keep us from being obedient and doing the Lord's will.

Today's Prayer

Father God, you have assigned to each of us a calling, a unique way in which we serve you and others. You understand the many distractions we face every day. We can't avoid interruptions, but help us discern the important from the unimportant. Show each of us the ways we lose focus and become sidetracked from our mission. Remind us daily that being with you in prayer and intimacy is our first and highest calling. Without anchoring ourselves in Jesus we often lose our center and are hindered in knowing your will. I pray we not worry and fret over things that rob us of our effectiveness. We fix our eyes on the prize. In Jesus' name. Amen.

Today's Scriptures

Proverbs 4:25–27; Luke 10:38–42; Colossians 4:17; Hebrews 12:1

May 9

Today's Thought

Jesus extends a most appealing invitation in Matthew 11. It appeals to the human spirit and body; it has been water to my thirsty soul many times. I have been wearied in body, emotions and mind. How about you? In these three verses in Matthew 11, Jesus reaches out to us with a lifeline of pure oxygen. He extends to us an invitation, *"Come to me, all you who are weary and burdened, and I will give you rest. Take my yoke upon you and learn from me, for I am gentle and humble in heart, and you will find rest for your souls"* (Matthew 11:28–29). Take notice of how Jesus wants us to see him. *Gentle and humble in heart.* That speaks volumes to me in my weariness. He will not berate me for being weary. He is not out to whip me into shape. He understands and affirms my weariness, because he himself experienced exhaustion and fatigue. He is drawing me to his loving and gentle heart so I can find my rest in the One who understands.

Today's Prayer

Precious Jesus, we are grateful that you experienced all the feelings and emotions we go through. You lived as one of us so we could know that you understand and empathize in our weaknesses. Lord, I pray today that we learn to lean into the promise of Matthew 11:28–30. You give us all we need to take that next step as we find our rest in you. You light up our path so we take courage to rest when needed and to move ahead when needed. Even in our weariness you have a purpose and a plan. May we have eyes to see, ears to hear and a heart that understands all you want to teach us in our weaknesses and weariness. In the name of our Great High Priest. Amen.

Today's Scriptures

Psalm 73:23; Matthew 11:28–30; 2 Corinthians 12:9–10; Hebrews 4:14–16

May 10

Today's Thought

One Sunday morning as I was teaching a first grade Sunday school class, a certain little girl looked up at me and with all sincerity said, *"Miss Fern, God sees you just as if you are a little girl like me."* Wow, I let that truth sink in and embraced it fully; out of the mouth of babes! That sweet reflection has always stayed with me. After all, Jesus did say that unless we change and become as little children, we will not enter the kingdom. So, what are the childlike qualities Jesus is looking for in his children? Certainly, meekness and trust would top the list. A joyful heart would most likely describe a childlike quality. A child is not tarnished by the rhetoric and seduction of the world. Children are still in awe of the wonders of nature as they explore the creation of God. On and on I could go, but I think we can see Jesus' implication. He wants us to see life through the eyes of innocence and trust. This does not mean blind trust or ignorant innocence. Of course, we need to be wise and discerning, but before our God, let us dance and sing with abandonment of a child.

Today's Prayer

Papa God, you are looking for children who know what it means to be childlike. Lord, help us to change so that we can be the children you desire. Thank you for Jesus and the words he left us. May we grow more childlike every day, trusting, believing, and exploring our world through the eyes of the great Creator. Help us learn to play again, even as we carry out the work you have assigned to us. Teach us the joy of discovery and the wonder of you. Let us make the world our playground and the beach, the sandbox you built for us. In the name of our Papa God. Amen.

Today's Scriptures

Matthew 18:1–4; Matthew 21:14–16; Luke 22:24–26; 1 Peter 2:1–3

May 11

Today's Thought

I admire folks who can take a piece of worthless trash and turn it into something of value. Good money is paid for a fine repurposed piece. The prophet Jeremiah was told by the Lord to make a visit to the potter's house. Once there, he observed the potter at work reforming a marred piece of clay. We sometimes need to be reminded that God is the master potter and we are the clay. He can form and shape us into whatever seems best to him. He uses the wheel of trials, suffering and temptations to test the clay, to see what we are made of. When something within the clay does not please him, he will put that clay back on the wheel and reshape and remold into his desired vessel. Our Divine Potter never leaves the wheel or takes his eyes off the clay. The Potter knows his clay and knows when to remove it from the wheel of affliction. When pain and sorrow come to us through circumstances, we must trust that our Potter, our Creator God, is forming a masterpiece through which his glory and honor can shine.

Today's Prayer

Father God, you created Adam from the clay of the ground. Then you lovingly breathed your own breath of life into him. We are the clay, you are the Potter, the One who molds and shapes us. You take an intense interest in every aspect of our lives. You desire vessels fit for the Master's use. You always do what seems best to you. We praise you that you take even the scarred and broken shards of our lives and form them into something of great value and worth. Nothing is wasted with you, Lord. Every mistake, every wrong move, every hurt and abuse we experience is raw material for your precious wheel. Thanks be to you, Lord. Amen.

Today's Scriptures

Genesis 2:7; Isaiah 64:8; Jeremiah 18:1–6; 2 Corinthians 4:7

Today's Thought

When I was young, I wanted to save the world. Now that I am older and hopefully wiser, I will be content to have contributed to one changed life. God calls us to make an impact on the world around us, and we do. The strange thing is, we never know when it happens. Once in a while, perhaps, someone will share how we made a difference, but we can't count on it. The most we can do is live lives that please God and leave the results up to him. Nonetheless, everything we do and say leaves an impression one way or another. As I write today, I wonder how these devotions will help someone see or understand themselves and God in richer ways. I may never know. The important thing is that I trust God will take what is his and use it for good. Go forth today, trusting that you will somehow make an impact. Heaven will tell the full story. Until then be the salt and light in a world that desperately needs to be impacted for Christ.

Today's Prayer

Father God, we thank you for the people and the situations in our lives that made an impact on us. You used it all to draw us to yourself. You often hide from our eyes the difference we are making, perhaps to keep us from pride. Then there are times when you clearly show us the good we do in this world. Lord, we want to make an impact for godliness. Use our lives today as we go forth in serving you and others. Keep us aware of our words and our actions, how they affect others. We thank you that we do not have to have great power or position to be an influencer. We are sufficient in Christ in affecting change in our corner of the world. Amen.

Today's Scriptures

Matthew 5:13–16; Philippians 2:14–16; Colossians 4:5–6; 1 Peter 2:12

May 13

Today's Thought

After Jesus was resurrected, He showed himself to Mary in the garden. She quickly ran to the place where his disciples were hiding behind locked doors. *"While they were still talking about this, Jesus himself stood among them and said to them,'" peace be with you'"* (Luke 24:36). Yes! The Prince of Peace himself came to them at their darkest hour. Jesus showed them the scars on his hands and sides. It was only then that they became overjoyed seeing that it truly was the Lord. The now resurrected, glorified Jesus had visible scars. Imagine the scars of his great sacrifice clearly visible. A scar means the hurt is over and the wound is closed. It means you conquered the pain, learned a lesson, grew stronger, and are now moving forward. The question I have for us today is this, even as Jesus was willing to expose his scars to us, are we willing to allow him access to ours? Are we keeping our painful past locked up for fear of exposure? Jesus can use every part of our life, good and bad, crowns and scars, to reach those in a hurting world who are hiding their hearts behind locked doors.

Today's Prayer

Lord Jesus, what an amazing risen Savior you are! You invade all the dark places in our lives. You walk right into the woundedness and you understand all the brokenness. Lord, help us to have the trust to invite you into every part of our past and present. Help us to stop trying to hide our scars from you and from the world. They need to see that we are not perfect and that we understand life's trauma. Only then will they find courage to say, *"Me too."* In the name of the Risen Resurrected Lord. Amen.

Today's Scriptures

Isaiah 53:5; John 20:19–20; John 20:26–28; 2 Corinthians 1:3–5

May 14

Today's Thought

How do you view your trials? Do you wince every time God sends a test your way? Do you attempt to fix it quickly so as to avoid the pain? I am learning that God does not test us without first preparing us, just as a teacher presents the material before the pop quiz. That truth should greatly relieve our anxiety as we see the storm clouds approaching. Scripture clearly teaches God's purposes for trials. They are stepping stones to deeper faith. They draw us to God's Word. They are opportunities to draw closer to Jesus. They create a deeper longing for heaven. Trials are meant to humble us and keep our hearts soft and pliable in the hands of God. Trials teach us that obedience is always the best choice. Struggles grow us in godliness and Christ-like character. Next time you experience a battle that seems to drown you, keep in mind that you will come out on the other side, stronger and healthier than when you went in.

Today's Prayer

Father God, we thank you for the past struggles of life and how they worked to grow us. I pray we learn to trust you as we enter future places that are not comfortable. You will be testing us until the day you call us home. You are never out to harm us, only to help us be a better version of ourselves, more like Christ. We thank you for the dark times when we knew our only hope was you. We thank you for the hard times that opened our eyes to the truth of your Word. We thank you for the humbling of trials that keep our hearts soft in your hands. Lord, help us to embrace all you allow into our lives as means that draw us closer to you and keep our affections on things above. In the name of the One we trust. Amen.

Today's Scriptures

2 Corinthians 4:16–18; James 1:2–4; 1 Peter 1:6–7; 1 Peter 5:10–11

May 15

Today's Thought

I am quickly approaching a landmark birthday. The years are piling up. A child recently asked my age. I told her; she sweetly responded, *"Those are some big numbers."* Yes, those are some very big numbers. In light of this reality, I sat this morning and wrote out my goals for the next five years, should God grant me time. As I looked over my musings, I realized that I can make all the plans my heart desires, but what I really want is for the Lord to direct my steps. He promises to do that if I will let him. None of us know what the future holds; our days are numbered by the Lord. I believe we should live expectantly, dreaming and planning for the future, but we need to hold those desires loosely. The Lord could return at any time, or when we least expect it, we might be called home to heaven. Either way, we belong to a Father who cares deeply for us and wants us to live out our days being productive and flourishing. The Lord knows the plans he has for us today, tomorrow and forever. As we daily seek him and submit our plans to him, he lovingly directs our steps.

Today's Prayer

Father God, you call us to live as if we will dwell here for many years. Likewise you advise us to be prepared at any time to exit planet Earth. Lord, help us to find the balance in it all. Help us to hold our goals, desires and plans loosely. You alone hold the master blueprint of our days, and we trust that you know best because you see the beginning to the end. You are our Alpha and Omega and everything in between. Lord, prepare us for the future plans you have for us. I pray that we are open and pliable in your loving hands. Lord, have your way. In Jesus' name. Amen.

Today's Scriptures

Psalm 37:23; Psalm 90:12; Proverbs 16:9; James 4:13–15

Today's Thought

"So heavenly-minded, no earthly good." We've all heard it said. But is it true? Quite the contrary. God's Word clearly indicates that we are to be heavenly minded as we journey through this earthly life. Paul said in Colossians 3:2, *"Set your minds on things above, not on earthly things."* Another version renders, *"set your affections."* The word *"affection"* means to be mentally disposed in a certain direction. It also involves *"to think about and to savor."* When we compare the brevity of this life with the eternal, we should be setting our affections on the place where it most matters. What we seek after, where we seek and where we lay up our treasures ... there we will find our hearts. If Jesus is our treasure, we should be setting our full affection on where he is. This life is simply a journey to his arms. When we are heavenly-minded it changes our perspective on this life. Looking toward heaven keeps us from being entangled in the affairs of this world. It gives us the courage and strength to endure the hardships we face now.

Today's Prayer

Father of heaven, you are always thinking about us. You have set your heart and your affection on us. In return we should *"set our affection"* on you and our eternal home. You say that we are already raised and seated with Christ in the heavenly places; so, God, help us to live in that reality as best we can. I pray we savor, taste and see that you are good and you have a good and perfect life waiting for us in your presence. Lord, help us keep and maintain that heavenly perspective as we travel through this life in anticipation of all that awaits us there. I pray our lives reflect that our affections are set on you. In the name of our heavenly Savior. Amen.

Today's Scripture

2 Corinthians 4:16–18; Ephesians 2:6–7; Colossians 3:1–4; Hebrews 11:13–16

Today's Thought

Do we understand that the kingdoms of this world now belong to Satan? It is with God's permission that he is the ruler of earthly kingdoms. It's no wonder the world is in such chaos and disarray. Every worldly kingdom will eventually fall. Many nations have already seen their day and no longer exist. In the wilderness experience Jesus was offered the glory of all the kingdoms of the world if he would bow down and worship Satan. The devil was able to make the offer because in a sense, they were his to give. Jesus knew his appointed mission. It was not to set up an earthly throne. He came to gather a people who looked toward the heavenly kingdom, willing to renounce the treasures of this world. Jesus trusted God in the waiting and so must we. In Revelation 11 a trumpet is blown and the seventh angel shouts with a loud voice, *"The kingdom of the world has become the kingdom of our Lord and of his Christ, and he will reign forever and ever!"* (Revelation 11:15).

Today's Prayer

Father God, all power and authority have been given to your Son, Jesus Christ. For now, your plan must be played out in this world. Meanwhile, you have supreme control of all things. Lord, help us to embrace the truth that we belong to a different kingdom. We do not place our trust in human systems or governments; they will all fall and pass away. Our kingdom is an everlasting one full of peace and righteousness. Lord, I pray we never set our hopes in this life, in the kingdoms of this world. May we truly understand that we are citizens of a kingdom with one ruler and one God. Amen.

Today's Scriptures

Luke 4:5–8; John 18:36; 2 Corinthians 4:4; Revelation 11:15

Today's Thought

Do you like shortcuts? You know, like that back road that seems to be a better, faster way. Sometimes shortcuts work out, and sometimes they turn into a train wreck. I have many regrets over attempting to short circuit the tough work that goes into success. In contrast, some of us take the long way home, around the same old mountain again and again. Somewhere between the two, there is a path called, *"Doing It God's Way."* In Jeremiah's day, the religious leaders were handing God's people a quick fix to the problems they created for themselves. They promised a false peace in spite of their rebellion; God was calling for repentance. They promised superficial healing for their wounds; God offered them the healing balm of the Messiah. They promised an easy road to freedom; God wanted them to do it the right way, even though it was a longer and harder road. When we forsake God's chosen path, it never ends well. His Word is our compass, our road map, our assurance that we are heading in the right direction. God's way leads to victory and freedom.

Today's Prayer

Father God, there will always be a way that seems best to us, but it is not always your way. Our stubborn ways often lead to regrets. Help us to get it right the first time through obedience to your Word and the sensitivity to your Holy Spirit. Lord, you never leave us to figure life out on our own. You have given us a sure foundation on which to build our lives ... your holy Word. We thank you that when we do go in the wrong direction, you lovingly guide us back to true north. Help us to turn around quickly when we see that we are missing the mark. In Jesus' name. Amen.

Today's Scriptures

Psalm 32:8; Proverbs 14:12; Isaiah 30:21; Isaiah 48:17–18

Today's Thought

One of my first Bible teachers made a statement that has stuck with me. She said, *"If God showed us all that is in our heart at one time, we could not endure it."* Jeremiah recorded these words, *"The heart is deceitful above all things, and beyond all cure. Who can understand it?"* (Jeremiah 17:9). I could not believe that my heart was in such a wretched condition, but as the years passed, I understood that my teacher was right. Just when I think I have arrived spiritually, God uses people and circumstances to expose more sin in my heart. I am eternally grateful that he did not show me the truth about my heart all at once. I would have been undone. But our God, who is rich in mercy, will not do that. When he does expose sin in us, it is always out of love and concern for our spiritual well-being. He is a gentle refiner of the heart, never wanting to hurt or destroy us. He is simply looking to change us into the amazing men and women of God that he knows we can be.

Today's Prayer

Father God, we are grateful that you now see us through the redeeming blood of Jesus. Right now, we stand justified and holy before you in the heavenlies. We do know that your plan in this life is to sanctify us and continually cleanse our hearts so we can live holy lives. We confess that our hearts will need work until the day you call us home. Then, we will be perfect and complete in your presence. Until then, Lord, we invite you to continue searching our hearts and exposing those sins, attitudes and motives that do not line up with your ideals. Thank you that you never overwhelm or shame us. I pray we fully cooperate with your desire to conform us into the likeness of Jesus. In his name. Amen.

Today's Scriptures

Psalm 26:2; Psalm 139:23–24; Jeremiah 17:9–10; 2 Corinthians 7:1

Today's Thought

The gospels of Matthew and Mark both include the story of a poor widow who was praised by Jesus for her meager offering, equivalent to a fraction of a penny. Let's unpack this a bit. First, Jesus deliberately positioned himself opposite the offering box in the temple as offerings were being made. One after another they came with their coins, placing them in the box. They all knew Jesus was watching and made a great show of impressing him. Clink, clink, clink, in went the coins. Great sums into the temple treasury. Lastly, the poor widow came. I imagine her embarrassment, trying to be inconspicuous, with her two tiny coins. Then as she walks away, Jesus turns to his disciples with this lesson of truth. *"I tell you the truth, this poor widow has put more into the treasury than all the others. They all gave out of their wealth, but she, out of her poverty, put in everything, all she had to live on"* (Mark 12:43–44). I don't think the main point is the amount they gave, but how they gave; the attitude of giving that came from the heart. As we give, whether of our finances, resources or time, we need to search our hearts as to our motive. Is it to be seen and praised by others, or is it to be wholly pleasing the Lord?

Today's Prayer

Father God, every good and perfect gift is from you. When we give, we are only giving back what already belongs to you. All things are yours, and we are stewards of your blessings. We know you love a cheerful giver. Lord, help us to be of the fellowship that loves to give back. I pray you create in us the widow's heart of giving, not from our excess, but from the top, the first fruits. May we never make a show when we give, but always give simply, as unto you. In the name of the One who owns all things. Amen.

Today's Scriptures

1 Chronicles 29:14; Matthew 6:1–4; Mark 12:41–44; 2 Corinthians 9:6–7

Today's Thought

Yes, God owns the cattle on a thousand hills, but that does not mean he will give them to you. Be assured though, he will always give you what you need. Wants and needs are not the same. Our needs are basic: air; food; water; clothing; and a roof over our heads. Our wants go beyond: fine dining; the best shoes; a vast wardrobe to choose from; and a bigger, more modern home. Nothing wrong with any of that, if our reasons are right and our desires line up with God's will. Make no mistake; God loves to bless his children just as we love giving to ours. When we are grateful for what we have, and find our contentment in knowing God as a loving, generous Father, he is free to pile on more. God owns everything and all is his to give or withhold. When we desire Jesus above all earthly gifts, we truly have all we need. Let us wake up every day grateful for God's provision of all our basic essentials, and for everything else he so lavishly imparts.

Today's Prayer

Father God, what a good and generous God you are. There is nothing that we need that you will not provide. Yes, you own the cattle on a thousand hills; and, you own the hills too! No good thing will you withhold from those who love you. Lord, help us to discern our wants from our needs. Help us to be content and grateful for all you have given us without demanding more. You know how much is too much. Father, give us only what we need. Excess may make us proud, and poverty may cause us to steal. Lord, I pray we never desire anything that would turn our hearts away from you. In the name of the God who owns it all. Amen.

Today's Scriptures

Psalm 50:9–12; Psalm 84:11–12; Romans 8:32; Philippians 4:19

Today's Thought

As soon as we seek our approval from man, we are in trouble. The minute we look to others for affirmation, we are in for disappointment. The moment we enter a relationship for validation and acceptance, greater is the fall when it ends. How do I know this? First and foremost the Bible tells me so; and, I have personally experienced the letdown of looking to others for what only God can give me. Our approval can never be grounded in the opinions of others. It can never come from what we do, who we know or our position in life. Our approval must come from God alone. The good news is, we do not have to earn his love and approval. We are already accepted in the Beloved Son of God. Nothing can change that. It is anchored in the Word of God which does not lie. It is assured us in the character and nature of God which does not change. Because Christ is accepted, we are accepted. Because Christ is worthy before God, we are worthy before him. Our value is rooted and grounded in whose we are, children of the Living God. Our worth shines from the inside, not from outside opinion. Christ in us, the hope of glory.

Today's Prayer

Father God, Jesus secured our position with you. We are beloved children. You have accepted us into your divine family and we are forever loved and accepted. We do not need the approval of man. We desire to live a life in which Christ is evident, and we do not set our hearts on the validation of others. Lord, I pray that we not depend on the opinions of others as an endorsement of our value. We make it our aim to please you, Lord. Help us to find our total security in you. In the name of the Beloved. Amen.

Today's Scripture

John 12:42–43; Galatians 1:10; Colossians 3:22–24; 1 Thessalonians 2:3–6

May 23

Today's Thought

I like crime shows that take us through the process of cracking a case. It fascinates me to see how modern technology brings criminals to justice. About 58% of crimes are solved eventually; but many still go unsolved. I applaud justice being secured for the victims. My heart goes out to those still awaiting justice for their loved ones. In Luke 18 Jesus tells a story about a widow's encounter with a judge who did not fear God or care about people. She was asking for justice against her adversary. The judge refused to hear her case, but because she kept bothering him and wearing him out, he eventually saw that she got justice. Then Jesus says this, *"And will not God bring about justice for his chosen ones, who cry out to him day and night? Will he keep putting them off? I tell you; he will see that they get justice, and quickly"* (Luke 18:7–8). Our God is a righteous Judge. We may not always see our cause resolved quickly, and maybe not even in this lifetime. But rest assured that God, our faithful Judge, keeps good records. In his justice, all things will be resolved in our favor.

Today's Prayer

Father God, your justice is sure. We will be vindicated either here or in the life to come. All things are naked and bare before you and nothing is hidden from your eyes. No one is getting away with anything. You fight for us and our cause is of utmost importance to you. Lord, you expect us to conduct our affairs with the same justice you demonstrate. I pray that we come to see your justice through the lens of scripture so we can know to do right in every situation. Thank you that you are on our side. In the name of our Righteous Judge. Amen.

Today's Scriptures

Ecclesiastes 3:16–17; Luke 18:1–8; Romans 12:19; Hebrews 10:30

Today's Thought

Chapter 11 of Hebrews is often referred to as the Christian Hall of Faith. The writer is commending each person for his trust in God, even when enduring the worst of circumstances. Abel was murdered by his brother because of his devotion to God. Noah obeyed God in spite of ridicule and harassment. Abraham left all he knew in obedience to God even when he did not know where he was going. Moses chose to be mistreated along with the people of God rather than enjoy the pleasures of Egypt. Some were stoned, flogged, tortured and wrongfully imprisoned. These faith heroes still speak today, even though they are dead. Their testimonies are immortal. How will our lives speak after we are gone? We can be sure we are being watched now; and, after we are gone our lives will still speak. Will our names be included in God's Hall of the Faithful?

Today's Prayer

Father God, thank you for these shining examples. They teach us that faith is not about everything turning out as we hope. It's about trusting you even when things go contrary to what we would expect. Lord, help us to understand true faith; trusting you when we don't see results, when we don't understand, when we feel our prayers are not heard. Abel was murdered for his faith; in contrast, Enoch never experienced death but was taken up by you as he lived by faith. You are a sovereign God; you do what seems good to you. You are a just God; may we not question how you work in our lives. Father, I pray each of us have the kind of faith that lives long after we are gone … faith that speaks even from the grave. In Jesus' name. Amen.

Today's Scriptures

Proverbs 3:5–6; Romans 8:28; Hebrews 11:1–4; Hebrews 11:32–40

May 25

Today's Thought

"Faith is taking the first step even when you don't see the whole staircase." Were you ever so excited about beginning something only to discover it involved a lot more than you anticipated? Refinishing a piece of furniture, reading through the Bible in a year, writing a book? I am feeling that way right now as I complete this day's devotion. How will I ever get through writing 365 days! It will take commitment, perseverance and endurance. Often, I have to look back and remember how God got me through other endeavors that I undertook. Journeys are not always easy or quick. They require determination and dedication. Some days will be harder than others. We do what we can and keep moving ahead. The best way to eat an elephant is one bite at a time. Sometimes we take on more than we are capable of; but that's no reason to quit. It's okay to revisit the plan and make adjustments. It's only impossible if you never begin.

Today's Prayer

Jesus, what a journey you embarked upon. You left your Father and all the glory of heaven to come to live where we live and dwell among us for a while. You walked the dusty roads of your homeland, one step, one joy, one heartache at a time. You demonstrated commitment and perseverance. Even as you journeyed up Golgotha's hill, you faltered at times, just as we do; but, you kept walking all the way to the cross. You overcame every obstacle and persevered through the pain and suffering. No journey we ever undertake will cost us as much as the price you paid. Lord, thank you for the example you left for us as we complete our journey. Amen.

Today's Scriptures

Galatians 6:9; Philippians 4:13; Hebrews 12:1–3; James 1:12

Today's Thought

It took me too many years to learn that love is a decision; it is more about what we do than how we feel. On some level, I think that truth should be included in wedding vows. Perhaps it already is and we just don't hear it. Our culture has promoted a sappy kind of love, one built on erotic passion and feelings. Marriages would be more secure and enduring if each partner made a daily decision to love regardless of feelings. Choice is a powerful privilege God has given us. Choice is a discipline we must exercise every day. If we want our relationships to be amazing, we need to nurture them as if they are amazing. If we want our relationships to be of substance, we must base them on God's definition of love. God has made a covenant of love with us. He will never leave us or forsake us. He says we are his forever. That's the kind of love we are to imitate.

Today's Prayer

Father God, you demonstrated your love in the person of Jesus Christ. When he cried out to you in the garden, he did not *feel* a desire to endure the cross; but nevertheless, he walked out his love for you and for us, all the way to Calvary. Lord, we need to be different than a culture that so easily breaks commitment; a culture that makes love decisions based on feelings. God, we need a deeper understanding of covenant love. Help us to grasp this biblical truth. Your Word and your Son have given us the blueprint. I pray, Lord, that any way in which our minds need to be renewed in understanding authentic love, that your Spirit would accomplish that in us. We thank you that you hear and respond. In the name of our covenant God. Amen.

Today's Scriptures

John 15:9–13; Romans 5:6–8; Roman 12:9–10; 1 John 4:7–12

Today's Thought

Jesus promises to never leave us or abandon us. How does that speak to you? What it says to me is this; everything that Jesus is and all he has is forever mine. His strength, his power, his love; everything I will ever need, is always available to me. Because he is with me always, all of his nature, attributes and character are at my disposal. Because Christ is in me, I have access to everything I need in him. Peace does not come and go; he is the Prince of Peace and he lives in me. Security does not desert me; he is my security and he lives in me. When we open Jesus' statement to its fullest meaning, we see that we are never alone or abandoned. Never, ever, will he remove his glorious presence from us. He goes where we go. He lives where we live. He is in our going out and our coming in, our rising up and our sitting down. What a blessed assurance, Jesus is mine!

Today's Prayer

Father God, our minds cannot begin to comprehend a divine Savior who is always with each of us; but we know your Word is true. We hold to your amazing truth. Lord, today we confess that we believe that we are never alone, never forsaken, never forgotten. All that Jesus is, he is for us. All that he has, he has for us. Lord, help us to seize upon this truth every day; to draw from the well of living water all we need to satisfy our spiritual thirst. I ask that we gain a fuller understanding of these truths. I pray we never again feel alone or abandoned. May we hold to the reality of Jesus' promise that we are forever his and he is forever ours. He is ever with us now and forever. In his name. Amen.

Today's Scriptures

Deuteronomy 31:8; Joshua 1:9; Psalm 73:23–26; Isaiah 41:13

Today's Thought

Is there a way to do less but accomplish more? Yes, but it will cost something. It may require rearranging your morning schedule and realigning priorities. May I suggest a time of rest before you begin your day ... a Sabbath rest, a time spent with the Father. God created Adam on the sixth day, then, on the seventh day, God rested. I have to assume that Adam rested with God on that seventh day. It was only after they rested together that Adam went forth to do what God created him to do. I believe the principle behind this is the need to rest with our Creator before launching into our day. If we make the beginning of our day, every day, a Sabbath Rest, we can accomplish so much more with a lot less energy. I know for myself personally, if I give the best part of my day to being with the Lord, the rest of my day goes a lot smoother. I receive guidance, direction and often correction. When I wake up to a full, demanding schedule and plan to meet with the Lord later, it often does not happen. Christ gave us his first and his best. How can we give him any less?

Today's Prayer

Father God, you created us for yourself. Forgive us for the times we rush into the day, leaving you behind in the wake of our busyness. Lord, teach us the rich truth of resting with you before we launch into our day. Time rushes at us like a fast-moving locomotive; we need the quiet time spent with you so we do not get run over by schedules, demands and distractions. Jesus, you gave everything you had so we could be with you, both now and in the life to come. God, help us to make time with you our daily dependency. In the name of Jesus, our Rest. Amen.

Today's Scriptures

Mark 1:35; John 15:4–5; Hebrews 4:1; Hebrews 4:9–11

May 29

Today's Thought

The prophet Isaiah was commissioned by God to deliver devastating news to King Hezekiah; his illness would end in death. Hezekiah sought the Lord with bitter tears for his life and God granted mercy; he gave Hezekiah fifteen more years. In the very next chapter however, Hezekiah does a very foolish thing and is reprimanded by Isaiah. First he asks Hezekiah what he did when the king of Babylon paid him a visit. In his pride King Hezekiah had shown all his glory and wealth to the king of Babylon, God's enemy. Isaiah now had to pronounce the price for his disobedience. *"The time will come when everything in your palace and all that your fathers have stored up until this day will be carried off to Babylon, nothing will be left"* (Isaiah 39:6). King Hezekiah's response is mind-boggling and selfish. He tells Isaiah, *"'The word of the Lord you have spoken is good,' for he thought, 'there will be peace and security in my lifetime. What you have spoken is good'"* (Isaiah 39:8). Beloved, this is no time in world history to cease praying for the generations that will come. They need our support and prayers. What they will be up against will be horrendous. God forbid we think only of our own peace.

Today's Prayer

Father God, may we never be as Hezekiah, so caught up in our own finite lifetime that we neglect the responsibility of praying for our children, grandchildren and all future generations. How much they will need the strength and hope to live in a world that is getting more and more depraved. Lord, we pray you guide us in how to pray for them. Equip us to be godly examples in every way. Lord, help us to remember to tell the next generation of your unfailing love and your great salvation. In the name of God who hears us. Amen.

Today's Scriptures

Genesis 17:7; Psalm 22:30–31; Psalm 78:1–4; Isaiah 39:5–8

Today's Thought

I love looking into the book of Acts. It's our history lesson on the amazing things performed by the Holy Spirit through the early church. These were courageous men and women who did not back down or in any way renounce their faith in Jesus. They faced great persecution and even death, but they were not turned aside from their mission of proclaiming the gospel. In Chapter 4 of Acts, Peter and John were seized by the religious leaders and asked by what power and what name they proclaimed salvation and performed healings. They boldly confessed, *"Know this, it is by the name of Jesus Christ of Nazareth … that this man stands before you healed"* (Acts 4:10). The leaders saw the courage of Peter and John and saw that they were unschooled, ordinary men; they took note that these men had been with Jesus. The point I want to make is this: do those around us see that we have been with Jesus? Can they see that we have been sitting at the Master's feet as Peter and John had done? Will they want what we have because they perceive that we have found all that really matters?

Today's Prayer

Father God, we are grateful that the confidence and boldness we have for the gospel is because of Jesus. The light that shines from us comes from our time and devotion to him. Lord, I pray that when others encounter us, they can plainly see that we have been taught by Jesus, that we walk with Jesus and that we know him personally. I pray that our lives of devotion be a sweet fragrance that draws others to the Savior. May we become more and more like the One we worship. As we walk with the wise Teacher, may we become wise. In the name of Jesus. Amen.

Today's Scriptures

Acts 4:13; 2 Corinthians 3:18; Ephesians 5:1–2; 1 John 2:5–6

Today's Thought

My friend Cindy and I have a running banter between us; contending for the position of "Chief Sinner." I don't know how it started, but we sure do have fun with it. There is however, a serious side to all of it. Both of us know our past, who we were before the Savior captured our hearts. Our lives were not pretty; but, that's who we use to be, not who we are. Praise be to God for his unfailing mercy. Every time we converse through mail or text, we make sure we sign off as "Chief Sinner." Actually, we consider being the "Chief Sinner" not a badge of honor, but a witness of the awesome power of Christ to reach into the lowest, vilest pit to save and redeem. You may be wondering what we base our branding on. We all admire and respect the life and writings of the apostle Paul. Listen to what he says to Timothy, *"Here is a trustworthy saying … Christ Jesus came into the world to save sinners, of whom I am the worst … That in me, the chief of sinners, Christ Jesus might display his unlimited patience as an example for those who would believe on him and receive eternal life"* (1 Timothy 1:15–16). That's our story; and, we want Christ to use his patience toward us and the miracle of our salvation to draw others. Our lives are trophies of the rich grace of God for all sinners, of whom I am chief.

Today's Prayer

Father God, what a wonderful Savior you sent us. While we were yet the vilest of sinners, Christ died for us. Because of your great patience and love we all have a chance. No one is ever too far gone that you cannot reach and redeem. Lord, we are all the worst of sinners. We are all your trophies of grace, and we are on display for all the world to see how merciful you are. Amen.

Today's Scriptures

1 Corinthians 6:9–11; Ephesians 2:1–9; Ephesians 5:8; 1 Timothy 1:13–16

June 1

Today's Thought

What thrills your heart? I what do you delight? God has indeed given us all things on this earth to enjoy and I hope you are enjoying the life God has given you. I delight in my grandbabies. What a miracle a baby is. A new member of the family. One whom we can love on, tickle and hold close to our hearts. Children are the continuation of our family and heritage. Mine are all grown up now, but the memories of those growing up years are priceless. Psalm 37:4 invites us to make the Lord our delight. David goes on to tell us that he, the Lord, will give us the desires of our heart. I use to think the verse meant that when I delight myself in the Lord, he will give me the *things* that I desire. Now that I am older, and hopefully wiser, I see this in a new light. I no longer see the verse saying *"delight myself in the Lord, so that he will give me the desires of my heart."* When I delight myself in him, and keep delighting, then I will have the desire and longing of my heart. You see, the deepest longing and desire of our hearts is him. The more we delight in him, the more he will give us of himself. After that, everything else is simply added blessing.

Today's Prayer

Father God, today and every day we delight in you. We delight through talking with you, listening to you, reading and obeying your Word. We rejoice in your creation and all the beauty around us. We delight in watching you work in our lives and the lives of those we love. We delight in answered prayers and in anticipation of answered prayers to come. You created us for your pleasure and we will enjoy you forever. You created our hearts to delight in you before all else Amen.

Today's Scriptures

Psalm 1:1–3; Psalm 37:4; Psalm 84:2; Mark 12:28–30

Today's Thought

Who would you call in a crisis? Why would he or she be the one? I myself often consider that question. I have several in mind. Each of them has the qualities needed in an emergency. They are people who think before acting. They know how to stay calm while they evaluate the situation. They do not act impulsively or irrationally. They are men and women of prayer and know how to seek the wisdom of God. I have seen how they respond in their own times of crisis. 2 Timothy 4:5a cautions us, *"Keep your head in all situations ..."* I sincerely hope that others would see me as a person who can be depended upon in a crisis; someone who keeps her wits about her when others need a calming presence. How about you? Would you like to see your name at the top of someone's list?

Today's Prayer

Father God, you are our Rock and Anchor in the midst of every storm. It is good to know that you also provide people who we can confidently call upon when we just don't know what to do. We thank you for those who have the fortitude and wisdom to bring a comforting word, or a nugget of insight to a frightening situation. Lord, we want to be someone else's choice, someone who can be depended upon. Help us first to learn to keep a calm spirit when misfortune and adversity invades our homes and families. Teach us to imitate the quiet and gentle spirit of Jesus. Lord, help us to see that we can only see and think clearly when we allow your Spirit to take hold of us in difficult times. May we be a people who know how to be still and know our God will help us. In the name of our Refuge in times of trouble. Amen

Today's Scriptures

Psalm 46:1–5; Psalm 112:7; Ecclesiastes 4:9–12; 2 Timothy 4:5a

June 3

Today's Thought

How many times have we entreated the Lord for a good word? In desperate times and situations, we often cry out to him, *"Lord, I need to hear from you!"* Just recently I sought the Lord about three different sets of circumstances and decisions I was facing. I needed to know if I should move ahead. In response to each request the Lord clearly said, *"No."* I was disappointed because I wanted to carry out my plans. Now came the hard part. Would I obey, or would I act contrary to the word I received from the Lord? Many times in scripture the kings of Israel would ask the prophets to seek God for direction. Often the king did not like God's answer; so, to his great misfortune, he went against the words of God's anointed prophets. It never went well for him. We must be careful when we seek God on a matter. Before we ask, we must settle it in our hearts that we will listen carefully for God's answer and be ready and willing to obey. This is the key to being in the sweet spot of his will.

Today's Prayer

Father God, your ears are always open to our prayers, cries and requests. You are neither deaf nor silent, you always hear and you always respond. Lord, give us well-trained listening ears and obedient hearts when we come to you for direction and guidance. Often, we hear what we want to hear and do exactly as we want to do, even against our better judgment. Teach us to wait quietly and patiently for your wisdom and direction. May we not run ahead of you, or lag behind as we hear from you. I pray we learn to stay in step with you and your plans, through loving obedience. In the name of the Only Wise God. Amen.

Today's Scriptures

1 Samuel 15:22; Psalm 34:15; Luke 11:27–28; James 1:22–25

Today's Thought

Imagine the tremendous disappointment the twelve disciples felt. They thought Jesus would abolish the Roman Empire and set up his earthly kingdom. They would be the royal cabinet of his earthly realm. It all fell apart as they watched their beloved master die on a Roman cross. So much for their political dreams. Even after Jesus rose from the dead, they still did not understand why he did not seize control of the nation. So, some reverted back to what they knew ... fishing. In his disappointment, Peter said to the others, *"'I am going out to fish', and they said,' We will go with you.' So, they went out and got into the boat, but that night they caught nothing"* (John 21:3). With their teacher gone, they set out on their own, fishing all night. In the morning, Jesus stood on the shore and called out, *"Friends, haven't you any fish?"* (John 21:5). In essence he was chiding them. *"How is this working for you?"* No fish. He told them to cast their nets on the right side of the boat, and when they did there were so many fish they could not haul in the net. When they went ahead with their own plans they did not prosper. When Jesus was invited into the situation, wonderful things happened.

Today's Prayer

Father God, help us to remember this story when we are tempted to think we can be move ahead on our own without your counsel. When we feel abandoned, may we remember that you said you would never leave us. God, in all our endeavors may we invite you in so we can have the best outcomes. I ask that we always pray and seek your wisdom and will before moving ahead with our own plans. Thank you that you always want to be in the boat with us, helping us to succeed. In the name of Jesus. Amen.

Today's Scriptures

John 15:5; John 18:36; John 21:1–6; Philippians 2:12–13

June 5

Today's Thought

In 1990 Bette Midler recorded the well-loved song, *From a Distance*. She sings these words, *"God is watching us, from a distance."* Those words always disturbed me. The writer's theology is off-center to say the least. The God of the Bible is anything but distant. As well-meaning as the writer of those lyrics, the sentiment is entirely wrong. Our God is not a distant God. He is as close as our heartbeat and our next breath. He is intimately involved in every detail of our lives. He has not left us here on our own to figure it out. Our Father God is lovingly and intimately involved with his creation. He is an interactive God; he listens to us, and he responds to us. He demonstrated his involvement by sending his own Son to die in our place. Jesus came without reservation or hesitation to live among us, walk with us, eat with us and teach us. He even dared to touch the leper! That's a close-up encounter of the most divine nature. We are told that not even a tiny sparrow will fall to the ground without his notice. How much more does he lovingly watch over us.

Today's Prayer

Father God, we praise you for being what we need, a God who is involved with every aspect of life on this planet, and even more, with every moment of each life you created. We crave intimacy and you give it. We long for your involvement in our everyday circumstances; and you give it. God, may we never feel distant from you, as you are never distant from us. Lord, you came the distance for us. You closed the wide divide between a holy God and sinful humanity. Yes, Lord, you are watching us, but never from a distance. Amen.

Today's Scriptures

Isaiah 57:15; Matthew 10:29; John 1:14; Romans 5:8

June 6

Today's Thought

Mark 14 records a sad night in Jesus' ministry. As he and his disciples reclined at the table of the Passover meal, Jesus said to them, *"Truly I tell you, one of you will betray me, one who is eating with me"* (Mark 16:18). The disciples were saddened by Jesus' words. One-by-one they asked, *"Surely not I?"* (Mark 16:19). I am struck by the tenderness of the men. Each one concerned that somehow he had offended the Master. I can picture John, hand covering his heart, hardly breathing, *"Surely you don't mean me?"* Yesterday I had a visit with a dear friend who loves Christ. In the course of our conversation she emphasized the fact that she would never deny her Lord, no matter what. That got me to thinking, when was the last time I made that declaration? The Bible warns us to take be careful when we think we stand; for we may fall. With persecution on the rise around the world, perhaps it's a good time to sincerely think about our own loyalty to Christ. Am I anchored deeply enough in my love and devotion to him that I would never deny him, even in the face of death?

Today's Prayer

Father God, as Christians face perilous times in America and around the world, how much we need to take heed to your warnings. I pray you help us to stay strong and loyal so we not fall into apathy and complacency, becoming susceptible to deceit and betrayal. May we not be presumptuous in thinking we would not deny you in the face of danger. God, I pray we keep short accounts with you in regard to sin and our faithfulness to Jesus, especially as times grow difficult and dangerous. Lord, may we not hesitate to ask, *"Lord, is it I?"* Amen.

Today's Scriptures

Mark 14:17–19; Mark 14:37–38; 1 Corinthians 10:11–12; 2 Timothy 2:11–12

Today's Thought

I love great questions; they help us discover truth; and truth discover for oneself is truth that makes a lasting difference. Jesus was a master at asking the right question at the right time. In the John 20 account, Mary is crying outside Jesus' empty tomb. As she turns to leave, the risen Christ approaches her, but she does not recognize him. He now asks one of those great questions, *"Woman,* he ask, *why are you crying? Who is it you are looking for?"* Thinking he was the gardener, she said, *"Sir, if you have carried him away, tell me where you have put him and I will get him"* (John 20:15). Jesus knew exactly why Mary was crying. Why did he ask? Mary was so blinded by her grief she could not see the answer to her question standing right in front of her. When he spoke her name, she recognized her living Lord. Sometimes the answer to our sorrow, grief and questions is right in front of us. As we experience the empty tomb of unanswered questions, Jesus will meet us there if our hearts are receptive, our eyes open and our ears attentive to hear him softly whisper our name.

Today's Prayer

Father God, you hold the answer to our questions when our hearts are hurting and our hope seems gone. In times of sorrow, you meet us at the tomb of our brokenness and unanswered questions. As we invite you into our hearts and lives, you come to dwell and abide forever. Lord, we thank you that we are never left alone; we are never without hope. As we call out your name, you come to us and you never turn us away. Jesus, you are the answer. When all else fails and we are at the end, we have an anchor of the soul to sustain us. It's you, Lord, the answer to every question.

Today's Scriptures

Psalm 34:18; Psalm 139:11–12; John 20:10–16; I Peter 5:7

June 8

Today's Thought

I don't know about you, but when someone expresses words of praise about me, I am all ears. Who doesn't like to be spoken well of? The Bible permits us to receive praise. *"Let another praise you and not your own mouth"* (Proverbs 27:2a). It's okay to listen as others applaud us. The key is not to be puffed up over praise. Likewise, scripture gives us 248 references urging us to praise God. The anchor verse that bonds all our praises together is the declaration that, *"Yet you are enthroned as the Holy One; you are praise of Israel"* (Psalm 22:3). He is all ears and all heart when he hears our praise; he draws near so as not to miss a word. The Bible gives us many trustworthy purposes in praising God. Praise ushers in the presence of God and chases away despair. Praise puts the devil to flight and brings victory in our battles. Praise settles our hearts and calms our spirit. It helps us to see our situation from heaven's perspective. When you are at your wit's end and don't know what to do, lift your voice in praise to God and he will show up to be the glory and lifter of your head.

Today's Prayer

Father God, we praise you for you are worthy of all praise. You command us to praise you, and we offer our adoration to you willingly. Help us to take you at your Word and expect wonderful things to happen when we praise you. Chains fall off, despair takes flight, and victory is at the other end. We praise you for who are, what you do, and for our great salvation in Jesus Christ. I pray the praises of all your people come up to you continually as a sweet concert of agreement that you are most worthy of all praise and glory. In the name of the One and Only Worthy God. Amen.

Today' Scripture

Nehemiah 9:4–6; Psalm 22:3; Psalm 34:1–3; Psalm 150:1–6

June 9

Today's Thought

As I write, we, as a nation are still bearing up under the effects of Covid-19. As I shopped today, I was distressed at how empty the shelves were. I grumbled about wearing a mask in the summer heat. As I walked to my car I began to think about my attitude. Not good. I realized how negative I was in my thinking. To be honest, I have been talking trash, how bad things are, will they ever get better? Rehearsing over and over again that things may get worse. As I write today, I am determined to stop all this negativity. I am going to begin to talk about all the blessings I still enjoy in America. To anyone who will listen I am going to encourage rather than discourage. I want to be someone who makes a difference for good. I can be realistic without being fatalistic. The Apostle Paul wrote the book of Philippians from a Roman prison cell, yet his letter is saturated with encouraging and uplifting messages to the readers. In his chains, he overflowed with joy.

Today's Prayer

Father God, we have so much to be thankful for, but the pressures of life often squeeze the joy out of us. Some days are difficult when we don't know what the future holds. Lord, we can only change our outlook as your Spirit enables us. Help us to be intentional in being bearers of good things. I pray that we settle it in our minds to look on current events and our future with the hope we find in Christ. Help us to see your goodness rather than focus on all the things that are wrong. You are good to us; may we spread that goodness all around. In the name of our God who gives us abundant life. Amen.

Today's Scripture

John 14:27; Philippians 2:14–16; Philippians 4:4–9; Hebrews 10:24–25

June 10

Today's Thought

In the classic story of *Snow White*, only a kiss from her prince charming could bring her back from the grip of death. He shows up right in time, kisses her, and she rises up from her deep slumber. Off they go on his white stallion, galloping up to his castle fair. That got me to thinking about the spiritual apathy that I sometimes experience. Lately I have been feeling a numbness in my spirit. At times I feel as if I am just going through the motions, you know, lip service. I think it happens to all of us at one time or another. It creeps up on us so subtly that we hardly notice. My devotion times get shortchanged, my prayer life has no fervency, I feel as if a spiritual slumber has overtaken me. The difficult part of it is I cannot shake myself out of it. I need someone to come and revive my soul. Have you ever felt this way? I have come to learn that the only hope we have in this spiritual slumber is a move of the Holy Spirit in our soul. We are impotent in shaking ourselves loose from the chains of spiritual sleepiness. The Word entreats us to wake up! Then I cry out, *"Oh Lord, come and kiss my soul into wakefulness, lest I sleep the sleep of apathy."*

Today's Prayer

Father God, you know how easily we fall into spiritual stupor. You know the trappings and distractions that lull our souls to sleep. God, we are at your mercy in these times of spiritual dullness. Lord Jesus, you raise the dead, and by your power you can revive our spiritual fervor. I pray for those who are struggling to believe and those who are wrestling for hope. I pray the power that raised Jesus from the dead be active in raising those who long for an awakening. In the name of our Resurrected Lord. Amen.

Today's Scriptures

Matthew 25:5; Romans 8:11; Romans 13:11–12; Ephesians 5:13–14

June 11

Today's Thought

My friend and I talked over coffee. She had struggled most of her life, trying to figure out her roles and goals in life. She was diligent in reading her Bible, praying and seeking wise counsel. Still, she felt a void, something she could not quit define, almost as if a part of her was deeply flawed. As I listened, I prayed God would show me what to say, how to minister to her. As she talked, I thought about all the love she had shown me over the years. She was always there for me when I was in crisis mode. She loved her husband in spite of many years of helping him cope with bouts of depression. She helped her parents out of financial difficulty several times and gave to anyone in need. She cared for my ailing mother when I had to work out of state for a season. My friend is one of the most caring and loving women I am honored to know. It was in light of this important revelation, I turned to her and said, *"You have spent so much of your life trying to 'figure it out,' but you grasped the truth a long time ago. You instinctively knew that the most important thing is love."* Before we stand before the throne of God, we must ask ourselves, *"How well did I love those God gave to me?"*

Today's Prayer

Father God, you are our example of genuine unfeigned love. How are we loving? Are we doing what you commanded us to do? Lord, love does not come naturally to most of us; teach us your kind of love. Help us to remember that the world will know us by the love we have for one another. We want to follow your example of loving well at all times. In the name of our God, who is Love. Amen.

Today's Scriptures

Romans 13:8–10; 1 Corinthians 13:13; Colossians 3:12–14; 1 John 4:16

June 12

Today's Thought

Love alone is not enough. Here's my point. I love my kids and grandkids; with everything in me, I love them. If I love them all my life but never apply discipline, I create little monsters who eventually become dictators of the home. I am sure I do not have to paint a more vivid picture; we have all seen this sad scenario in action. That brand of love can blow up right in our faces. But love coupled with correction can produce the results we want to see in our children's lives. It brings peace to our homes and joy to our hearts as we see them emerge as responsible adults. So it is with God and his children. If all we ever received from him is love, love, and more love, without needed discipline, how shallow and vain we would be. God's discipline flows from his love; they go hand-in-hand. The Bible actually says that if we are not disciplined by God, we do not belong to him. Let us not despise godly discipline, for it produces in us the fruit of a righteous and godly life.

Today's Prayer

Father God, your love for us is without question, but it is not without discipline. Your perfect plan was put into motion at the very beginning, in the Garden of Eden. When Adam and Eve disobeyed you, you applied the discipline of consequences. From Eden we learn that disobedience never pays. Lord, we are grateful for your love and your correction. You want to see results in our lives that bring glory to you and a good reputation to our families. We praise you that you call us yours and prove that claim by being the perfect Parent. Help us grow up into the image of your perfect Son. In the name of Jesus. Amen.

Today's Scriptures

Job 5:17–18; Proverbs 3:11–12; Hebrews 12:5–11; Revelation 3:19

Today's Thought

Yesterday we examined the truth of God's discipline. Today I want us to look at self-discipline. If we exercise self-discipline in our lives, we will need less of God's discipline. Self-control is a fruit of the Spirit. It grows in us as we apply it to our daily lives. Thankfully, we don't have to struggle to produce this fruit on our own. God has generously poured out on us his Spirit, who is our Helper and Advocate. As we set up healthy boundaries in our lives, we are better able to discern that which is good for us, that which is bad and that which is excess. We have human appetites that can lead into over indulgence; food, sexual immorality, spending, alcohol, illegal drugs, uncontrolled anger and much more. Paul reminds us that we are in a race. Unless we train our bodies to come under control of the Spirit, we can be disqualified. There is so much unbridled self-indulgence all around us. God calls us to be different, a people in control of our passions. God has given us all things here to enjoy, and we can truly enjoy life and its many joys when we practice holy restraint on a daily basis.

Today's Prayer

Father God, we thank you that you have not left us on our own to accomplish the things you ask of us. We are upheld by your Spirit, and through him there is always hope of success in our struggle for self-control. God, I pray that you help each of us as we endeavor to bring the flesh into subjection to the Spirit. In all the temptations we face daily, you make a way of escape, a way to bear up under the pressures that war against our better judgment. Lord, we desire to be under the control of your good and gracious Spirit. In the name of the One who bears us up. Amen.

Today's Scriptures

Proverbs 25:28; 1 Corinthians 9:24–27; 1 Corinthians 10:13; Titus 2:11–14

June 14

Today's Thought

In Psalm 136, the response *"His steadfast love endures forever" (ESV)* is repeated 26 times. It got me to thinking about why the psalmist included the words *steadfast* and *endures*. There are several definitions of the word *endure*. To continue in the same state. To remain firm. To regard with acceptance and tolerance. *Steadfast* speaks of the changeless, immutable nature of God. All of this conveys a message of permanence, dependability and acceptance. Now allow me to paraphrase this verse. *"God's love for us is rock solid. It is firmly established and nothing can ever change the fact that he loves us."* His love endures with us through all the mess, all the struggles, all the rebellion, all the doubt and unbelief; he never gives up on us, walks away or ceases to love us. Through all the ages, all history of mankind, all of our personal lives, and on into eternity, his steadfast love endures it all. Because of God's steadfast enduring love, we are now encouraged by the psalmist to give thanks to the Lord. We learn best through repetition and Psalm 136 is one that we should embrace.

Today's Prayer

Father of steadfast enduring love, we give thanks to you for all your mighty and awesome deeds. Every day we need the assurance that your enduring steadfast love is for us. These precious words give us a solid and sure foundation on which we build our trust in you. I pray the power of these words sink so deeply into our souls that we can truly say, *"I will not be moved, I am loved with a steadfast enduring love."* We can live with confident hope because we are greatly loved by a great God. Amen.

Today's Scriptures

Psalm 86:15; Psalm 136; Lamentations 3:22–24; Ephesians 2:4–5

Today's Thought

I sometimes wonder if we know the difference between a right and a privilege. We live in a culture that screams *"rights"* at every turn. As human beings created in the image of God, we certainly have immutable rights. Our Declaration of Independence states, *"We hold these truths to be self-evident, that all men are created equal, that they are endowed by their Creator with certain unalienable rights, that among these are life, liberty and the pursuit of happiness …"* So much of what we enjoy in life is a privilege. Regardless of how we view the difference, as a people of God there are two important points for us to remember. With privileges and rights, comes responsibility. It is our responsibility to exercise rights and privileges as God-given. As the Son of God, Jesus set the example for us. He set aside his rights and humbled himself. He never demanded or arm wrestled his way in any situation. With Jesus it was always about what he could give, not what he could get. The second thing of importance is attitude. It's always that attitude of the heart that matters to God. Paul certainly exhibits an attitude of servanthood in all his writings. Let's be reminded that love does not insist on its own rights or in having its own way.

Today's Prayer

Father God, we thank you that you have endowed us with certain privileges and rights. Every good and perfect gift is from you. I pray we use these gifts in responsible ways. Lord, keep us humble in our words, actions and attitudes. May we be ones who serve with the same mind that Christ had in serving. I pray we be willing to forfeit our rights at times when it serves the higher good. Lord Jesus, what really matters is that your gospel goes forth in power. In your humble and exalted name. Amen.

Today's Scriptures

Mark 8:34–35; 1 Corinthians 8:9; 1 Corinthians 9:12; Philippians 2:3–4

June 16

Today's Thought

Is there a song that spills forth from your soul, one that plays in your head over and over again? Maybe one from your childhood, or the bridal song played at your wedding? Songs that bring back happy memories are so precious. These songs are deeply rooted in our hearts, becoming a part of who we are. Every time I hear the oldie, *"That'll Be the Day"* by the Crickets, I remember dancing with a boy for the first time in eighth grade. I still know that song by heart. What we harbor in our hearts will always spill out sooner or later. When a crisis strikes, that which is in our hearts will come out. When we feel we are sitting in darkness, what is in our hearts will determine our response. Praise for God will rise up even in the worst of times if we have been trusting in him. If we have been harboring bitterness and resentment it will surely come out of our mouths. I am always taken back when someone makes a critical comment then says, *"I was only joking."* The truth has already been spoken from the heart. It's no joke, from the overflow of the heart, the mouth speaks. Our words are a good indicator of what we are harboring in our hearts.

Today's Prayer

Father God, your heart overflows with everything good. Our hearts can so easily fill up with the residue of stuff that does not bless you or those around us. God, I pray you help us to really hear what comes forth from our hearts and mouths. We understand that the heart and mouth are always connected; they work together. I pray we continually examine what we allow in and what we speak forth. In the name of the One who purifies our hearts. Amen.

Today's Scriptures

Psalm 19:14; Matthew 12:33–37; Ephesians 4:29; James 3:5–10

June 17

Today's Thought

If only Abraham and Sarah had waited on God's timing; what heartache could have been avoided? If only King Saul had waited for Samuel to show up before he went to war; his reign as king could have turned out so differently. If only I had waited on God in so many of my life's decisions, I could have avoided the high cost of disobedience. The wonderful thing about our God is that he still brought something good out of it all. Then again, why suffer the end result of a hurried decision? There is so much wisdom in waiting on God, so many benefits; but, so many consequences in running ahead of him. Waiting on God is one of the spiritual disciplines we talked about a few days ago. We are so prone to impatience; or, is it just me? We so quickly grow weary and make the terrible mistake of taking matters into our own hands. We can always trust that God knows best and always has our best interest in mind. Sometimes God's delay is because he has to work something in someone else; it's not always only about us. Dear one, trust and believe that when you are seeking something from God that not only has he heard you, but he has also put things in motion on your behalf.

Today's Prayer

Father God, you know our frames, you understand our human tendency to rush into decisions when you ask us to wait. Lord, forgive us for those times when we ran ahead of you, disobeyed, or have taken matters into our own hands. Help us to trust in your good judgment. You have shown us again and again that you know best. You are never too early, never too late; you are always on time. We pray that you teach us how much better it is to allow you to work things in your way and in your time. Lord, when we are impatient and in a hurry, help us to remember that nothing good comes from our impulsiveness. In the name of the One on whom we wait. Amen.

Today's Scriptures

Psalm 27:14; Psalm 103:13–14; Isaiah 40:29–31; Micah 7:7

June 18

Today's Thought

I was at a point in my life where I just wanted to die. I told the Lord I was willing to be martyred for his sake. The response of his still small voice stunned me, *"I don't want you to die for me; I want you to live for me."* That was many years ago, and those words from the Lord have helped me through many difficult days. I have concluded that at times it would seem easier to escape the trials and tribulation that life brings. God has not called us to cheap escapism. He calls us to live quiet and peaceable lives for him. We may never accomplish anything spectacular or stunning during our days on earth, but as we live out the common days of our lives, he looks on us with approval. The Lord is not necessarily looking for martyrs or spiritual giants; he searches for those whose hearts are yielded wholly to him, and those who live boldly and courageously in a world that can be extremely trying at times. If you are in a place where you would like to give up, remember James 1:12, *"Blessed is the man who perseveres under trial, because when he has stood the test, he will receive the crown of life that God has promised to those who love him."*

Today's Prayer

Father God, we have much need for endurance. You are well aware of all we are up against as we await the glorious return of our Lord. Life can be trying and we need your grace poured out on us as we struggle from day-to-day in a world that resists goodness and righteousness. Help us to live in such a way that those in our corner of the world will see the wonderful difference that Jesus makes in a life. I pray for the endurance that perseveres till the end. In his name we pray. Amen.

Today's Scripture

Matthew 24:12–13; Philippians 1:20–24; Hebrews 10:35–39; James 1:12

Today's Thought

I am a rule-keeper by nature. I drive the speed limit, well maybe a few mph over. I never cross over the solid white line, drive too closely to the vehicle in front of me or pass on the right. You get the picture. I try my best to obey the posted signs. Rule-keepers get into a lot less trouble than ones who like to push the envelope. God has laid down his rules in his Word. He is not out to spoil our fun; he wants to keep us safe in all situations. Road signs are warnings and cautions to keep us safe on the road. God's Word is designed to keep us safe in life. When we bend the rules to suit the lifestyle we want to live, trouble will surely meet us up the road. When we line our lifestyle up with God's Word, we always come out ahead. God is always giving us sign posts as we journey through life. Do not lie, do not steal, do not commit adultery, and the other commandments are intended to bring blessing and peace. When we ignore his posted rules, we suffer the consequence; when we obey, we reap a harvest of righteousness. It's not always easy to be a rule-keeper, but God never calls us to that which Jesus himself did not live.

Today's Prayer

Father God, thank you that we do not journey alone. We are supported by your own Holy Spirit. We are grateful that you have given us commands, warnings and cautions to help us live the best life we can. Your high aim is to keep us safe in a dangerous world. As our loving Father you want the best for us, and that requires obedience on our part. God, I pray we not grow neglectful in the study of scripture that clearly points us in the right direction. In the name of our wise Law-Giver. Amen.

Today's Scriptures

Deuteronomy 30:11–16; Psalm 119:35; 2 Timothy 3:16; 1 John 5:2–3

June 20

Today's Thought

All quiet time is not created equal. My quiet time may look very different from yours. Your quiet time may be in the evening, mine in the morning. Some use worship music and others take up notebook and pen. Even the versions of our Bibles are chosen to uniquely minister to our individual needs. Many enjoy using a devotional such as you are reading now, while others prefer a study book. My point is this, just as we are all unique, so is our quiet time with the Lord. As soon as we try to imitate someone else and their distinctive way of connecting with God, we lose our individuality. The important thing is that we have a daily routine of meeting with the Lord in sweet communion. That's going to look different for all of us. Likewise, the environment we choose as our personal sanctuary is a matter of where we feel comfortable. God is comfortable in every room of your home. God is not particular in how we come to him; he just wants us to come. We need not compare our quiet time with others; the Lord takes us just as we are.

Today's Prayer

Father God, you love your time with us; we love it too. It's good to know we don't have to imitate anyone else or compare our quiet times. We love being your irreplaceable child with unique tastes and different choices. When we are with you in that sacred space, it's as if we are the only child you have to love on and give all your attention too. I think you enjoy the variety we offer you, as you created your world with so much diversity. We thank you that we can come to you in our own special way and be fully accepted by you. In the name of God who meets us where we are. Amen.

Today's Scripture

Psalm 119:147–148; Matthew 6:6; Matthew 14:23; Mark 1:35

Today's Thought

If we don't know where we are going, we'll end up somewhere else. It's always good to have a plan. I have learned that the Holy Spirit works best in an environment of order. There have been times when I decided to randomly open my Bible and search for a verse that would bless me. Most of the time, I was disappointed because that's not generally the way God works. When I begin the year with a Bible reading plan, the Holy Spirit meets me there every day within my reading strategy. Isn't that true in all areas of life? Things just work better when we have a plan. Asking the Lord daily to guide, to give direction and lead us in his will is the key to a better day. The Word tells us to do all things decently and in order. What would our world look like if God did not command order in nature? The sun would rise in its own good time and the moon would do its own thing. The seasons would have no time lines or boundaries. All things that God created have purpose and arrangement, and in the same way our day-to-day lives should be ones of preparation and order.

Today's Prayer

Father God, you created all things with specific design and directive. All of nature follows your divine plan day after day, season after season. What a beautiful picture you give of how life is best lived. Lord, show us any areas where we lack order. Help us to be effective planners from the beginning of our day until the end. When unexpected situations interrupt our day, the Holy Spirit comes and works within our plans. You tell us that our times are in your hands, so I pray that we are wise stewards of the time you give us. Help us be wise planners. In the name of the God of order. Amen.

Today's Scriptures

Proverbs 21:5; Luke 1:3–4; 1 Corinthians 14:40; Colossians 2:5

June 22

Today's Thought

What a thoughtful God, that he would give us each other as gifts in navigating this unstable world. Winds pommel us from every direction. Winds of change. Winds of temptation. The wind of an ungodly culture. How do we remain true and faithful in our Christian journey? I devised a plan for myself years ago and it has been a safeguard for me through the years. I call it the three women safety-net. We all need other women in our lives; that's how God designed us. The three women I want to introduce to you today are my safety-net. These women keep me grounded, balanced and accountable. The first woman is the one who I look to for spiritual guidance. She is ahead of me on the journey and sharing her experiences helps me to avoid trappings that may be awaiting me. She mentors me, supports me and lives life with me. The second woman is my peer. We are walking side-by-side on our journey, in the same season of life. We can share mutual friendships, lifestyles and help each other through the struggles. The third woman is one who is coming up behind me on the road. I have the joy and privilege of being a spiritual mother to her, one in whom she can look to for guidance and direction when life gets difficult. This plan has helped keep me stable in an unstable world.

Today's Prayer

Father God, I pray that you provide for each of us today a three women safety-net. May they be godly women who will be a comfort, safeguard and blessing in our lives. You never intended for us to do life on our own. We need the encouragement of fellow travelers to help us navigate the narrow path of faith. Thank you for this essential provision. Amen.

Today's Scriptures

Ecclesiastes 4:9–12; Romans 12:5; Galatians 6:2; Hebrews 10:24–25

Today's Thought

When Bible reading was still allowed in schools, my teacher read from Psalm 24 frequently. I never forgot that Psalm. As a curious reader of God's Word, I have struggled over verses 3–5. The question is posed, *"Who may ascend the hill of the Lord? Who may stand in his Holy place?"* (Psalm 24:3). The Psalm describes that person; one who is without fault, has clean hands, a pure heart, and is honest and free of idolatry. But no one can meet these conditions! So, where does that leave me? I want to ascend the hill of the Lord. I want to stand before his holiness. I want to be heard on high. God in his love and mercy made a way for sinners to come before his holy throne. Jesus is the way; no one can come to the Father except through him. The pure One, the One with clean hands intercedes on our behalf. Now, under the new covenant, in Christ, we can boldly and confidently ascend the hill of the Lord and stand in his holy presence.

Today's Prayer

Father God, you are holy, we are unholy. Your hands are clean; our hands are stained with sin. In the natural, we have no right nor do we meet any conditions to stand in your presence. How can we receive vindication? Praise be to God, you sent us One who did it all for us. Jesus lived a sinless life so we could be made perfect in him. How can we ever show you our gratitude? We desire to honor you by allowing your Holy Spirit to do his sanctifying and purifying work in our hearts and lives. We will never acquire perfection in this life, but we can always stand in your presence even as you continue to work the life of Jesus in us. It's in his glorious name we praise and thank you. Amen.

Today's Scriptures

Psalm 24:3–6; John 14:6; Romans 5:9–11; Hebrews 4:14–16

June 24

Today's Thought

In a recent message my Pastor, said this, *"Urgency forces us out of complacency into dependency."* Who hasn't experienced complacency at one time or another? A few years ago, I had a health issue that literally brought me to my knees. I was just sailing along, everything going great, then wham! I was having my quiet time every day, reading my Bible, going to church, all of that, but a deep complacency had set in. It was as if I was going through the motions. Then sudden illness totally rocked my world, and not in a good way. I began to pray and seek God as I had not done in a long time. I desperately needed him to help, give me direction and relief. There was a real living breathing urgency that invaded my life; it shook me to my core and left me absolutely at the mercy of God. Urgent circumstances are one of the ways God works to get our attention and remind us that we are always in need of him. We ought to guard against complacency by recognizing and confessing our ongoing dependency on the Lord. The moment we think we are self-sufficient, we start down a road that eventually leads to complacency and apathy; not a good path to take.

Today's Prayer

Father God, we love smooth sailing. You love our dependency on you. Help us to discover the balance between feelings of well-being and understanding that we need you every moment. Forgive us when we try to live independently of you. You created us for reliance on you and communion with you regardless of our circumstances. I pray we cling to you through all the good times and all the hard times. Lord, we confess we need you every moment. In the name of the God we depend upon. Amen.

Today's Scriptures

Proverbs 1:32; Luke 21:34–36; Hebrews 6:12; Revelation 3:15–16

Today's Thought

For over 30 years my husband and I enjoyed boating on Lake Erie. If I had a dollar for every time I pulled up that 50 pound anchor I could buy a new pair of Jimmy Choo's. It certainly was worth the effort because we would have lost the boat a hundred times over without that secure anchor. It causes me to think about Hebrews 6:19, *"We have this hope as an anchor for the soul, firm and secure ..."* The anchor of hope the writer refers to is the reassurance we have in the finished work of Christ, who now sits in the very presence of God on our behalf. The anchor is the symbol of the confidence we have in God's promises; sure, and steadfast; they keep us from being tossed about by winds that suddenly come about to shake our faith. Anchors prevent a ship from being swept away by storms and wind just as our faith in God's promises keep us anchored securely in the heavenlies rather than placing our confidence in a world that is as unsteady and as uncertain as shifting sand. Since our hope is anchored in the person of Jesus Christ, and the absolute unchanging nature of God, we can be a people of confident assurance no matter how the storms of life rock our boats.

Today's Prayer

Father God, your Son now sits at your right hand, ever living to intercede on our behalf. This gives us full assurance that our salvation is anchored firmly upon his finished work on the cross. We can add nothing to that and nothing can ever separate us from your love and acceptance. Our faith in Christ holds fast no matter how the storms rage. Jesus, you are our anchor and our eternal trust is in you. We praise your glorious name. Amen.

Today's Scriptures

Psalm 62:5; Romans 8:34–39; Hebrews 6:19–20; Hebrews 11:13–16

Today's Thought

Life is like a jigsaw puzzle; all the pieces randomly scattered about. Puzzles can be very challenging. One missing piece can mar the entire picture. Not so with God. When I mess up in my Christian journey, I think the Lord is disgusted, fed up and done with me; but, here is the truth. God always chooses to see the big picture. He takes all of our life into account. The character change that we resist is no problem; he will work on that. He makes a way out of that doubt and confusion we experience. That jam we got ourselves into, he can help us make it right. God sees the whole picture and at the end of the day, he sees our good intentions and helps us find that missing piece. He sees the kindnesses we extended, the ones we served in his name, the prisoner we visited, the cup of cold water we gave. God never stays focused on our mistakes. He helps us learn through them and moves us on. Ultimately, when we are home safe in his arms, he slips that last puzzle piece into place and says, *"It is finished. Welcome home, child."*

Today's Prayer

Father God, we are so grateful that you are a big picture God; and at the same time a most close up and intimate Father. Lord, you are on our side, you are not against us. You are always for us. When we need correction, you give it. When we need encouragement, you are generous in giving. When we mess up, you remind us of who we are, but more important, you show us who you are. You are a mighty Savior, a God full of mercy and grace. You are firm but always kind. You see the full picture of who you created us to be and you will finish the good work you began in us. In your glorious name. Amen.

Today's Scripture

Psalm 138:8; Romans 8:31–32; Philippians 1:6; Hebrews 6:10

June 27

Today's Thought

I get down on the floor and stretch almost every day. It's amazing how much these simple exercises keep me limber and able to do the things I enjoy. I must admit, it was really painful at first, but after several weeks, it got easier. God wants to stretch us in a spiritual sense; he wants us to move outside the box of our comfortable postage stamp existence. Life can be difficult at times. Can we assume together that God intends our trials and sufferings to challenge us to reflect outside the borders of our perfectly ordered lives? Predictability feels safe. Could it be that stretching us through hardship is God's way of drawing us to bigger and better things; things that are for our higher good; things that have eternal weight? Yes, it can be painful, but the gain of eternal perspective far outweighs the momentary discomfort. When we are being stretched by God, we would do well in accepting it with the expectation that he is up to something good. When our spiritual muscles of faith are tried, tested and stretched, we come out spiritually stronger and healthier. Isn't that what we all want?

Today's Prayer

Father God, in your infinite goodness, you do not save us and then leave us as babes. You know how to grow your children into mature believers who can run the Christian race with endurance and perseverance. Lord, we pray for the stretching and the shaping that keeps us fit for the kingdom. We know you are not out to harm us. When we are tried, we will come forth as gold and as children who can patiently endure the struggles that strengthen our faith. You are a divine coach and you are always cheering us on to victory. In the name of the God who grows us. Amen.

Today's Scriptures

Job 23:10; 2 Corinthians 4:16–18; Hebrews 5:13–14; Hebrews 12:11

Today's Thought

Matthew Chapter 6 contains three elements that are clearly Christianity 101. Jesus is instructing his disciples on important issues, including prayer, giving and fasting. In all three he never says, *if* you give, *if* you pray or *if* you fast. He states plainly that *when* we give, *when* we pray and *when* we fast. He then gives them guidelines in practicing these spiritual disciplines. Don't do them to impress others. Don't seek honor and recognition. Don't go about looking as if you are making some great sacrifice. Do them humbly and in secret as unto God and not as a way to gain the attention of those around you. Jesus calls these three disciplines, acts of righteousness. He cautions us to avoid making a pretense of giving, praying, and fasting, as some do. Their reward is a worldly reward which is shallow and temporary. Jesus goes on to encourage with these words. *"Then your Father who sees what is done in secret, will reward you"* (Matthew 6:4).

Today's Prayer

Father God, your commands for righteous and godly living are so clear. Your guiding principles on giving, prayer and fasting are not difficult to follow. Sometimes we need to be reminded of how crucial these disciplines are to our spiritual growth and well-being. Most importantly, we want to please you and imitate Jesus in every area of our lives. Lord, teach us to give, to pray and to fast as if no one sees but you. In prayer, help us to be mindful of the motives of our hearts. Keep us generous in giving knowing that we can never out give you. And Lord, when we fast, I pray for the strength of Holy Spirit to uphold and encourage us. I pray in the name of Jesus our great reward. Amen.

Today's Scriptures

Matthew 6:1–18; 2 Corinthians 9:6–11; 1 Timothy 4:7–8; 2 Timothy 2:15

Today's Thought

How would you react if an angel of the Lord suddenly visited you and said, *"The Lord is with you mighty warrior"* (Judges 6:12). It happened to Gideon, a timid man of the tribe of Manasseh. Gideon's reaction was one of surprise, disbelief and mistrust. Nonetheless, God stood by the angel's proclamation and used this fearful man to be exactly what God called him to be, a mighty warrior. God is calling out mighty warriors today. He is looking for men and women who will believe they have power from on high to do great exploits in Jesus' name. Every time we engage in prayer we are in battle. A war is taking place in the unseen realms that are driven by our fervent effectual prayers for our prodigals, our addicted, and our lost and broken loved ones. Let us rise up as mighty warriors and together do battle in prayer. God can work through even the most timid among us. It's a fact that all through scripture God uses the most unlikely of men and women to accomplish his purposes. All he needs is a willing vessel who knows the battle belongs to the Lord.

Today's Prayer

Father God, in these last days we know and believe there is an urgent need for intercessory prayer. Our country, our families and our churches are under attack by the god of this world who hates us because he hates you and your Son. We know and believe that you have given us power and authority over these dark forces in Jesus' name. Lord, call each of us to take our place on the battlefield of prayer. Call us out of our timidity, our fears and our doubts. Raise up an army of mighty warriors who will defeat the enemy on our knees. In the name of our Mighty Warrior Jesus. Amen.

Today's Scriptures

Judges 6:11–12; Luke 21:36; Ephesians 6:10–13; James 5:16

June 30

Today's Thought

Oh, the lies we believe! I am not enough. God could never use me because of my past. God could never love me. I will never change. Women who work outside the home are more fulfilled. God does not hear me when I pray on and on. Perhaps you can relate to some of these, or have a few self-spoken lies of your own. Satan is a liar and the father of lies. Father God is the God of all truth. It's our choice to whom we listen. In God's eyes we are always enough, always have been and always will be. He forgives our sins and remembers them no more. The Holy Spirit is always working on the inside to bring needed change whether we feel it or not. Being a mom and creating a beautiful and peaceful home for your family is the highest calling for a woman. God always hears when you call out to him in prayer. Now, my dear friends, I challenge you to address the lies you believe and find God's truth and record it in your journal. Choose you this day whom you will believe and whom you will serve.

Today's Prayer

Father God, your truth is forever settled in heaven, it will never change. Your truth about who we are in Christ Jesus is founded upon the reality that we are created in your image and that makes us precious and priceless in your sight. Lord, I pray we have the courage to lay down all the lies and begin the scriptural search for our true identity. All of who you created us to be was declared by you while we were yet in our mother's womb. The lies we believe have marred that God-ordained image and we now want the truth of who we are to rule in our minds and hearts. In Jesus' name. Amen.

Today's Scriptures

1 Samuel 16:7; Psalm 139:14–18; Proverbs 31:10, 29–30; John 17:17

July 1

Today's Thought

I recently was faced with a decision, either take a well needed trip to visit family or stay home. I prayed, then, left the decision with the Lord. It was only a matter of days before I felt very sure in my spirit that I was not to take the trip. After my decision, an offer was made to facilitate a healing Bible study that would cover the next eight weeks, including the time I would have been away. I tell you this because once again I am impressed with how the Lord leads when we ask. God sees the beginning to the end; we do not. We never see far enough up the road to make important decisions on our own. God knows the plans he has for us, and by his Spirit he leads as we ask. I always want to be in that sweet spot, the center of God's will. I will miss the family visit, but God has different plans for me right now. When we settle it in our hearts that his thoughts and ways are higher than ours, we will be more ready to hear from him. We are faced with decision every day; we to always be ready to hear. There will be times when we will miss the mark, but God brings good out of everything.

Today's Prayer

Father God, you do indeed know the plans you have for us. You tell us that you will lead, direct and counsel us with your eye upon us. Your thoughts and ways are so much higher and better than ours. Lord, I pray we desire to be more in tune with your plans instead of running ahead with our own. I ask that we see the wisdom in coming to you for direction and instruction in regard to future intentions. Lord, we sincerely desire your help in avoiding those pitfalls of self will. In the name of our Great Shepherd who leads us. Amen.

Today's Scriptures

Psalm 32:8; Isaiah 55:8–9; Jeremiah 29:11; Ephesians 5:15–17

Today's Thought

The Lord sings over you today. He is singing a song that is for you alone. Do you hear it? Can you perceive the words? Can you sense the joy and delight he has in you? Envision this beautiful picture God painted for his beloved Israel. I believe it is also a truth for his church and for each of us individually. Listen to what he says, *"The Lord your God is in your midst, the Mighty one, will save; He will rejoice over you with gladness, he will quiet you with his love, he will rejoice over you with singing"* (Zephaniah 3:17; NKJV). When my children were born, I sang over them; I quieted them as I rocked them in love. I rejoiced over the precious gift God had given me. I think of God like this at times. I like to imagine the tenderness and joy he feels as he watches us grow into all he created us to be. Today let's open our spiritual ears and receive the unique song he sings over us. In return, let us sing our song of love and joy to him.

Today's Prayer

Father God, what a blessing we have in this verse. To think your love is so intimate, so tender that you sing and rejoice over us as a mother would over her child. Lord, I pray for those of us who need to be quieted in your love. Cause your Spirit to settle deep within and bring that peace that passes understanding. For those of us who need a deeper revelation of your personal intimate love, I pray you help us to open our hearts to the truth of this verse. For those who are under condemnation and feeling inferior or inadequate, remind us that it is not about us, what we did or did not do, but it's about you and what you did for us. Help us to believe in a love so grand. In the name of Jesus, who sings over us. Amen.

Today's Scriptures

Psalm 5:11–12; Isaiah 49:15–16; Zephaniah 3:17; Ephesians 3:16–19

Today's Thought

How deep is the sea? Who has ever ventured to the very deepest depth of it? Who knows where the farthest reaches are? God knows, and he said that he has put our sins into the deepest place where no one can go and bring them back. When we confess our sins, he is faithful and just and fully forgive. He puts our sins behind his back; he remembers them no more. He sweeps them away forever. The most profound truth is that along with Jesus, our sins were nailed to the cross. There is no need for us to ever dredge them up again. We need not work to *"forgive ourselves,"* because his work was complete and final. It was enough. Why do we forget this truth? Why is it we still pull our past sins up from our memory bank and allow them to taunt us? God never intended us to carry this heavy burden. He has banished them from his sight and wants us to fully release them. If today you still see your sins floating on the surface of the sea, I urge you to let them sink to the depths where they belong.

Today's Prayer

Father God, how merciful you are. You forgive, you forget, you cast all our sins behind you and remember them no more. Lord, in our humanness we struggle with the truth of being fully and forever forgiven. Help us to practice forgetting those sins that we have confessed, turned from and left with you at the cross. It is a new day for us; we are under a new covenant. We do not have to visit our sins every year and beg for atonement. The atonement came in the person of your Son. We do not have to be weighed down with a relentless burden of shame and guilt. In the name of the Sinless Lamb of Calvary. Amen.

Today's Scriptures

Psalm 32:1–5; Micah 7:18–19; Colossians 2:13–14; Hebrews 8:12

Today's Thought

Imagine if someone tried to dress you in clothes that were five sizes too large. It paints a pretty ridiculous picture. It would be difficult for you to move about and do things you needed to do. Let's go back to a time when a teenage boy named David was clothed in a suit of armor that was so oversized and heavy, he couldn't stand. He was expected to go forth and slay a giant with his helmet covering his eyes. He refused the ill-fitting armor and went out in the power of God to slay his giant. David focused not on the size of the giant, but the size of his God. The mighty power of God is our armor when we face our giants. We cannot dress up in the world's methods and ill-flitting garments of pride, arrogance and self-sufficiency. Giants are real; they come in all shapes and sizes. They are sins, fears and emotional wounds. Our giants need a supernatural power that lays them flat once and for all. I don't know what challenges you are facing today, or will face tomorrow, but this I know; *in Christ we are more than conquerors through him who loves us and gave his life for us.*

Today's Prayer

Father God, we are reminded once again that the weapons of our battle are not worldly and carnal, but the giants we face are real. How we need the protection you provide as we engage in the warfare of our lives. Lord, I thank you that you have equipped us with spiritual weapons as we fight the battles of daily living. On our own we are ill equipped to slay the nit-picking fights that come our way, let alone giants. Lord, we thank you that you know all about our giants, and they are already defeated in Christ. In Jesus' name. Amen.

Today's Scriptures

Deuteronomy 3:22; 1 Samuel 17:45; Isaiah 41:10; Romans 8:36

July 5

Today's Thought

Let's think about the last words we would want to speak before we draw our last breath? I know I would want to carefully consider those words. What would be the most important expressions I could leave in the hearts of those I love? Before the beginning of time, Jesus knew the words he wanted to leave us with as he faced his death on the cross. The night he was betrayed his words comforted us. He was going away, but he would come for us again so we could be where he is. He told us he would send the Holy Spirit to be our Helper. He encouraged us to remain in his love and obey him. Over and over again he spoke of his great love for us. He warned us that we would face persecution for our faith; but, we must stay strong. Jesus emphatically called us to love him and each other with selfless devotion. That night, in his last open prayer he asked the Father to unify us. Jesus was never desperate, but he was passionate in those last hours to reach us with the things that were dearest to his heart.

Today's Prayer

Father God, you have not left us as orphans to figure things out for ourselves. You have given us your Holy Spirit to remind us of Jesus' every word. All he said is of utmost importance; but oh, those last heartfelt words are so precious to us. He knew the suffering of the cross was waiting for him. He knew he was soon returning to you. Yet his foremost thoughts were of us. He cared more about our well-being and our future than the agony he was facing. What a wonderful Savior he is! Lord, I pray we pour over those last hours of Jesus' life and really hear, really feel, truly know his heart. In the name of Jesus, your beautiful Son. Amen.

Today's Scriptures

John 14:1–3; John 14:15–18; John 15:9–12; John 16:33

July 6

Today's Thought

To know our weaknesses is a strength. Sometimes we are tested so we can see our weaknesses; sometimes tested to discover our strengths. Our weaknesses are flaws God can use to grow us in our faith. When we come face-to-face with our frailties, God can build a strength in us. When we have the courage to face our feeble humanity, we put ourselves in a position for growth. God is intentional in exposing our weaknesses. As we see them for what they are, he will lead us into victory. He gives us the strength of his Holy Spirit to help us conquer. Jesus was at his most vulnerable in Gethsemane, yet he turned that helplessness into a cry to his Father. He bore up under the agony of the cross because he knew all the good fruit that would come forth. Isaiah the prophet records these words for us, *"For this is what the high and lofty One says, 'I live in a high and holy place, but also with him who is contrite and lowly in spirit, to revive the spirit of the lowly and to revive the spirit of the contrite'"* (Isaiah 57:15).

Today's Prayer

Father God, you know our weaknesses and our strengths. We cannot hide any part of our mind, body or soul from you. The One who created us, knows our name and knows our frame. You created man from the dust of the earth, and your breath gave him life. Just like Adam and Eve, we try to hide our weaknesses from you. Lord, help us to embrace all of who we are, knowing that you love us too much to leave us in a defenseless condition. When we are acknowledging our dependence on you, we please you and move you to act on our behalf. Thank you for your Holy Spirit who dwells in us, producing the life of Christ in us. In His name we pray, Amen.

Today's Scriptures

Isaiah 57:15; Isaiah 66:2; 2 Corinthians 12:7–10; 1 Peter 5:6–7

Today's Thought

Last week as I was walked to the check out, I glanced at the wrapped piece of salmon in my hand and realized that I was undercharged by several dollars. Instinctively, I kept walking to the checkout, thinking, oh well, it's her error. That thought only lasted a second or two. I quickly came to my senses and made the long walk back to the other end of the store to correct the error. I tell you this because we need to see how easy it is to resort to our old nature. Though I was tempted, I ultimately did the right thing. Why did I make that choice? As I read several verses in Romans 6, I see that although I used to be a slave to sin, in Christ, I have been made a slave to righteousness. This means I can be tempted to sin, but because of my new nature, I can cooperate with the Holy Spirit and choose righteousness. Why? Because I am a slave to righteousness. This is the kind of slave I want to be. In every temptation, may we remember that we are bound to righteousness because He dwells in us.

Today's Prayer

Father God, you tell us there will always be temptations in this world. Our fallen nature so easily succumbs, but your Spirit in us is greater than our humanity. We praise you that you provide everything we need for godly living, and you cause us to triumph in Christ Jesus. When we do fall, you never leave us there. Your mercy and grace comes to us, lifts us up, and helps us to start again. Thank you for your forgiveness that covers a multitude of sins. Lord, we know and believe that we are overcomers in Christ, we are slaves to righteousness. I pray that we always choose the good and shun the evil. In the name of Jesus, the Righteous One. Amen.

Today's Scriptures

Romans 6:15–18; Romans 7:21–25; 1 Corinthians 10:13; Hebrews 9:14

July 8

Today's Thought

What's concerning you today? What are your frustrations? What is it you want God to do for you? God once told the prophet Samuel, *"The Lord does not look at the things man looks at. Man looks at the outward appearance, but the Lord looks at the heart"* (1 Samuel 16:7b). Judging by outward appearance we may think we need one thing, but God sees our true need. With God, it's always about the heart. The heart, which represents our inner, true self, can be in one of many states. It can be restless or asleep in a spiritual sense. It may be wounded, grieved or broken. The heart can be anxious, fearful or hardened. We often place blame for our condition on the outward circumstances when it's really a heart issue. The situations in our lives need to be addressed, absolutely; but, if we come to God in an attitude of, *"First examine my heart, Lord,"* the circumstances can become clear as God searches the heart. He wants to resolve those painful issues we have struggle with. Deep down we long for wholeness. God wants to accomplish that in each of us.

Today's Prayer's

Father God, you are the Maker and Keeper of our hearts. You are always looking at and searching the heart. I pray we remain still long enough so you can expose the condition of our hearts. You are not out to harm or condemn us; you desire to heal us at every level. You make for yourself a home in our hearts. We want you to dwell there as if it is your very throne. As each of us give you access to the very core of our being, we trust you to do what only a good and loving Father can do. Change us where we need to be changed. In Jesus' name, the keeper of our heart. Amen.

Today's Scripture

1 Samuel 16:7; Psalm 26:2; Proverbs 4:23; Hebrews 4:12–13

Today's Thought

It's such a great feeling when that plane begins its descent, the landing wheels come down and I feel the security of the tarmac beneath me. I have arrived! What a terrific feeling. We like arrivals: arriving at our destination; arrival of a newborn; arrivals of our friends and family to dinner. It's a feeling of completeness and well-being; all is well in my world. The one arrival we can never enjoy now however is a spiritual arrival. No matter how long, deep or how passionate our walk with God, we will never attain spiritual perfection until we reach our final destination, heaven. This is a good plan. God does not want us to ever come to a place where we do not know our desperate need and dependency on him. I use to think I knew a lot, but the older I get, the more I realize how little I know. But the few things I do know, I know with absolute certainty. God loves me, Jesus died for me, and I am always safe in his everlasting arms. He has a perfect home waiting for me and he greatly anticipates my arrival.

Today's Prayer

Father God, we are grateful that you do not expect perfection in us. We would all be in serious trouble if that were so. You are a Father who is ever patient with us. You encourage us to keep pressing on to the goal to win the prize for which you have called us heavenward. You continually work the character of Christ in us. You use all the circumstances in our lives to grow us and stretch us into spiritual maturity. This is your goal, that we be conformed to Christ's image. We will enter heaven one day to stand in your presence and we will finally have arrived in every sense of the word. How glorious that will be. Our feet will land on that street of gold and when we see your arms wide open to receive us. We will then know that we have truly arrived!

Today's Scriptures

Philippians 3:12–14; 2 Timothy 4:6–8; Hebrews 13:14; Revelation 22:1–5

Today's Thought

Can we know the Lord's voice? That's a question we all wrestle with at times. I have often envied the fathers of the faith who heard so clearly from God, often in an audible voice from heaven. After really thinking about that, I have reconsidered my viewpoint. After all, only a select few heard directly from God in specific circumstances and for specific purposes. Now, with the Holy Spirit living in each of us, we can all hear from God. Secondly, we have the benefit of the entire Word of God, the whole counsel of God; they did not. God has provided so many ways to know his voice. Our pastors speak to us as they hear from God. Lyrics to Christian songs are saturated with doctrine. A word spoken by a friend or loved one reaches into our hearts and we know it is God. A walk into nature inspires such awe and joy, we feel God walking alongside of us showing off his wonders. We are hearing from God all the time, whether we know it, hear it or feel it. He is always speaking through his Word into our inmost being. At just the right time, that which he whispered into the quiet of our hearts will burst forth and become just what we need at just the right time.

Today's Prayer

Father God, since the beginning of time it has always been your intention for us to know your voice. You display the grandeur of your voice everywhere from the highest heavens to the depths of the sea. Psalm 29 teaches us that your voice is powerful and gentle. It is majestic and simple. At your rebuke the desert shakes and by your love the heart is made quiet. There is no where we can go that your voice is not heard. The heavens declare your glory and the skies proclaim the work of your hands. Your words go out to the ends of the earth. Our hearts are created to hear you; our ears made to receive your word into our inner being. Lord, we wait quietly in your presence today; speak Lord, your servant hears.

Today's Scriptures

Psalm 19:1–4; Psalm 29:3–9; Jeremiah 33:2–3; John 10:1–4, 27

July 11

Today's Thought

I went to watch my daughter run in a half marathon. How exciting to see all the runners warm up and toe up to the starting line. I waited at the finish line ready to applaud each runner as they finished their course. But the one my eyes sought was my daughter. Suddenly, out of the crowd, there she came. She looked quite different than when she began. I snapped a picture of her as she sat utterly exhausted beneath a tree. I love that picture! In it I see a champion, not because she placed, but because she ran and gave it all she had. After catching her breath, she looked up and saw me waiting, applauding and welcoming her into my arms. Dear one, we are in a race; it's not a sprint; it's a marathon. It's our spiritual race of life. Our faith is the starting line; heaven our finish line. We must never give up the pursuit. We have so much waiting for us at the end. A crown of life, the applause of heaven, and Jesus' arms ready to enfold us.

Today's Prayer

Father God, as we run our race, I pray we run well. No running ahead of you or lagging behind. May our steps be right in sync with yours. I pray we follow where you lead and avoid those things that trip us up and hinder our progress. Give us eyes to recognize obstacles that the enemy places in our path. Help us to follow our coach and example, the Lord Jesus. You have carved out each race with care and intention. Lord, may we not attempt to run another's race, only our own. I pray we cease from comparing our journey with any other. We thank you for the uniqueness with which you created us. We thank you that you run right beside us. Lord, help us to know our pace; when we need to pick it up and when to slow down. Continually remind us that there is One waiting at the finish line. One who is cheering us on every step of the way. In the name of our forerunner, Jesus Christ. Amen.

Today's Scriptures

1 Corinthians 9:24–27; Philippians 3:12–14; 2 Timothy 4:6–8; Hebrews 12:1

Today's Thought

The Old Testament is teeming with stories warning Israel of Baal worship. Simply put, the god Baal dictated the lifestyle of the ones who worshipped at his altar. Baal represents the culture of the day. Israel's heart was continually bent in following the gods of the other nations. Every time Israel went into captivity, they succumbed to the pagan culture in which they lived. Think of it, they had the most powerful, the greatest, the One True God, yet they always slid into bowing the knee to the cheap imitations. The Old Testament records Israel's history as an example for us. Human nature does not change apart from Christ. Our culture has forsaken the One True God for every frivolous whim and trendy god that comes along. Baal comes in many seductive forms, shapes and sizes. We are not immune to blending into the ungodly culture of our day. We must know God and know his Word so as not to be led astray by the enticements and lies of Baal: power; position; acceptance by the culture; moral compromise; and so many others. The line has been drawn. Who will we follow? To whom will we bow?

Today's Prayer

Father God, you have not left us in a dark place, stumbling around for truth. You have made it abundantly clear who and what we are to believe. Your Word is our guide for our times and forever. Your truth will never shift and change as the culture does. We are grateful and secure in knowing you as the One True God. We do not have to pick and choose among the gods of pagans. You have made it so simple for us. Jesus is the way, the truth and the life. Lord, I pray you give your church a discerning heart that we may know to separate the holy from the profane. I pray that we may be the salt and light in our world and resist the pull to compromise our holy calling. In the name of Jesus, our King. Amen.

Today's Scriptures

Jeremiah 11:13; Ezekiel 44:23; John 17:14–16; 1 John 2:15–17

Today's Thought

Feeling overwhelmed? I have been there many times and it's a place I do my best to avoid. Being overwhelmed paralyzes me, thus little to nothing gets done. I feel squeezed into a self-imposed box from which I cannot escape. As I resort to doing nothing, the daily tasks pile up and the feelings of being trapped increase, moment-by-moment. If you have been there, you understand what I am saying. How does it happen? Most times the problem stems from the inability to distinguish the important from the unimportant, the temporal from the eternal. We struggle to know what God has called us to, what others demand of us, or believe that "good Christians" need to say yes to every request. God wants us to know that it's okay to say, "No." "No" is a beautiful and freeing word and "no" is a complete sentence. We need boundaries and the word "no" is a good one. Another trap is unrealistic expectations that leave us feeling like failures when we cannot achieve what we set out to do. God is never behind our feelings of being overwhelmed. He did not design us to pile one thing on top of another until we are crushed under the weight. An overwhelmed schedule will often result in the barrenness of an overwhelmed soul.

Today's Prayer

Father God, thank you that you know our limitations. Often, we do not. Pressures to perform come from all directions: our own expectations; demands of others; and the culture of our day. Lord, we need your guidance every day as we make our choices. As we place our calendars and lives before you, help us to discern the important from the unimportant, those actions that will have eternal value as opposed to commitments that will only serve temporal purposes. Help us to know when to say *"yes"* and when to say *"no."* I pray we learn to be careful stewards of the time you give us. In Jesus' name, the One who is keeper of our time. Amen.

Today's Scriptures

Psalm 90:12; Psalm 127:1–2; Ephesians 5:15–17; James 4:13–15

Today's Thought

Do you have a favorite pair of walking shoes? What makes them the best? For me, my walking shoes fit my feet in such a way that they work in harmony with the rest of my body. Shoes that are too tight will pinch the toes. Those that are too loose will cause blisters. How we walk is as important as what we choose to walk in. The apostle John attempts to get that very message across to us in a spiritual sense. He uses the analogy of walking ten times in his three short epistles. Jesus used the walking illustration himself in the four gospels. Walking in the spiritual sense refers to our lifestyle. John admonishes us to walk in the truth. We are to walk in the light while it is day. We are to walk in a manner worthy of the God who calls us. Paul urges us to walk by the Spirit, in the newness of life. We are to walk honestly, sincerely and according to love. Let us walk by faith and not by sight. Also, we are to walk in wisdom toward those outside the faith. If we say we know Christ then we also should walk as he walked and live in the light of his commands. All of these truths refer to a consistent godly lifestyle. How are we walking these days? Does our faith-walk fit us well and do others see how comfortable we are in our relationship and walk with Christ? Always remember, you never walk alone.

Today's Prayer

Father God, how we conduct ourselves in this world is of utmost concern to you. We are reminded today that we were once darkness, but now we are light. Lord, help us to walk as children of the light so the world can see Jesus in us. Thank you for your Holy Spirit who guides our steps and leads us into the truth of what a Christ-like walk of faith should be. Lord, I pray you help us carefully examine our spiritual walk and show us any ways in which our lifestyle is out of sync with your truth. Show us any ways that we may be following after the culture of the day. In Jesus' name. Amen.

Today's Scriptures

Galatians 5:25; Ephesian 5:8–10; 1 John 1:5–7; 1 John 2:3–6

July 15

Today's Thought

At one time we had well water; then we had to bring in city water because the well water had become polluted and was causing rust everywhere. My white cloths were beginning to turn orange. Yuk! Have you ever noticed how many life changing meetings happened at a well? Rebekah met Abraham's servant at a well and soon became Isaac's wife. Rachael met Jacob at a well and seven years later became his wife. Moses met Zipporah at a well and she became his wife. Who can forget that life-changing encounter with Jesus and the Samaritan woman at the well! Wells in Bible times were most crucial. Without them there was no water. Where there was no water, life could not be sustained. I think it was intentional that all these significant events happened at a well. Our greatest physical need is water; our greatest spiritual need is living water. Jesus is the only one who can satisfy our spiritual thirst; he alone can fill the emptiness and longing of the heart. He made it very clear to the dear woman at the well and to us, that when we drink deeply of him it will quench that thirst once and for all and will spring up into eternal life. What is your well of need today? The well of God's love is pure, holy and unpolluted and He calls us to drink to the full.

Today's Prayer

Father God, you supply our every need, both physical and spiritual. Still, we have a hunger of the heart and longings of the soul that need a divine touch. Lord, when we are running on empty, remind us that Jesus is still the answer. Thank you for making it abundantly clear that the world has nothing that can permanently satisfy. You bid us come for rest and refreshing. Your living water springs up in us to eternal life. Help us to cease from striving after the things that do not provide the fulfillment and contentment we crave. In the name of Jesus, our living water. Amen.

Today's Scriptures

John 4:4–15; John 7:37–39; Revelation 21:6; Revelation 22:17

July 16

Today's Thought

I often wonder why inwardly I still feel like a young girl. I look in the mirror every day and it tells me differently. I question this contradiction. The only conclusion I come to is this: the part of me that will live forever is ageless and timeless. It's the soul; some call it the spirit. No matter how we look at it, it is an amazing truth. Our bodies will age. Our minds will grow dim and forgetful, but our soul is forever young. God gave us our spirit and breathed life into us at conception. He breathed eternal life into us as we gave ourselves to Christ. Ecclesiastes 12:7 says, *"And the dust returns to the ground it came from, and the spirit returns to God who gave it."* We are on loan here on earth. We belong to God and one day he will claim us back to himself forever. It is our spirit that returns to him, unharmed, undamaged, whole, blameless and complete. I encourage you to embrace the ageless and timeless spirit-woman that you are. Let her run free and unencumbered; she is but a young girl and she will live forever!

Today's Prayer

Father God, you are amazing! You thought of everything when you created man and woman in your image. You breathed your own breath into us, and placed your own spirit within us. You created us to live forever. We are glad these bodies of flesh will wither away with age, because you have new bodies prepared for us, eternal bodies. Our minds will falter and forget but the part of us that lives forever cannot be destroyed. Lord, some of us are feeling the ravages of age, stiff joints when we stand, back aches when we sit. We cannot do the things we could do when younger. Still deep inside we can leap, sing and rejoice because inwardly we are being renewed day-by-day. Father, help each of us to embrace our season of life, and also embrace the truth that is timeless. In the name of our ageless God. Amen.

Today's Scriptures

Ecclesiastes 12:7; 2 Corinthians 4:16; Philippians 3:20–21; Jude 24–25

July 17

Today's Thought

How we love the familiar. It's comfortable and safe. However, God does not call us to be cozy and sheltered. Read the book of Acts. God loves diversity and variety; just look around and see all the distinct differences in nations and cultures. So it is in our lives. God is always up to something new, but often we resist, resorting to that which worked in the past. The way he saved me is so unique and unlike your salvation experience. We can never fully comprehend God and his methods. At this point in your life, God is up to something. It may be in the way he worked in the past; or, it may be a totally new and unique way you have not experienced before. Are you open to that possibility? Are you willing to be stretched and pushed out of your comfort zone, like a bird pushed from the nest of its mother? God wants us to soar. He wants us to fly above the norm and predictable. What grand adventures he has for us. Someone once said, *"You cannot swim to new horizons until you have the courage to lose sight of the shore."* Yes, it feels safe to hover around the shore line; but oh what joy awaits the one who dives into the depths of new places in Christ.

Today's Prayer

Father God, how you love doing new things in our lives? We open our arms and lives to receive the new thing you want to work in and through us. Likewise, we embrace the old paths, the ancient way that is tested and true. Father, forgive us for the ways we try to confine you, looking for you to work the same way today as you did yesterday. We trust you in all you do even when it seems new and strange. You have brought the former things to pass and you also declare new things. You always make a way where there seems to be no way. You alone know how to lead us in the path we should go. So now, Lord, we let go of all that needs to be released and we embrace all you have waiting for us. In Jesus' name. Amen.

Today's Scriptures

Isaiah 42:9; Isaiah 43:18–19; Isaiah 55:8–9; Romans 11:33–34

Today's Thought

Hope. It's a universal quest, from hungry children in Africa to the grieving widow sitting in the penthouse suite in New York City. In my lifetime I have hoped for many things. Many of my dreams were realized and many were not. Without hope, we are lost. I recently listened to a story told by a young husband about his wife's diagnosis of stage 4 cancer. I was astonished as he shared that his hope was not first and foremost in her healing. He talked about the ultimate hope, the hope of heaven. He said many things about their health crisis, but the truth that most spoke to me was this, *"God has already cured us of our greatest sickness, sin."* How true. Being lost without God is our most grievous darkness. Since Jesus bridged the gap of that separation, we are never without hope. When our sights are set on being with Christ forever, being made perfect in his presence, every other challenge loses its power over us. Yes, we will have trials and tests. We will hurt and find ourselves broken at times. This is life. But God ... He gave us the gift of eternal hope in Jesus Christ his Son. God did not create us to cling to this earth life. We are destined for something far greater, something that is better by far ... an eternal hope in Christ Jesus, an eternal life in heaven.

Today's Prayer

Father God, you do all things well. Your plan for mankind and our redemption is the greatest healing we will ever know. Once we were lost, but now we are found. We do cling to this life, we do hope for good things to come, but help us to remember that this life is not all there is. This earth is not our home. When crisis hits us the hardest, when we do not know how we will meet the challenge, may we look to the cross where our true hope lies, where by his strips our souls are healed. Lord Jesus, you do not simply provide hope, you are our hope. In your precious name, Amen.

Today's Scriptures

John 6:67–69; Philippians 1:22–26; Colossians 3:3–6; Hebrews 6:17–20

Today's Thought

How many times have I gone to God with the broken pieces of my life in my hands? More than I can count. Why do I wait so long? How much easier it would be for all concerned if I would go as soon as I make the mess. God is bigger and greater than any situation I bring to him. He created the universe; that makes him bigger than the universe and everything in it. He knows all about my sin, my poor decisions, my brokenness and shattered relationships. Like a little child afraid to show Daddy her broken toy, we often think we can hide our predicament until we can figure a way out. Our Father is the God of broken things. He delights in helping us out of the pits we fall into and the confusion we have brought on ourselves. He longs for us to cease striving in our own strength and energy. He waits with hands outstretched, ready to take from us what we can no longer endure. His trustworthy hands can mend the most grievous of circumstances. The longer we wait to go to him the wider the chasm grows. Why not take what you have been holding behind your back to him now. You will find his love and peace there.

Today's Prayer

Father God, how wonderful is the truth that you never abandon us in our messes. Instead, you are at work rebuilding those broken places in our lives. You take every part of us that we offer up to you and you make all the crooked places straight. You build up the weak areas and you strengthen our feeble spirits. You are the glory and lifter of our heads. You restore relationships and you mend broken hearts. Nothing is too difficult for you. Lord, forgive us for thinking we can handle life on our own. With great hope and expectation, we relinquish those things that have us confused and trapped. Thank you for being a Father who loves to restore and rebuild. In the name of the One whose hands are open to us. Amen.

Today's Scriptures

Psalm 3:3–4; Psalm 71:20–21; Matthew 11:28–30; 1 Peter 5:10–11

Today's Thought

When is the last time you tasted a new food or created an original recipe? Some of us are braver than others when it comes to new and exotic flavors. We are invited to, *"Taste and see that the Lord is good; blessed is the man who takes refuge in him"* (Psalm 34:8). There is so much meaning packed into that challenge. Surrounding that summons is the psalmist's declaration that he lacks no good thing because he has made the Lord his refuge. The word *"taste"* in this context is loaded with meaning. It includes, *discern, perceive, sample in order to evaluate.* It also suggests *"the capacity to choose and delight in good things."* The word *good* embraces the meaning, *"possesses desirable qualities."* What does this all have to do with us? To paraphrase I would conclude, *"Come to the Lord and see how good he is. Try him out. Discern and perceive that he is the right choice. Look at his attributes and see that he has all the desirable qualities you are seeking after."* When a new and different flavor is set before us, we carefully, with small bites of course, examine, smell and partake. Once we know we like the new fare, we begin to take it in with delight. So it is with the Lord and his Word. Little by little, as we savor him, we come to know him and delight in him as the good God that he is.

Today's Prayer

Father God, you have invited us to your banqueting table, and all you have waiting for us there is good. You have laid out all the best qualities we could ever hope for in our God: love; faithfulness; peace; and delightful joy. Father, you are all you say you are and so much more. Lord, I pray you quicken our appetite for your Word because it is good and is like honey to our souls. Jesus, you are the bread of heaven and we are full and satisfied in you. In your Word we dine on the finest of wheat and the purest of milk. Help us to grow up into healthy mature believers. In the name of our God and Father, Jesus Christ and the Holy Spirit. Amen.

Today's Scriptures

Psalm 34:8–10; Psalm 119:103; Song of Solomon 2:3–4; 1 Peter 2:1–3

Today's Thought

Does it sometimes seem as if you are the only one on which the rain falls? One winter my daughter and I drove to Florida. Every time she got behind the wheel it started to rain. As soon as it was my turn to drive, the rain stopped. We still get a good laugh over that. Sometimes it seems as if everyone else is doing well and we are hit with struggle after struggle. We can become so discouraged we may begin to question God's love. Am I the unloved one? Did I do something to lose favor with God? In our humanity, we sometimes go to those dark places. Truth is, God is not partial in any way toward his children. The Word tells us that God causes the sun to rise on the evil and the good, and sends rain on the righteous and the unrighteous. The reality is that God treats all of us better than we deserve. The minute we think we deserve only good from God and are not willing to accept the hardships we are treading on dangerous ground. In the midst of Job's suffering his wife suggested that he curse God and die. Job's response is a truth we all must embrace. *"You are talking like a foolish woman, shall we accept good from God, and not trouble?"* (Job 2:10).

Today's Prayer

Father God, you told us that in this life we would have trouble, but Jesus told us we could take heart; he has overcome all the difficulties we will face in the world. Because he conquered, we are victors with him. Lord, when we feel alone, afraid and forgotten, remind us of your promise that we are never alone. You love each of us deeply and completely. You hurt when we hurt; you rejoice with us in our victories. You favor each of us as if we are the only child you have. You are never partial in your love and attention. I pray for those who are feeling overwhelmed with trials. Lord, remind them today that your love remains. In the name of Jesus, the One who loves us equally. Amen.

Today's Scriptures

Jeremiah 31:2–3; Luke 12:6–7; John 16:33; Romans 8:37–39

Today's Thought

Does God care about the state of our relationships? In Philippians 4, Paul is pleading with two women who had at one time ministered side-by-side with Paul and with each other. Seems as if the women had a falling out, a disagreement over something not mentioned in the passage. Think about it, Euodia and Syntyche had labored side-by-side with Paul for the cause of Christ and the gospel, and now here they are miles apart. Paul is urging someone to intervene and help these women find their way back. The fact that this rift in the body of Christ is mentioned by Paul gives weight to what God thinks about unity among believers. I hope that due to Paul's plea the women were reconciled. Now I must pose the obvious question. Are you currently at odds with another brother or sister in Christ? If so, what would the Lord call you to do in light of Philippians 4:2–3? Are you willing to take the first step of humility toward reconciliation? God has called us to peace. He says that as much as it is up to you, be at peace with others. Sometimes reconciliation is not possible because of another's resistance and unforgiveness; but, we must try. After trying our best, we leave the results in God's hands. I never regret the times I took the first step in the healing of a broken relationship. Is there someone you need to call or write a letter to today?

Today's Prayer

Father God, you love your family, and just as we love harmony in our families, so do you. Lord, you understand the complexities of human relationships and how fragile they can be. We make mistakes and say things that are damaging, things that separate us. It is not your will that we be at odds with others in the body of Christ. You have called us to peace and to be peacemakers. Lord, help us to take the steps we need to be in right relationship with others. In the name of Jesus our reconciler. Amen.

Today's Scriptures

Matthew 5:9; Romans 12:18; 1 Corinthians 1:10; Philippians 4:2–3

Today's Thought

We hear and read a lot concerning our identity in Christ. God's Word makes it quite clear that we are a new creation. Today I want to look at one of many passages that speak to this new identity. It's found in 1 Peter 2:9–10. Peter gives us three distinctive characteristics of our new nature. First Peter assures us that we are God's chosen possession. Just as the Jewish race was chosen by God as a unique people unto himself, we, as Gentiles, are also his chosen believers. As chosen vessels, we pour out the aroma and life of Christ everywhere we go. Second, we are a royal priesthood, chosen by God to intercede for the people just as those of the Levitical priesthood. What an honor! Third, we are a holy nation. We are not holy in our own right; we are holy because we are in Christ Jesus, the Holy One. We are the holy nation scripture speaks of. God has created a new nation, different and unique from any earthly nation. We may call ourselves Americans or Canadians, or go by the name of any other nation, but the church of Jesus Christ makes up a brand new nation that is truly under God and his authority. Let us now walk in this new identity: a chosen people; a royal priesthood; and a holy nation.

Today's Prayer

Father God, you have called us out of darkness into your marvelous light. We were once alienated from you, but in your love and mercy you now call us your special possession. We make up a new nation, a holy people. Once we were not a people, but now we are yours. Once we did not have mercy, but now we have received mercy. Now we have the honor of being a royal priesthood that intercedes before your throne on behalf of those who still walk in darkness. What a grand position we have before you on this earth. May we walk in all that you call us to be. In the name of the One who called us out of darkness into his wonderful light. Amen.

Today's Scriptures

1 Corinthians 5:17–18; Titus 2:11–14; 1 Peter 2:9–10; Revelation 1:4–6

July 24

Today's Thought

Who or what rules your decisions? Who rules where you go and who you go with? What rules your attitudes and motives? Quite probing questions. These are questions I must ask myself, and I challenge you to consider as well. We can be ruled by many things, our emotions, our own good ideas and the demands of others. When I am ruled by my fleshly desires, it usually does not end well. My old nature likes what it likes and does what it pleases. Sadly, what pleases my carnal nature does not always please God. After all, isn't that our aim, to please Christ? I always resort to God's Word when attempting to answer questions concerning my Christian walk. Our Father has set down some healthy guidelines that help us stay within the safety zone of his protection. My favorite is Galatians 5:16–25. I encourage you to read it in its entirety, and to engrave it on your heart. What Paul is saying here is that daily we must choose between two ways to live. If we live according to the flesh, we reap death. In contrast if we live according to the Spirit, we reap a life of love, joy and peace. I love that God understands our weakness to give into the flesh, and so provides his Holy Spirit to help us keep in step with the Lord's will. All we need to do is call upon him in the weakness of our old nature and he will surely respond with the help he promised, the help of the Holy Spirit.

Today's Prayer

Father God, I pray that we will allow your Word to change our minds, to rule over our emotions and guide our hearts, our words and our actions. How much our lives will flourish under the control of your Holy Spirit. Cause us to cleave to you and your good Word of truth that brings life to our souls. Lord, we desire to be transformed from the inside out. We aspire to holy living. We long for good and effective fruit to spring from our lives. In Jesus' name, the One in whom is our new identity. Amen.

Today's Scriptures

Romans 8:5–10; Romans 8:13–14; Galatians 5:16–25; 1 Peter 2:11–12

Today's Thought

God's presence in our lives is a foretaste of heaven. Oh, how we long for the full reality of seeing him face-to-face. We can however have as much as we want in this life. God promised to be with us, until the end of this age, then into eternity. By his Spirit we are in continual communion with the Father and Son. His presence in us is our greatest joy on earth. Imagine, God with us! What does this mean for us? We are never alone. Jesus' indwelling presence is a guarantee, no matter our circumstances. Even when we stumble through temptation, he is there to pick us up and give us a fresh start. When we need direction and guidance, the presence of the Holy Spirit will come alongside of us and advocate for us. When we feel we can no longer go on and want to give up, the Lord himself encourages us to take heart; he will strengthen us in the journey. One day we will be in the reality of God's presence, but even now, we can experience his presence moment-by-moment. We only need to believe the truth that he will never leave us, never forsake us.

Today's Prayer

Father God, you reign over all creation. You fill all of heaven and your glory is over all the earth. We love your presence in our lives. It is like a sweet fragrance to our spirit. Like honey to our soul. You lift us up to a place of peace and comfort. Your presence is heaven to us. Lord, I pray you reign in righteousness over our day. I pray for that one who especially needs to feel your presence today; the one who needs your nearness and comfort. I pray you uphold her with your strong but gentle arms. May her eyes be opened to see you working in her heart, her life and her day. Lord, we thank you that you have not left us alone, we are not orphans; we belong to you and have a unique place in your forever family. In Jesus' name, our ever-present God. Amen.

Today's Scriptures

Exodus 33:14; Psalm 16:11; Psalm 139:7–10; Zephaniah 3:17

Today's Thought

The morning headline unsettled me. One of the top religious leaders of the world condoned a sinful practice. I am saddened that some we look up to have come to this, placing stamps of approval on what God calls sin. I know we are to love the sinner and hate the sin, but it seems as if those lines are blurred these days. I don't mean to be a downer today, but my heart is so grieved I must write through my disappointment. When we cease to consult the Word of God for our spiritual direction, we will embrace any deceptive practice. We can expect the world to cave into sin, because they are only doing what they know how to do. My grief is over the fallen state of some religious leaders who are leading the sheep astray. The church is meant to be a safe place where we hear the full counsel of God preached. When we witness misled shepherds peddling their own thoughts and opinions rather than God's commands, we are heading in a dangerous direction. I am by no means legalistic, but I do believe the church should be holy and living a life that draws the culture to God's moral standard. I hope you are in a church where the Word of God is the final authority, where truth and Jesus Christ are both preached from the pulpit.

Today's Prayer

Father God, you sent your Son, the Word made flesh, to show us your righteous path. Your Word is crystal clear on sin and its ravages on society. You do not give us guidelines to confine us, rather your righteous laws are for our protection. The church of Jesus Christ needs shepherds who will nurture and love the sheep, leading them into truth and freedom. Lord, we pray for those men and women who have such a grave responsibility to teach and rightly divide the Word of God, teaching us right from wrong. We pray that your Word would have final authority over our lives and how we live. In Jesus' name, the way the truth and the life. Amen.

Today's Scriptures

Jeremiah 3:15; Matthew 5:17–19; 2 Timothy 2:15; 2 Timothy 4:3–4

July 27

Today's Thought

Our mother Eve was quite a woman. We often want to focus on her disobedience in eating from the forbidden tree. Today I want to spotlight three significant attributes we have inherited from her. It will be simple to remember, as simple as ABC. A: A is for adventure. Just as Eve was, we were created for adventure. When God gave the pair their earthly assignments, he clearly referred to *"them."* He appointed *them* to rule over all creation. Eve was totally included in the great adventure awaiting the couple in the garden. As Eve's daughters, we were born for adventure. B: Eve was born for beauty. When Adam saw her for the first time, he was awed and said in essence, *"She is beautiful and she is mine!"* You and I were born for beauty. Some have had their beauty marred by sin, our own sin and the sin that others have committed against us. God is well able to restore our God-given beauty when we allow him. C: Eve was born for courage. It took great courage to continue life after the fall. She gave birth and raised children even though it would be difficult and painful. Today I encourage each of us to walk in adventure, beauty and courage. That's what we were created for.

Today's Prayer

Father God, you made all things, you made woman and declared her good. You made us for yourself and for your pleasure and delight. Father, I pray you help us to see ourselves as you see us. Thank you for granting us an adventurous life. I pray we rise up to live a bold life of meeting our challenges head on. Thank you for the beauty you place within each of us. I pray we take off the garments of shame brought on by sin and put on the beautiful garment of praise. Lord, thank you for the courage you give us in Christ Jesus. I pray we face every day as brave women ready to do exploits for our King. In Jesus' name, our perfect Creator. Amen.

Today's Scriptures

Genesis 1:26–28; Proverbs 31:25–31; Isaiah 61:1–3; 2 Timothy 1:7

Today's Thought

Have you noticed how the darkness flees when light is turned on in a dark room? It's as if the darkness was never there. That's the concept the Apostle John shares with us in John 1:5. *"The light shines in the darkness, and the darkness has not understood it."* That light is Jesus and his truth. Jesus came into a world shrouded in darkness and turned on the lights. When we allow the light of truth to enter our souls, the darkness of lies is dispelled and defeated. Morning dawn brings with it a brightness that chases away night, and then when the gloom of a dark sky surrounds us, the moon shines on our path. Are we able to grasp the essential importance of light? Imagine a world without the sun, moon, or lamp light. Imagine if Jesus had never come into the world. We would be in the deepest darkness. But praise be to God, he did send Jesus, and he shattered the great darkness of our world and the blackness of our souls. This leaves us with a mission. Our pursuit should be that of shining the light that is in us all around to a people still sitting in the chains of lies and darkness. This Jesus light of ours is no trivial insignificant gift. The light in us is The Light who can light up and change the whole world.

Today's Prayer

Father God, you not only call us to walk in the light, you commission us to be the light in a world that is bound in darkness. Cause us, your people to shine bright in these last days. I pray that you use our lives to turn many from the shadows of sin and lies to the glorious freedom that comes through Jesus. One day, Father, we will not need earthly light, for the Lamb will be our everlasting light. As we wait for that day, I pray we hold the truth of Jesus and your Word high so that the true light can shine into every nook and cranny of our world. May the light in us expel the darkness that binds those we love. In the name of Jesus, the light of the world. Amen.

Today's Scriptures

Psalm 18:28; Matthew 4:16; Matthew 5:14–16; John 3:19–21

Today's Thought

In John 15 Jesus uses the word, *"abide"* eight times. Today I want to explore this word in order to help us understand what Jesus' words imply for us today. The Lord wants us to live a fruitful life. He uses the illustration of a vine and its branches to help us understand how high-quality fruit comes about. Jesus is the Vine and we are the branches. The branches can produce nothing on their own. Their productivity is completely dependent on the vine. This is a picture of a life-giving union. The branch can only get its life-giving sap from the Vine. Secondly, must we continue to abide. Jesus makes it clear when he says, *"Abide in Me, and I in you. As the branch cannot bear fruit of itself, unless it abides in the vine, neither can you, unless you abide in Me"* (John 15:4; NKJV). Some versions render "abide" as to *"remain or continue."* Quite simply, we need Jesus and we need to remain connected to him and his Word if we want to grow, mature, and bring forth fruit for the kingdom. While we are abiding, the fruit is growing all by itself. Think about it, in a garden you don't see how the seeds turn into beautiful flowers or how the apple tree brings forth its fragrant fruit; but, we always see the results. As we silently abide in his love, he does for us what only the Vine can do, that which we cannot do for ourselves.

Today's Prayer

Father God, you are the keeper of all things, you are the keeper of our hearts. You have shown us how to keep our hearts in the love of Christ. You call us to abide. I pray you help us to grasp the deep truth of John 15. Help us to understand how crucial this life-giving connection is to our spiritual growth. We confess that apart from Jesus, our Vine, we can accomplish nothing of eternal value. We cannot grow ourselves or produce the fruit that your Holy Spirit provides. We are simply called to come to your vineyard, abide in your love and obey your commands.

Today's Scriptures

John 15:1–17; Galatians 5:22–23; 1 John 2:27–28; 1 John 3:24

Today's Thought

Many people say that Christianity is for the weak; but, it takes courage to follow Christ. Just look at the lives of the prophets of old and the disciples who followed Jesus to the cross and beyond. They were persecuted beyond anything we can imagine; still they persisted in proclaiming the God they served. It's in the hard and scary places that we learn to trust God in greater measure. As we face our fiery trials, we find that we have more opportunities to rely solely on God. It takes courage to say "no" to the things in which the modern-day culture would have us indulge. It takes courage to witness for Christ when we face rejection and persecution. Somedays it takes courage simply to get through another day when we see no change in our circumstances. God calls us to meekness which is translated, "strength under control." It takes courage to make those hard choices between what we want and what God wants. Simply put, courage equals trust. The saints of the past and the saints of the presence are the bravest people I know. We believe that living for God takes fortitude, faith and courage and that he is the one who supplies everything we need to live a godly life in this ungodly world.

Today's Prayer

Father God, in this day and culture in which we now live, you are calling upon men and women who are willing to go against the tide of ungodliness. You call us out from among those who cave to the culture. You Word tells us that you choose the weak things of this world to shame the strong. This is not a contradiction. We are considered weak by those who consider themselves strong. You have turned that upside down. You have made the wisdom of this world as foolishness. Lord, keep us brave; keep us walking in courage and trust as we face these difficult days on earth. In Jesus' name, our Victorious King. Amen.

Today's Scriptures

Psalm 56:1–4; 1 Corinthians 1:26–29; 2 Timothy 1:7; 2 Peter 1:3–4

Today's Thought

Humility is a magnet for God's approval. Let's look at the scriptural proof for that statement. God commended Moses as being the meekest man on earth. Unassuming Abraham was called a friend of God. Job humbled himself under God's mighty hand and was rewarded with twice as much as he started with. These are just a few examples. The Bible is full of stories of men and women whom God choose because of their humility. We cannot overstate the greatest model of humility we have in Jesus himself. Philippians 2:6–7 states, *"Who, being in very nature God, did not consider equality with God something to be grasped, but made himself nothing, taking the very nature of a servant, and being made in human likeness."* Jesus knew exactly who he was. He was God incarnate;, yet he made himself low so we could be lifted up. Humility is not thinking less of oneself; it is thinking of oneself less. Jesus did that. He considered his own life as nothing, taking on the nature of a servant. He laid down his earth life so we could have eternal life. The difficult thing about humility is we don't know when we have it. As soon as we think we have it, we lose it. However, God knows because he alone knows the heart. The most we can do is continually pray for humility and allow the Holy Spirit to do his silent work in us as we respond to our circumstances in meekness and in surrender to the will of God.

Today's Prayer

Father God, you love to see humility in your people. It is the greatest way we can imitate the life of Christ. Lord, grant us the grace to desire a humble life before you and others. You tell us that humility is required of us. Father, deliver us from the love of self. Lord, help us learn to esteem others above ourselves. Grant us a humble spirit. Help us see that we don't have anything good apart from you or that we deserve anything because of our own goodness. In the name of the lowly Jesus. Amen.

Today's Scriptures

Micah 6:8; Ephesians 4:1–3; Philippians 2:5–8; 1 Peter 5:6–7

Today's Thought

Who or what defines you? Is it your physical appearance, your wealth or position? Maybe it's people such as parents, husband or boyfriend. Even your own thoughts about who you are will affect your behavior and how you respond in relationships. Whatever defines you controls you. We ultimately decide who or what we believe about ourselves. There is only one place we can go to know the truth about our identity, God's Word. All of the realities revealed about you and me are found within those timeless pages. Okay, here we go. You are forgiven and set free. You are accepted. You are chosen in the beloved Christ, and that makes you the beloved of God. You are created in his image and you are known by God. You were wonderfully made and fashioned by God before your birth. You are lavishly loved because you were bought with a price, the precious blood of Christ. You are a new person, the old is gone. You are cherished and beautiful in his sight. Need I go on? The question now is this, who or what will you believe about yourself? Who or what will you allow to define you? The choice is always yours.

Today's Prayer

Father God, when we attempt to define our personhood by worldly standards, we will always fall short. When we allow our own self-talk dictate how we feel about ourselves, we will be deceived. You alone define us. You alone complete us. Lord, we do not have to determine your love for us by our own goodness or virtue. You look past all of that and see us through the cross, the death and resurrection of your Son. We are defined by what your Word declares. We look outside of ourselves to a hill called Calvary and there we see who we are, a child worth dying for, a child forgiven and redeemed. Love's arms are open wide. We no longer hang our heads in shame. It's all nailed to the cross. Praise his wonderful name.

Today's Scriptures

Psalm 45:10–11; Psalm 139:13–18; John 1:11–13; 1 John 3:1–2

Today's Thought

For many years I was a part of a ministry that helped women heal from past-abortions, past and current sexual issues and other grief-related pain. At one point we were in need of a private facility where women could feel safe as we came together for our studies. A local church offered a badly water-damaged parsonage that had not been in use for years. Needless to say, it was wrecked. The church and the ministry began a joint renovation project that took over a year to complete. Finally, we moved into a beautifully restored home where God could do his healing work in the lives of hurting women. What a stunning image of what God does in our ravaged hearts and lives damaged by sin. He does not simply make it better; he comes in and utterly restores all the broken places. He lays a new foundation, knocks down a few walls, over hauls every bit of flooring, ceiling and crevasses of our being. He is building a place where his very presence will dwell. The Word promises that nothing can ever separate us from God's love. Your see, dearly beloved, in Christ it's never separation, it's always restoration.

Today's Prayer

Father God, you are the restorer of all things. Even now you are restoring us, redeeming us for yourself and your glory. Lord, I pray for those today who are damaged and hurting from past sins and the sins committed against them. Help each one to trust and believe in your willingness and power to restore every facet of their brokenness. You never desire separation from those you love, you always long for restoration and wholeness. Father, I ask for those hurting today who see no way out of their pain, lead them to the help they need. Bring them into contact with godly ministries that offer biblical healing and restoration from the damage that life can bring. In the name of Jesus, our Healer and Restorer. Amen.

Today's Scriptures

Hosea 6:1–3; Romans 8:38–39; 2 Corinthians 5:17; 1 Peter 5:10–11

August 3

Today's Thought

For what high purpose were you created? God has many noble purposes for having created us. We all have a unique calling on our lives and God will use our individual gifts and talents in diverse ways. There is one purpose however that we all have in common. God created you and me for intimacy. What exactly does that mean? Authentic intimacy involves vulnerability and risk because it encompasses being fully known by another. We often hide ourselves from that kind of familiarity. Another aspect of intimacy is to know another on that deep, personal and private level. This mutual knowing of each other requires a deep-seated trust that only comes with time. Where do we find this intimacy that our soul longs for? We often seek it in casual emotional and sexual relationships; but, intimacy is not necessarily about sex. In fact, the truest intimacy, the intimacy we were born for is the highest and purest we will ever know. It is the intimacy we find in our holy communion with God. God delights in you and wants you and me to delight in him. God knows us inside out and wants us to desire to know him in the same way. This, dear sister, is true and authentic intimacy. As we make knowing Christ our most noble aim, the intimacy we yearn for will surely come.

Today's Prayer

Father God, from the beginning you created man and woman to know you and delight in you. Sadly, we attempt to fill our deep need for intimacy with that which will never satisfy. We try everything in order fill our God- shaped heart, and we miss that for which we were created, to know you and be known by you, in a pure and holy communion. Lord, I pray you touch us today with the truth of authentic intimacy, and what that means to each of us personally. May we now reach for that high and noble purpose. In the name of our intimate and holy God. Amen.

Today's Scriptures

Jeremiah 9:23–24; Jeremiah 29:13; John 17:3; Philippians 3:10

August 4

Today's Thought

Every choice has consequences. Our day-to-day decisions may not seem like a big deal, but they are. As one who is now in the twilight years of life, I still experience consequences that I made as a teen and as an adult. The aftermath of bad choices is not pleasant. I also enjoy the benefits of the good and righteous choices I have made. Most of my good choices were made after I surrendered my life to Christ. Knowing God and his Word takes us a long way in discerning how to choose the right and reject the wrong. How do we know the better choice? First, we go to the Word of God. Most choices are made clear within the pages of this Spirit-breathed guide. *"Thou shall not,"* passages are not optional, or multiple choice. God's Word means exactly what it says. There are however, gray areas where it can be a bit cloudy. In these cases, we need to take into account the whole counsel of God and his character. We must ask, is the decision I am about to make in line with all of scripture and does it reflect the character of the God of the Bible. Still other areas of life's choices involve neither right or wrong. In these cases, we must allow our consciences to guide. I make it a personal rule to never violate my conscience. If I have any doubt, I throw it out. Encompassing all of this is the leading and conviction of the Holy Spirit.

Today's Prayer

Father God, thank you that you have not left us alone, as orphans, to figure life out on our own. You guide and direct our life choices in so many ways. Your Word is lamp to our feet and a light to our path. Your holy counsel is a sure foundation on which we build our daily choices. You tell us that all things are lawful, but not all things are beneficial. I pray as we continue on this Christian path as followers of Christ, that we learn to listen, study and obey. Help us to avoid the pitfall of unpleasant consequences. In the name of our righteous guide. Amen.

Today's Scriptures

Psalm 119:105; Romans 14:1–8; Galatians 6:7–8; 2 Timothy 3:16–17

Today's Thought

I recently attended a conference that centered on biblical healing for past wounds. I heard many stories of redemption and restoration shared by a wide diversity of women. There is just something about stories that grab our attention and reach to the core of our souls. Perhaps this is because we each have a story. I don't know where you are on your spiritual and emotional journey, but I know your story is not finished; and, I know your story is sacred. Jesus reached women throughout the ages with the stories he told. The story of the sinful woman who washed Jesus' feet with her tears personally resonates with me. Most of our stories are not pretty; in fact they are largely filled with sinful choices and the resulting consequences. The amazing thing about sharing your story is that others gather the courage to step out of their silence and open up their hearts to the healing light of God's grace. Many years ago I heard a woman tell her story of a past abortion and how she found healing at a pregnancy resource center. After hearing her story I was able to open up about an abortion I had kept locked within me for almost 30 years. I was liberated after attending a biblical healing group. I was set free from my shameful secret sin. That may have never happened if not for one brave woman. What's your story? Who might benefit by your sharing? What might you gain?

Today's Prayer

Father God, thank you that you can take the worst, the most tragic story and use it to bring forgiveness, healing and restoration to our lives. I pray for anyone today who needs to hear a story or needs to tell her story so others may be reached. I pray we know the proper time and the proper setting to reveal our hearts and stories to others. We know you will bring good things when we share our journey. We know that in your hands our stories are sacred and our stories are safe. In Jesus' name. Amen.

Today's Scriptures

Isaiah 9:2; Luke 7:44–50; John 5:6; Ephesians 5:8–9

Today's Thought

"Obedience" can be a scary word. As a child I dreaded hearing my father say, *"Fern, you need to obey me!"* When I first read about obedience in the Bible it had a heavy tone for me. Disobedience has dire consequences, like King Saul losing his kingship over disobedience. Our fallen nature rebels against obedience; just ask Adam and Eve. We like being our own boss. I don't know about you, but that's not working for me. When I attempt to run my own affairs, I end up in places I never wanted to be. One day I heard some really good news. God does not call us to obedience and then leave us alone to figure it out. No, he comes right alongside us and gives us the grace and strength to obey that which he asks of us. When he calls us to turn away from evil, his Spirit within us walks it out with us. Obedience need not be a hard or a heavy burden to bear. God is our burden-bearer and we can cast all our cares upon him because he cares for us. When my sons were young and learning to obey me, I entered the situation with them and taught them the benefits and joys of obedience. Even the human Jesus learned obedience. Dear friends, obedience always pays off and we are never left on our own in learning to obey God.

Today's Prayer

Father God, you call us to obedience, as a good Father who wants the best for us. In grace, you have provided your Holy Spirit to help us carry through. Lord, I pray that we are quick learners; that we learn to obey without having to go through stern discipline. You never ask more of us than we have to give. As we obey you one step at a time, you show us our next step. You are always cheering us on to higher levels of obedience because you love us. Obedience is a high form of worship, and we desire that level of honoring you. I pray that our growth in obedience comes from our deep devotion and love for you. In the name of your obedient Son, Jesus. Amen.

Today's Scriptures

1 Samuel 15:22–23; Luke 11:27–28; Hebrews 5:7–10; 1 John 5:1–4

August 7

Today's Thought

Yesterday I really messed up. I made some bad choices. I could have just kicked myself, because I know better. Of course, I know better. Knowing better does not keep us from the human experience of messing up. However, it was an amazing feeling to wake up this morning and remind myself that it's a new day. I can learn from yesterday and make better choices today. With God, all things are redeemable. He can take our worse mistakes and salvage them for his use and purpose. Lamentations 3:22–23 tell us that because of his great love, we are not consumed by our past mistakes. His compassions never fail, they are new every morning. God is for us, not against us. He is rooting for us, always cheering us on. When we fail, it's not fatal. I am most grateful that a day lasts only 24 hours. I always need a new day, a new 24 hours to recoup my losses. Friends, we do not have to wake up each morning in dread and regret over yesterday's poor judgments; we can leap and sing for joy that God is the God of a new day, new opportunities, and new choices. As sure as the dawn, the Lord is ready to meet and greet you and together with him you gain a new and fresh beginning.

Today's Prayer

Father God, your mercies never fail us. Great is your faithfulness to meet us each day as yesterday's slate is wiped clean. We know we have consequences to those choices we made, but with you, it's always a new beginning, a chance to rise up and choose the better and higher way. You infuse us with fresh hope and renewed strength to walk in righteous paths. Today is the first day of the rest of our lives. Lord, I pray we learn from yesterday and its pitfalls. I ask that you use all of those wrong decisions as teaching tools for today. With you Lord, nothing is wasted. We look up to you as our restoring God. In the name of Jesus, our Redeemer. Amen.

Today's Scriptures

Isaiah 40:30–31; Isaiah 43:18–19; Lamentations 3:19–24; Philippians 3:12–14

Today's Thought

When I read the finished product of *As Sure as the Dawn*, I know I will be wishing I had done some things differently; I should have said this or should not have said that. It has happened to me many times. After I have delivered a presentation, I almost always rethink what I said and how I said it. I think this is a human condition; our quest for perfection. However, at the end of the day, I will place this devotional in God's hands and leave the results to him. All we can do in this life is our best. I will not do another author's best, or presenter's best, just my best. I believe that as we do God's will with the tools and gifts we have, we please him. When God assigns us a task, he joins us in the venture. He does not leave us on our own to figure it out. Many times in Scripture Jesus invites people to enter into their own healing, to have a part in what he wants to do. When Lazarus was called from his grave, Jesus had others roll away the stone. Then he called on others to unwrap the grave cloths. He could have done all that by his very spoken Word, but he wants us to partner with him in what he is doing. When the Lord calls you to an undertaking, it's really his, but he wants you to share in the glory. Next time you feel overwhelmed with your calling, remember, ultimately it belongs to God. Do your best and leave the results in his hands. Then let it go because it never really belonged to you.

Today's Prayers ...

Father God, what a joy it is to serve you. We do that in small ways and in in very big ways, but it's all yours from the smallest task to the greatest. How we are honored to be called into the work you are doing on earth. Help us to remember that it is you who initiates every good work whether it be serving tables or leading a Bible study, writing a book or writing a song. Thank you for inviting us into your grand story and for giving us a part in this great adventure called life. In Jesus' name. Amen.

Today's Scriptures

Ecclesiastes 4:9–12; John 11:38–44; 1 Corinthians 3:5–9; Philippians 4:13

August 9

Today's Thought

I find it easier to weep with those who weep than to rejoice with those who rejoice, especially when they have received something from the Lord that I have been asking for. For example, years ago my friend's husband built her a beautiful office in their downstairs family room. She invited me over so we could gush over it together, and we did. Secretly however, I was envious and resentful because I had wanted my husband to add an addition onto our tiny house so I could have an office. I was writing Bible studies back then and I REALLY needed an office. I was operating everything from my tiny bedroom. I was not able to truly rejoice with her because my resentment got in the way. Why did she get the office I so desperately needed? Finally, God got hold of me and exposed my self-centered attitude, and that I was violating his command to rejoice. Hopefully I have turned away from that covetous attitude, but honestly, there are still times when I have a hard time rejoicing with a sister when she gets what I want. God is helping me. Just because we pray for a thing does not mean God will capitulate to our demands. Eventually my husband and I bought a bigger house and I now have an entire room as my office. I am writing from it right now. All in God's own good and perfect time.

Today's Prayer

Father God, thank you that you do not give us everything we ask for when we ask for it. You are not raising up a bunch of insistent children. In your gracious love you will give us what we need, when we need it. Lord, I pray for us, that we would learn to rejoice with others, especially when you grant them something we have longed for. With you there is no partiality or favoritism. Help us to remember that the sooner we learn our lessons, the sooner your blessings can be released. In Jesus' name. Amen.

Today's Scriptures

Luke 12:13–15; Romans 12:15; 1 Timothy 6:6–10; James 4:1–3

August 10

Today's Thought

What voices are you listening to? That could be difficult to answer as there are many voices coming at us every day. With so much noise screaming at us, it's no wonder we are hindered in hearing God's voice. Newspapers, social media, TV news programs, magazines along with all other sources. It boggles the mind when I think of the noise level we are continually exposed to, and it's getting louder and louder. We are continually plugged into noise and distraction. It makes it so easy to check out. All of this makes it difficult to discern the voice of God. The first guard we have against noise pollution is of course God's Word. That is the first line of defense we have in sorting through the chaos. Listening to his voice through his Word gives us a sieve through which we can eliminate the lies from the truth, the better from the best and his voice from the rest. If we begin our day in silence before God, we have a good chance of breaking through the barriers of all the demands that pound at us throughout our day. God does want us to be engaged in world events, but not entangled. As his children we are to rise above the chatter by disconnecting when necessary. It's about balance. It's about knowing God and his Word and understanding the difference between the important and the tyranny of worldly urgency.

Today's Prayer

Father God, we live in a world of distractions. Sometimes we lose our focus as we listen to all the sources, all the voices that bombard us each day. I pray we remember to come to you first, to hear what you have to say and know your voice through communion with you and your Word. Help us to unplug from the demands of a culture that is set on separating us from you and hindering us from discerning your will. Bring us back to the delight of being silent and still, of waiting on you and loving your voice above all others. In the name of our God who speaks to us. Amen.

Today's Scriptures

Psalm 46:10; Mark 6:30–31; Romans 12:2; Hebrews 12:1–2

August 11

Today's Thought

Getting even can feel good for a while. In the long run, it does not bring the satisfaction we hoped for. When we look at scriptures and the stories of revenge, no one wins. Today I want to look at the story of Joseph and how he opposed the mindset of his day and took the high road rather than revenge. Beginning in Genesis 37 a tale unfolds that is almost unbelievable. Joseph is the favored son of his father Jacob. Ten of his brothers were so jealous of him they threw him into a pit and left him for dead. He was found by a band of merciless vagabonds who sold him into Egyptian slavery. Joseph's saga includes false accusations, false imprisonment, sexual temptation and betrayal. In the course of time, according to God's plan, he landed in the position of second in charge of all of Egypt. Many years later because of a famine in their land, his ruthless brothers came to Egypt in search of food. Joseph had the power to feed them or kill them. The brothers were terrified that Joseph would now take his revenge on them for what they had done. At the end they threw themselves down before him and said, *"'We are your slaves.' But Joseph said to them, 'Don't be afraid. Am I in the place of God?'"* (Genesis 50:18–19).

Today's Prayer

Father God, thank you for Joseph's story. It teaches us so much about integrity, morality, forgiveness and leaving room for God's vengeance. When others hurt and harm us, our human tendency is to "get back." Revenge seems to be a sweet answer to life's wounds. Lord, we thank you that your Word leaves no room for personal vengeance. It is not an option for us. You settled the matter when you clearly said, *"It is mine to avenge; I will repay"* Help us to always stand back and get out of your way so you can correct the wrong. Help us to do our part in forgiving and leave the results up to you. In the name of our Defender, Jesus. Amen.

Today's Scriptures

Genesis 50:18–21; Proverbs 20:22; Romans 12:17–21; 1 Peter 3:8–9

August 12

Today's Thought

When was the last time you remember being carried? When I was a child, I loved it when my dad would scoop me up in his big arms and carry me. Sometimes he would put me on his broad shoulders and lug me around the back yard. With my father now gone, those are some sweet memories. Do you know that at times your Father God carries you? He carried young Israel through the howling desert. He bore them up on eagle's wings. The Shepherd holds the lambs in his arms, and in our gray hair and old age, he promises to carry us. I especially love that. I can be sure that as I age he will bear me up, strengthen me and carry me when I no longer have the strength of my youth. That time is quickly approaching for me. These precious promises keep us from despair when the body can no longer enjoy the vigor it once enjoyed. In his love, God has made provision for every season of life. In the poem *Footprints* a beautiful portrait unfolds of two sets of footprints in the sand. At one point one set of prints disappears. The writer questions God," *Why did you leave me when I needed you most?"* God answers, *"My child, I did not leave you, that's when I carried you."* We can be sure, God walks all the way with us and in the times when we falter, he lifts us up and carries us.

Today's Prayer

Father God, what a good Father you are. You are always with us on this life's journey. You carried us from our mother's womb and you carry us in our old age. How you love your little ones, your gray-haired saints, and everyone in between. You carried your beloved Israel and you carry your church. You will not let us go or leave us to fend for ourselves. Yours are the everlasting arms, the sheltering arms. I pray we remember your promises when our strength wanes. I pray we lift our arms to you in surrender to your strong arms. In Jesus' name. Amen.

Today's Scriptures

Deuteronomy 32:10–11; Isaiah 40:11; Isaiah 46:3–4; Mark 10:14–16

August 13

Today's Thought

Is your past dictating your present? Our past has a way of catching up with us. Amazingly, God has made provision for those times. He forgives and restores as we confess and repent. He wipes the slate clean and we begin anew. The problem arises when our minds have not received the memo. Those memories and regrets can come in like a flood to condemn and hinder us in the present and hijack our future. When we gaze into the rear-view mirror long enough it convinces us that we are no different than we were. The past does not determine who we are today. When we come to Christ, old things are gone, the new has come. When God called you to himself, it was with plan and purpose. We must learn from the past, but we must not live there. There are steps we can take that can help us move on. Forgiving those who hurt us is a big stride toward leaving the past behind. Stop focusing on the "what ifs." The Lord wants us to make new memories as he leads us in our ongoing journey. Being aware of the devil's tactics can help. He comes to steal, kill and destroy. We can defeat him through honesty with God about our past and know that God provides everything we need to move on. As we do our part, God does his beautiful work of freedom and restoration. Dwelling on the past robs us of the present. Living in the present insures a great future.

Today's Prayer

Father God, you make all things new through your Son Jesus. Thank you that we are not defined by our past mistakes. We are set free, redeemed and restored through your faithful mercies. Lord, when our minds and emotions take us to those past places that would hold us hostage, we pray that we look to you and the truth that *"whom the Son sets free is free indeed."* We are forgiven and now walk in the newness of life. All praise to you, Jesus, our Kinsman Redeemer. Amen.

Today's Scriptures

John 8:36; John 10:7–10; 2 Corinthians 5:17; Philippians 3:12–14

Today's Thought

Spiritual growth is always linked to suffering. That may not be the good news you want to hear today, but stay with me. Among the 12 disciples, Peter bristled the most against the thought of suffering for his faith. He fully expected Jesus to set up an earthly kingdom, overthrowing the Roman government. Peter wanted nothing to do with suffering and spoke out against Jesus when he spoke of his imminent suffering and death. We like accusing Peter for his bumbling brashness, but who among us looks forward to suffering for righteousness's sake. Fast forward to Peter's first epistle. This five-chapter book is super charged with verses on suffering. Peter mentions the theme no less than 16 times. Peter seems to make it his mission to encourage and empower Christians as they suffer for the sake of the gospel. He admonished us to come to grips with the truth that we will suffer, but to also rely on God's grace in the midst of persecution. How different now is Peter's perspective as he faces his own death on a cross? What does this mean for us today? We can be sure that suffering and persecution will come. Peter assures us that to suffer for Christ is a glorious honor. He reminds us that without suffering there is no spiritual growth. He encourages us that this present world is passing away and we are aliens in a place that is not our home. So, we look up and praise God for the honor to suffer for his name's sake.

Today's Prayer

Father God, we do not like suffering, yet we want to grow up in Christ. Lord, help us to count the cost of living for you. May we be willing to pay the price for spiritual maturity. I pray we not shrink from the sacrifice needed to identify with our Lord Jesus. When our own family members come against us because of our faith, may we rise up as Peter did, fully relying on the grace of God to persevere. In the name of Jesus. Amen.

Today's Scriptures

1 Peter 1:3–7; 1 Peter 2:19–21; 1 Peter 3:13–17; 1 Peter 5:10–11

August 15

Today's Thought

I recently counseled a woman who tearfully confessed that she feels as if she is invisible. Sadly, this is not as uncommon as we may think. Even in a crowd one can feel alone, isolated and alienated. I once read a quote that exposed an awful truth, *"Loneliness is the worse pain in the world."* A poet friend of mine said it this way, *"Uninvited ... loneliness creeps into my soul, reaching its tentacles around my aching heart but who will ever see my unshed tears?"* How aware are we of those around us who are experiencing the loneliness, and the anguish of feeling invisible? Perhaps you have felt this way, or feel its sting even today. God's truth can bring us freedom from the captivity of the lie that we are alone. Over and over, he assures us that his presence goes with us and he will never leave us. The beautiful reality is, we are seen, we are heard, we are known by the God who created us and loves us. There are those around us who need to hear this liberating word. We are the vessels that God wants to use in relieving those who are hurting because of the lies. First, we must believe it for ourselves at the deepest recesses of our being. Then we go forth to proclaim the truth that sets the captive free. We are seen, we are heard, we are completely known by God. We are never invisible to the Lord who died for us. He looked down from the cross, he spanned across the ages and he saw us. He heard our cry. He knows us.

Today's Prayer

Father God, while we were yet sinners, Christ died for us. You will not withhold any good thing from us? You never close your eyes to us; you never shut your ears to our cries. You tell us that you know us through and through. I pray that when we feel lonely and invisible, we remember that you are near. I pray that when we experience the feelings of loneliness, we allow it to cause us to draw near to you. In Jesus' name. Amen.

Today's Scriptures

Exodus 33:14; Psalm 34:15; Psalm 139:1–3; 1 Corinthians 12:13

Today's Thought

There is a very old song that most of my readers are too young to remember. The chorus went like this, *"Detour, there's a muddy road ahead, detour."* I cringe when on a long trip I come across a detour in an area that is not familiar to me. It can be very unsettling and it feels like a great waste of time. I have gone around and around at times figuring my way out. We encounter road detours because something ahead is under construction. That got me to thinking that perhaps when God ordains a detour, could it be that he wants to overhaul something in us? As the Israelites left Egypt, they embarked on an 11-day journey that took them 40 years. That's quite a detour! They were under construction. God's people had many lessons to learn as they wandered that desert. The old ways they learned in Egypt had to be transformed to God's ways. The cultural attitudes, the mindset of indifference, even the food they became accustomed to, all of it was not appropriate for God's chosen people. In those 40 years he was renewing, restoring and preparing for himself a people who would turn the world upside down. Let's think about our detours. What could God possibly be up to when life takes an unexpected turn? When unforeseen events turn your world upside down, place a seal over your heart which reads, *"Under Construction."*

Today's Prayer

Father God, we do not like change that upsets our neatly ordered world. We do not like detours. Why are we so surprised when unexpected events takes us to places we would rather not go? Lord, I pray we learn to trust you in these disconcerting times. I pray we embrace the new direction and know that you have good things in store for us. Help us to let go of our plans so we can enjoy what you desire for us. You always go ahead of us, what have we to fear. Lead on, O' King Eternal. In Jesus' name. Amen.

Today's Scriptures

Isaiah 30:21; Isaiah 55:8–9; Jeremiah 29:11; Romans 11:33–34

Today's Thought

Aren't you glad God keeps his Word? Can you imagine what life would be like if God changed his mind? What if God suddenly took all his precious promises and did a recall? There are times in scripture when God relented and didn't bring disaster on Israel due to the intercession of his prophets. One thing is certain, he never changed his mind about his love for them, and he will never change his mind about his love for us. Just as God is a keeper of his Word, so should we hold our word in high esteem. God expects us to keep our word. The thought of that should cause us to be careful about what we speak and the promises we make. I tend to commit to more than I can handle. I cannot count the times I suffered burn out trying to keep up with all the things I said I would do. Are you relating? Here is what I learned. Know your limits, set boundaries on your time. It always seems that we have more time than we really do, so we fill up our calendars and then wonder why we are exhausted and overwhelmed. God did not create us for the hectic lifestyles we tend to establish for ourselves. In the end, we often have to renege on our word because we committed to something we just can't fit in. It takes integrity and character to keep our word. Let's be more Christ-like in that. Let's think before we speak. Let's not be too hasty in saying yes, and not afraid to say no.

Today's Prayer's

Father God, your Word is firmly established. With you there is no variableness, neither shadow of turning. You are our immutable God. This quality in you gives us peace and assurance that what you say you will do. Lord, we are not always like that. We make promises and obligations we are not able to keep. Father, help us to consider our word as sacred. Give us pause in filling our calendars and committing impulsively to every request. In the name of the God who keeps his Word. Amen.

Today's Scriptures

Psalm 119:89–90; Proverbs 20:25; Ecclesiastes 5:5; Matthew 5:37

Today's Thought

This may be a challenging day for you? It will be for me. We can face the day in one of two ways. We can see it as an opportunity to rely on the power and strength God promised us, or we can spend the day wringing our hands in anticipation of crashing and burning. My preference is to stand on what God tells me in Deuteronomy 33:25. *"The bolts of your gates will be iron and bronze, and your strength will equal your days."* This is a promise that supports me throughout each and every day, the easy ones and the challenging ones. God empowers us according to the need. I don't need strength for tomorrow, I need it for today and he will give it. As I depend on him one day at a time, I find all the grace, strength and fortitude I need to meet every task. God never leaves us to push through on our own. He graciously grants the strength we ask for. Our part is to reach out by faith and receive all the help he offers. Don't be shy about showing him your neediness. In our weakness, he loves showing off his power. This is where his glory shines through as he works in us and through us.

Today's Prayer

Father God, you never disappoint us; you never let us down. When we humble ourselves before your mighty power, you respond in granting us that which we most need. Help us to live one day at a time so we can receive your daily provision as needed. The strength you give you give lavishly. Sometimes we need the blessing to rest, and you offer that as well. Lord, thank you that we are never on our own. I pray for each of us today that we not be afraid to reveal our neediness. It is in this place of necessity that you come in and lift us up to meet the challenges. Father, we rely on you in every way, physically, mentally, and spiritually. You are well able to meet all those needs. Thank you for strength for the weak and power for the powerless. In Jesus' name. Amen.

Today's Scriptures

Psalm 73:26; Isaiah 40:29–31; Isaiah 41:10; Philippians 4:13

August 19

Today's Thought

Though None Go with Me. This is the title of a book I read many years ago. It resonated with me because for 30 years I attended church and served the Lord without any family members by my side. This made for many lonely Sunday mornings, sitting alone in my pew. The Lord in his goodness provided many wonderful brothers and sisters in the Lord with whom I could share my spiritual journey. Still, there is something precious in worshipping God alongside our God-given biological family. I watched as so many families worshipped together and often shed tears as I sat alone. We regularly sang these words, *"Though none go with me, still I will follow."* Those words helped build up my resolve to follow Jesus, no matter what. That's what many Christians must do when family members refuse to give Jesus a chance. There will be times for all of us when God calls us to walk alone. Circumstances happen and suddenly we look around and wonder what happened, why are we left alone? These moments are God ordained. We must all pass through the testing of the depth of our commitment in following Christ. Though none go with us … will you decide to persevere, or will you cave to the aloneness? You decide.

Today's Prayer

Father God, as we follow in the footsteps of Jesus, at times, we must walk through those lonely places. We never walk alone, though our feelings often tell us differently. Lord, today I pray for those going through the fire of testing. I ask that you strengthen their resolve to follow you no matter what. I pray we all remember that one day when we decided to whole- heartedly follow Jesus, and that there is now no turning back. We set our face toward the cross where we find our identity. We set our hope on your ability to provide comfort when we feel unconnected. In the name of Jesus, our constant companion. Amen.

Today's Scriptures

Deuteronomy 31:8; Matthew 12:46–50; Luke 9:62; Luke 14:25–27

August 20

Today's Thought

We all love authenticity. If you had the money and the chance to snag a genuine Coach bag or a knock off, which would you take? Counterfeits are everywhere, tempting us to compromise on quality and value. I am guilty. There is an area however, that needs to always be real and genuine. It's our personal time and communion with God. If we are getting our spiritual tank filled only on Sunday mornings, we are settling for a spiritual knock off. Don't misunderstand me, I love my pastor and his messages always edify and build up. But if I rely wholly on what he receives from God, and neglect what God wants to give me in my own quiet personal prayer time, I am robbing myself of the one-on-one experience God wants to have with me. No one can give us what only God gives in our personal holy communion with him. I don't know about you, but I don't want to continually feed on someone else's God-time experiences. I want my own time with the One I love; and, I hope you do too.

Today's Prayer

Father God, when you sent Jesus, you did not send a cheap imitation; you sent the real thing. In all of his glory, he is the express image of the Father. When you gave us your Word you did not have to borrow from other writers; you wrote and sent the original masterpiece. You are the God of the authentic. Lord, I pray that we have a heart for making our own memories of personal times with you. That is where you call us by name; it is where you whisper things meant only for our hearts to hear. Lord, may we never compromise on the quality of relationship we can only find in our private time with you. We thank you for pastors, teachers and those who present and represent you so well; but, help us to understand that they cannot give us what only you can, a personal encounter with the living God. In Jesus' name. Amen.

Today's Scriptures

Exodus 33:11a; Matthew 6:6; Mark 1:35; Revelation 3:20

Today's Thought

Do you remember the first time you fell in love? For me it was a feeling like no other. I was sure I would never love anyone but him. Well, life happens and that puppy love soon cooled off and I was onto the next handsome darling. So it goes until we meet that one that we commit to for life. Sadly, even then it does not turn out to be forever after. I once had a bumper sticker that said, *"Jesus is forever."* It was when I met Jesus that I finally discovered a forever love. I walked on cloud nine after I gave my heart to him. As my Christian walk took on all the twists and turns that life brings, my fervor for Jesus cooled. My love for him was as strong as ever, but my expression of that love waned. I found myself caught up in serving him, doing for him, rather than fanning the flame of passion I once had. By his grace and passion, he always drew me back. He lovingly called me back to first love. Jesus himself warns us in Revelation 2:4 that we are prone to forsake our first love. I think we are inclined to slacken in fervency for the Lord. We can so easily begin to do for him rather than just being for him and with him in intimate communion. We need to tell Jesus regularly that he is still our first love. Even when we do not feel the passion, we need to tell him. Our hearts need to be reminded that he is still, and always will be our first love. Why not tell him now.

Today's Prayer

Jesus, you are still our first love. You are our forever darling of heaven. Lord, when our fervor turns to duty, quicken us to fan the flame of desire for you. Help us to continue to abide. Even in the busyness of life I pray we always take the time to just be with you in the garden of love. There is so much of your life you want to share with us. We don't want to miss out on one precious moment. You are the lover of our souls and we need to cleave to you always. In the name of Jesus, our first love. Amen.

Today's Scriptures

Song of Solomon 2:3–4; Zephaniah 3:17; 1 John 4:19; Revelation 2:3–4

Today's Thought

Wherever you are today, the Lord saw you long before you got there. If you are in a difficult place emotionally, he saw it coming. If your issues are health-related, he knows all about it. If your concerns are of a spiritual nature, he's got you. He is God of the past, present and future. He told Israel that he would send his angel ahead to guard them along the way and that he would prepare a place for them. The place you are in right now was long ago arranged for you. God does not lead us into uncharted territory. He goes ahead and scouts out all the dangers, all the trappings and he equips us for whatever lies ahead. He arrives before us and walks our unknown future. Who better than God to lead us into the next great adventure? It makes me think of the pioneers of the Old West who went ahead of the settlers insuring a safe passage. Jesus did that for us when he walked Calvary's hill and tasted death for us. Then he rose from the tomb to ensure eternal life for us. He said he was going ahead of us to prepare a place in his Father's house. Jesus surely will be the forerunner for us now. He carves out our path long before we know the course. He is faithful to be there waiting for you when you walk into those new and strange circumstances.

Today's Prayer

Father God, you are our omnipresent God. You were present in our past; you are present in our daily living; and, you are now present in our future. What peace it gives us to know that nothing will ever take you by surprise. We can rest in the truth that you go ahead of us in every situation. In your love you have prepared for us a glorious future both now and forever. When we face difficulties, we can be sure that you faced them first. We are confident that you will take us by the hand and lead us on. We trust in your Father's heart that never means us harm, but only good. In the name of our Forerunner, Jesus. Amen.

Today's Scriptures

Deuteronomy 31:8; Psalm 139:7–10; Isaiah 45:2; Jeremiah 23:23–24

August 23

Today's Thought

Think about the people in your life who influence you. Are they drawing you closer to the Lord or are they causing you doubt and confusion? Are you being strengthened in your faith, or being weakened in your resolve to be whole-heartedly serving God? Who we hang out with matters? Don't be limited by the opinion of others. Don't be swayed by those who want you to get in on the fun when it goes against God's will for you. Your best friends and confidants should not be unbelievers. The special people in your life should be of the household of faith, sharing the same values you hold dear. We need to befriend those outside the faith; who knows that our influence may lead them to Christ. We are called salt and light on the earth, and we should be. Often though, we need to make a distinction between people who are safe for us and those who are unsafe; between those who build us up and those who bring us down. I challenge you and I challenge myself to examine our closest friendships to see if any adjustments need to be made.

Today's Prayer

Father God, thank you for friendships, especially those that affirm us and help us to be better people. Thank you for godly influences within the body of Christ. Lord, I pray you help us examine our current friendships and how they may be affecting us. If there be any way in which we have moved off-center with relationships that do not draw us to Christ and his lifestyle of love, give us wisdom to make corrections. I pray we are always open to reaching out to those who do not know Jesus; that we are willing to befriend them as we reflect Christ in the way we live. We know that you are not willing that any perish and we want to be a part of building your kingdom on earth. Help us to know who and what to embrace and those whom we need to hold loosely. Lord, grant us balance. In the name of Jesus, the Head over the household of God. Amen.

Today's Scriptures

Proverbs 13:20; Proverbs 22:24–25; 1 Corinthians 15:33; 1 John 1:7

August 24

Today's Thought

One of the most frequently asked question by Christians is, *"Have I committed the unpardonable sin?"* To truly understand any difficult passage, it must be taken in the context in which it was spoken. Jesus went about casting out demons. The scribes of the day, akin to our modern-day lawyers, accused Jesus of being possessed by Beelzebub, another name for Satan. Jesus rebuked them saying, *"How can Satan drive out Satan?"* (Mark 3:23). These men were attributing the work of the Holy Spirit to Satan, thus blaspheming. Jesus said, *"Truly I tell you, people can be forgiven all their sins and every slander they utter, but whoever blasphemes against the Holy Spirit will never be forgiven; they are guilty of an eternal sin"* (Mark 3:28–29). The Holy Spirit is pure and clean and always points to Jesus. It is he who witnesses of Jesus. What hope can there be when one continually rejects the witness of Jesus by the Holy Spirit? There is no other way to the Father except by Jesus. These scribes accused Jesus of being possessed by Satan. They are what the Bible describes as reprobate, which is a mind set against the holiness of God. Questioning if you have committed this sin is clear evidence that you have not, for those who commit it are so hardened in their hearts they do not care that they commit it. Rest assured, dear one, no one can snatch you out of your Father's hand.

Today's Prayer

Father God, we thank you that we have the hope of forgiveness and eternal life in Christ Jesus. Our hearts are yours and nothing can separate us from you and your love. We praise you for a soft heart, one that will never reject Christ or reject the work of your Holy Spirit. When we came to Jesus you sealed our hearts. As we accept the witness of Jesus by the Holy Spirit, we know that we are beyond committing the unpardonable sin. We attribute this totally to your grace and mercy that saved us. Lord, we purpose to never again question our salvation. In Jesus' name. Amen.

Today's Scriptures

Mark 3:22–30; John 10:28–30; Romans 8:38–39; Ephesians 1:13–14

Today's Thought

Someone once said, *"I think God would rather hear us say I trust you, than hear us say I love you."* Loving God is not optional of course. We love him by accepting his Son and our obedience to all Jesus taught. Three times the Lord asked Peter, *"Do you love me?"* (John 21:15–17). Then he placed on him the call to feed his sheep. The truth Jesus was expressing was that all we do for the Lord must be motivated by love. Obedience is born of love. Now let's look at trust. To trust someone there must be a long history of knowing that person in many diverse sets of circumstances. It takes time and experience to trust someone. It takes knowing their very heart and motives behind their actions. This is why it is crucial that we know God in intimate personal communion. We get to know our loved ones by being with them, sharing conversation and opening our hearts to one another. That is what our relationship with God should look like. In that way, we get to not only know him, but we can truly know his heart. When we know the heart of God, we can then believe in his Word and his character. We can trust that his heart is for us and that love is at the core of his motives in orchestrating the events of our lives. Trust God and trust his heart.

Today's Prayer

Father God, your Word tells us that we cannot put our trust in man. Our fallen nature does not always live up to what is promised. Our intentions may be good, but we mostly fall short. Not so with you. We can always trust your Word and who you say you are. We can trust your Father's heart that you always work in our best interest. We may not always understand, but trusting you can give us peace in the midst of any storm. Lord, I pray you deepen our trust level. Take our faith in your goodness to the deepest places of our hearts. I pray that in all circumstances we learn to say, *"I trust you; I trust your heart."* In the name of our trustworthy God. Amen.

Today's Scriptures

Psalm 118:8–9; Proverbs 3:5–6; Isaiah 26:3–4; John 14:1

Today's Thought

She said to me, *"God promised me that she would live, but she died."* This dear woman was speaking of her adult daughter who had recently passed due to a long-term illness. I looked at her and said, *"If it was a promise God made, and she died, then God lied to you. The Word tells us that God cannot lie, so then we must believe that he did not make you that promise."* My words stunned her. Too many trusting Christians are confused about God's promises. Just because we see a promise in scriptures does not mean it is meant for us and our situation. Many of God's promises were made to specific people at specific times for specific purposes. A good example is when the jailer was told that he and his entire household would be saved. We often want to "claim" this for our family. Hopefully your entire household will be saved, and we certainly pray for that, but it does not work that way. However, there are many promises that we can all rely upon. God promises salvation to all who trust in Jesus. He promises wisdom to those who ask for it. He promises to provide a way out of temptation. Jesus promised that he will come back. The key is distinguishing promises from principles. Promises are 100% fulfilled. A principle is a general truth. Proverbs is mostly principles, not blanket promises. These nuggets of wisdom are good to practice, but not guarantees. Let's not put words in God's mouth.

Today's Prayer

Father God, help us to rightly divide and interpret your Word. Help us to discern promises from principles. Lord, I pray we not read something into scripture that is out of context. Help us to avoid the pitfall of believing something that is not meant for us. We thank you for all the precious promises you have given us, those we can rely on 100%. Help us also to practice the principles you give so life will go well for us. In the name of our God who keeps his promises. Amen.

Today's Scriptures

Joshua 23:14; 2 Corinthians 1:18–20; Hebrew 10:23; 2 Peter 1:3–4

Today's Thought

In an old Dennis the Menace cartoon, Dennis and his little friend Joey are leaving Mrs. Wilson's house, their hands full of cookies. Joey says, *"I wonder what we did to deserve this."* Dennis answers, *"Look, Joey. Mrs. Wilson gives us cookies not because we're nice, but because SHE'S nice."* What a glorious picture of the grace and goodness of God. Let's be honest, if God gave us what we deserve, not one of us would be able to stand. But at just the right time, God sent us a Savior, his own Son, Jesus Christ. It is in him that we found our true selves and our true lives. Because of Jesus, we not only are spared eternal separation from God, we are given heaven. What mercy and grace! All of our goodness is like filthy rags compared to his goodness shown to us. We could never earn the free gift of salvation God has so graciously offered. Why do we still try? Just as Joey assumed, we also often think we did something to earn God's favor. Maybe it helps us feel better about all the goodness we receive from him. Mercy and grace are free gifts, never to be earned. If we could earn them, they would no longer be gifts. If we could be good enough, there would be no need for grace. I think we would do well to hold each and every gift up to God and declare, *"Not because I am good, but because you are good."*

Today's Prayer

Father God, how we need and appreciate your goodness. Help us to fight against our human thinking that we somehow can earn your good gifts or that we did something to deserve your mercy. No act of serving you or others can pay the price for our salvation. No act of kindness or goodness could ever buy our way into heaven. Only the blood of Jesus and your goodness makes us worthy. We do good things because of what you already did for us. Our love and service flow from our grateful hearts. What an indescribable gift of mercy and grace you give!

Today's Scriptures

Isaiah 64:6; Romans 5:6–8; Romans 11:5–6; Ephesians 2:4–9

August 28

Today's Thought

America has about 256 embassies scattered across the globe. They represent the US, our President and our governing authorities. The official resident of the embassy is an ambassador. He or she remains in the foreign country and lives in or near the embassy. Ambassadors represent the policies and interests of their home country. They are the President's highest ranking authority abroad and represent him and his governing power. Let's put that into a spiritual context. As citizens of heaven, we are living as foreigners in this world. Paul says that since we have been reconciled to God, he has committed to us the message of reconciliation. Therefore that makes us ambassadors as God makes his appeal to the world through us. Just as the Father sent the Son into the world to be his perfect representation, he sends us into this world to proclaim that there can be reconciliation and peace with God for the one who believes. Are we acting as his ambassadors? Are we representing him and his kingdom accurately? Are we about our King's business in this land where his salvation is so desperately needed? Are we allowing God to make his appeal to a broken world through us? May we be his best ambassadors!

Today's Prayer

Father God, what a privilege and responsibility you have granted us. To represent you well in our corner of the world is indeed an awesome position. Lord, our prayer is that we exemplify you and your kingdom accurately. May we impart your Word truthfully; that we serve all without partiality. I pray our attitude be one of humility. I pray the world sees the One True God through our witness. Lord, help us lift you high so the world may be drawn to you. We are your ambassadors, and we are honored to serve you on earth. In the name of the One who sends us, Amen.

Today's Scriptures

2 Corinthians 5:17–20; Ephesians 5:15–16; 1 Peter 2:11–12; 1 Peter 4:11

Today's Thought

Do you know the difference between conviction and condemnation? Too many of God's children come under condemnation, thinking it is from God. First let's look at what it is. Condemnation is an accusation, scolding or punishment for a bad act. It is damnation; it leaves no room for grace. Condemnation says, *"You are bad, you will never be better, give it up because you are guilty and doomed."* Now let's look at conviction. Conviction is defined as admonishment, convincing of sin, to tell of a fault, reprove or rebuke. In essence, conviction says, *"What you did was wrong. You need to make correction. Let's work on this together."* The Holy Spirit brings conviction; Satan brings condemnation. The key for us is to discern what voice we are hearing. Conviction is firm but gentle; condemnation is cruel and harsh. Conviction brings with it the desire to do better. Condemnation brings with it a sense of hopelessness. God sends conviction out of his love for us; Satan brings condemnation out of his hatred for God. When the Holy Spirit convicts us, we confess, repent and move on in our faith-walk. When Satan condemns us, we become stuck and paralyzed. When we are in Christ Jesus, there is therefore now no condemnation. Praise God!

Today's Prayer

Father God, we thank you for the Holy Spirit who helps us discern right from wrong, sin from obedience. We want to grow up in our faith and you use conviction to keep us moving forward in truth and righteousness. We thank you that we are no longer under condemnation, but we are under grace. This does not give us a license to sin, but it gives us freedom from beating ourselves up when we stumble. Lord, help us to discern your voice from the enemy's voice and even our own human voice. I pray we be most sensitive to Holy Spirit who is our wise counsel and guide as we grow in our faith. In the name of Jesus who is always for us. Amen.

Today's Scripture

John 16:7–11; Romans 8:1–2; 1 Peter 5:8–9; 1 John 1:8–9

Today's Thought

It's a good day when I have no expected commitments. I can sleep in, lounge around in my robe, have a nice leisurely breakfast and do nothing except what pleases me. These days are few and far between, as it should be. God never intended us to be do-nothings. We are called to rest of course but we are also called to be productive. If I made it a habit to spend my days being idle, with no goals or dreams to reach for, what a sad life that would be. On the other hand, if I worked myself ragged and into a frenzy, what good would I be to anyone? Balance is the key. How can God exceed my expectations if I don't have any? God wants us to have dreams, ambitions and expectations. Then he loves to take our aspirations and do exceedingly abundantly above all we ask or think. That's who our gracious God is. He has dreams for us. We need only to seek him and ask him to reveal his heart to us. He says he wants to give us the desires of our heart, but we must first know the desires of his heart. Sometime, he needs to make adjustments so our longings line up with his will. God loves for us to live expectantly, sitting on the edge of our seat in anticipation of that next thing he will lead us into.

Today's Prayer

Father God, help us to live the expectant life. As we wake up every day, I pray we look heavenward for your guidance and counsel. Cause us to balance our times of rest with times of productivity. Lord, you are first and foremost our every expectation. Fill our hearts with your dreams and your will for our lives. Help us to live hopefully knowing that you have exciting pursuits for us. You created us for adventure and we want to live that way. Give us courage to step out of our comfortable places and into the breathtaking places you have prepared for us. In Jesus' name. Amen.

Today's Scriptures

Genesis 2:15; Psalm 62:5; Proverbs 14:23; Colossians 3:23–24

August 31

Today's Thought

There is a small book in the Old Testament written by the prophet Habakkuk. He was deeply troubled by the violence taking place in his day and began to question God. In the midst of famine, disease, pestilence and death, his heart was broken. Sounds a bit like life in America. Today we are going to look at some of his questions, how God responded and how Habakkuk trusted God in those perilous times. He began by asking, *"Oh Lord, how long must I cry for help, but you do not listen?"* (Habakkuk 1:2a). He wondered where God was. He longed for God to act. This is God's reply, *"Look at the nations and watch, and be utterly amazed. For I am going to do something in your day that you would not believe, even if you were told"* (Habakkuk 1:5). God had a plan, and it was amazing. Now listen to Habakkuk's response. The Word says he trembled; his legs gave way beneath him. In humility, he said he would wait on the Lord. Then he declared to God that even if everything in his life fell apart, yet he would rejoice in the Lord. He maintained his belief in God to be sovereign and the Lord of his strength. He knew that his God would lift him above the circumstances. Where are you today? Is there some way in which you need to tell God that "even though," you will trust him in your circumstances? Do you believe he is doing something in your life that will surprise and delight you?

Today's Prayer

Father God, we are to thank you in all circumstances. I pray we learn to echo the prophet's hopeful expectation that even though we do not understand what you are doing, we trust, hope and wait on you. When nothing in our world makes sense, you remain our safe place, our refuge. You are looking for childlike trust in your people. It is in your embrace that we find quietness, confidence and calm. Your love lifts us up on eagle's wings and carries us far above these present troubles.

Today's Scriptures

Psalm 3:3–4; Psalm 46:1–5; Habakkuk 3:17–19; 1 Thessalonians 5:16–18

September 1

Today's Thought

God loves a cheerful giver. We often associated this passage with the giving of finances, and Paul may have well had that in mind as he wrote, but I think we can apply it to all giving. Often it is easier to give our money than give our time. Some would rather give to missions than do a short-term mission trip. That phone call that comes in unexpectedly; and we feel we just don't have the time for it. That winter coat that has hung in the closet for the past three winters and we just can't part with it. That need in the church nursery that we ignore week after week. Well, you get my drift. I am right there with you. We can be so good at excuses and justifications. But God does love a cheerful and generous giver. Paul qualifies this statement by saying, *"Each man should give what he has decided in his heart to give, not reluctantly or under compulsion, for God loves a cheerful giver"* (2 Corinthians 9:7). God leaves the giving up to us. If we cannot truly give cheerfully, what does anyone gain? On the other hand, when we give out of a glad heart, God is pleased because he loves to watch us imitate him in joyful giving. I don't know about you, but I want that kind of jubilant giving cultivated in my heart.

Today's Prayer

Father God, you give lavishly. You provide without reservation and supply not only our daily needs, but you give above and beyond what we ask or think. Never have you ever given grudgingly or resentfully. You do not withhold from us any good thing. Lord, we want to be like that. Teach our hearts the joy of giving. Help us to believe that it is indeed better to give than to receive. When we are presented with a need, may we respond with wisdom through the prompting of the Holy Spirit. You do not call us to give to every request, but may we discern what you are asking of us and I pray we respond out of a joyful heart. That's what you love!

Today's Scriptures

Proverbs 11:24–25; Matthew 6:19–21; Luke 6:38; 2 Corinthians 9:6–7

September 2

Today's Thought

I am learning not to be surprised when sin abounds. After all, sinners are doing what comes naturally. When one is in darkness, darkness is what they do. Before Christ invaded my life, I walked after the inclination of my carnal heart. Sin came instinctively to me. I did not even have to think about it, there was no debate. Ephesians 5:8 confirms my claim, *"For you were once darkness, but now you are light in the Lord. Live as children of the light."* So, why do we often expect the unbeliever to act as if they are in the light? Why do we sit in our little Christian circles and complain about the neighbors, or gossip about our coworker who spends her weekends at the corner bar? Have we forgotten that we were once darkness? Paul has some very good advice on how to relate to our unbelieving loved ones, friends, neighbors and coworkers. *"Be wise in the way you act toward outsiders; make the most of every opportunity. Let your conversation be always full of grace, seasoned with salt, so that you may know how to answer everyone"* (Colossians 4:5–6). God wants us to conduct ourselves with wisdom toward unbelievers. In spite of what we see them do, or how they revile us, we are to remain humble, loving and caring. Jesus was humble even to the cross. He asked the Father to forgive those who crucified him. This is good for us to remember as we interact with unbelievers, remembering that we were once in darkness, but now we are the salt and light in a broken world.

Today's Prayer

Father God, forgive us when we expect those outside the faith to act holy. Lord, I pray we are always gracious to those who do not know you, so that perhaps, by our lifestyle and conversation they may be attracted to you. You say we are the fragrance of Christ to those who are perishing. You call us to be salt and light. Help us, Lord, to be a lifeline to those who are drowning in darkness. In the name of Jesus, the light of the world. Amen.

Today's Scriptures

Mark 2:15–17; Ephesians 2:1–5; Ephesians 5:8; Colossians 4:5–6

Today's Thought

When you don't understand, you can trust God. Why? Because his entire being loves your entire being. Love does no harm. Love does not keep a record of your sins and failings. Everything God has done for us from the cross to the empty tomb is born of his love. The future he has waiting for us on the other side has been promised by his love. God the Father, Jesus the Son, and the Holy Spirit all agree on their deep love for you. Their love is the only perfect love you will ever know on earth. God designed us with a deep need for unconditional love; then, he provided it in himself. What this means for us is that when the storms of life overtake us and threaten to drown and sweep us away, we can look to that perfect love and even though we feel overwhelmed, we can trust in a love so grand. The key is to get that truth into every recess of our being. We do that by hiding his Word in our hearts and allowing it to dwell there richly. It comes through experiences in which we see the Lord come through for us. As we look to all he has done for us, and look at all the future promises, we can be sure of this one thing, Jesus loves me, this I know!

Today's Prayer

Father God, when times are good and when times are hard, we can be confident in your love. We are learning to trust you through our life experiences, one day at a time. The more we know you, the more we understand a love that does not always give us what we want, but always gives us what we need. Even in times of discipline, your motive is always love. The entrance of your Word gives light so that we can understand and believe in your great love. Who else would die for us? Who else could have risen from the grave so we could trust in resurrection? Who would dare give his own Son for the love of sinners? Lord, I pray that each of us would lay hold of the eternal truth of your eternal love. In Jesus' name. Amen.

Today's Scriptures

Zephaniah 3:17; Romans 8:35–39; Ephesians 2:4–5; 1 John 4:9–10

September 4

Today's Thought

Let's think about the concept of "being *in Christ*." This truth is so profound we will never fully understand it this side of heaven. However, there are some realities we can grasp as we study scripture. We are dead to sin and alive to God because we are *in Christ*. We could not ever do that for ourselves. We can stand before God holy and righteous without sin, justified by the blood of Christ. We are not condemned. *In Christ* we are forgiven and redeemed. There is so much more we enjoy because of our position *in Christ* before God. To sum up, our position before God is blameless and secure for all of eternity. On the other hand, when we think about *Christ in us*, we are talking about our position before others, how we conduct ourselves in this world. Because of *Christ in us*, we can reflect his life through our lives. So, being *in Christ* is our position before God; *Christ in us* is our position before others in this world. Praise God for his marvelous plan for our present life in this world and the life to come.

Today's Prayer

Father God, what amazing plans you had for us all along, ever since the Garden of Eden you intended to have a people for yourself. You knew we could never come to you on our own terms, in our own strength or in our own goodness. Thank you that *in Christ* we have been given all we need to stand before the Most High and holy God. You also knew we would need power to live out our lives as representatives of Christ on earth. *Christ in us,* our hope of glory. Lord, I pray we never hesitate to come before your throne, knowing that you now tell us we can come in confidence and boldness because we are *in Christ*. I pray we walk worthy in this world knowing that Christ is in us working his good pleasure on the earth. Our position before you and our position in this life is a miracle of your master design. We give you our deep gratitude in Jesus' name. Amen.

Today's Scriptures

Romans 8:1; 2 Corinthians 5:17; Galatians 2:20; Colossians 1:27

Today's Thought

People will treat you the way you let them. Taking this truth to heart can set you free from the relentless fear of rejection. When we are in captivity to the opinion of others, we will allow them to treat us badly. When we seek our validation from others, ultimately, we set ourselves up for the very rejection we fear. At the root of this fear is the belief that in some way, we are inadequate, so we launch into a campaign to prove our value through the acceptance of others. The more we devalue ourselves the more others will take advantage of our fears. What's the answer to overcoming the fear of rejection? We need look no further than Jesus' life. When he was rejected, he did not respond in a way that encouraged more rejection. He shook the dust off his feet and moved on. He went to those who took notice of him, valued him, listened to him and held him in high esteem. Jesus knew he had his Father's full acceptance and he never needed to fear the rejection of people. Beloved of God, you have always had God's full acceptance and love. He will never reject you and he has assigned the highest value on you. Believe what God says about you, embrace it, and reject the rejection.

Today's Prayer

Father God, you know all about rejection. You know where it comes from and why we tolerate it. Lord, I pray today for each precious one who lives under the fear of rejection. I ask that you begin to reverse those feelings of inadequacy and sense of low worth. Your Word is our starting place. The truth of our value is without question as we search the scriptures. We are precious and honored. Teach us to place boundaries around those relationships that devalue and set us up for rejection. As we look at the life of Jesus, I pray we imitate all the ways he moved pass the rejection and looked solely to his Father for approval. It's in his name I pray. Amen.

Today's Scriptures

Psalm 27:10; Psalm 139:14–18; John 1:10–11; John 15:18–19

September 6

Today's Thought

Engagement rings! Who doesn't love them? Have you experienced the thrill of receiving yours and couldn't wait to show it off? That ring represented a declaration. Someone loved you and wanted to spend the rest of his life with you. That little band represented a pledge and a promise of wonderful things to come. Perhaps an engagement party when loved ones and friends could celebrate with the happy couple. It told of a beautiful future event where each of you would take wedding vows and seal your holy communion before God. There is a forever after that is guaranteed to you and me. When God gave us his Holy Spirit it was like an engagement ring from God. 2 Corinthians 1:21–22 confirms that, *"Now it is God who makes both us and you stand firm in Christ. He anointed us, set his seal of ownership on us, and put his Holy Spirit in our hearts as a deposit, guaranteeing what is to come."* Jesus is our betrothed, we are engaged to him and one day we will be his glorious bride. The indwelling presence of the Holy Spirit, assures us that the marriage will come. His responsibility is to bring us safely to the Bridegroom. There will be a wedding feast and Jesus will take us to be with him forever in the Father's house. Someone loves you and wants you by his side for all eternity.

Today's Prayer

Father God, nothing could ever be added to your plan to make it more perfect. From the beginning of eternity past you desired a bride and a marriage for your beloved Son. You choose us, the least likely to be a pure and spotless bride. In your mercy, you selected us from every nation, tribe and tongue. In spite of our unworthiness, you wanted us. You saved us and placed your seal of promise on us ... your Holy Spirit. We wear him like a beautiful promise of the glory that will be revealed in us. Lord, we do not have words to express our joy and gratitude. We praise you. Amen.

Today's Scriptures

John 14:1–3; 2 Corinthians 1:21–22; 2 Corinthians 11:2; Revelation 19:6–9

September 7

Today's Thought

What do you consider your greatest blessings? Your family, friends, good health, and daily provision surely come to the top of the list. There are two little verses in Romans 4:7–8 that come to mind when I think of my greatest blessings. *"Blessed are they whose transgressions are forgiven; whose sins are covered. Blessed is the one whose sin the Lord will never count against him."* Aside from love, our greatest need is the need for forgiveness. Forgiveness is something we all need along with love. God in his mercy provided both for us in the person of his Son Jesus. If not for forgiveness we would all be walking around under burdens of shame and guilt. When it comes to counting our blessings, we often miss this one, perhaps because we tend to forget how much we need it. No forgiveness, no salvation. No forgiveness, no freedom to live for Christ. As we think about all the many blessings we have received, let's remind ourselves and each other of this incredible gift, thanking God for forgiveness, redemption and reconciliation. The grave is defeated. Heaven awaits. The grave is empty. Forgiveness has been secured.

Today's Prayer

Father God, how merciful you are! When we deserved your wrath, you sent your Son so we could be spared. His death on the cross secured our forgiveness, and oh how we needed it. From your love flows forgiveness. When Jesus took our sins upon himself on the cross, he also took the burden, the guilt and the shame of that sin. Lord, I pray we remember the marvelous gifts we have in your Son. We have freedom because you have assured us that, *"If we confess our sins, you are faithful and just and will forgive us our sin and purify us from all unrighteousness"* (1 John 1:9). We thank you Father, Son and Holy Spirit for every good and perfect gift. In Jesus' name Amen.

Today's Scriptures

Matthew 26:27–28; Ephesians 1:7–8; Hebrews 10:16–18; 1 John 1:9

September 8

Today's Thought

In Psalm 11 David presents this question, *"When the foundations are being destroyed, what can the righteous do?"* (Psalm 11:3). I can ask it another way which is relevant today, *"When the flood of ungodliness overtakes us, what can God's people do?"* We are facing this most distressing truth in our day. In verse 1 David declares, *"In the Lord I take refuge; how then can you say to me, flee like a bird to your mountain"* (Psalm 11:1). There is a truth in his confession that we must take to heart. We are not to turn a blind eye and hide in our church pew. We can run to God for he is our refuge and hiding place. As we hide in him, he instructs us as to our role and purpose in this present age. More than ever, we are to go out with compassion and begin to invite lost sinners to know the Savior. When the earth is being shaken to its very core, we have the stability others need. We have a Rock of Refuge we can introduce to them. We have the answer to their fears and uncertainty. As the foundations are crumbling all around, as the flood of ungodliness swirls around us, the last thing we want to do is turn a Pharisaical back on those outside the church who are drowning in the flood. I encourage each of us to think outside the church; go to them and invite them to experience his saving grace. If each of us does our small part, many can come to know Jesus.

Today's Prayer

Father God, you are preparing a great banquet and you want every person to receive the invitation. You told us to go out into the streets and alleys and invite the least likely: the poor; crippled; blind; and lame. As the foundations crumble we have neighbors who are lost and have no hope. As our world is being shaken, you are more than ever a safe haven for those who believe. Lord, give us the courage and compassion we need to step outside our comfortable circles and reach the lost for you. In the name of the One who is not willing that any should perish. Amen.

Today's Scriptures

Psalm 11:1–3; Proverbs 11:30; Luke 14:15–24; 1 Corinthians 9:22–23

September 9

Today's Thought

This morning, due to a sudden medical issue, I had to cancel a long-anticipated trip. What a disappointment. I had been asking the Lord to direct and guide. He did. Just not in the way I had hoped. When we seek the Lord in any situation, we need to be prepared to surrender to his leading, even when it does not line up with what we want. This is such a valuable lesson to learn. In Psalm 32:8 God assure us with these words, *"I will instruct you and teach you in the way you should go; I will counsel you and watch over you."* God has done that very thing for me so many times. The Palmist goes on to warn, *"Do not be like the horse or the mule which have no understanding"* (Psalm 32:9a). The horse runs ahead while the mule lags behind. Once God has shown us the way to go, we need to then stay in step with him. Our dreams and plans do not always line up with God's. That's a good reason for us to hold our desires loosely. God is never out to harm or hurt us. He always has good intentions toward us. This can be hard to remember when we face roadblocks or detours. I have been learning that my disappointments are often his divine appointments. If we can hold to that outlook, we can discover great joy on the other side of our setbacks.

Today's Prayer

Father God, you always know the plans you have for us, plans to benefit us and not harm us. In your infinite goodness you lead and guide us when we seek you. Lord, I pray that we are open to plans that change so that it is your will being accomplished in our lives. When you graciously reveal your plan, I pray we keep in step with you rather than attempt to force our own way. Your thoughts are so much higher and purer than ours, and you always act in love toward us. Father, your direction and guidance are so dear to us. In it we find that peace we long for. Being in the center of your will is the sweetest place we can be.

Today's Scriptures

Psalm 32:8–9; Isaiah 55:8–9; Jeremiah 29:11; John 10:27

September 10

Today's Thought

When the children of Israel were in the wilderness, they craved meat even though God had given them the food of angels. They cried out to God, complaining about having the same food day after day. God finally gave them the cravings of their heart, but it brought leanness to their souls. They were now physically satisfied, but spiritually empty. They were God's chosen ones, called out to live differently. He miraculously brought them out of Egypt, the pagan nation they loved. They wanted to continue living in the worldly Egyptian fashion they had learned. God wanted to take them to a land flowing with milk and honey. How much we too want what we want! Sadly, after we get what we want we realize it's not as gratifying as we had hoped. We must be careful in what we ask for. If we beg God often enough for what we think we need, he may just let us have it. If what we desire does not line up with God's will, it can be disastrous. We may get what we want but lose what we need. Insisting on having our own way is foolishness. Allowing God to have his way may be the narrow way but it leads to eternal life and the best life we can live here on earth. Let's do our best to follow Jesus on the path he desires and our souls will flourish.

Today's Prayer

Father God, your Word shines a light on our path. When we follow your wisdom, we are safe and our souls prosper in spiritual health. When we go our own way, we bring leanness to our souls. Lord, we do not always know the right way to go. We often confuse your voice with our voice or the voice of others. We sometimes want to revert to our old ways; we want the things the world once offered us. Father, forgive us for the carnal cravings we cling to. Help us to fill our souls with all the good things you pour out upon us each day. In the name of the True Bread from heaven. Amen.

Today's Scriptures

Psalm 92:12–14; Psalm 106:14–15; Ephesians 5:15–17; James 1:17

Today's Thought

Nothing brings out the Lord's jealousy more than when other things take his place in our hearts. God warns us about idolatry more than any other sin. He declares himself to be a jealous God, even going so far as to reveal one of his names as Jealous. When we think of human jealousy it brings images of an angry green-eyed monster. It can then be challenging to think of God's jealousy. This is where we need to understand a love so great that it will not allow anything or anyone to take its place. The Lord jealously guards what is rightfully his. All our love and devotion need to be first to him. When we place him in the highest position, we are safe from the sin of idolatry. When we allow other things to crowd him out, we are setting ourselves up for disaster. God will discipline the child who displaces him with people, places and things that were never meant to satisfy or fulfill. Does he want us to enjoy all things? Absolutely. The Word tells us that he has given us all things to enjoy. The problem arises when we push him to a lower position in our hearts. When we consistently hold him as our dearest, most loved possession, everything else brings great pleasure.

Today's Prayer

Father God, you desire to rule and reign in our hearts and lives. You alone are worthy of that position. Your jealousy over us is a gift that keeps us living in right relationship with you. When other things compete for our hearts, you are swift to correct. Indeed, your name is Jealous. We are yours and you alone have secured our salvation. You are our Kinsman Redeemer and have bought us out of slavery. We have left behind the things of the world that use to control us. We now serve you in the newness of the Spirit. All of us belongs to all of you. May we guard our hearts against any foreign invasion. May we live as your treasured possession. In the name of him who bought us with his own blood. Amen.

Today's Scriptures

Exodus 34:14; Jonah 2:8–9; Galatians 4:8–9; Colossians 3:5–10

September 12

Today's Thought

Today I thought about you and wondered how I could encourage you. I don't know where you are in your journey but I do know that God is in it with you. You never walk alone. This new day brings renewed hope and is full of promise. The Lord watched over you as you slept and carved out a beautiful plan for your day. As you seek him, he will be faithful to let you in on his purposes. He wants that for you; he does not play games. His intentions toward you are always for good. He knows how to bring you out of discouragement. He knows how to heal your ailing body or your broken heart. He will provide all you need today so you can fully live for him. He is great, and greatly to be praised. When we praise and thank him before we see any results, we are exercising a faith that he rewards. Our faith will be continually tested because it is so precious to God. My dear sister in Christ, why not begin to lift up your heart and voice right now in gratitude to a Savior who wants to freely give you all good things. He held nothing back on the cross and even now he will not withhold what you most need today.

Today's Prayer

Father God, I lift up to you this precious one. I thank you that you know exactly where she is and what she needs. Out of your storehouse of love you will provide. From your great throne in heaven, you are able to empathize with all the feelings and emotions of her heart. You are her Great High Priest who wrapped himself in human flesh so she could know that you hear and understand. Help her to know that she is not alone. You have gone before her today and you watch over her every step. I pray that as she seeks you this day, your faithful love will surround her like a shield. I pray that your Word will be a light to her path and a lamp to her every step. Lord, be the glory and lifter of her head. In Jesus' name. Amen.

Today's Scriptures

Psalm 3:1–4; Psalm 84:11–12; Romans 8:31–32; Hebrews 4:14–16

September 13

Today's Thought

How do you spell L- O- V- E? In a culture that has watered down such a beautiful concept there is a need to hit the pause button and think about what love really is and what fills our personal love tank. T- I- M-E. For many, the giving of time spells love. T -R- U- S -T. When we find someone we can trust with our deepest thoughts, desires, hurts and disappointments, that spells love for us. P- R O- V- I- S- I- O- N and P- R- O -T- E -C- T- I- O -N. Meeting our basic needs and calming our fears translate into love for some. G- I- F- T- S. Who doesn't like to receive gifts that are unique to our personality and particular dreams? N- O. Every good parent will in love say N -O to anything that can bring harm to a cherished child. Y- E- S. Oh, what a delight when we ask a loved one for special favor and receive it tenfold. God is the fulfillment of all the many ways we spell L- O- V- E. The gift of his Son sent to redeem our soul from sin's captivity is the greatest expression of love we will ever know. *"Greater love has no one than this, that he lay down his life for his friends"* (John 15:13).

Today's Prayer

Father God, how desperate we are for genuine love. This world is offering us cheap imitations. Its love is erotic, sentimental, impure and unfaithful, leaving our souls empty and unfulfilled. Lord, you are the wellspring of all love. From you emanates the purest and truest love we can ever know. You place the highest value on love and demonstrated it in the person of your Son Jesus. You show your love to us in a hundred million ways, and then some. We see your love in all you created, in your Word and in all you are doing in our world today. Your love is shown to each of us uniquely, as you know our hearts, our desires and dreams. You bring us great joy by the myriad ways you love on us every day. I pray we reveal that same love to those who need to know it. In Jesus' name. Amen.

Today's Scriptures

Isaiah 54:10; John 15:13; Ephesians 2:4–5; 1 John 4:7–10

September 14

Today's Thought

I was nervous as I clutched the dozen red roses in my hand. After 40 years I would be seeing the woman who first shared the gospel with me and led me to Christ. She was my Sunday school teacher when I was 12 years old. I never forgot her. I tracked her down through my aunt and now 40 years later I was sitting in her church. The pastor had graciously given me 10 minutes at the pulpit to honor her. She had no idea I was there or who I was. I shared with the congregation how as a child I was introduced to the Savior and my deep gratitude for the woman who unselfishly gave of herself in that little Sunday school room. Then I called out her name. Of course, she had no idea I had been talking about her. She vaguely remembered me, but that did not matter; I know I will never forget her. Afterwards, several folks in the church told me how they were inspired to go to someone who had influenced their lives and thank them. How about you? Is there someone in your past who would be immensely blessed with a heartfelt "Thank you." Perhaps a neighbor, a teacher, a pastor or an aunt? I encourage you today to think about that and make a plan to do it soon. You will be blessed and so will they.

Today's Prayer

Father God, thank you for the people you bring into our lives who have had a powerful impact on us. They cannot know how our lives were changed by their words or actions unless we tell them. I pray for each of us today that you will stir us to think back over our lives and remember those who influenced us in our spiritual journey. I pray you give us opportunity to somehow communicate with them, even if it has been many years. I thank you that I found Jean and was able to honor her before her church family. Jesus, I thank you for teachers, pastors, neighbors and family members who take the time to minister to children, even as you did.

Today's Scriptures

Leviticus 19:32; Matthew 19:14; Romans 12:10; Romans 13:7

September 15

Today's Thought

As we navigate through the difficult times in which we live, what is God asking of us? We pray to understand the times. But do we take it to the next level and ask the Lord what he would have us to do with the knowledge we have? What we have gained and learned in our spiritual journey is not meant to be horded as hidden treasure. God wants us to share the pearl of great price we have found in him. If ever people need to know truth it is now in this fallen world that is crumbling around us more and more each day. So many are searching for the answers to despair, hopelessness, fear, depression and bondage. We have the answer. His name is Jesus. That may sound quite cliquish, but it is an eternal truth. Jesus was the remedy to the ills of his generation and for every generation after. He calls all who are weary and burdened to come to him for rest and restoration. As we pray to understand the times in which we live let us also ask the Lord what he would have us do with the understanding and knowledge we have. Who needs to hear your story of redemption? Who needs to hear about the answer you have found for our broken world?

Today's Prayer

Father God, when the world in solemn slumber lay, you sent your Son as the answer for a sinful broken world. While we were dead in our sins and trespasses, you revived us and made us alive in Christ Jesus. In the times in which we are living, many are still broken and awaiting someone to bring them the good news that a Savior is born, the answer has come. As we approach in a few months another joyous Christmas season, I pray our own hearts are quickened and revived as we remember who we celebrate. He was the answer to our sin problem and is still the answer for the whole world. Help us to reach our corner of the world with the hope of the world, Jesus Christ. In his name we pray. Amen.

Today's Scriptures

1 Chronicles 12:32; Matthew 11:28–30; Matthew 13:45–46; 2 Corinthians 4:7

September 16

Today's Thought

Our thoughts can take us headlong into a train wreck. Have you heard the expression, *"I lost my train of thought?"* As I camp on that idea, I realize how much truth lies there. A train will take us where it says it will take us. If I get on a train in Ohio that is headed for Florida, I will end up in Florida. So it is with our thoughts. We get on a train of thought and the end result is the destination we imagined. If our thoughts are good, positive, biblical and godly, we will arrive at a place that blesses God, ourselves and others. If our train of thought is negative, ungodly, self-defeating, the end is not good. What we think about most of the time, we become. If we think on God and his Word, our hearts, our attitudes and our actions will reflect his heart and life. When we allow our thoughts to take us down unbiblical roads, we will encounter pitfalls, snares and deception. The ending is a train wreck of sin and disappointment. It is so hard to get back on the right track. Let's think about our thoughts today. Let's pay close attention to where we allow them take us. Let's stop those thoughts in their tracks that are opposed to the knowledge of God. Let's take them captive to the truth of God's Word.

Today's Prayer

Father God, you have given us freedom over our thoughts. We know how unruly they can be. We fantasize, we imagine, we romanticize and contrive things that ought not to be. Lord, help us to be the master over our thoughts. I pray we learn to quickly filter out those thoughts that set us up for disaster. Help us to be aware of the tracks our thoughts are choosing. Help us climb out of the rut of bad thinking. Lord, we desire to think biblically so we can act biblically. We want to become all you created us to be. Today we choose the mind of Christ. Today we choose to use our freedom wisely. In Jesus' name. Amen.

Today's Scriptures

Romans 12:2; 2 Corinthians 10:5; 2 Corinthians 11:3; Philippians 4:8–9

September 17

Today's Thought

When we are flat on our backs, the only way to look is up. I have been there; so low I could hardly breathe. I thought the dark night of my soul would never end. I wondered if God heard me, saw me or cared about my pain. It involved a broken relationship that included betrayal. I went into a depression so deep, I questioned if I wanted to live. I thought my pain was connected to the breakup. At the end of it all, I saw clearly that it was not about the man, it was all about me. For many months my emotions were all over the place. I was being ruled by them. As a child of God, my emotions should have been ruled by the Holy Spirit. That was what I needed to hear, that is what I needed to learn. As I spent that time spiritually on my back, I learned to look up. I looked up scriptures and I looked up to God, begging him to teach me what it was I needed to learn. I learned to turn my human emotions over to the control of the Holy Spirit. As I recovered, I began to see God's plan in it all. He did see, he did hear, he did care. He never took his eyes off of me. The gentle Refiner was relentless in teaching me a lesson I could have learned no other way.

Today's Prayer

Father God, everything you allow in our lives brings a precious lesson with it. You will always be intentional in growing us and maturing us to reflect the character of your Son. Lord, when we find ourselves in a dark, hard, painful place, help us to cry out the words you want to hear, *"Lord, what is it you want to teach me in this?"* We know that in your love and faithfulness, you will not disappoint us. When we are in the lowest valley on our backs, you are there with us. As we look up, you respond gently but firmly. Father, you are never out to hurt us, but you are determined to work out of us those things that do not accurately reflect you. Lord, we trust you even in the darkest of times. In Jesus' name. Amen.

Today's Scriptures

Psalm 23:4; Psalm 46:1–5; Psalm 119:71; Proverbs 18:10

September 18

Today's Thought

After every shower I pick up that little circle-like screen that catches the hair from going down the drain. I am amazed at all the hair that can be lost in one shower session. What mystifies me even more is that every one of those hairs are numbered by God. In Matthew 10, Jesus warns his disciples that persecution would come. When he saw that fear was about to overtake them, he reassured them by reminding them of the tiniest aspects of life; sparrows falling to the ground and the hairs on their head. In the same breath he admonished them not to fear men, but to fear God who has power to destroy both body and soul. What a contrast. Nothing is so great as to be beyond his control. Nothing is too small or insignificant to escape his all-seeing eye. There is never a situation that comes upon us that we should feel abandoned by the Father. He who pre-ordained the number of hairs on our heads continually keeps record. He knows what is around the corner and has made provision. He is involved and concerned over the big issues and the smallest matters we face. There is no situation you will ever face that God is not fully aware of. He observes all things that concern you. Fear not, you have a Father who is intimately involved in every aspect of your life. Next time you scrap those fallen hairs off of your shower drain, thank the One who knows and counts every single one.

Today's Prayer

Father God, thank you that you are current and up-to-date on every aspect of our lives. Nothing shocks you or comes as a surprise. The little sparrow that falls from her perch is in your loving hands. At the same time, you control and run the entire universe. Lord, as you count and record the hairs of our head, so you intimately watch over every move we make. I pray that when fear threatens to overtake us, we will not fear for we are of utmost value to you, Lord. In Jesus' name. Amen.

Today's Scriptures

Psalm 138:8; Psalm 139:17–18; Psalm 147:4–5; Matthew 10:28–31

September 19

Today's Thought

God was totally fed up with Israel's unfaithful shepherds. In Ezekiel 34 the prophet speaks for God in rebuking those who shepherd his people. They are accused of feeding themselves and starving the sheep. They have neglected to care for the weak and have not tended to their injuries. The appointed shepherds had not sought out the lost and rescued them from their enemies. They ruled over the people with force and harshness. The end result was a flock of sheep that were lost and scattered over the face of the earth. Because of their unbridled neglect, God rejected them as shepherds. Then God makes an astounding promise. He tells his people that he himself will shepherd them. He will search them out and rescue them from all the places where they have wandered. He will feed them and provide good pasture for them. He will bind up their wounds and heal them. God keeps his promise and in John 10 Jesus fulfills God's Word as the Good Shepherd who knows his sheep and calls them all by name. He says he will feed his sheep and bind up their wounds. The Good Shepherd will even lay down his life for the sheep.

Today's Prayer

Father God, how we needed a Shepherd who tends according to your heart. We are grateful that you keep all your promises and for providing a Shepherd who truly loves the sheep. The Lord is our Shepherd, we lack no good thing. Jesus seeks and saves the lost, just as you promised. He knows us and calls each of us by name; what an intimate love. We are secure and safe in his arms. The Good Shepherd secures eternal life for us. Father, we pray for those lost sheep who still wander. Many are our loved ones and friends. May the Good Shepherd seek them out and bring them safely into your fold. In the name of the Great Shepherd of the sheep. Amen.

Today's Scriptures

Psalm 23; Ezekiel 34; John 10:1–18; Hebrews 13:20–21

September 20

Today's Thought

Behind every difficult situation is a hidden blessing. I have experienced this truth many times. I recently had a health crisis that was painful and difficult to endure. As I came through and looked back, I saw that the things I learned about my body and better ways to care for it far outweighed the discomfort I experienced. A hidden blessing is exactly that, hidden. Lessons are not always evident; often we need to search them out. For the most part, we resist hard places, preferring to remain comfortable. It's a human tendency that we all face from time-to-time. If we open our heart when difficult trials invade our lives, eventually we will see a silver lining. When I face an uninvited situation, I begin to thank God in advance for all the good that will come from the trial because his Word tells me that," *We know that in all things God works for the good of those who love him, who have been called according to his purpose"* (Romans 8:28). God makes no mistakes and he always has the best intentions toward us. What are you going through right now? Would you be willing to express gratitude to God for the blessing he has in store for you at the end of the trial?

Today's Prayer

Father God, your ways are perfect, and your love for us is pure. You are never out to do us harm. As we look at this truth, we can be sure that every hard place we encounter is for our good and your glory. We thank you for the many lessons we've learned as we've endured the trials of life. When it seems as if no good can come through our circumstances, remind us that you are working it all for our benefit. Open the eyes of our understanding so that we may see your good intentions toward us. Open our spiritual ears to hear what your Spirit desires to speak to us. Most of all, I pray we yield to Christ being more fully formed in us. This is and always will be your highest purpose for us. in In Jesus' name. Amen.

Today's Scriptures

Romans 8:28; 2 Corinthians 4:17–18; Philippians 3:7–8; James 1:2–4

September 21

Today's Thought

Life can be a rear-view mirror or it can be a light at the end of the tunnel. When we gaze too long in the rear-view mirror, we lose perspective of the present. When we fix our sights on the glorious future God has waiting for us, we live and walk in the light of hope and victory. God does not want us panting after bygone days. Today is the good day. Today is to be lived to the fullest. Today God wants to fill your heart with happy memories that will sustain you in future disappointments. Are you continually looking behind you with regrets and "what ifs"? Are you still living as a victim because of past betrayals and hurts? Of course, God wants to heal and restore us. He will use Bible studies, trusted pastors, counselors and friends in bringing restoration. Gazing too long in that rear-view mirror however, will keep us stuck in a place that is not healthy. As we fix our attention on the good things to come, on who God is, on his great love, we live in the light that brings healing and health. There is a time to look over our shoulders, watching the generation coming up behind us. How are we influencing them for Christ? How do they view our walk with Jesus? Do they see us moving ahead with each new day or wallowing in the past? Let's live for them. Let's be intentional in leading the generation coming up into a rock-solid faith.

Today's Prayer

Father God, as we leave behind us the hurts and disappointments of the past, I pray you help us move fully into living for you today. I pray that we look more toward the future than to the past. I pray that we live for the next generation, just as the past generation of godly men and women lived for us. Lord, you are our light both now and at the end of the tunnel of life. You know the hearts of those coming up behind us, and we pray mercy and grace for those who are seeking after you. In Jesus' name. Amen.

Today's Scripture

Psalm 78:5–7; Ecclesiastes 7:10; Isaiah 60:19–20; Philippians 3:12–14

September 22

Today's Thought

I love to daydream about heaven. Our human language is inadequate in describing what we have never seen. Nonetheless, I spend much time trying to fit it all together from the little I see in scripture. The Father has a house and there are rooms being prepared for us. Pain, sorrow and tears will be a thing of the past. It will be full of the light of God and of the Lamb. Scripture talks of pearly gates and a street of gold. Righteousness will dwell there and no one who does harm will gain entrance. Jewels of all kinds and colors sparkle and adorn our forever home. There will be trees laden with lush leaves and fruit. A glorious throne, golden crowns, innumerable angels, colors of flashing light, voices raised in worship and continual praise. The Father, Son and Holy Spirit will be forever present in the midst of it all. A river pure as crystal flows from the throne of God. It's breathtaking just to imagine. The one thing though that will make it heaven for me is the purity, the sinlessness, the holiness that will never be tainted by anything that corrupts or blemishes. That is what I long for more than anything ... being in the presence of a holy God who forbids anything sinful to ever touch us again.

Today's Prayer

Father God, thank you for the hope we have in Christ your Son. He did so much in saving us, and beyond that you have prepared for us a place free of danger, sin and heartache. We know that heaven is our eternal resting place and we will enjoy you forever in a place where only righteousness and holiness dwell. Lord, as we wait to enter this glorious city of God, I pray that we are mindful of living a holy life in the present. We know temptations will be with us here. Help us to be overcomers in every sense. We look toward the day when we are in the city not made with human hands, whose designer and builder is God. In Jesus' name. Amen.

Today's Scriptures

John 14:1–3; 1 Corinthians 2:9–10; Hebrews 11:10; Revelation 21:1–5

September 23

Today's Thought

Your God does not miss a thing. The tiniest sparrow that falls from her nest is in his sight. You have never been overlooked by your heavenly Father. In all your joys and all your sorrows, he has been there. He knows you by name. He hears the thoughts in your head and the cries of your heart. That is such an intimate love, knowing someone inside and out. We do not have to fear that God knows us so well; we should rejoice in it. No one on earth will ever fully know us. Because of that, no one on earth is able to help us and heal us. Sometimes we feel so alone; we can feel forgotten or overlooked. It's in those times that we can comfort ourselves with these words from the prophet Isaiah, *"Can a woman forget her nursing child, that she should have no compassion on the son of her womb? Even these may forget, yet I will not forget you. Behold, I have engraved you on the palms of my hands; your walls are continually before me"*(Isaiah 49:15–16; ESV). God is always mindful of your condition. It can be difficult to wrap our minds around this astonishing truth, but that does not make it any less true. We believe by faith which, in the sight of God, is most precious. Keep in mind today that his eye is on the sparrow and his eye is on you.

Today's Prayer

Father God, we praise you that there is no valley too low, no mountain too high you cannot see us or reach us. We know by your Word of truth that we will never be forgotten or overlooked. Your purposes for us today will be performed. Lead us and guide us into a deeper level of understanding of your all-seeing eye, your all-loving heart and your all- hearing ear. We confess that we are needy and we require 24/7 care. You are the Father God, the only one who can perform that mission. In love we now turn to you in complete trust. In faith we go forth today, knowing we do not go unnoticed. In Jesus' name. Amen.

Today's Scriptures

Psalm 12:8; Psalm 139:1–4; Isaiah 49:15–16; Matthew 6:25–33

September 24

Today's Thought

What is troubling you today? A broken relationship? Finances? Children? Aging parents? Career concerns? Relentless temptation? In this life we will have trouble. But Jesus said, *"I have told you these things, so that in me you may have peace. In this world you will have trouble. But take heart! I have overcome the world"* (John 16:33). We can relax, he has it, he has us. We can go about our day in trust believing that he is in control of every situation we encounter. Right now, he is about the business of putting all things into place for you. If he seems to be slow in acting on your behalf, it is because he is making all the proper arrangements that he may show you favor. Waiting goes against the human tendency that says, *"I want it now."* The only alternative is to run ahead of him, take matters into our own hands; that often puts us back to square one. God is bigger than anything you are facing. He alone has all the answers and solutions to your dilemma. It would be wise to take the position of waiting on God, the one who has the keys, the solutions and resources to work all things together for your good. Trust him today.

Today's Prayer

Father God, you alone can untangle all the knots of my life. All the consequences I am facing from my past choices, all the brokenness others have caused me, every troubling situation I am facing today, you've got it. I choose to wait on your good timing. I choose to trust you with my past, my present and my future. You alone can bring about good in the worst circumstances. Lord, today I will wait quietly and patiently for you to act on my behalf. I will trust you to orchestrate and arrange for deliverance from the perplexities I face. I will rest in your great love for me. Jesus, you hold the answer; and, you are the answer. I look to you, I wait on you, my hope is in you. In Jesus' name. Amen.

Today's Scriptures

Psalm 121:1–4; Psalm 131:1–2; Isaiah 30:18; Romans 8:28

September 25

Today's Thought

One of the greatest blessings that came with my faith in Christ was freedom. It was for freedom that Christ set me free. This freedom is not a license to sin. God's Word leaves no room for that. The freedom I have is to make my choices and then live with the results. As children and then teens, our parents made most of the tough choices for us, or at least led us into the better option. When we became adults, we became responsible for our own choices. Now let's talk about control issues. Just as God gives us freedom of choice, ought we not to do the same for others? How many of us want to control our husbands' choices, our children's choices, our parents' choices, our friends' choices? We tend to think we know better, and sometimes we do, but we must give those we care about the freedom to choose, even the freedom to fail. When we attempt to take control of the choices of the adults in our lives, we are robbing them of their freedom. God never intended for us to operate in this way. From the very beginning God gave Adam and Eve the freedom to obey or disobey. When they disobeyed, they paid a dear price; but, they learned. Isn't it the same with us? God allows our bad choices, then, hopefully we learn to walk in a better way. Yes, I thank God for the freedom to choose.

Today's Prayer

Father God, we are grateful that you did not create us as robots. We have freedom in Christ Jesus. I pray we learn to use our freedom with wisdom and that we give others their freedom to succeed or fail. Lord, release us from the pride that attempts to control and play God in another's life. You alone know your child. You're the one who knows how to teach the lessons that need to be learned through wrong choices and bad decisions. Just as you give us freedom, so we purpose to do the same for others. In Jesus' name. Amen.

Today's Scriptures

Deuteronomy 30:19; Romans 14:1–4; Galatians 5:1; 1 Peter 3:1–2

September 26

Today's Thought

Some words used to define the word "common" are, *regular, ordinary, plain, unsophisticated and routine.* I wonder if the word common should even be a part of our language. Nothing God created is common. Every creation of God is magnificent and beautiful, from the brilliant flashing lights of the outer universe to the tiniest sparrow. Jesus himself told of the little brown bird that is always under the watchful eye of the Father. Do you tend to think of your life as common? Think of the intricacy in which you exist. You are one of a kind, a masterpiece of God. There is absolutely nothing common about you. You have been hand-crafted by a Master Designer. Your life is not routine. Every day is an adventure as you walk hand-in-hand with your Lord. Yes, some days, months and years may seem the same, but beneath it all, God is doing things in and through your life that you cannot see now, but one day will be revealed in heaven. I recently finished a novel where the heroin got a tattoo of a tiny brown sparrow. It was to be a constant reminder that *"His eye is on the sparrow, and I know he watches me."* I have never had a tattoo but if I were to take the leap, it would be of a tiny brown sparrow.

Today's Prayer

Father God, we all need to know that someone is watching out for us. We need to believe that nothing you ever created is common, plain or ordinary. Everything that exists from your hand is intricate, sophisticated and magnificent. Your ever watchful eye never slumbers or sleeps. We can never be lost to you. There is no life on earth that does not matter to you. There is no activity under heaven that is unimportant. Wherever we are in our lives matters to you. Lord, you are a great God and greatly to be praised. We lift our voices and hearts to you today in gratitude for our extraordinary lives and for your watchful eye upon us. All praise to Jesus. Amen.

Today's Scriptures

Luke 12:6–7; Ephesians 2:10; 1 Timothy 4:4; Revelation 4:11

September 27

Today's Thought

"Who are you to judge someone else's servant ..." (Romans 14:4). As I read these words, I had to pause and consider to whom Paul was referring. I came to conclude that his words represented all of us who serve the Lord Jesus Christ. Of course, I was convicted because there are many occasions when I want to evaluate and judge those who do not act as I act, or agree with what I believe. This happens especially in the church. How many times do we judge the sermon, or the style of worship? Perhaps we don't like the selection of music or songs. Judging God's servants is serious business, and God calls it a haughty spirit. The worst of it is when in our hearts we pass judgment and we feel somehow superior. I sure don't want others to judge my decisions or motives. The Lord wants us to all get along, without demanding that we all agree on certain matters. Paul calls it the unity of the Spirit. We can be joined together by the Spirit and still have differences. We can agree to peaceably disagree. God alone is the final judge of his servants and we must leave that in his just hands. Together let's purpose in our hearts to be more aware of judging one another and with God's help we can overcome this haughty attitude.

Today's Prayer

Father God, forgive us our trespasses. Forgive us for indulging in the judgment of others. We do not want to be judged, for you alone know and understand the motives of the heart. To you alone we stand or fall. To you alone we must give account. We are your servants and we serve the Lord Jesus Christ as best we can. Sometimes we make mistakes and others make mistakes as well. May we allow grace to rule in our hearts. When we disagree, I pray we make room for differing opinions. I pray in regard to biblical doctrine that we be in unity, and when correction is needed, it be done with patience and humility. In Jesus' name. Amen.

Today's Scriptures

Matthew 7:1–5; John 17:20–23; Romans 14:1–4; Ephesians 4:1–6

September 28

Today's Thought

I have observed two types of older women. There is the cranky one. She complains to everyone, gossips and is convinced the world should revolve around her. Nothing in her life goes as she thinks it should. Everyone around her has been made aware of how badly life has treated her. Then there is the woman who is growing old with grace. She has many friends because we all like being around her. She is grateful for the smallest blessings. She speaks well of others and defends the underdog. Her world revolves around others and their needs. She is quick to embrace younger women and help them better navigate marriage and parenting. Which would you like to grow into? I want to be a godly gracious older woman. God is still working on that. The latter woman I described did not wake up one day and find herself living the life of the Proverbs 31 woman. No, she grew into a lovely admired woman one good choice at a time. She chose to study God's Word and obey it. She sought out those scriptures that address what a godly woman's behavior should be. She was easily corrected by her mentors. She put the needs of others above her own and only ever spoke well of others. She is not perfect by any means; she knows her weaknesses which is one of her strengths. She guards her mouth, her heart and her actions. She is a blessing in her generation.

Today's Prayer

Father God, you made women to be help mates, not only to our husbands, but to all who need the nurturing touch of care and compassion. When I think of a helper, I am reminded that Jesus introduced the Holy Spirit as the Helper. Lord, I pray that we move through our world as gently and wisely as the Holy Spirit; that we imitate him in character and action. I pray we desire to be the godly women you created us to be. In Jesus' name. Amen.

Today's Scriptures

Proverbs 21:19; Proverbs 31:10–31; Ephesians 5:1; Titus 2:3–5

Today's Thought

I use to cringe when I read 1 Corinthians 7. It's Paul's guidelines for marriage, remarriage and widowhood. I was single, and I wanted to be married. Paul was admonishing me to be content in the life in which God had called me. He qualifies that by telling me that those who marry will have distress, being anxious over worldly matters. Those who remain unmarried will be free to concern themselves with the things of the Lord, serving him unhindered. My desire to be married far outweighed Paul's advice to remain unmarried. Let's sort this out. Paul is not against marriage. We know this because we judge 1 Corinthians 7 with the rest of scripture which applauds marriage as a holy communion instituted and blessed by God. Ultimately Paul recognizes both marriage and singleness as being good. As a married woman of 33 years, I now see 1 Corinthians 7 through older and wiser eyes. Marriage is hard. Just look at the divorce rate. It takes many years of trudging through the tough stuff to get to a place where partners settle into a place of true peace and contentment in marriage. I sometimes think that if I ever face widowhood, I may choose to follow Paul's counsel to remain single and have the freedom to serve my Lord unconstrained.

Today's Prayer

Father God, when you joined Adam together with Eve, you declared their union to be very good. You have given us many examples of singles and widows who were in a place where you used them mightily. You also raised up married men and women whose lives were lived for you, through which you accomplished much good. You bless them all, the married, the single and the widows. Lord, I pray that as each of us face this life-changing decision, we would seriously consider Paul's wisdom and earnestly seek you to show us your will in marriage. In Jesus' name. Amen.

Today's Scriptures

Genesis 2:18; Proverbs 18:22; Mark 10:6–9; 1 Corinthians 7:39–40

September 30

Today's Thought

I had dream. A man called me on the phone and began to pour out all his sorrows and sadness. Nothing in his life was right. I had no idea what I could say to this over-distraught man. As I listened, the Lord spoke into my heart and said, *"Give him hope."* Three simple words; but oh so powerful. If ever our world needs hope infused into its soul it is now. Hope to our spirit is as crucial as oxygen to our lungs. The enemies of hope threaten to do us in: fear; worry; anxiety; even hatred. In a world where hope is a rare commodity, the Lord is calling us to infuse encouragement into the lives of those who feel hopeless. First, however, we ourselves need to be a people of confidence. As we fill our souls with scriptures full of reassurance, we have a reservoir to draw from and extend to others. Are there any ways in which your aspirations have dried up? Hope simply put is *"an expectation of a better future; trusting in good things to come."* Hope is contagious. Let's first fill ourselves with biblical hope, then, help others trust God for those better things to come.

Today's Prayer

Father God, we find our rest and our hope in you alone. Our every expectation is in you. You know the plans you have for each of us, plans to give us a future hope. Your intentions toward us are for peace and courage for our souls. Lord, as we allow your Spirit to fill us to overflowing with confidence, I pray we go forth and allow that fountain of expectation to overflow into the hearts of others. We find all we need within your Word to anchor us in the truth that you are our hope and our confidence. In the name of our Hope and Refuge. Amen.

Today's Scriptures

Psalm 39:7; Psalm 62:5–8; Jeremiah 29:11; Romans 15:4

October 1

Today's Thought

Daniel 7 is a fascinating but challenging chapter. Thrones were put in place and the Ancient of Days took his seat. The court was in session and the books were opened. God brings final judgment. The world's dominions are seized and given to the Son of Man, Christ. To him was given everlasting dominion and glory, so that all nations should serve him. His kingdom shall never pass away and shall never be destroyed. Then a most astounding declaration, *"Then the sovereignty, and power and greatness of the kingdoms under heaven will be handed over to the saints, the people of the Most High"* (Daniel 7:27). The saints of all the ages will be given the kingdom, the everlasting kingdom. Luke confirms this truth in chapter 12 of his gospel, *"Do not be afraid little flock, for your Father has been pleased to give you the kingdom"* (Luke 12:32). The world is full of kingdoms that do not judge righteously, nor do they rule according to God's Word. They will eventually fall; all that will remain is the everlasting kingdom of Christ and his saints. Fear not what is coming upon this world! Our Father's will is supreme and his will prevails!

Today's Prayer

Father God, you are the great Ancient of Days. You keep all the books and you keep perfect accounts. One glorious day the worldly kings and kingdoms will be judged with your righteous judgment. When all the shaking is done, all that will remain is Christ and his everlasting kingdom. As his saints we will rule and reign with him. Lord, I pray we prepare ourselves now for that time when we will judge with Christ according to your Word. I pray we let your Word dwell in us richly as we look forward to governing with Christ. To him will be given all the kingdoms of the world. We look with great joy toward that day.

Today's Scriptures

Daniel 7:9–14; 27 Luke 12:32; Revelation 5:10; Revelation 11:15

October 2

Today's Thought

Saint Augustine said of God, *"Our heart is restless until it rests in you."* What does a restless heart look like? It never feels satisfied. A restless heart wanders from place to place looking for something that will fill it. It is easily agitated and fearful. It's a hungry heart but cannot find food that satisfies. It gropes in the dark for something elusive. It's like a little bird that cannot find a place in which to nest and settle. A wandering heart hates the dark and despises the light. It has nowhere to land. Are you relating in anyway? A heart at rest knows its Maker. It trusts in the One who formed it. A heart at rest is not easily provoked, is not fearful or shallow. A rested heart finds meaning in all things and does not fear man, but fears the God who promises eternal life. It knows it has purpose and longs to bring forth fruit for the kingdom of God. It is an occupied heart, being about the Father's business. It bursts forth with praise and worship for its Creator. Rest fully in the only One who can transform your heart into a heart like his. Be at peace with your God in all things and you will find joy and satisfaction in all of life. Pursue God's heart and you will find your own.

Today's Prayer

Father God, we are truly restless until we find our rest in you. No one will ever know or understand the empty heart as you do. No one can fill those vacant places except the Holy Trinity of God. Together, Father, Son and Holy Spirit work in us a contentment of rest. Jesus, you have invited us to come to you and find rest for our wandering, restless souls. Today we come. Every day we set ourselves apart in a place with you where we can be filled to overflowing with all the goodness you have for us. Lord, I pray for those who do not have a heart at rest. I ask that you bid them come to that quiet place of the heart where you can meet them and fill them with the peace and contentment their hearts craves. In Jesus' name. Amen.

Today's Scriptures

Psalm 4:8; Isaiah 26:3–4; Mark 6:31; 1 Timothy 6:6–8

October 3

Today's Thought

When I visit my brother in Florida, I enjoy the company of his calico cat Jazzy. I use to think she really liked me, until I realized she only likes the kitty snacks I give her. She hangs around me, showing her belly, giving me those sad kitty eyes. As soon as she gets her snack, she's gone. I realized I can sometimes be like that with God. I go to him in desperation and ask him to fix the mess I made. Sometimes I go to him for things I want that are not really needs; and, often he grants my desires. He is a good and generous God, always aware of our longings. Like Jazzy, I am often gone and on my way after I get what I want, rather than remaining in his presence with the sole longing of just wanting to be with him. I have to wonder how often we go to the Lord wanting only to be near him, enjoying his companionship. I wonder if we could make it a consistent practice of going to the Father with no agenda except to know him better. We were created to know God intimately and to enjoy him forever. Let's make that a cry of our heart. The Lord loves when we go to him for help, or provision or healing. We demonstrate our dependence on him, and he rewards our trust. We express our desire to know him and be near him when we go asking for nothing but his glorious presence.

Today's Prayer

Father God, your presence is heaven to us. When we draw near to you, you draw near to us. Spending time with you is never a waste of time. Being with you is the best investment we can ever build into our day. Lord, I pray we are aware of our hidden agendas as we come to you in prayer. Lord, purify the motivations of our hearts. We are grateful that you are willing to hear our pleas and provide our needs so lavishly. Even more so, we are blessed that you want to be with us in sweet fellowship. We pray to know you more in the quiet places where we meet with you. In Jesus' name. Amen.

Today's Scriptures

Jeremiah 9:23–24; Hosea 6:3; John 17:3; James 4:8a

Today's Thought

The greatest gift ever given is forgiveness. The Bethlehem babe became a man and the Savior of the world through his sacrifice. On the cross he took it all for us. God's wrath against our sin was fully satisfied in Jesus' atoning death. Forgiveness has come and we no longer have to live under the guilt and punishment of it. Why is it some struggle with believing that it is finished? I wonder if it may be because of the aftermath that follows our sin. Yes, it's as if we never sinned and God will never hold our sin against us. However, every sin has consequences attached to it. As we work through those effects of sin it can feel as if, maybe, we were not forgiven after all. Our feelings can deceive us, because consequences do not equal unforgiveness. My experience is that in walking out my consequences, God's mercy far outweighs the price I pay as the result of sin. Even as we live with the effects of our sins, God comes to us with the comfort and assurance of his love. He reminds us that His grace is sufficient. As fully as he has forgiven so will he fully uphold us as we work out the devastation and loss caused by sin. His mercy triumphs over judgment.

Today's Prayer

Father God, how merciful you are! We need your mercy today and every day. It is always there waiting for us, with each new dawn. As we confess and repent you fully forgive and we are free to walk in the newness of life. Even in the consequences of our sin, you give us a safe place where we can find peace and hope for the future. One day the ravages of sin will be over and forgotten as we enter into eternal rest with you. Lord, I pray for that one who is now struggling with the after effects of sin. I ask that you hold and comfort her with your promise of unconditional forgiveness and your great mercy over her life. Remind her that Calvary covers it all. In Jesus' name. Amen.

Today's Scriptures

Lamentations 3:19–24; Romans 8:1; Hebrews 8:12; 1 Peter 5:6–7

Today's Thought

Recently I injured my left arm in a fall. Why am I so surprised that I still struggle to do those tasks I did so easily with two hands and arms available to me? I have taken for granted how marvelously God has knitted me together. All my body parts have been designed to work harmoniously, accomplishing the daily tasks required of them. It only takes one minor injury to throw it all out of balance and a major injury can be devastating to the entire body. So it is within the body of Christ. Paul likens the effectiveness of the body of Christ as every joint and ligament being fitly joined together. This is God's way of using us all as we function as one. We are held together by the faith-love we have in Christ Jesus. When even one body part fails to do its job, the whole body suffers. We are called to give more care to those parts that are weaker. I find myself sheltering my left arm so as not to do more harm and give it rest so it can fully heal. Let us show that same compassion with each other as we are all part of the same body. When a brother or sister in Christ is hurting, we who are well need to rush to their sides and help them stand again. When we all do our part, Christ, who is our head is pleased and the kingdom prospers.

Today's Prayer

Father God, in your infinite wisdom you formed a body of believers with Christ as our head. Anything that affects his body comes through him. You designed us to function as one. Just as the parts of our physical body work together in harmony, so you desire us to work together in love. I pray we all recognize our particular function, take our place and do our part. I pray for those who are weaker by nature, faint hearted or battle weary. May those of us who are stronger honor the more fragile parts. I pray we all grown up into maturity in Christ. In Jesus' name. Amen.

Today's Scriptures

Psalm 139:13–14; Romans 12:3–5; 1 Corinthians 12:12–13; Ephesians 4:15–16

October 6

Today's Thought

Have you ever felt an empty disappointment? You know; that feeling of major letdown. You were sure that something or someone would be that "thing" that would fill you. You thought if you could just have it, it would bring lasting gratification. Have you discovered that life just doesn't work that way? Have you wondered why? People, places and good things have their place in our lives, and God has given us all good things to enjoy. The problems arise when we set our hopes and expectations on them, anticipating lasting fulfillment. Every time I buy something new, I am sure I will love it forever. It does not take long for that thing to lose its luster. Last year's amazing favorite dress now hangs on the back rack of my closet as I go out looking for a new one. We have inner expectations that often don't line up with outer reality. Human nature is always searching for that elusive everlasting pleasure. God designed us that way so that we would seek and pursue him as our chief joy. What we need to realize is the cavern in our hearts is meant to be filled only by him. Yes, we have a God-hole in our heart. When we try to cram other things in, we are left emptier than when we began. When we make Jesus our uttermost expectation and joy, we will never be left empty or disappointed.

Today's Prayer

Father God, you created us for yourself. We have spiritual senses that crave to be filled with your presence. Forgive us when we try to satisfy the longings of our hearts with outward trappings that leave us empty. You have given us a world with unlimited pleasures that fill our natural senses. I pray you continue to remind us that these delights are only temporary. Only you can give us the lasting joy we search for. Our inner expectations will be satisfied when they are set on you. We thank you for all things good, but mostly we place our greatest expectation in you.

Today's Scriptures

Psalm 62:5; Matthew 6:33; 1 Timothy 6:17; 1 John 2:15–17

Today's Thought

Is it just my imagination or is the world getting worldlier? Sin abounds and is even proudly applauded by those who practice it. We are not the judge of people's hearts, but we are to recognize that which compromises the Word of God and call sin what it is. Many shake their fists at God and call him old fashion, obsolete and just not with the times. They say his Word is outdated and can't possibly apply to us now as it did when written. Others go so far as to say the Bible is just a book written by men, not divinely inspired. God has not changed his mind about righteousness. Some blame God for all the ills coming upon the world and assert that he is the problem. If Jesus would just keep his judgment on sin to himself, we could all just get on with living any way we wish. As the prophet Isaiah declared, *"So justice is driven back, and righteousness stands at a distance; truth has stumbled in the streets, honesty cannot enter"* (Isaiah 59:14). What a sad state of affairs for Isaiah's time; how much more is it true in our day. In the book of Revelation, as the plagues of destruction are poured out, mankind has the audacity to curse and blame God for all the suffering and problems of the world. Those of us who know our God know differently. We know that Jesus is the answer, not the problem. We are to take this truth and shine it into the darkness. The time is growing short. Let's reach out to those trapped in lies and give them truth in the person of Jesus Christ.

Today's Prayer

Father God, help us to be the witnesses and ambassadors of truth you call us to be. Rather than sit by and pass judgment, I pray we will speak up in love and boldness to those who sit in darkness. The night is far spent; the Day of the Lord is at hand. I pray we put on the armor of light, the righteous life that exposes the deeds of darkness. In Jesus' name, the light of the world. Amen.

Today's Scripture

Isaiah 59:14–15; Romans 13:12; Ephesians 6:10–13; Philippians 2:14–16

October 8

Today's Thought

Have you experienced the thrill of knowing you were at the right place at the right time? This should be common for the follower who is walking close to Jesus and obeying his will. *"My times are in your hands; deliver me from my enemies and from those who pursue me"* (Psalm 31:15). David was up against the ropes of life. In Psalm 31 he cries out to God for relief from the grief and distress of being pursued by relentless adversity. At one point he declares God to be his refuge, and trustingly commits his spirit into the hands of God. Fast forward to where Jesus calls out to his Father, *"Into your hands I commit my spirit, then he breathed his last "*(Luke 23:46). David and Jesus knew their God and that even in the valley of the shadow of death they could trust him. Why? Because they knew that they could trust God in every moment, every day and every year of their lives. In both the time of rejoicing and the time of weeping, they were always in the faithful hand of God. Their destiny lay in the hand of the One who lives outside of time. And still, he enters time to orchestrate all the events of our lives, placing us at the right place at the right time. He is the Alpha and Omega of our days, and he is everything in between. He is the author and finisher, and all your moments are in his hand.

Today's Prayer

Father God, you are the keeper of every moment of our lives. You began a good work in us and you will complete it. You watch over our days to guide our steps into our destiny and your eternal purposes. When we are afraid, we will trust in you. Your steadfast love encompasses us as long as we live. Your hands are trustworthy and gentle, always leading us to the right place at the right time. To you we commit all the days of our lives. We are always safe with you. Have your way, Father God, as you lead us into life eternal. In Jesus' name, the keeper of all our days. Amen.

Today's Scriptures

Job 12:10; Psalm 31:14–15; Luke 23:46; Philippians 1:6

Today's Thought

Jesus was at the right place at the right time when he encountered the woman at the well. No self-respecting Jew would deliberately go through Samaria. Jesus was no ordinary Jew; he was on a mission from his Father. He had a divine appointment with a needy woman at a Samaritan well. From a human standpoint, one would think he was sent there to expose her sin and rebuke her for living an adulterous lifestyle. We really do not know what happened to end all those marriages, but surely the pain of it all made her cynical and distrustful enough not to marry again. Instead she chose to simply live with her current man. Jesus broke straight through her defenses and got right to the root of her problem, the inability to remain in a committed relationship; always looking for the "one" who would stay or be worth staying for. Maybe this one will be the right one? Can you imagine the pain of all those broken vows? Her bucket was empty and Jesus knew she needed water that would finally satisfy her; the living water of One who would never leave her or forsake her. Jesus did not come to her that day with condemnation. He came to offer her a way out. He offered himself, the Messiah, the one she had long been waiting for.

Today's Prayer

Father God, we are grateful that you are not a superficial God. You always go right to the heart of the matter if we are willing to listen. You know all about the things that have bruised and wounded us. You understand the emptiness inside that drives us to make one bad choice after another. Jesus, you are the living water who goes into our inmost being and begins to fill up all those empty places. In this woman's story and Jesus' love for her, we find hope. Thank you that you do not come to us with condemnation, but with the truth that heals us and sets us free. In Jesus' name, our Living Water. Amen.

Today's Scriptures

Isaiah 61:1–3; Luke 19:10; John 4:13–15; Romans 8:1–2

Today's Thought

Life is certainly challenging. Just when we think we have pulled it all together we get slammed with another opportunity to have our faith stretched. With the right attitude during a trial, we can come out with so much more than what we went in with. Spiritual growth does not happen while we are singing on the mountain top. I love being in that place and it is where I can joyfully bless the Lord. Being in the valley of distress is a whole other story. That is the place where I learn to praise him in the dark. When I cannot see him nor feel him, I know I need to go to his Word and cling to his promises. I have discovered through my toughest trials that God is working in me levels of deeper trust. God is always looking for that most important question when we are being stretched, *"What is it I need to learn through this difficult time?"* When I come out on the other side, I can contemplate all the lessons discovered. As we seek his purposes in every trial, we grow in the knowledge of Christ and his ways. The sooner we learn the lesson, the sooner he can bring us out into that wide and spacious place of spiritual maturity. Whatever challenges you are facing right now, remember, you do not walk alone. Jesus promised to send you a Comforter and he is there with you. Life is challenging, but we have the promise of a great Helper and Teacher.

Today's Prayer

Father God, your highest purposes for all of us have to do with learning and growing into the character of Christ. We do not always welcome trials and challenges as friends; but, your intentions toward us are always good, especially when the path is tough and uncertain. Lord, I pray today that whatever we are facing, we will remember that we do not face it alone. You go into those tough places with us, you remain in it with us, and you come out the other end with us. In Jesus' name. Amen.

Today's Scriptures

Psalm 18:19; Proverbs 3:5–6; John 14:25–27; 2 Peter 3:18

October 11

Today's Thought

Who knows your middle name? How many people truly know you? I mean that deep down fully knowing. Who knows what makes you laugh and what makes you cry; what genre of music you like and what causes you to be curious? Who knows about your secret dreams and desires? Who knows your weaknesses and the things with which you struggle? I have a friend like that. She knows more about me than anyone. I can tell her anything and never feel judged. As much as we know each other and feel able to share anything, there are still things that she will never know about me or, that I will know about her. There are things about me that only God can know because the one who created me knows me best. There are things about me that I don't even know. The Word tells us that we are fully known by God. I don't know how you feel about that, but I love being known by the One who knows even the motives and intentions of my heart. Your middle name is not insignificant to God, nor any other infinitesimal detail of who you are and what makes you uniquely you.

Today's Prayer

Father God, we are fully known and fully loved by you. We are blessed to belong to a Father who created us to be known. No detail of our lives is too small or insignificant in your sight. Even those closest to us will never fully know our heart as you do. We know that the day will come when we will fully know you, even as you know us. What a glorious day that will be. We will see you face-to-face and our redemption will be complete and perfect. While we wait, Lord, I pray we lay hold of the truth that we are never ignored, rejected or abandoned by you. You know those who belong to you, and you know how to care for those who come to you. You know us fully and you love us completely. You are acquainted with all our ways. May we seek to know you more and more. In Jesus' name. Amen.

Today's Scriptures

Psalm 139:1–4; John 10:14–15; 1 Corinthians 13:12; 1 Samuel 16:7

October 12

Today's Thought

Oxygen is crucial in sustaining physical life? Without it our bodies could not survive. As important as that may be, how often do we think about our spiritual oxygen? There are elements our spirit needs in order to sustain itself. When folks visit an oxygen bar, they want to infuse their bodies with greater pep and vitality through piped infusions of oxygen. When we engage in spiritual activities and build spiritual disciplines into our daily lives, we are getting massive doses of life for our eternal souls. When we take in God's Word, we are partaking of the bread of heaven, nourishing our spirit lives. When we pray, we are infused with the faith that causes God to move on our behalf. When we fellowship with other believers, we are building up the body of Christ. When we give into God's kingdom, we sow seeds of blessing in our own lives and the lives of others. When we serve one another in love, we better understand the servant heart of God. What is supplying your spiritual oxygen? Our souls will shrivel up without these crucial life-giving disciplines. They are the oxygen that fuels a healthy and balanced Christian lifestyle.

Today's Prayer

Father God, you desire spiritual health for us. You have given us tried and true guidelines to keep us fully alive in Christ. You have provided heavenly bread in your Word and spiritual drink by your Spirit. Just as we need physical sustenance, even more we need spiritual sustenance. You have done your part; you have provided all we need for godly living. Now you call us to do our part by partaking of the crucial elements of spiritual vigor. Lord, I pray we feed on your Word, stay connected to the body of Christ, serve you and others in love, and give of our talents and resources in advancing the kingdom of Jesus Christ. In his name we pray. Amen.

Today's Scriptures

Proverbs 4:20–23; John 6:32–35; Acts 2:42; 2 Peter 1:3

October 13

Today's Thought

Faith pleases God. What is faith? We can look to Hebrews 11 as a reliable definition. In this chapter God shows us clearly what he considers to be the purest faith. He parades men and women before us as examples of what he looks for in his people. Each of them testifies to us that trust in God and his Word can bring us through all circumstances. To understand faith, we need to closely examine verse 1. *"Now faith is the substance of things hoped for, the evidence of things not seen"* (Hebrews 11:1; NKJV). We see that faith must have substance, something tangible and believable. Where do we find that assurance? God's Word is the tangible substance of our faith. When we hide his Word in our hearts, we place the reality of truth there that we can draw on when the going gets tough. God's Word has substance. It is real, it is divinely inspired, it is tangible, it is alive and quickening. Trials are fleeting but God's Word is forever. God's Word will not fail and will not disappoint. It is the truth we cling to, it's the reality of our faith. God's Word is built on the rock-solid foundation of his character. His character and his Word are the assurance of good things to come.

Today's Prayer

Father God, grow our faith as we hide your Word in our hearts. I pray the certainty of your Word dwell in us richly. I pray that we have that living water to draw from when trials hit. When we need a faith that we can stand on, I pray we look to your Word and not our feelings. Our feelings have little substance; they give us no lasting reassurance or hope. Thank you for giving us the shining examples of genuine faith in Hebrews 11. I pray we hold these faithful ones up as models of the faith that you applaud. Lord, we do not want a shallow faith that depends on our emotions. We want a faith that has substance and is available to us in every way and at all times. In Jesus' name. Amen.

Today's Scriptures

Romans 10:17; 2 Corinthians 5:7; Hebrews 4:12; Hebrews 11:1–6

October 14

Today's Thought

We once were dead but now we are alive. Think of that, before we came to Christ, we were spiritually dead in our sins. We had no power to redeem ourselves from our empty way of life. Then the miracle happened, we were quickened and became spiritually alive to the things of God. Jesus called that miracle, "being born again." Another biblical term is regeneration. When our mothers gave us birth, we were physically born into this world. We belonged to the family into which we were born. We became citizens of whatever country into which we were born. Our natural birth alone could never give us access to heaven. God wanted a family so he determined to give us a second birth, one of adoption into his family. We could never do that for ourselves, we were dead in our sinful nature. When we came to faith in Christ, we were made alive and are now citizens of heaven. There will also come a day for each of us when this physical body will die, then we will be resurrected into eternal life. So, God gives us a spiritual resurrection and a physical resurrection. What a gracious God he is. He did not leave us dead in our sins, nor will he leave us dead in the grave. We are children of the resurrection. Praise our great God and Father.

Today's Prayer

Father God, in your love and grace you did for us what we could never do for ourselves. By the quickening of your Spirit, eternal life was breathed into us. While we existed, before Christ we were not spiritually alive. Now, we are alive in Christ Jesus. We have put him on and in him we live and move and have our being. You have made us your children and given us citizenship in heaven, our eternal home. We now look to the resurrection of our mortal bodies which will be made like Jesus' glorious body. We once were lost but now we are found. We once were dead but now we are alive. In Jesus' name. Amen.

Today's Scriptures

John 3:1–6; Act 17:28; Ephesians 2:1–5; Philippians 3:20–21

October 15

Today's Thought

I have always been fascinated with contrasts in the Bible: light and dark; righteousness and evil; wisdom and foolishness. I recently read through the book of Esther and was struck once again by the contrast between the two women in chapters 1 and 2: Queen Vashti and Queen Esther. Queen Vashti was summoned to the king's celebration. She adamantly refused. The king's advisors informed him that if word of her refusal got out within the kingdom, all the women would follow her example and refuse obedience to their husbands. Because of her rebellious behavior she lost favor with the king and his officials. Come onto the stage, Esther. This beautiful and wise Jewish woman found favor with the king and was chosen queen in place of Vashti. It is not recorded in the book of Esther, but I am sure her godly example to the women of the kingdom was one that also pleased the king. That brings me to my point. We as women have powerful influence. Our influence is far reaching and can work for good or work for evil. Whether we are aware or not, we influence every person who comes across our path. Our speech, our manners, our actions affect our surroundings and the people around us. We can use our influence to encourage other women to respect and honor their husbands. How different than the Vashti's of our day. Let's resolve to be like Esther, coloring our world with wisdom, godly behavior and influence.

Today's Prayer

Father God, we are pleased to be women and want to use the influence you grant us for the good of our world. Lord, show us the quality of our influence. Are we pleasing our King? Are we influencing other women toward Christ and godly living? Do we act modestly toward the men in our lives? I pray we think about these things today and have ears to hear what you may be saying to us. In the name of Jesus our King. Amen.

Today's Scriptures

Esther 1:10–18; Esther 2:15–17; Proverbs 31:28–31; Titus 2:3–5

October 16

Today's Thought

The hand of the Lord is upon you. This is a truth repeated throughout scripture. Ezekiel, Ezra, Isaiah, to name a few, declared that the hand of the Lord was upon them. What does it mean to have the hand of the Lord upon you? You have been chosen and called by God for a reason. You were created with purpose on purpose for a purpose. He has placed His hand on you for His will. God's hand represents divine approval. All who are God's children have his hand on their lives. Here are a few scriptural truths in regard to the hand of the Lord. His hand is mighty to save. The hand of the Lord empowers us. The hand of the Lord helps us and delivers us. The good hand of the Lord is on us to prosper us. The hand of the Lord is on us to discipline us and to drive away our enemies. His hand is always on us, regardless of where we are in life. When we stray, his divine hand leads us back to safe pasture. When we are afraid his loving hand comforts us. Do you see the hand of God working in your life today? You can be sure that his hand is there, always upon you for good. Tell him what you need today. We can always be sure that we are chosen and called by God for his purposes and he will guide us into our destiny by the power of his mighty determined hand.

Today's Prayer

Father God, your hand is sure, fixed and determined to guide us in the way you would have us go. What have we to fear? Nothing! Your hand of love is always upon us to save, deliver, comfort and guide. We trust in your Word, not our emotions. When we are up against the ropes, your hand remains. When our lives go well, your hand remains. I pray that with our spirit eyes we would see your hand moving us into our calling and divine purpose. I pray we see that your hand is on us for good, even when it does not feel that way.

Today's Scriptures

Ezra 8:31; Psalm 138:8; Acts 11:21; 1 Peter 5:6–7

Today's Thought

In my years of mentoring young women, I have heard my share of sad stories. *"How did I get here?" "Where did I go wrong?" "How can this be fixed?"* The first thing we did together was go back to see where she had been. I asked about her thoughts, what she had been listening to, what she had been watching, what activities she engaged in, and who was she hanging around with. The point I was trying to make was this, *"You are where you are because of where you have been."* When our thoughts are fearful and negative, we will end up in despair and depression. When we listen to what the culture is saying about world events, we can lose hope in a bright future. When the music we listen to pulls us down rather than draw us to Christ, we end up feeling distant from him. When we let the voice of the world's system define us, we will always fall short. When we visit the dark places of our past, the light in us begins to wane. When we spend our time with people who curse God rather than bless him, we learn their ways. There is only one way to reverse this destructive pattern; create a new path that leads to a better outcome. Reading God's Word, listening to godly music, thinking right thoughts, being with people who encourage and engaging in activities that are appropriate and faith-building will make the difference.

Today's Prayer

Father God, show us any ways in which we are walking on a destructive path. Forgive us and help us to turn this around. I pray we are aware of our thoughts, what we say, what we listen to, where we spend our time and with whom we spend the majority of our time. Lord, we want good outcomes and we understand that we have a responsibility in making that happen. We are grateful that you are willing to help us turn this around. We put our hand in yours as you lead us into the better way. In Jesus' name. Amen.

Today's Scriptures

Psalm 1:1–3; Matthew 15:10–11; Romans 12:2; 1 Corinthians 15:33

October 18

Today's Thoughts …

Who doesn't like honey, or cookies or cake? There's just something about sweet things that appeal to our taste buds. Solomon warns us in Proverbs 27:7 not to eat too much honey lest we get sick. I have experienced that at times, especially around the holidays when all the sugary goodies abound. God loves using things in the natural to teach us spiritual lessons. In scripture, God's Word is often referred to as *"a sweetness."* Psalm 19:10 compares it to the drippings from the honeycomb. Psalm 119:103 tells us that God's Word is sweetness in our mouths. Proverbs 16:24 goes as far as to tell us that his sweet and pleasant words are health to our bones. Ezekiel ate the scroll and said it was as sweet as honey in his mouth. Just as we must be careful not to eat too many sweets lest we get sick, the Word of God's proves to have the opposite effect. The more we partake, the sweeter it gets. The more we dine on God's Word, the more we want. Too many sweets can turn bitter in our stomachs, but God's Word provides the sweetness of wisdom to our souls and nourishes our faith. It fully satisfies. The true mark of Christ in one's life is our attitude toward his Word. God's Word will satisfy you like nothing else on earth.

Today's Prayer

Father God, your Word became flesh and dwelt among us. Jesus, the Word, came to bring satisfaction to our hungry souls. We can so easily relate to your Word being like honey, sweet and sustaining. We love the sweetness of your presence and the sweet communion we share with you. I pray we not neglect reading and obeying your Word. It is spiritual honey to our souls, supplying wisdom and insight as we apply it to every aspect of our lives. As we partake of your Word daily, may we take on the sweetness of Christ and offer the delight of him to those around us. In Jesus' name. Amen.

Today's Scriptures

Psalm 19:7–11; Psalm 119:103; Proverbs 24:13–14; Ezekiel 3:13

Today's Thought

Today I read through the book of Titus. Paul was writing to his true child in the common faith. The greeting alone gives me a beautiful picture of Paul's love for this young man. Paul is encouraging Titus to appoint elders in Crete and is giving him clear guidelines as to what to look for in men and women who will be in positions of influence. As I read it dawned on me that the qualities Paul is expounding on are those that we should all exhibit in our faith-walk. Let's look at a few. One should be above reproach, not arrogant or quick tempered. Not greedy or given to much wine. A true child of God should not be argumentative or controversial. Now let's look at the characteristics of one who is pleasing to God. She should be hospitable, a lover of good, self-controlled, upright, holy and disciplined. She must hold to sound doctrine and able to teach what is good. She must be reverent in behavior and encourage younger women to love their husbands and children. We are to be models of good works showing integrity in all things. This little book is truly a Christian's guide to godly behavior. I love that Paul also gives us the long-range benefits of living according to God's standards. He tells us that when we live this way our opponents will be put to shame, having nothing evil to say against us. He then says that when we live this way, we adorn the doctrine of God our Savior. What a beautiful picture, adorning the gospel of Christ!

Today's Prayer

Father God, as we read this precious book today, I pray we take to heart all that Paul has to say to us. I pray we purpose to live the lifestyle that you require of us no matter our position in the body of Christ. We may not be an elder or an elder's wife, but you call each of us to adorn the gospel of Christ and in this way, we avoid reproach from those inside and outside the faith. Lord, help us to live holy lives. In Jesus' name. Amen.

Today's Scripture

Matthew 5:14–16; Colossians 3:17; Titus 2:1–8; Hebrews 13:7

October 20

Today's Thought

David and Jonathan. Ruth and Naomi. Paul and Timothy. Jesus and Lazarus. What comes to your mind? I think of friendship, very special friendship. These men and women of the Bible did not have to go it alone. They were faithful companions on life's journey. They shared each other's joys and sorrows. They had intimate knowledge of each other's struggles. They were vulnerable and transparent in their relationships. They were great encouragers to their friends. They were fellow companions in advancing God's work in the world. They were there to remind each other of the faithfulness and goodness of God. What a blessing! Indeed, it is one of God's greatest gifts. Is there someone who is walking with you through life as a sacred companion? I hope you have been granted that priceless gift. If that is what you are praying for, I pray that with you and for you.

Today's Prayer

Father God, those of us who have been given the gift of a special friendship thank you deeply. We know our friendships have been divinely appointed. Thank you for the ones who encourage us and walk through every season of life with us. Lord, I pray for those who have not yet encountered relationships that fill that deep need. I pray Jesus, that by your Spirit you would arrange those divine appointments, bringing the right people together at the right time for your glory and your purposes. You know how much we need encouragers in our lives … ones who will walk with us until the end … ones who will be faithful companions now, and with whom we will share eternity. Lord, it was said that you loved Lazarus. The people recognized this special friendship and declared, *"See how he loved him."* You wept over his death. Lord, we all are in need of that kind of love from another human. Thank you that you recognize this and you are more than able to provide. In Jesus' name. Amen.

Today's Scriptures

1 Samuel 18:1–4; Ruth 1:16–17; John 11:32–36; 2 Timothy 1:1–4

October 21

Today's Thought

Why is it we feel we have the right to understand life and its circumstances? God has given us much truth in his Word that helps us sort things out and come to reasonable conclusions. But what about those things that just make no sense: the death of a child; loss of health; betrayal of a loved one; those unexpected turns of events that rock our world? When we search the Word, we find no answers that adequately explain how God is working. Friends and family are not able to offer comfortable answers. It just seems as if there is no reasonable explanation for sudden tragedy, loss and upheaval. There are always going to be times in our lives when we simply have to give up our perceived right to understand. It is in these times when we have no other recourse but to run to the Father and let him hold us while the storms rage. It is during these times when we come to know God in deeper ways, learn to trust him and allow him to change us. We are so limited in our perspective, so short- sighted in our viewpoint. Trust in the revealed God of the Bible is what we have to cling to during those times that make no sense.

Today's Prayer

Father God, When the storms of life rage, help me to remember all the times pasts when you have been with me and carried me through. Remind me of your faithfulness and goodness. I cannot do life on my own. I need you every moment. I need your strength and courage in the eye of the storm. Uphold me now, precious Lord. God, grant me the eternal perspective in my sorrows. You truly are a refuge to whom I can run in times of confusion and grief. You are my anchor as the earth shifts beneath me. You are the rock that is higher than all my circumstances. When I do not understand life, I can trust that you are in every situation with me, and you will never walk out on me. In Jesus' name. Amen.

Today's Scriptures

Psalm 61:1–2; Isaiah 26:3–4; Romans 11:33–36; 1 Peter 1:6–7

October 22

Today's Thought

When I think about some of the scariest moments in my life, I always go back to that sudden unexpected snow storm the day before Thanksgiving. I had to travel one and a half hours to pick up my blind and mentally- challenged brother so he could be with us for the holiday. He and I were on our way back home, travelling on a back country road when a blinding snow storm hit and I had all I could do to keep us safely on the road. It was an unfamiliar area with a low ditch on the side of the road. If there were any other vehicles around me, I could not see them. Just when I thought it couldn't get worse, the rubber attachment on the driver's side of my windshield wiper flew off. The ice and snow began to accumulate and now I was truly blinded. My brother was oblivious to our peril, but God was not. God is never blinded to our needs. He is never mentally-challenged in giving us guidance. As I began to urgently call on him, I felt a peace come over me that was unexplainable. I continued driving slowly, praying and depending on the Lord to bring us through this unexpected squall. After a while, the snow began to let up and I was again able to see. With the Lord's guiding hand, we made it home safely and celebrated a wonderful Thanksgiving together.

Today's Prayer

Father God, when we cannot see what lies ahead of us, or cannot understand the storm raging around us, you see us. When we call upon you for help, you rush to meet us. We are never alone and we are never without your presence, no matter how challenging the situation. Lord, you promise us peace in the midst of trouble, I pray we remember that when the storm rages around us. Holy Spirit, remind us to praise God when we find ourselves in a dark place. Lord, you will light up our paths and you will be a sure anchor for our souls at all times. In Jesus' name. Amen.

Today's Scriptures

Psalm 91:1–2; Isaiah 43:1–3; Isaiah 54:10; John 14:27

Today's Thought

Have you ever wondered why some women you know seem to soar spiritually while others lag behind and never seem to reach those higher places? I have an idea of what the problem may be: lack of consistency. The one who daily applies the spiritual disciplines will keep moving ahead in a steady pattern of growth. Just as we need to nourish our bodies daily with good food, our soul needs a daily dose of the sustenance of God's Word. If I devour 10 chapters one day but fail to dive in for the next week or two, I will not thrive. If I isolate myself from fellowship for long periods of time, my spirit will begin to shrivel. When I neglect time in prayer with my Lord I will begin to feel the distance in my soul. Consistency is the key to spiritual success. What is true in the natural realm is even more in the spirit realm. When I neglect my natural daily disciplines, my whole life suffers. The same is true in my spiritual life. We cannot afford to be inconsistent in matters of spiritual growth. If we are not moving ahead, we are sliding backwards. Let's take inventory today to determine where our priorities lie. I want to keep moving ahead, climbing higher and growing closer to the Lord every day. How about you?

Today's Prayer

Father God, you have provided everything we need for godly living. Our responsibility is to apply those good and necessary disciplines daily to our lives. Lord, we want to grow up spiritually and we know you want that too, just as any good parent would. Help us to be consistent and unswerving in those most crucial habits. Give us a heart for growth. Help us to find stability by following the guidelines you give us in your Word. Where we lack, I pray you fill those spaces with the power of your Spirit to make the necessary changes. Lord, empower us to desire more consistency. In Jesus' name. Amen.

Today's Scriptures

Proverbs 4:20–23; 1 Corinthians 9:24–27; 1 Timothy 4:8; 2 Timothy 2:15

October 24

Today's Thought

Remember the bumper sticker, *"God is my co-pilot?"* I use to love that until the Holy Spirit set me straight. If God is not in the driver's seat, I will crash. God will have nothing to do with being in second place. When I rely on God only after I put forth my own efforts, it usually does not end well. Why is it we come running to God after we have led ourselves into a mess? We think we know what we want and what is good for us, only to discover that we have a huge problem. How would it look if we had avoided the predicament in the first place? God claims first place, the driver's seat, the pilot's chair at all times. We are so limited when it comes to making those crucial life decisions. Only God sees far enough up the road to know what is best for us. What I so love about him is that even after I have stubbornly dived headlong into having my own way, God is always faithful to lead me out and set my path straight again. It is the goodness of God that helps us navigate through these sticky situations and land safely back into his will. Are you ready to let go of the reins and allow God to be the captain of your life and your destiny?

Today's Prayer

Father God, you know the plans you have for us; they are good plans. Forgive us for thinking we know best when we are so limited in knowing what the future holds. You are God of the future, and you always know what's best for us at any given time. Help us to seek you first, to give you your rightful place in our daily choices and decisions. Lord, keep us from the folly of believing we can steer our own ship. By faith we place you above all our desires and we acknowledge that we should not make moves without your guidance. Thank you for all the times you rescued us from the messes we made due to our foolish pride. We now relinquish our self-reliance and surrender our future plans to you. In Jesus' name. Amen.

Today's Scriptures

Psalm 25:4–5; Psalm 32:8; Psalm 37:23–24; Proverbs 3:5–6

October 25

Today's Thought

The second epistle of Peter is a sobering little book. In it he glorifies God, confirms our calling, warns us of false prophets and teachers and tells us what to expect when God brings down all the evildoers. Some of the pictures he paints are quite frightening. As I read through this book, I see clearly that we are living under the same ungodliness that righteous Lot endured in his day. At one point Peter describes Lot as being greatly distressed by the sensual conduct of the wicked and that his righteous soul was daily tormented over their lawless deeds. I cannot imagine all this man had to bear up under living in wicked Sodom. You can read the account of what I assume to be the worst events of Lot's life in Genesis 19:1–29. We are now living in our own Sodom and Gomorrah. I don't know about you but I am disturbed in my soul every day as I see America sinking lower and lower into depravity. Peter makes it very clear that the day of the Lord will come like a thief and that all the works done on the earth will be exposed. I am so glad Peter did not leave us on that ominous note. In his final words he encourages us to be diligent, patient and remain stable in times of shaking. God is our refuge and an ever-present help in trouble.

Today's Prayer

Father God, in these troublesome times, we are told by your Holy Spirit through Peter to continually grow in the grace and knowledge of our Lord and Savior Jesus Christ. We have peace and hope with him through our personal relationship with him through his Word. As we know him more and walk in his ways, we escape being carried away with the lies of lawless people. Lord, we know there is a great deception overtaking the ones who refuse to know the truth. Help us to remember our mission. As men and women are drowning in a sea of deception, I pray we reach out to them in urgency, with the lifesaving gospel of salvation. In Jesus' name. Amen.

Today's Scriptures

Matthew 24:1–14; Mark 16:15–16; 2 Timothy 3:1–9; 2 Peter 3:10–14

October 26

Today's Thought

Yesterday God gave us insight into Peter's second epistle. My hope was to leave you with a godly urgency to be alert toward the times in which we live, but also to leave you with great encouragement. Today I want to solely focus in on the last two verses of 2 Peter 3:17–18. Peter sums up his writing with two important thoughts. First of all, he wants to remind us that because we have been warned about the coming destruction of evildoers, we are to take care that we do not get carried away by the error they promote. Peter exhorts us to cling to our stability in Christ during these turbulent times. Then he tells us how to maintain that spiritual steadfastness. We are to continually grow in knowing Christ. We do that by reading His Word and being obedient to all that Jesus taught. And, we are to grow in the grace of our Lord and Savior Jesus Christ. What does that mean? God's grace is our escape route from present and future dangers. When we receive God's grace we can live courageously in the midst of a perverse and evil culture. Apart from God's grace we cannot maintain an eternal perspective. Apart from God's grace we lose our stability in a world of chaos that is being shaken to its very core. As we grow in our knowledge of Christ and live in his grace, we are able to stand firm and unmovable in these treacherous times.

Today's Prayer

Father God, your Word contains all we need in order to navigate troubled waters. Your promises of sufficient grace provide us with strength and wisdom for all situations. As we search the scriptures, I pray we begin to understand your plans and purposes for the times in which we live. Lord, help each of us to discern how you would have us respond to the events taking place in our lifetime. We were born into your kingdom for this time and purpose. I pray we continually grow in the knowledge and grace of our Lord and Savior Jesus Christ. In his name we pray. Amen.

Today's Scriptures

Esther 4:14; Daniel 2:21–22; 2 Corinthians 12:9–10; 2 Peter 3:17–18

October 27

Today's Thought

As I was praying for an unsaved loved one today, I found myself asking the Lord to show her that she is indeed a sinner. That surprised me because that is not my usual prayer for the unsaved. I then realized that until we are convicted of how great a sinner we are, we will never understand our great need for a Savior. Why is it so hard to see ourselves as sinners? We like to think we are okay because after all, we are good people. Many believe salvation is for those who sin themselves into a pit of addiction and depravity. The Bible teaches that all have sinned and come short of the glory of God. We are born sinners, having inherited Adam's fallen DNA. Human pride is the culprit. Pride tells us that the other guy is the one in need of being saved, but we fail to look into our own neediness. Pride tells us that we are self-sufficient and well able to do life on our own. Pride is the greatest stumbling block to salvation. Until one understands the gospel of Jesus Christ, that it was for his or her sins for which he suffered and died, there is no other way to eternal life. I am a great sinner; Jesus Christ is a great Savior.

Today's Prayer

Father God, as we pray for the unbelievers we know and love, we pray your Holy Spirit deeply convicts them of their desperate condition as sinners. Until that reality is confronted, they are without hope. Lord, how you rush to rescue the one who knows his or her great need for repentance and forgiveness. Your mission was to seek and save the lost. We now live in the age of grace and redemption and you are not willing that any should perish but that all be saved through repentance. We lift up our unsaved loved ones and together we ask that by your Spirit you bring the needed awareness for salvation through repentance of sin and acceptance of the blessed salvation you have provided through your Son Jesus. Amen.

Today's Scriptures

Luke 19:9–10; Romans 3:23–24; Romans 5:8; Ephesians 1:7

October 28

Today's Thought

Have you ever built a sand castle at the ocean's shore? I love watching the children with their little plastic buckets forming their own personal palaces of sand. They place their little flags on top and claim their positions as kings or queens. It sort of reminds me of the castles we build on the shores of our lives. We gather together all the things that make us happy and give us security. Homes, careers, bank accounts, travel and all the possessions that fill up our pleasure buckets. These are all good things and God does not condemn us for desiring them. The problem comes when we fail to realize that they are only castles in the sand. Just as the children's castles are soon washed away by the waves of the ocean, even so our earthly accumulations will be washed away by the waves of time. All the work and effort we put into accumulation, and bam, it's no longer ours because after we are gone, someone else gets it all. We build things here on earth thinking it will last forever. Time and death will steal away all the treasures we store up on earth. There is however something that will outlast misfortune, time and death … relationships. All we can take into eternity with us are the believing friends and family we love and enjoy on earth. Today, let's purpose to build our castles in the heavenlies where they will never fade or be washed away.

Today's Prayer

Father God, you make it very clear that we are to lay up our dearest treasures in heaven. As we build our earthly relationships, I pray we handle them as if they are going right into heaven with us. Help us to build wisely, lovingly, fervently and generously. Remind us continually that we are only here for a short time and everything we do matters. I pray we hold life dear and as something fragile and fleeting. Lord, help us to understand your priorities and to make them ours. In Jesus' name. Amen.

Today's Scriptures

Matthew 6:19–21; Matthew 7:24–27; 2 Corinthians 5:1; Hebrews 11:13–16

Today's Thought

Is what you are watching and listening to producing faith or fear in your life? It really matters. The world and its systems desire to fill us with fear of the present and of the future. Pandemics, wars, terrorism, political upheaval, violence, racism, financial ruin; you name it, all those things are inclined to fill us with fear. The evening news leaves us with little hope for the future of our children and grandchildren. On the contrary, if we are listening to God's voice through his Word, we will be left with a deeper faith and an enduring hope. Too many Christians have given into fear and one of the consequences of fear is a wavering faith. As we allow the voice of the world system to influence our thinking and our emotions, fear and the loss of peace will always be the end result. God's truth produces life, peace and hope in our hearts. I encourage you to rejoice. Jesus has overcome all things in heaven and on earth.

Today's Prayer

Father God, we are living in treacherous times. There are so many dangers surrounding us and our loved ones. Your Word warns us that in these last days there would be challenging events overtaking the world. Your Word gives us direction in navigating the times. You are very clear in exhorting us to be a people of faith and hope. We need not live in fear of the things coming on the earth. You are our ever-present help and a sure refuge in times of trouble. Lord, when unexpected events come upon us, I pray we not panic as the world does. We know we have a Father who cares daily for us and watches over us with an all-seeing eye. I ask that we be a comfort and source of hope to those around us who feel they are drowning in worry and stress. I pray we not forsake the gathering of ourselves together so that we may bring great hope and encouragement to one another. In the name of Jesus, the hope of the world. Amen.

Today's Scriptures

Psalm 46:1–5; Luke 21:25–28; Hebrews 10:24–25; 1 John 2:15–17

Today's Thought

One of my favorite artist's renderings of Jesus is the Shepherd with the sheep grazing around his feet. He is lovingly holding a little lamb in his arms. I often wonder about that little lamb. Did something frighten him? Was he injured or ill? Did he lose his way for a season and now he is found? Did he simply need some special attention from his shepherd? One thing we can know for sure is that the shepherd loves the lamb and the lamb trusts his shepherd. Imagine that you are the little lamb in the arms of the Shepherd. He knows your needs today. He knows the circumstances and the emotions you are experiencing. He knows you intimately. His arms are always ready to hold and comfort you if you trust him enough to let him pick you up and carry you. Think about that picture again. What do you need today? You are the little lamb in the Shepherd's arms.

Today's Prayer

Father God, in scripture, you have lovingly given us the picture of the Good Shepherd who loves his sheep. Jesus willingly laid down his life for us. He knows us and calls us by name. When we are lost, he finds us. When we are injured or sick, he nurses us. He warns us of dangers and guides us to safe pasture. When we are too weary to go on, he picks us up and carries us. We are grateful that we have a Shepherd who sees to all of our needs. When we walk through the valley of the shadow of death, he is with us. He restores us and refreshes us. Even his discipline is done with great love and care for our souls. Our Shepherd was first a lamb himself … a spotless and sinless lamb. Who better to understand the sheep? Who else could ever be a Savior Shepherd? Lord, I pray over your little lambs today. On behalf of those who are weary and feel unable to carry on, I ask that you scoop them up in your strong arms today and carry them close to your heart. In the name of Jesus, our Shepherd. Amen.

Today's Scriptures

Isaiah 40:11; John 10:11; Hebrews 13:20–21; 1 Peter 2:24–25

Today's Thought

One of the most read passages of the Bible is Jesus' Sermon on the Mount; we know it as the Beatitudes. For the next several days we will look at the blessings about which Jesus taught. These powerful words are relevant for every age and apply in every generation. We find this sermon in Matthew 5:1–12. It helps me to think of the Beatitudes as "Beautiful Attitudes." Each verse is introduced with the words, *"blessed are those."* The word blessed in this context involves the favor upon one with whom God is pleased. Our culture often diminishes the word "blessing" by watering it down and using it frivolously. God takes his promised blessings seriously and does not pronounce them flippantly. So, as we study the nine blessings of Jesus, let us come to these passages with the seriousness they deserve. Keep in mind that with each pronouncement, Jesus is turning the cultural mindset of the day upside down. In a society of proud macho men and vain competitive women, he comes along offering a more blessed way to live. Even today, in the church of Jesus Christ, these nine blessing can be stunning to our way of thinking. Our own cultural mindset may need to be dismantled if we desire the true blessings of God.

Today's Prayer

Father God, as we dive into the nine blessings in Matthew 5, we pray for illumination and a greater understanding of Jesus' heart as he walked up that mountain to teach. Lord, we want all the blessings you have for us. We want to live the life you call us to live, even when it calls us to give up our pride and self-protections. Holy Spirit of God, come alongside us to help us lay hold of the treasure we have in these verses. Help us to study with a heart that desires to obey what our Lord teaches. We know he has our best interest in mind and we know he guides us out of his love for us. In Jesus' name. Amen.

Today's Scriptures

Matthew 5:1–2; Romans 12:1–2; 2 Corinthians 5:17; Ephesians 4:1–2

November 1

Today's Thought

"Blessed are the poor in spirit, for theirs is the kingdom of heaven" (Matthew 5:3). This is a concept we don't hear much about in our get-rich-quick culture. But Jesus was not talking about financial poverty in this passage. He refers to a spiritual poverty. The closest I can come to understanding spiritual poverty is from my own personal experience. I had to come to the place in my life where I realized I had nothing of worth to offer God. I know there is nothing I can do to secure eternal life for myself or pick myself up by my own boot straps and make myself right before God. Without God involved in the saving and prospering of my soul, I am spiritually bankrupt. Our soul needs God every moment, every day and in every way. When we know this at the very core of our being, we are poor in spirit and ready for the kingdom of heaven. You see, heaven is being prepared for those who truly understand that there is nothing they can do to earn the blessing of eternal life with Christ. The proud, arrogant and self-sufficient will never enter the kingdom of heaven. Only the poor in spirit receive that blessing.

Today's Prayer

Father God, we long to be poor in spirit because we long for the blessing of inheriting the kingdom of heaven. No matter how appealing, we know we will never be satisfied with what the world has to offer. We are desperate for you and continually desire more of you. We long for heaven, our eternal home, knowing that no home on earth will ever fully satisfy. We confess our spiritual hunger and dependence on your Holy Spirit to fill us. Lord, show us what it means to each of us personally to be poor in spirit. Open our eyes when we attempt to be self-reliant, independent, spiritually proud and self-righteous. We desire the blessing of the kingdom of heaven, both now and in the life to come. Bring us to the childlike humility that pleases you. In Jesus' name. Amen.

Today's Scriptures

Matthew 5:3; Matthew 18:1–3; Luke 1:46–53; Luke 18:9–14

November 2

Today's Thought

"Blessed are those who mourn, for they will be comforted" (Matthew 5:4). This beatitude contains several spiritual truths. God reveals to us that when we grieve over a great loss, he will surely comfort us. I think however that Jesus' words in Matthew 5:4 also refer to a deep conviction of the Holy Spirit over our sin. When we realize how much our sin offends a holy God, there should be a heartfelt sorrow and repentance. When we respond to our sin in this way, God will not only forgive us, but he will come alongside of us and comfort us with hope. He assures us that he is at work in every area of our lives, ready to deliver and restore. It is fitting that mourning over our sin follows being poor in spirit. Once again, a spirit of humility is required. Another aspect of mourning is in regard to the sin of the world. God calls us to intercede on behalf of our family, city, nation and the whole world. As we do this, an overwhelming sense of grief and mourning will overtake us as we think about the judgment coming upon the earth. As we cry out on behalf of mankind, God joins us and pulls us in close with the comfort only he can give.

Today's Prayer

Father God, we know that Jesus was a man of sorrows, acquainted with grief. Jesus never sinned, but he is well able to comfort us as we mourn our own sin. You are holy and our sins offend you deeply. Our sins also bring us a sense of separation from your presence. We want to be as close to you as we can, at all times. Thank you for your patient love for us. We pray we come to a place where we are able to recognize sin in our lives and repent from a sincere heart of love for you. We also pray for a heart to mourn over the sins of the whole world, knowing that you are not willing that any should perish, but your desire is for all to be saved. In the name of our great Comforter, Jesus. Amen.

Today's Scriptures

Job 5:8–11; Psalm 51:1–12; Isaiah 53:3; Matthew 5:4

Today's Thought

"Blessed are the meek, for they will inherit the earth" (Matthew 5:5). The world offers a false concept of meekness; they interpret it as weakness. Jesus wants us to understand it from his perspective. Jesus was meek; he was *"strength under control."* In his life, Jesus portrayed both power and gentleness. He never sought to overwhelm or control although he possessed the authority to do so. The world desires to win its battles on its own terms, sometimes by brute force. Jesus calls us to live differently. He calls us to use the influence and power we have in mercy and gentleness. In our relationships and encounters with unbelievers, we are to put aside our right to be right and trust God to work for justice on our behalf. This does not make us doormats, but it will certainly speak to others of a power within us that is stronger than the self-seeking ambition the world puts on display. As we live as Jesus calls us to live, we move into position to inherit the earth and all its kingdoms with the Lord when all are given to him by the Father.

Today's Prayer

Father God, you are seeking a people who stand out in the world, not because they forcefully promote themselves, but because they know how to stand back and allow you to fight their battles. We know that you will secure justice for us when we look to you and face the world with a gentle and meek spirit. Along with Jesus we are the true inheritors of the earth because you purpose it to be so. Lord, help us to understand the concept of meekness, to be strong, but tender and to allow your Holy Spirit to control our spirit. Teach us how to carry ourselves in meekness in the face of the pride and arrogance we encounter. Lord, we want to be different. We want to respond in every situation as you would respond. We thank you for the wonderful future we have, ruling and reigning with you forever. In Jesus' name. Amen.

Today's Scriptures

Matthew 5:5; Titus 3:1–2; James 3:13; 1 Peter 3:15–17

November 4

Today's Thought

"Blessed are those who hunger and thirst for righteousness, for they will be filled" (Matthew 5:6). The first important thing for us to know is that in Christ we are already righteous before God. He made the great exchange on the cross, our sins for his holiness. His sacrifice placed his robe of righteousness on us. That position is forever secure in the heavenlies. Apart from that amazing truth is the reality that we are called by God to walk out the righteousness of Christ here on earth. Our walk of an upright life is characterized by a heart that aims to please God by honoring and obeying his Word. If we already have the righteousness of Christ, why do we still hunger and thirst for it? Could it be that after all he has done for us, we know we fall quite short of imitating the life of Christ. We know there is a huge gap between the life he lived and the life we live in the flesh. God is calling out a people to be different, influential and attractive in holiness. Deep in our souls we want that too. So, we hunger and thirst for it. He has given us his Holy Spirit to create that hunger and to do the necessary work, thus bringing us a contentment that only a righteous life can bring.

Today's Prayer

Father God, Jesus has already done the work of imputing his righteousness onto us. Before you we are forgiven and free. When you look at us you see the obedience and holiness of your Son. We are grateful and out of that gratitude we want to walk out that truth in our lives. We want the work he did to be made visible in our lives. Lord, create in us a hunger and a thirst for righteous lives. We long for souls that are satisfied. We know that our lives are not perfect, but we know that by your Holy Spirit we are being renewed day-by-day. Help us to walk in the Spirit so we do not fulfill the lust of the flesh. In Jesus' name. Amen.

Today's Scriptures

Matthew 5:6; 2 Corinthians 5:21; Galatians 5:16–17; 1 John 2:29

November 5

Today's Thought

"Blessed are the merciful, for they will be shown mercy" (Matthew 5:7). I don't know about you, but do I ever need mercy, every day! First from God and then from those I interact with daily. How about you? Simply put, mercy is not receiving the punishment we deserve. Every one of us is in dire need of mercy. Talk about being counter-cultural. How much mercy do you see in your corner of the world? Vengeance and pay back is more of what I see. Jesus wants us to be different in the way we return mistreatment. Our culture still lives by the rule, *"an eye for an eye, a tooth for a tooth."* Jesus came along and told his disciples, no, this is not the rule I want my followers to live by. I desire mercy. I came to offer mercy and I want you to do the same. What a beautiful heart attitude. How sweet to receive underserved mercy when we do wrong, how precious to extend mercy to those who wrong us, to those who do not live up to our expectations. The opposite of mercy is justice. The Word teaches us that justice belongs to our God. He will repay. When we have been wronged and mistreated, we are to extend mercy. God will secure justice for us when justice is called for.

Today's Prayer

Father God, you know what we are up against here in this fallen world. We suffer the abuse, rejection and exploitation of others. It hurts, and we know, Jesus, that you understand because you suffered all of it. Still, you extended mercy, even to the cross, even to your last breath. Lord, I pray we learn to walk in your ways of mercy. We know you will one day make all things right; justice belongs to you and you alone. We understand that as we walk in mercy, mercy will be shown to us. We could never add up all the times we received your mercy for all our wrongdoing. Rather than receiving what we deserved, we received undeserved forgiveness and mercy. Teach us to walk in deeper levels of mercy. In Jesus' name. Amen.

Today's Scriptures

Matthew 5:7; Matthew 5:38–42; Romans 12:21; 1 Timothy 1:15–17

Today's Thought

"Blessed are the pure in heart, for they will see God" (Matthew 5:8). A pure heart … what a beautiful quality. But, what is a pure heart? I could never fully describe a pure heart; it encompasses so much. A pure heart is a deep mystery. There could never be an adequate description, only God understands its reality. It does however, have a spiritual beginning. Without God taking residence in one's heart, there can be no purity. When Christ is invited into the life of a sinner, he begins a process of purification. It is entirely up to us how far we will allow the Lord to go in cleaning up our hearts and lives. A pure heart comes about only through surrender to the sanctifying work of the Holy Spirit. Going halfway with God will not produce a pure heart. It is for those willing to go all the way with God. He works from the inside out and he alone can do the refining of our rebellious hearts. A pure heart can be trusted. It is honest, sincere and reliable. It is a heart full of warmth, sexual purity and is generous, and so much more. It is filled with the goodness of Christ. This is the one who will see God working in all areas of her life. This is the one who knows his presence in the most intimate of ways.

Today's Prayer

Father God, we now know that you seek out the pure in heart that you may reveal yourself to them in exceptional ways. Lord, we understand that purification is a work of your Holy Spirit, and we know we must co-operate. Help us to desire a heart that reflects Christ. We want a heart that is trustworthy, honest, sincere and yielded to righteousness. We cannot do this on our own, so we ask that you do for us that which we cannot do for ourselves as we surrender our hearts to you. We want to see you; we want to experience your glory. We want to know you in deeper ways. We want our hearts to shine forth your glory. In Jesus' name. Amen.

Today's Scriptures

Psalm 51:10; Matthew 5:8; 1 Thessalonians 5:23–24; 2 Timothy 2:22

Today's Thought

"Blessed are the peacemakers, for they will be called the sons of God" (Matthew 5:9). We are not born peacemakers. My siblings and I are proof of that. We fought over everything. He has more ice cream than me. He touched me. She breathed on me. Her room is bigger than mine; and, on and on. Good parents help us get over these childish squabbles, but do we really get over them? Too many adults have carried these petty grievances into their adult relationships. We are a competitive culture. Sadly, we like arguments and feel the need to always be right; often at the cost of our friendships. It was no different in Jesus' day when he called out for peacemakers. Peacemakers take the initiative toward peace. They pursue peace. They love peace. Peacemakers strive for peace at every opportunity. It does not mean they compromise their beliefs, but in love, endeavor to bring the disagreement to a win-win situation. Sometimes they are willing to come out on the bottom, just so peace can reign. These are the children that God looks for. He calls them his sons and daughters because they imitate Jesus, the greatest peacemaker. Through his atoning death he reconciled us to God having made peace for us with God. Now we are called to promote peace.

Today's Prayer

Father God, while we were yet your enemies, Christ died for us, satisfying your wrath. Now we are at peace with you. Lord, we want to imitate Jesus, the great peacemaker. Help us to recognize every opportunity into which we can bring harmony. I pray we learn to keep peace and pursue tranquility. We want to be the ones who walk in peace, and who brings reconciliation into difficult situations. Help us in our marriages, our friendships and all relationships to be gentle and peace-loving. We want to be known as children of the living God as we pursue peace as a recognizable quality in our lives.

Today's Scriptures

Matthew 5:9; Romans 12:18; Ephesians 2:14; Colossians 1:19–20

November 8

Today's Thought

"Blessed are those who are persecuted because of righteousness, for theirs is the kingdom of heaven" (Matthew 5:10). What do you think of when you hear the word "persecution"? Sadly we often have a really lame idea of what it is. If you google *"Christian persecution around the world,"* you will gain a broader perspective of all its implications. We tend to think of persecution as a co-worker using Christian slurs against us or a family member ridiculing us for loving Jesus. No doubt about it, these insensitive words of others hurt, but is it the persecution Jesus talked about? Most of the suffering mentioned in the Bible has to do with being maligned and experiencing great loss and pain for the testimony of Jesus Christ. The early Christians often surrendered to death rather than deny Christ. In America today we still enjoy religious freedom and are not jailed, killed or beaten for our faith. I pray we remain in such a position. But, dear one, we must be ready to possibly face some harsh treatment from those who oppose the God we love and serve. We are living in a time where good is called evil and evil is called good. We must be prepared to stand firm for the cause of Christ no matter the cost. Remember, Jesus promises us the kingdom of heaven where all pain and sorrow will flee away and he will wipe away every tear.

Today's Prayer

Father God, we are grateful for the religious freedoms we enjoy as your people. We pray that it continues. Lord, we also want to be prepared to stand firm for what we believe and in whom we believe. Search our hearts and see if there is any compromise in us. Help us to evaluate our resolve and willingness to confess Christ when we are put to the test. Father, we join our hearts in lifting up the persecuted Christians around the world and pray you strengthen and encourage them as they fight the good fight of faith. In Jesus' name. Amen.

Today's Scriptures

Matthew 5:10; John 15:18–21; Hebrews 11:35–38; 1 Peter 4:12–14

November 9

Today's Thought

"Blessed are you when people insult you, persecute you and falsely say all kinds of evil against you because of me. Rejoice and be glad, because great is your reward in heaven, for in the same way they persecuted the prophets who were before you" (Matthew 5:11–12). Jesus now makes further comments on persecution. In the ninth beatitude he develops his thoughts on persecution. This is the type of persecution we can relate to. Being reviled and spoken evil of is something we all have experienced if we are truly following Christ. Jesus' focus here is on our response to these accusations. Surprisingly, he calls us to rejoice and be exceedingly glad. Our human instinct is to fight back, defend ourselves or retreat inward and engage in self-pity. None of that is what Jesus had in mind. He is calling us to a celebration; keeping before us the awareness of heaven awaiting with all of its rewards. I want to enter glory with my head held high, knowing I never denied my Lord and that I responded as he asked me to. This version from the Message Bible blesses my heart, *"Not only that-count yourselves blessed every time people put you down or throw you out or speak lies about you to discredit me. What it means is the truth is too close for comfort and they are uncomfortable. You can be glad when that happens, give a cheer even, for though they don't like it, I do! And all heaven applauds. And know that you are in good company. My prophets and witnesses have always gotten into this kind of trouble"* (Matthew 5:11–12).

Today's Prayer

Father God, we pray that we come to a place in our faith where we can truly rejoice and be glad when we are suffering for the sake of our Lord and his name. We thank you that our current persecution is not unto death. As long as we have breath we pray for the courage and fortitude to be faithful witnesses for Jesus Christ. In faith, we rejoice now in anticipation of what we may face at any given time. We know our reward in heaven will be amazing. In Jesus' name. Amen.

Today's Scriptures

Matthew 5:11–12; Acts 5:41; Romans 8:16–17; Revelation 3:11–13

November 10

Today's Thought

As I conclude the lessons on the beatitudes, I can see that they are all about attitudes and issues of the heart. Jesus' words call us to live and think differently than the world. The goodness that Jesus requires of us must emanate from a heart that loves God above all else. As we love him in this way it will manifest itself in how we live, how we treat others and how we respond to mistreatment. The Lord is always watching for our responses. When he sees the mature ways in which we handle ourselves with others and the situations that arise, he applauds us and will give us the courage and strength needed to spiritually survive and thrive in a culture that has, for the most part, rejected him and his commands. In Matthew 5, Jesus continues his exhortation by telling us we are the light of the world. It's as if the world is shrouded in a great darkness and we are the light that brings freedom and hope to those held captive by a culture that has rejected Christ.

Today's Prayer

Father God, thank you for sending Jesus. Fill us with the wisdom we need to survive these last days on earth. How we need his words to light our path and teach us how to live in good times and in evil times. Lord, we want to be the peacemakers of our day. We desire to be humble and to have contrite hearts. We need to mourn over our sins and the sins of the nation. We long for meekness and we hunger and thirst for righteousness. We pray to be merciful toward others so that we can obtain mercy when needed. We pray for courage in the face of reviling and persecution. Most importantly, we pray for pure hearts, by which we can see you, hear you and obey you in all things. We want to be the lights that you call us to be, in our families, our communities and our world. In Jesus' name. Amen.

Today's Scriptures

Psalm 91:14–16; Proverbs 10:25; Matthew 5:14–16; Colossians 1:9–11

Today's Thought

When I came to Christ in 1981, the first proof of my transformation was a deep repentance for my many sins. I can still vividly recall the sense of forgiveness and cleansing I experience. I learned early on that once I confessed and repented, I never had to revisit those sins again. It is finished. Jesus has accomplished full forgiveness for us. I soon learned that when my conscience wanted to accuse me of forgiven sin, it was condemnation, and that is never from God. I learned to rebuke those thoughts of guilt and shame. I also learned about conviction, that's always from the Holy Spirit and it is God's way of making us holy. So, conviction is good and tells us we have done wrong and we need to talk to God about it. Condemnation is from Satan and is meant to rob us of our peace with God. I encountered another aspect connected with my sin, contrition. I often wondered why I would suddenly feel deeply sorry for the sin I committed and how it hurt God and others. I learned that contrition was a godly sorrow over my past sin. It is not quilt or shame for past sin. Contrition is a reminder to me of how my sin hurt God's heart, did damage to others and left me broken. I don't live in regret or wallow in the mire of past sins, but I always want to have a godly heartfelt sorrow for having sinned against God. During those moments, God holds me close and comforts me because I am his forgiven child.

Today's Prayer

Father God, what a merciful God you are. You bring us to confession and repentance through conviction of the Holy Spirit. You teach us to reject any condemnation that comes from Satan or our own thoughts. You also give us a contrite heart so that when appropriate we can remember how we hurt you, ourselves and others. Thank you for godly sorrow that keeps us from pride and repeating our sin. In Jesus' name. Amen.

Today's Scriptures

Psalm 34:18; Psalm 51:17; Isaiah 57:15; Isaiah 66:2b

November 12

Today's Thought

Who doesn't like thinking about the future? That wonderful man God will bring as a future husband. The beautiful children God may give. A new and bigger home, a career boost, debts paid off. It's good to think ahead, to dream and plan. In Psalm 119:11 the psalmist shares with us his future plans for avoiding sin. He says, *"I have hidden your Word in my heart that I might not sin against you."* Here we find a safeguard against future sin. As we store his commands in our hearts, they are there to remind us of who we belong to and who it is we love and serve. Because he is holy, he calls us to holiness. We don't have to achieve holiness on our own. The Holy Spirit continually performs the sanctifying work of God in us. We must, however, do our part in depositing his truth in our hearts and receiving the engrafted Word of God with all meekness. We have a future; we have dreams. Let's remind each other that our future will only be as good as the abundance of truth we have stored up in our hearts.

Today's Prayer

Father God, your Word is meant to warn, correct, convict and lead us in the paths of righteousness. James calls it a mirror by which we examine ourselves and see where changes need to be made. Lord, we know that everyone is tempted by sin. In our humanness we can easily be seduced by urges that are not holy. Thank you for giving us strategies within your Word to combat the desires that war against our spirits. You say that we are more than conquerors through Christ who loves us. We must, however, do our part in the battle for our souls. I pray that you impress deeply upon our minds and hearts the need to pick up you Word, the sword of the Spirit, which can cut through the sin that easily trips us up. We purpose now to continue to store up your Word in our hearts that we not sin against you or others. In Jesus' name, the Word made flesh. Amen.

Today's Scriptures

Romans 8:36–37; 1 Corinthians 10:13; 2 Timothy 3:16–17; James 1:23–25

Today's Thought

Wouldn't it be awesome if your household pet suddenly spoke to you? That's exactly what happened to Balaam in Numbers 22. Balaam was on the road, on his way to curse Israel by request of the king of Moab. God however, had his own plan to prevent Balaam from carrying out his assignment. As Balaam traveled, his donkey encountered an angel of the Lord with a drawn sword in his hand. After three attempts to stop Balaam, the donkey laid down in the road. As Balaam began to beat his donkey for the third time, the Lord opened the mouth of the donkey and the donkey spoke to Balaam. *"What have I done to you to make you beat me these three times?"* (Numbers 22:28). After a heated argument with the donkey, the Lord opened the eyes of Balaam to see the angel who gave Balaam instructions on what he was to do. I hope the amazement of this story is not lost on us. A donkey talking! A simple beast of burden being used by the Lord to save his people! How much more will God use his own child to accomplish his eternal purposes? God loves to take the ordinary and use it to accomplish extraordinary things. That includes each of us!

Today's Prayer

Father God, thank you that everything and every person are of use to you in your grand design. Your marvelous story includes each and every one of us. Whether we are called to visit a neighbor with a tray of freshly baked cookies, go to the furthest regions of the earth to share the gospel, or anything in between, your desire for us is to have a part in the story you are telling. Lord, help us to remember that it is the most ordinary and common people you chose to be a part of the extraordinary. We open our hearts and lives to the truth that we are your vessels, chosen to do the works of God. Even as you received glory from a common donkey, so receive glory from all you do in and through us. In Jesus' name. Amen.

Today's Scriptures

Numbers 22:21–33; John 14:12; 1 Corinthians 1:26–29; Ephesians 2:10

November 14

Today's Thought

Yesterday we saw how God used a donkey in accomplishing his purposes for Israel. As we think about that, let's consider the different ways God chooses to speak to us. He used a donkey to correct the path of Balaam; and, he can speak to us in different ways as well. But our ears must be open to hear. When Jesus wanted his disciples to get the lesson, he called out, *"He who has an ear, let him hear"* (Luke 8:8). This was his way of telling us that what he just said is of utmost importance; *"don't miss it."* We have all encountered ways that God speaks. He speaks through creation and nature. There are numerous illustrations in the Bible that point to certain behaviors in the animal world that are life lessons for us. Plant life, flowers, farming, sowing and reaping, all have something to say to us. God also uses sermons, Bible teachings, radio and TV programs to get his messages across. He will use friends and even not-so-friendly people to reprove, correct and encourage us. The greatest way however, to hear God's voice, is through his Son, the Word made flesh. We go there first to study how we are to live, how we are to conduct ourselves in a world hostile to God. Nature, people and God's Word give us all we need to understand and know a God who longs to be known and heard.

Today's Prayer

Father God, you are not a distant or silent God. You are a hearing and a speaking God. Your voice comes to us in so many ways that it would be impossible not to hear the message you have for the world you created. We want to have ears to hear what you are speaking into our world today and what you are speaking into our individual lives. We trust your Word above all else. From that starting point, you can now reach us in many other ways. Lord, help us to hear as never before. We don't want to miss anything you have to say to us. In Jesus' name. Amen.

Today's Scriptures

Exodus 19:16–19; Psalm 19:1–4; Romans 10:17–18; Hebrews 1:1–3

November 15

Today's Thought

I love to dream about heaven. After all, it's my future forever home, just as it became yours when you placed your faith in Christ Jesus. I have come to discover that the Bible has more to say about what will not be in heaven than what we will actually see and experience. Today I want to share about some things that will never be in heaven. God's trustworthy Word tell us that no one who's name is not written in the Lamb's book of life will enter heaven; nor, will sorcerers, murders, the sexually immoral, idolaters and all who practice and love falsehood. There will be no tears or mourning or pain or crying or fear. There will be no more night or anything that frightens. There will never be sin in heaven. Death is swallowed up and will be no more! Anyone who does not confess that Jesus Christ is Lord will be allowed to enter heaven's gates. Sounds very exclusive; and it is. Jesus said, *"Small is the gate and narrow the road that leads to life, and only a few find it"* (Matthew 7:14). He also told us that he is the only way to the Father. We must trust that God is a God of justice and he knows those who belong to him. Inside or outside the kingdom, it will ultimately be an individual choice.

Today's Prayer

Father God, you are not willing that any should perish, but that all should be saved. In love and agreement, we say amen. You have made it very clear that only those wrapped in the righteous robe of Jesus Christ will enter your beautiful heaven. We thank you that our forever home will be pure, holy and unstained by death and sin. You alone are sovereign over the heaven that is your home. You sent your Son to save the whole world; no one is without the hope of salvation. We thank you that you give us the freedom of choice. In your love you have opened wide the gates of heaven to whosoever will to enter in. In the name of Jesus, the Holy One. Amen.

Today's Scriptures

Matthew 7:13–14; John 14:6; 2 Peter 3:9; Revelation 22:14–15

Today's Thought

God has so much waiting for us in heaven; it could never be recorded in all the books that could ever be written. Paul said that he knew a man who was caught up into the third heaven. He saw and heard things that could not be expressed in human language. I imagine that is why God did not go into greater detail about our future home. However, what he has revealed is enough for me. Heaven will be a place of eternal peace, joy and love in the purest sense. We will enjoy the eternal presence of Father, Son, and Holy Spirit. God will be our eternal light, and the Lamb will be our lamp. There will be food and drink and a tree that bears its fruit every month. The river of the water of life will flow freely from the throne of God. Heaven will be full of people from every tribe, people, language and nation, and together we will worship God forever. Rewards will be there for God's servants, those who followed the Lamb, and the rewards will be enjoyed forever. This is heaven, and the half has not yet been told!

Today's Prayer

Father God, we know that Jesus is preparing a place for us in the Father's house. We may not know everything waiting for us there, but we know enough. We know you are a good and generous Father who loves to bless us. You tell us that our faith and loyalty to your Son will be greatly rewarded. We look forward to all you have laid up for us; but, the most wonderful experience will be to live with you forever, to behold your glory and to worship you always. Lord, we are on our way home and the light of the Lamb is burning for us. We will be whole, perfect and holy as you are holy. As we complete our course here on earth, I pray you encourage and strengthen us for the journey ahead. Help us keep our eyes on the prize. Give us a heart for heaven and a longing to see you at last face-to-face. In Jesus' name. Amen.

Today's Scriptures

John 14:1–3; John 17:24; 2 Corinthians 12:2–4; 1 Corinthians 2:9

November 17

Today's Thought

One of the more difficult virtues I struggle with is generosity. It is taking me a long time to let loose of all that I think is rightfully mine. Just being honest here. I know all the scriptures, and I practice tithing and giving, but it is not always from a cheerful heart. Sometimes it feels like duty, plain and simple. God never intended for me to approach giving as something I had to do. I pray continually for a generous heart and little-by-little God is helping me to be the open-handed child he created me to be. My aim is to be a woman who gives hilariously. I want to laugh when I give because I know it is pleasing to my Lord. I want to laugh because I see the bondages of mistrust being broken. I want to know in the core of my being that I can never out give God. I want to give from a heart that knows I own nothing; I am simply a steward of all God has entrusted to me. When I generously give to the needs of others, I want all the praise and thanksgiving to go to God. I hope that you already know how to give out of a cheerful and grateful heart. If you struggle as I do, let's pray together for ourselves and for each other.

Today's Prayer

Father God, we first give from the grateful heart that knows you first gave to us. Help us to be the best little stewards we can be. We desire to obey your Word in giving cheerfully and generously. Help us to absorb the truth that all you have entrusted to us still belongs to you. We understand that we will give account for how we used the finances and resources given us from your generous hand. Lord, pry open our hands that hold ever so tightly to what we believe is ours. I pray that through the truth of your Word we see how wise and wonderful it is to be wildly generous. We want to go above and beyond giving cheerfully; we want to give hilariously. We trust you now for doing above all we ask or think. In Jesus' name. Amen.

Today's Scriptures

Proverbs 11:24–25; Acts 20:35; 2 Corinthians 9:6–8; Philippians 4:17–19

November 18

Today's Thought

How well do you know God? There are so many levels on which we can know him. It's good to know where we are in our understanding of him. First, it's possible to not know him at all. We all know folks like that. There are those who know him on a very superficial level. They acknowledge there is a God, and will perhaps engage in a conversation about him; but do not engage in a relationship with him. Some know him in a casual way, referring to him as a buddy or the man upstairs. He can be known for certain attributes like love and goodness, but many do not go deeper than that and when the storms come, they easily fall away. None can judge another's depth of relationship with the Lord, but he has shown us clearly how he desires to be known by all. In Jeremiah 9, he says, *"Let not the wise man boast of his wisdom, or the strong man boast of his strength, or the rich man boast of his riches, but let him who boasts boast about this, that he understands and knows me"* (Jeremiah 9:23–24). The word *"know"* in this verse is the kind of knowing as a husband and wife know each other, the most intimate of knowing. Notice the word *"understand"* in the verse. It implies that God wants us have an in-depth understanding of his character through experiencing him in an everyday loving relationship.

Today's Prayer

Father God, you want us to know you as deeply as you know us. You desire that we have a knowledge of you that comes from seeing you as you reveal yourself through your Word. You want us to understand your ways and how you work in our world and our lives. Lord, we want this too. I pray for each of us, that we go deeper into knowledge, understanding and love for you. I pray we experience you in a relationship that is deep, faithful and obedient. Holy Spirit, take us deeper in our knowledge of you, to places we have never been before. In Jesus' name. Amen.

Today's Scriptures

John 17:3; John 17:25–26; Philippians 3:10–11; 2 Peter 3:18

November 19

Today's Thought

Lies. We choose to believe them. First however, we need to recognize the lies we believe. I am not loved. I will never be good enough. If only I were prettier, smarted, richer. Each of us believe our own lies, we just don't know they are lies. Lies will take us into some very dark places and keep us there for a very long time. Most of the lies we believe originated in childhood; things carelessly spoken to us by people we trusted. TV ads, movies, magazines, social media, all are filled with lies that distort who and what we believe about ourselves. There is only one way to identify a lie. Does it line up with what God says in his Word? Who does God say I am? There can be nothing sadder than a woman, who belongs to Christ, who believes lies about herself. When we are in Christ, we embody all that he is. Christ in us helps us separate the lies from the truth. We have the divine power working in us to know truth. Yes, dearly beloved, when we need to know the truth and do not seek it out for ourselves, we deceive and rob ourselves of the glorious freedom Christ's death secured for us.

Today's Prayer

Father God, you have made known to us the source of every lie. Satan is a liar and the father of lies. Jesus is truth and the bearer of all truth. Lord, help us to choose truth and reject lies. I pray for each of us that we would seek out the truth of your Word and evaluate ourselves through that lens. There is not one single child of yours who is inferior in any way. There is none that is lesser or insignificant. You created us for truth, and you sent Jesus as our truth-bearer. Lord, we are guilty of believing and promoting lies. Please show us how we have fallen into the trap of mistaken identity; open our spiritual eyes to see the beauty you placed in us. Help us to know our great worth as revealed in your Word. In the name of all truth, Jesus Christ. Amen.

Today's Scriptures

Psalm 25:4–5; John 8:32; John 17:17; 2 Corinthians 10:5

Today's Thought

As we approach Thanksgiving Day, it's a good time to think about gratitude. The Christian should never wait for Thanksgiving Day to give thanks. Giving thanks needs to be an everyday habit of the heart. Have you counted the passages in the Bible that encourage us to bless God, give him praise and offer thanksgiving? Let's unpack those three different mandates, praise, blessing and thanksgiving. Praise is the highest form of acknowledging God. In praise, we are recounting his attributes, being grateful simply for who he is. Thanksgiving is our way to remember all his goodness to us, voicing our gratitude and being specific in the ways he has blessed us. When we bless God, we exalt him as the one and only God who is worthy of all glory and praise. It astounds me that in my frail humanity I can actually bless God. I can give him pleasure through my praise and thanksgiving. We mostly think of God blessing us; but, to have the honor and ability to bless him is truly amazing. In Psalm 103 David speaks to his very soul and cries out, *"Praise the Lord, O my soul; all my inmost being, praise his holy name"* (Psalm 103:1). He then goes on to tell of all the ways God has been good to him. All of this makes for a most intimate loving relationship. He gives to us and we give back. We give to him and he gives back.

Today's Prayer

Father God, we are a grateful people. We have so much to thank you for; we could begin our expressions of thanksgiving today and they would go on into eternity. We worship you for who you are. We thank you for all you have given us and done for us. We bless you because you are worthy. As we lift our hearts up to you today, I pray you are blessed and that our delight is in you. When we bless you, you desire to return the blessing. Beginning with our salvation, the gift of eternal life, and everything in between, we praise and thank you. In the name of Jesus, our forever praise. Amen.

Today's Scriptures

Psalm 69:30–31; Psalm 103:1–2; 1 Thessalonians 5:16; Hebrews 13:15

November 21

Today's Thought

Do you ever doubt? Do you beat yourself up when you have those doubts? Skepticism can come in all shapes and sizes. We can question our past decisions and wonder if we should have taken another path. We can doubt if God can love us after what we have done. We can have misgivings, wondering if we heard correctly from God after a major move or life change. You name it, we will have our doubts. Many stories in the Bible speak of the doubters and how God worked in them and through them in spite of their lack of faith. To doubt is not a sin. To doubt is human. The problem arises when we allow our troubling thoughts to turn into fear and mistrust. Fear is never a friend, never from God. Fear can cripple and paralyze us. As we take the doubts and entertain them apart from prayer, they can become unruly monsters that eat away at our sense of well-being. Doubts should always be taken to the Lord in prayer. He knows how to untangle all the knots of our thinking. Do you doubt your marriage, your parenting, a troubled relationship or even your faith? It's okay. God makes room for doubt. He uses doubt as an instrument to draw us and to teach us that we can trust him in the midst of our uncertainty.

Today's Prayer

Father God, doubt and fear are never from you. In your understanding of our human nature, you bear with us when we have doubts in our hearts. Your Word has the answer and cure for our misgivings. You continually remind us not to be afraid. And yet you help us overcome our anxieties and uncertainties with the encouragement and comfort of the scriptures. We can be so much like the questioning father who cried out *"Lord, I do believe, help me overcome my unbelief"* (Mark 9:24). We make this plea as well when doubt and fear want to overtake us. Lord we believe; help us in our doubts and uncertainties. In Jesus' name. Amen.

Today's Scriptures

Isaiah 41:10 Mark 9:23–24 Romans 15:4 Jude 1:22

November 22

Today's Thought

I quickly fail at cookie-cutter evangelism courses. I get all hyped-up, feeling equipped with all the right scriptures, all the tools of the trade, so to speak. But, as I attempt to put into practice what I learned, it doesn't turn out as I hoped. The problem isn't the program. We need to learn to present the gospel effectively. The problem I encountered was in using the methods I had learned. They did not fit my temperament or my personality. Like young David walking around in ill-fitting armor, I felt awkward and staged. Then I heard a great message on evangelism. I was encouraged to spend time discovering my own personal style of sharing Jesus with others. For me, asking the right questions was the best way to begin. I have an ardent interest in hearing people's stories. This feels very right and natural for me. I like to ask, *"Would you share with me your spiritual journey and where you are at this time?"* Most people love to talk about themselves and are more than ready to talk. How about you? Wouldn't evangelism be more exciting if you felt at ease and comfortable with a style of sharing that best fits you? I encourage you to seek God's wisdom in how you can most effectively share the good news of Jesus Christ within the framework of your unique personality.

Today's Prayer

Father God, you created us all with unique personalities and temperaments. We are all so different and we like that about ourselves. Lord, we pray today that you show each of us how we best interact with others and what approaches to sharing the gospel fit us well. We know we are called to evangelize, and we want to obey you in this. As we seek you, we thank you that you will reveal to us the special way you created us and want to use us in leading souls to Christ and his truth. In Jesus' name. Amen.

Today's Scriptures

Isaiah 6:8; Matthew 9:37–38; Mark 16:15; Romans 1:16

November 23

Today's Thought

William Shakespeare once said, *"My crown is in my heart, not on my head."* There are five crowns mentioned in scripture: the imperishable crown; the crown of rejoicing; the crown of righteousness; the crown of glory; and, the crown of life. These crowns speak of virtue rather than gold, silver and jewels. I do not know what these crowns will look like in heaven, but I do know we will be giving all the glory to our Lord and Savior. In Philippians 3:20–21, Paul encourages us to remember that our citizenship is in heaven; the Lord will transform our lowly bodies to be like his glorious body. Then he tells us that because of this we need to stand firm in the Lord. He joyfully confesses that his brothers (and sisters) whom he loves and longs for are his joy and crown. Paul establishes that while we are here on earth, people are to be our crowns. The good we bring into the lives of others become virtuous crowns of character and integrity that we wear on our hearts where only God can see. Proverbs reminds us that an excellent wife is the crown of her husband. Psalm 8 proclaims that after God created man, he crowned him with glory and honor. We have nothing else to do but cast these crowns at the feet of the One, who for us, wore the crown of thorns.

Today's Prayer

Father God, you are glorious in splendor, majesty and beauty. Likewise, you have adorned us with beauty, glory and honor. Lord, we pray that we begin now to wear our crowns upon our hearts and that we walk in this world as the royalty that we are. May we not be proud but humble, knowing we do not deserve the crowns that await us in heaven. All glory goes to Jesus Christ who is now transforming us and will one day transform our earthly bodies to be like his glorious body. Lord, in faith we now lay our crowns at your feet in praise and thanksgiving. In the name of Jesus. Amen.

Today's Scriptures

Psalm 8:3–5; Proverbs 12:4a; Philippians 4:1; Revelation 4:9–11

November 24

Today's Thought

Have you ever wondered why a holy God called a man of God to marry a prostitute? The book of Hosea starts out with a command to the prophet Hosea to go and take a wife of whoredom. And so, he went and took Gomer as his wife. Scripture hints at the idea that Gomer may have been raised in a home of sexual immorality and could have quite possibly been sold into prostitution by her family in order to pay the family debts. This was sadly acceptable for poor families in Israel; it could have been their only means of survival. How true this was in Gomer's case is not clear. However we can see that Gomer was now the wife of a godly, respected man, which changed her immoral identity to one of respectability. She was now Mrs. Hosea; but, her behavior was still of Gomer the prostitute. She never entered into her new identity but remained in her old identity. Paul tells us that in coming to Christ we take on a new identity, that of Jesus himself. We are to take off the old and put on the new. In Christ we have been made daughters of heaven, brides of Christ. Once we were darkness, now we are light; we ought to now walk in the light.

Today's Prayer

Father God, how lost we were, how dark our world. We needed someone to bring us out of the kingdom of darkness into the light. Jesus became our Savior, our light and our truth. We now cast off the works of darkness and we put on the Lord Jesus Christ. Lord, show us any ways in which we are clinging to the old identity, the old life. By your Spirit teach us how to walk fully in the light of Christ Jesus. As we take off the old and put on the new, I pray we live by the new way of the Spirit. May we no longer cling to our filthy rags of unrighteousness, but I pray we yield all of ourselves to righteous living. Old things are passed away, and we are continually becoming new. In Jesus' name. Amen.

Today's Scriptures

Hosea 1:2–3; 2 Corinthians 5:17; Ephesians 4:22–24; Ephesians 5:8–10

November 25

Today's Thought

Yesterday our focus was on Hosea, Gomer and new identity. Hosea's name means salvation. He became a savior to Gomer but she rejected his love. The prophet Hosea is a picture of God. The book of Hosea is a story about God and Israel, but it is also about you, me and God. Before Christ rescued us, we were living under the slavery of sin. God in his mercy called us to himself and made us his. Sadly, we are not always faithful to God. Often, like Gomer, we run back to our old gods, our sinful habits, addictions and methods of coping. God is harsh in his dealings with Gomer because he hates the sin; but, he also shows himself to be compassionate, tender and restorative. The attribute of God most clearly seen in this book is that of faithful and unfailing love. When I think of what Gomer deserved, and what I deserve, it is not a pretty picture. *But God ...* I love those words. *But God*, who is rich in mercy, took us as his own, in all our unfaithfulness and in our lostness, he woos us to himself and betroths himself to us forever. God gets us, even when we don't understand ourselves or know why we do the things we do. Hosea paid a high price to gain Gomer back. Jesus paid the ultimate price to win you and me back.

Today's Prayer

Father God, thank you for giving us the story of Hosea and Gomer. Many have said that it is one of the most powerful pictures of your love for Israel and for us. Only Christ's death on our behalf displays a greater love. Lord, we know that we are not worthy of a love so great; this is what makes it so amazing. Like Gomer we have played the harlot by chasing after other gods, looking for love and pleasure in sinful ways and dark places. Even when we were steeped in our sin, your unfailing love provided a way out. You wooed us and won us through the love of your Son. We are eternally grateful.

Today's Scriptures

Hosea 2:19–20; Hosea 3:1; John 15:13; Romans 5:6–8

November 26

Today's Thought

How many mirrors do you own? Mirrors are good; they let us know how we're holding up. When you gaze into your mirror, what do you see? If you are like me, you tend to focus on those flaws that seem to scream out from the glassy image. God's Word is a mirror. It reflects our lives and assesses how we are doing spiritually. This is how James says it, *"But whoever looks intently into the perfect law that gives freedom, and continues in it—not forgetting what they have heard, but doing it—they will be blessed in what they do"* (James 1:25). I recently discovered that how I looked into God's mirror needed a slight adjustment. I realized that when I looked at certain passages, I always camped out in those areas where I struggled and fell short. 2 Corinthians 13 is well known as the love chapter. Every time I read down through the list of what love should look like, I focused in on the one way in which I failed God's holy standard. I berated myself for my impatience and ignored all the ways I have succeeded in loving God and others. My point is this, dear sister, maybe we all need to read God's Word with more of an attitude of how well we are doing. I think God looks at us this way and he sees the bigger picture of our desire to please him.

Today's Prayer

Father God, your Word is truly a mirror by which we can examine our strengths and our weaknesses. You never intended it to be a hammer by which we beat ourselves up over our shortcomings. Your Word rebukes and corrects, but it is also your means of encouraging us in our successes. We are grateful that you want the best life possible for us and your Word leads us into that perfect law of liberty. Today I pray that we see more of your smiles, your approval, love and encouragement as we look into the mirror of your Word and see what your heart reflects back to us. In Jesus' name. Amen.

Today's Scriptures

Proverbs 31:29–31; Matthew 25:23; Hebrews 10:24–25; James 1:23–25

Today's Thought

Do you sometimes wake up feeling blah, as if you are in a deep spiritual slump, a blue haze, a pink funk? Praying and reading God's Word seems so far removed from what your heart wants. Often, these spiritual valleys can last for days, weeks or months. When I hit these lows, I begin to berate myself and wonder if I will ever emerge from the apathy of not caring. This can be very frightening for a Christian. Am I backslidden? Have I done something to lose favor with God? Am I truly saved? I sat alone one morning recently feeling just this way. I realized I had no human strength to pull myself up from the abyss. As I sat there in the dark, slowly the fog began to lift ever so slightly. Quietly and sweetly the Holy Spirit led me to Psalm 139. These words came to me on the wings of a dove. *"Where can I go from your Spirit? Where can I flee from your presence? If I go up to the heavens, you are there; if I make my bed in the depths, you are there. If I rise on the wings of the dawn, if I settle on the far side of the sea, even there your hand will guide me, your right hand will hold me fast"* (Psalm 139:7–10).

Today's Prayer

Father God, we thank and praise you that there is no place too high or too low that you do not see us. When we are on the mountain top rejoicing and flourishing, you are there dancing and singing with us. When we descend to a low and dark place, you are there! When we cannot see you, you see us. When we lose our way, you are the way back home. There is no place that can hide us from your presence. No darkness on earth can cover and consume us. Lord, we are forever secure in your love and faithfulness. You will not let us be buried in our indifference; you will not let us drown in our apathy. We are never lost or hidden from your sight. What a great God and faithful Father you are! I pray we never again believe the lie that you have forsaken or forgotten us. In Jesus' name. Amen.

Today's Scriptures

Deuteronomy 31:8; Psalm 139:7–12; Isaiah 41:10; Isaiah 43:2

November 28

Today's Thought

Prosperity, bring it on we say! Who does not want to realize the American Dream? I wonder how many of us understand that prosperity is not always a blessing; and, it's always a test from God. We hear a lot about prosperity these days; some of it is not in line with the truth of God's Word. Most people link prosperity to financial gain and good fortune. Biblical prosperity mostly relates to thriving spiritually as we grow into the person God created us to be. We can have all the wealth in the world, but if we are not being changed into his likeness, we are poor indeed. When one is blessed with wealth, God is going to test the stewardship, the attitude and the heart. Paul warns *"For the love of money is a root of all kinds of evil. Some people, eager for money, have wandered from the faith and pierced themselves with many griefs"* (1 Timothy 6:10). God knows those who can be entrusted with wealth and those who can be harmed by it. The rich young ruler had great wealth, but it stood in the way of his eternal well-being. Before we begin to ask God to prosper us materially, let's first pray for godliness and contentment with what we have. We must be aware that when we prosper, God is testing our hearts toward him and our attitude toward money.

Today's Prayer

Father God, you want so much for us, just as we want for our children. You know us so well. You understand our temperaments, desires and needs. You know how much wealth we can be trusted with; you know the things that steal our heart away from you. Lord, may our greatest desire be to thrive and prosper spiritually. Jesus, you said that you came to give us life, life more abundant. Help us to keep this in proper perspective. We know your highest goal for us is spiritual progress and growth. May we be content with what you have given us. May our souls prosper to the glory of God. In Jesus' name. Amen.

Today's Scriptures

Matthew 6:19–21; Matthew 6:24; Luke 12:15; 1 Timothy 6:6–10

November 29

Today's Thought

Location, location, location. What does location have to do with our spiritual well-being? All through scripture, men and women accomplished great things for God, all from being at the right place at right time. Young David for example. In 1 Samuel 17 David was obediently tending his father's sheep. At the same time three of his older brothers were in the Valley of Elah fighting the Philistines with the army of King Saul. The father sent David to the battle ground with provisions for his brothers. It was there that in God's providence David slayed the giant Goliath. At the right place, at the right time and the history of Israel was changed. Esther, living as Queen in a foreign palace, saved her people from the jaws of extinction. The right place at the right time. So it is with us. God has an ordained destiny for each of us, a special assignment within his kingdom, a divine purpose to be fulfilled. If we are not in the right place at the right time, we can miss it. I hope you are where you are supposed to be right now. If so, God will work mighty works through you. If not, adjustments need to be made. Whether you are now in the right place at the right time is between you and God. Why not seek him along with me. Let's be sure our decisions and our steps are being ordered of the Lord.

Today's Prayer

Father God, we do want your will and purposes to be fulfilled in our lives. This makes us utterly dependent on your direction and guidance. Give us ears to hear your voice of correction when we wander off the path you set for us. Give us discernment to know if we are in the right location to be used as you desire. Lord, we pray to be operating in whatever way and place you desire. May we trust you when we do not see or know why you have relocated us. Your ways are perfect and your heart is always for us. In Jesus' name. Amen.

Today's Scriptures

1 Samuel 17:17–20; Esther 4:14; Psalm 37:23–24; Proverbs 3:5–6

Today's Thought

Conviction and correction are such necessary ingredients for thriving spiritually and maturing into godliness. Today and tomorrow we are going to explore these two biblical truths. For now, let's consider conviction. It can be defined as the feeling of being convinced of doing wrong or the revelation of a sin operating in one's life. We can be so deceived by our sin it can only take the conviction of the Holy Spirit to convince us of our wrong. He takes the Word of God and applies it to our hearts, and shows us that God is not pleased with our thoughts or actions. When conviction comes, we have a choice. We can ignore the prompting or we can respond in an attitude of humility and repentance. When we ignore the conviction of the Holy Spirit, we start down a path where God will eventually have to judge that sin and deal harshly with our rebellion. Hard words, yes, but in reality, conviction is an aspect of God's love. Without the conviction of love, we step onto that slippery slope, spiraling out of control in sin. I recently heard a woman say, *"I covet the conviction of the Holy Spirit."* I want to embrace that same attitude.

Today's Prayer

Father God, what an amazing and divine parent you are! You always know exactly how to bring conviction to us so we can continue to grow and mature into godliness. Your desire for us is protection from the ravages of rebellion and sin. We are blessed children to have One who will not hesitate to deal with sin in our lives. Lord, we pray that we will never resist the working of your Holy Spirit in our hearts and lives. Thank you for your love that desires the best for us. I pray we avoid the sin that deceives and ravages. When we do error, we are grateful for your faithful Holy Spirit who brings conviction and we are blessed that he never brings condemnation. In Jesus' name. Amen.

Today's Scriptures

John 16:7–8; Romans 2:4; Romans 8:5–6; 2 Corinthians 7:9–10

December 1

Today's Thought

The same woman who said she covets conviction also said that she loves correction. That statement falls right in line with Proverbs 12:1 (MSG)." *If you love learning, you love the discipline that goes with it—how shortsighted to refuse correction!"* That's God's Word. I do not argue with him! Correction comes in many forms and through different sources. The first reliable source is God's Word. It can come by way of a trusted mentor, pastor or friend. Correction is God's means of making necessary adjustments to our attitudes, our words and our actions. God is continually training us in righteousness with the aim that we be thoroughly equipped for every good work. As we respond to correction, we gain wisdom and it shows our love of knowledge. When we ignore instruction, it shows that we despise ourselves and that we reject being trained in the righteous ways of God. It's not always easy to face correction and make the needed adjustments, but for the one who does receive, she is a wise woman indeed. She will be blessed in all her ways. Let's love correction; it's in this respect we show our love for Christ.

Today's Prayer

Father God, Jesus made it very clear, if we love him, we will obey him. By loving correction, we show ourselves wise. Again, we thank you for being a wise parent who does not coddle rebellion and foolishness. Lord, at times your discipline may seem harsh, but we know you always have our best interest in mind. If we are not disciplined, we are not your sons and daughters. We pray for teachable hearts that yield quickly to your correction. Give us the will to learn from your Word, from our mentors, pastors and teachers. You work in so many diverse ways in your determination to grow us into godly and wise women. May we love correction as we grow up in Christ. In Jesus' name. Amen.

Today's Scriptures

Job 5:17–18; Proverbs 15:31–32; 2 Timothy 3:16–17; Hebrews 12:7–11

December 2

Today's Thought

Today I write in honor and memory of my dear friend and sister in Christ, Jandy. Yesterday I received the news that she is now home safe with her Lord and Savior. I was hit with a twinge of jealousy. As I think about Jandy, so many happy memories of her flood my soul. She was bubbly, full of life, generous and oh so kind. She was one of the first women who reached out to me when I began attending church. After I moved away, she was faithful in writing beautiful letters and sending gifts on my birthday and Christmas. Those letters were full of praise, worship and love for her Lord. Every card or letter she ever sent me was stamped with these words, *"Jesus is the Answer."* I had 40 years of receiving that precious message from her. It took years for me to fully understand the profound implications of those simple but thought-provoking words. When the sorrows of life took their grip on me, the truth of those words reached out and sustained me in the worst of times. Jandy knew that in every expression of life, Jesus was the answer, and she lived as if she believed it. I will miss her. She loved God so completely, it adorned every part of her life with beauty and light. To God be the glory for all He has done.

Today's Prayer

Father God, we thank you for faithful sisters in Christ who share in our journey and we in theirs. As the song writer so beautifully expressed, *"I can only imagine."* As I think about my friend today, I know I cannot even begin to know the blissful joy she is experiencing in your presence. One day we who trust in your Son will know it as well. Thank you for the role models of godly women in our lives. Lord, help us to be an example to the women around us, always encouraging, lifting up and pointing to Jesus as the answer for all of our doubts and questions. In Jesus' name. Amen.

Today's Scriptures

John 14:1–3; 1 Corinthians 15:55–57; Philippians 1:21; 2 Timothy 4:7–8

Today's Thought

No matter where you are today, God will meet you there. There is no place, mental, physical, emotional or spiritual where his presence will fail you. He knows you so thoroughly and completely that he is able to plan for every event, circumstance, incident or surprise you could possibly encounter. Jesus was our burden-bearer on the cross and he continues to be the One who meets us right where we are today. No mountain is too high, no ocean too deep, no landmass so wide that he cannot rush to our side in a heartbeat. No one knows your deepest need like Jesus. No one can meet you there at the point of that need like Jesus. He may work through others or he may sovereignly meet your need himself; but, rest assured, he will meet you. What did you wake up with today? What is weighting your heart down or causing you concern? Give it to Jesus. Lay it at the cross. He knows your need today but he wants to hear your voice. By voicing your need you gain clarity. I can't promise you that your concerns will all be "fixed," but I know that he will meet your deepest need as you ask.

Today's Prayer

Father God, thank you for being a Father who is concerned with all that concerns us. We often cannot discern our deepest need. We think it is this, when really it is that. We want all our problems to just melt away. But there is purpose in our struggles. You are always at work in our lives. Even so, you know how to lift the heavy weight of our burdens. As we come to you in the early morning light, we can begin a new day with new mercies and compassion. You care about our every worry and apprehension. You desire for us to come to you with those daily needs so we can see your loving involvement in all aspects of our lives. Lord, we thank you for bearing our burdens, lifting our load and meeting us at our deepest level of need. In Jesus' name, Amen.

Today's Scriptures

Psalm 46:10–11; Isaiah 30:18; Philippians 4:19; 1 Peter 5:7

December 4

Today's Thought

She was 93 years old. As the story goes, she sat down one day and sketched out her goals for the next 10 years. At first, I laughed. Upon further thought, I realized she was living as God intended, believing for a long full life and being prepared. I later mused that I want to live with that kind of perspective. Many Bible verses speak about saints enjoying a long full life. The Old Testament men lived well beyond an age we can only imagine. Caleb achieved honor and recognition for the vigor and faith he displayed in his eighties. Saint John, the Lord's disciple, preached and wrote well into his nineties. God is not finished using our lives until we breathe our last. No bench sitting, no wallflowers in the kingdom of God. Many Bible verses speak to the aged and their ability in Christ to produce fruit in old age. Let's join our dear 93-year-old sister in Christ and continue in faith to lay out future goals at every age. After all, whether we live or we die, we belong to Christ and our lives are hidden in him. Let us serve him faithfully as long as he gives us breath.

Today's Prayer

Father God, life is beautiful and living for you is a wonderful honor. As long as you lend us breath, we can hope for a fruitful future. You have plans and dreams for us in every season of life. Help us to see long life as a gift that we offer back to you. By your Spirit may we continue to grow in grace and knowledge. We pray that you cause us to prosper in every way. Lord, fill us with hope as we contemplate your desire for our future. Whether we live serving you vigorously, or if we serve you in the quiet places at home, we will trust you to continue to bring glory to yourself through our humble lives. We thank you for every year of life you grant us. We praise you for all the ways you equip us to live for you throughout the years. In Jesus' name. Amen.

Today's Scriptures

Psalm 90:12; Psalm 91:14–16; Proverbs 22:4; Isaiah 46:3–4

December 5

Today's Thought

Some of the most chilling words spoken by Jesus are found in Matthew 7. Jesus wants his followers to understand the difference between attempting to impress him by works and the genuine desire to know him through serving him. Simply calling him Lord does not guarantee entrance into the kingdom of heaven. Jesus lets us know that one can do many things in his name, but they can be empty offerings void of any real relationship behind the actions. The lesson here comes down to the motive of our hearts. When we become doers only without heart-felt love for Jesus, we are like clanging cymbals, just making a lot of noise. Christ invites into his kingdom those who are serving him with pure motives and a desire to know and understand him. Matthew records Jesus' words, *"Many will say to me on that day, 'Lord, Lord, did we not prophesy in your name and in your name drive out demons and, in your name, perform many miracles?' Then I will tell them plainly, 'I never knew you. Away from me, you evildoers!'"* (Matthew 7:22–23). The word *knew* carries with it the reality of a relationship that exemplifies the intimate knowledge shared by a husband and wife. Today let's allow the Holy Spirit to search our heart motives in serving Christ.

Today's Prayer

Father God, you call us to serve you from a pure heart of genuine love and we want that. You have always desired a loving relationship with your creation. You want us to know you intimately and you have given us your Word where you reveal to us who you are. Father we are honored to be your servants and your friends. Lord, we pray that the Holy Spirit would search our hearts and expose any ways in which our works are not mixed with faith. We pray for the heart that blesses you through our service to you and others. We desire to feel your pleasure in this. In Jesus' name. Amen.

Today's Scriptures

Matthew 7:21–23; John 17:3; 1 Corinthians 13:1–3; James 2:14–26

Today's Thought

Wandering Israel. In Hoses 8:14a the prophet laments, *"Israel has forgotten his Maker, and built palaces; Judah has fortified many towns."* Rather than look to his God for provision and protection Israel has looked to his own hand to defend and deliver him. Before we judge, we need to look at where we place our confidence. God reminds us over and over that he is our stronghold, our fortress, our strong tower of defense. Still, we often run to other sources for what only God can give. We count on the court system to give us justice. We look to the world's methods for love, security, direction and assurance. We will never find what we are looking for if we are looking in the wrong place. The Word of God is the lamp to our feet and the light to our path. God has made every provision for protection, defense, safety and so much more. He declares that he is our Refuge in trouble, our Hiding Place from danger and a Sanctuary for the hurting. Why would we ever want to settle for a counterfeit? Dear sister, he is everything you need him to be today, tomorrow and forever. Our search is over. We have been given a Son, and in him is the fullness of God's love and provision.

Today's Prayer

Father God, you know how to take over when our human strength is gone and we lay it all down. You love being our Champion, our Rock of Refuge, our Defense. Lord, we now lay down those bricks of human effort with which we have built false securities for ourselves. We proclaim you to be our strength, our wisdom, our defense, our altogether lovely one. You are our safe place; we are always sheltered as we abide under the shadow of the Almighty. We acknowledge that we need you. You are the one we trust; you are the one who brings to us songs of deliverance in the night. Lord, cover us now as we lay our lives before you. In the name of the God of our security and prosperity. Amen.

Today's Scriptures

Psalm 32:6–7; Psalm 46:1–5; Psalm 91:1–4; 2 Corinthians 12:9–10

Today's Thought

What level of drama are you experiencing in your life? When unexpected circumstances overtake you, to whom do you run? Do you feel an urgent need to know about everything that is taking place around you? How often do you find yourself in the midst of a gab session, or on the phone, needing to know all about everything? I just described myself, the way I was some years ago. Truth be told, I had a deep-seated need to be in on the current scoop. Honestly, it wore me out. I discovered I could not keep up with all the latest talk, the intrigue in other people's lives, or worst of all, attempting to squeeze all the answers out of God. He brought me up short one day to let me know in no uncertain terms, that he operated on a need-to-know basis. I have come to discover that God will get to me the information that I need at any given time; as for the rest of it, I can let it go. He has proven to me again and again that this is the best way to live. It has freed up my time; improved my emotional state and has put me in a place of rest and trust. He has never let me down. What I need to know, he knows how to get to me.

Today's Prayer

Father God, we are grateful that we do not have to get caught up in the trap of needing to know everything. Lord, we want to be in a need-to-know relationship with you. We know that we can trust you to let us in on anything that pertains to us or those we love. Our souls can rest in the assurance that you will never let us down; you will not neglect to inform us or let us in on what concerns us. Lord, I pray for each of us that we would come into the relationship with you that you desire, one in which we can trust you to orchestrate our daily affairs and one that helps us navigate the murky waters of "having to know." Today we lay down the tendency to get involved in matters that are not our business. In Jesus' name. Amen.

Today's Scriptures

Proverbs 26:17; Ecclesiastes 4:6; 1 Thessalonians 4:11–12; 1 Timothy 5:13

Today's Thought

The tongue is a launching pad. Our words are missiles that can promote encouragement, inspiration and life, or discouragement, failure and death. As our words take off out of our mouths, they are like arrows we shoot into the hearts of others; they will wound or heal. Our words can be gentle or harsh, sweet or bitter. They can crush the spirit or uplift the crushed in spirit. Scripture likens our words to a bubbling brook, bringing refreshment when used for good. With our words we bless or curse. It's no wonder James warns us about the use of the tongue. He lets us know that it can be a roaring fire, destroying everything in its path. Our words can set our life on a course of success or failure. How we talk to ourselves will shape who we are, what we believe and how we live. What we speak to others will do the same for them. When we are in a position of influence, we have a great responsibility to speak words of life. We can only imagine then how speaking words of truth, the Word of God, can impact the hearer. From the smallest child to the oldest gray head, we all need life-giving words. Our words will live long after they have been spoken.

Today's Prayer

Father God, your Word is living and active. You sent Jesus so we could know your heart. As we listen well to his words, teach us to imitate speaking the truth in love. We know our words bring life or death. Help us to guard our tongues. Help us to think carefully before we speak. I pray we learn to carefully weigh our words before we launch them into the ears and hearts of others. Every word you have spoken to us through scripture is for our training, our correction, our encouragement. I pray we use your Word in the same way. May our words always be a blessing and never a curse. May our words be like soothing oil, poured into the heart of the hearer. In the name of the Word of God, Jesus, the Word made flesh. Amen.

Today's Scriptures

Proverbs 16:24; Proverbs 18:21; Matthew 12:36; Ephesians 4:29

December 9

Today's Thought

No one wants to see your life's purposes fulfilled more than your heavenly Father. However, it's not all up to him; we must cooperate in the process. How do we do that? It begins with prayer, asking God to lead us in the path of our eternal destiny. Then it requires laying down our own human desires that conflict with what God wants. My pastor puts it this way, *"Pray, Listen, Obey."* When I first began reading the Bible, I thought I had to obey everything therein all at once. God showed me otherwise. There is no way any of us can be immediately and completely obedient in all things God requires. What we can do is obey one step at a time. As we obey in that one thing, he will give us the next step. Yes, we will encounter detours and setbacks at times, as Jonah did, but he picks us up, puts us back on our feet, and we continue on the journey of obedience. God is not a taskmaster like the Egyptian Pharaoh was to Israel. He is a gentle, patient Father who knows our abilities and limitation. The Psalmist said it like this, *"He knows how we are formed; he remembers that we are dust"* (Psalm 103:14).

Today's Prayer

Father God, thank you for being a Father who has wonderful purposes for each of our lives. You are the true and only wise God who knows how to direct, lead and fulfill. You do all things well and what you determine will be accomplished. All of our days were written in your book before we lived even one. Now we are grown and you are looking for spiritual progress in our lives. Lord, teach us to pray, listen and obey. Help us to see the wisdom in obedience. Thank you that we don't have to get it all together all at once. Thank you for the space to fail and for the chance to begin again. You know our dispositions and our capacity for disobedience; and, you know how to bring us into alignment with your will and purposes. All the glory and praise to you. Amen.

Today's Scriptures

Psalm 32:8; Psalms 103:13–14; 1 Corinthians 13:11; Hebrews 5:8–9

December 10

Today's Thought

One of the hardest lessons I had to learn in my marriage was giving the gentle answer. I was always on the ready to argue back in a voice louder than my small frame called for. What is it about human nature that always needs to be right? Sometimes we are right, but the way in which we project our objection makes all the difference. When voices begin to rise, it's time step back and regroup. When personalities and differences clash, it can be an opportunity for growth. It took me a long time to understand that I had the power to bring about needed change when I handled myself in a mature manner, by giving a gentle answer, *gentle* being the key word. Proverbs 15 gives us this important principle. A principle does not guarantee a desired outcome, but it sure does give us the edge. *"A gentle answer turns away wrath, but a harsh word stirs up anger"* (Proverbs 15:1). When I push back against the words and objections of another, it can only escalate. When I give a soft answer, it can neutralize the atmosphere and disarm my opponent. A soft answer can turn a conflict into a win-win situation. A soft answer can teach others to see that there is a better way in disagreeing and solving conflict.

Today's Prayer

Father God, when you speak to your children, you are never harsh or cruel. You always speak truth in a manner that we can understand and receive. Lord, help us to learn the value of a soft answer. When conflicts arise, I pray we rise up in maturity and Christlikeness. We desire to be a godly influence in the lives of those who oppose us. When we know we are right, help us to voice that in gentleness, open to hearing the opinion of others. I pray we know when to speak and when to walk away. In our marriages, may we show our husbands that meek and gentle spirit that is very precious in your sight. In Jesus' name. Amen.

Today's Scriptures

Proverbs 15:1–2; Colossians 3:12–15; Titus 3:1–2; 1 Peter 3:3–4

December 11

Today's Thought

Our culture tends to be attracted to success, wealth, position and fame. I often wonder why that is. Could it be because that is what we want for ourselves? Consider Jesus. He did not surround himself with the rich and famous, the learned and the powerful. Rather, we see that those to whom he was attracted were the most marginalized; they were the outcasts, the sick and discarded of society. I can only conclude that Jesus is attracted to weakness. I believe the same is true today. When Jesus chose me out of my whole family, I was the youngest, the weakest, and the least powerful. Someone once said to me, *"You need Jesus. You are such a sinner."* She did not know how spot on she was. Jesus is most attracted to sinners, drawn to our weaknesses. He lived a life of low esteem and chose to be helpless against the powers of his day. Yet, his life was the most significant and powerful life ever lived.

Today's Prayer

Lord Jesus, as you hung on that cross and looked out over the crowd below, you saw the weak and the lost. Your heart of compassion reached out even while you were drawing your last earthly breath. We are grateful that you are attracted to us in our weaknesses, because we are indeed needy. You understand our vulnerability. Though you could have called down legions of angels to take you from the cross, you choose to endure it for our sakes. You choose powerlessness at that moment so we could know you understand our fragile condition. The story did not end there. You rose strong and victorious, and so shall we. Help us to remember that in our weakness, you are strong. In the name of our Strong Savior. Amen.

Today's Scripture

Isaiah 40:29; Matthew 9:36; 1 Corinthians 1:26–29; 2 Corinthians 12:9–10

December 12

Today's Thought

When was the last time you had a good laugh? Do you know that laughter is good, like a medicine? It's right there in God's Word in Proverbs 17:22. When we are laughing our entire body responds in the healthiest of ways. Laughter relaxes the whole body. It boosts the immune system. A good laugh triggers the release of feel-good chemicals. It improves the function of blood vessels which can protect against heart disease. The fun of laughter helps lift our burdens and burns calories. What's not to love about a good laugh! In his divine wisdom, God took everything into account when he created man. What a miracle we are! I have a few friends who I can call upon when I need a good laugh. They are funny women and can find the silliest things to giggle about. I always feel so good after spending time with them. Sometimes I have to be deliberate in reaching out to my fun friends, especially when I feel low. I hope you have a few people in your life that know how to bring joy into the room. If not, why not ask God for one right now.

Today's Prayer

Father God, you made us for laughter and fun. You fashioned our bodies to respond in wonderful way when we laugh. You made us in such a way that our entire being gets involved in the fun. I believe Jesus laughed a lot as he interacted with those who were fortunate enough to enjoy his physical presence. I can picture his laughter when he embraced the children or the joy he expressed when the blind received sight and the lamed walked. I believe heaven is full of laughter and fun. Your Word says that the angels rejoice in heaven, and that you rejoice over us with singing. Lord, I pray we follow those examples and learn to laugh more often. In the name of our Joyful Lord. Amen.

Today's Scripture

Psalm 126:2; Proverbs 17:22; Proverbs 31:25; Zephaniah 3:17

December 13

Today's Thought

When two nations battle, the loser must surrender to the winner. It's no wonder we have such a negative view of surrender. God turned the act of surrender upside down. When we submit to God and his will, we are not the loser, we are the winner. The Lord calls us to yield in many ways. We are to surrender our thoughts to his thoughts, our plans to his plans. Sometimes there are people in our lives we need to lay before the Lord. Most of all, the Lord calls us to surrender our will to his will. Relinquishing is not always easy, but the gains are priceless. We must understand that when we are experiencing emotional pain, it could be caused by something we are holding onto that needs to be relinquished. We come to him with our hands full of stuff that does not profit and over which we have no control. Our hands are gripped into a tight fist that God wants to pry open. When we allow him, we leave with hands empty of everything but his will. Now he can fill us with all that glorifies him and benefits us.

Today's Prayer

Father God, we all know that surrender to your will is not easy. We have our own stubborn wants and think we know best. We thank you that as our Father you are the One who knows best. The people, places and things that we cling to ever so tightly could be the very things that are hurting us. Lord, help us to recognize that which you are trying to pry from our clutching hands. Help us to understand the correct concept of biblical surrender. Help us to see that submission to your will is always in our best interest. Help us to see surrender to you as a win. We look to you today and open our hands and lift them to you so you can take what needs to be taken and give what needs to be given. In the name of the Sovereign One over our lives. Amen.

Today's Scripture

Proverbs 3:5–6; Isaiah 64:8; Luke 22:41–42; Galatians 5:24

Today's Thought

Have you ever found yourself in a dry and thirsty place? The Psalmist cried out to God, *"O God, you are my God, earnestly I seek you; my soul thirsts for you, my body longs for you, in a dry and weary land where there is no water"* (Psalm 63:1). We have all felt that overwhelming physical thirst at some point in time. Oh, the glorious feeling when we got our hands on that cold refreshing water and gulped it down. Our entire body responds to the inflow of the life-giving water. In Psalm 63:1 David was speaking of a different kind of thirst; a spiritual thirst. That reminds me of something Jesus said to his disciples in Matthew 10:42, *"And if anyone gives even cup of cold water to one of these little ones who is my disciple, truly I tell you, that person will certainly not lose their reward."* A simple offering … a cup of cold water. As I think about serving the Lord today, I am reminded that even the simplest act of service can be life-giving to someone who is dying of spiritual thirst. My words can be the living water that will help a struggling child of God find hope and purpose. The simplest act of service can help a weary fellow traveler find her way. We serve Jesus best by serving others.

Today's Prayer

Father God, we desire to serve you today. If we only have a few life-giving words today, I pray we speak them. If all we can do is visit a lonely shut-in, may we go. We understand that the little we have to offer turns into much in your hands. Even as the small lunch of the lad fed thousands, our little cup of cold water can save a life. Serving others in any capacity is serving you. Preparing a family meal, saying a kind word to the store clerk, sharing our faith journey with someone or praying over a newborn baby, all of it matters to you. Nothing is too small or too insignificant with you. Thank you for every opportunity you place in our hands today.

Today's Scriptures

Psalm 63:1; Proverbs 11:25; Matthew 10:42; Hebrews 6:10

December 15

Today's Thought

One day when I was 5-years-old my father took me downtown to enjoy the department store lights and windows decorated for Christmas. It was so exciting to that little girl so long ago. I was so small; I remember swarms of people pressing me on all sides. I clung tightly to my father's hand and tried my best to keep up with his long strides, my eyes looking everywhere, full of Christmas wonder. Suddenly I felt my hand slip away from his. In my panic I began to follow two legs that I thought were my dad's. Before too long, I looked up and realized I was not following my dad at all. Who was this strange man who did not know me? Where was my daddy in this mass of people? Tears began to run down my cold cheeks; I was so frightened. I felt so alone and lost. Just as I was about to fall into utter panic, two large arms came and scooped me up. It was my daddy! He may have seemed lost to me, but I was not lost to him. He knew how to find his child. No matter how lost we may seem at times, we are never out of God's sight. He has our hand and he's not letting go.

Today's Prayer

Father God, how secure I am! You hold me by your righteous right hand. I am never lost to you. If I try to hide in the darkness, you see me because all is light to you. When I lose sight of my dreams and goals, you've got them. When confusion and doubt set in, you give me clarity. If I try to run from you, it is futile because you meet me in my rebellion. If I neglect to acknowledge you, my name is still written in your book. Lord Jesus, help us to remember that you are as close as our next heartbeat. We can never be separated from you and your love. When we begin to lose our grip, scoop us up in your loving arms and shelter us. In the name of the One whose has engraved us on the palm of his hand. Amen.

Today's Scriptures

Psalm 27:10; Psalm 63:8; John 6:39–40; John 10:27–30

December 16

Today's Thought

I recently came across an interesting fact that is fulfilled in the birth of Christ. First, we must go back more than 1,000 years when God made a promise to King David that he would raise up his offspring to succeed him and he would establish his kingdom forever. There were indeed 21 kings from David's line, up through King Zedekiah. After Zedekiah, 1,000 years passed by with no king sitting on the throne from David's line. Imagine the discouragement of God's people. What happened to God's promise? Where is our long-awaited king from the line of our father David? For 1,000 years they waited, generation after generation. Then it happened, a young virgin was told, *"You will conceive and give birth to a son, and you are to call him Jesus. He will be great and will be called the Son of the Most High. The Lord God will give him the throne of his father David"* (Luke 1:31–32). There it was, the fulfillment of the promise made to David. From Solomon, David's son, came two Davidic lines, one leads to Joseph and the other to Mary, (Matthew 1:1). It happened just as it was told by Nathan the prophet. David's line never ended, and Jesus came forth as the promised heir of an eternal throne. Every time we encounter scripture that refers to Jesus as the son of David, we are reminded that God always keeps his promises.

Today's Prayer

Father God, every word you speak is truth and every promise you make is fulfilled. The whole world waited in anticipation for the long-awaited promised One who would sit on an eternal throne and who would reign in righteousness over an eternal kingdom. Jesus, the son of David came to us at just the right time. Born in David's city of Bethlehem, just as you said. Born of a virgin from the line of David. We stand in awe of our Christmas miracle, the Lamb of God who came to seek and save the lost. Today and every day we praise you, the God whose Word never fails.

Today's Scriptures

Isaiah 9:6–7; Matthew 1:1; Luke 1:26–33; Luke 2:8–11

December 17

Today's Thought

Nothing intensifies feelings of loss and grief like the holidays. That empty chair at the dinner table. Those missing gifts under the tree. The special phone call from far away. The loneliness and relentless depression amidst so much laughter. So many traditions that are forever changed, because we are forever changed. My intent today is to remind us that it's okay to be less than joyful during what can be a difficult time for many. Amidst all the festivities, parties and celebration, we can feel lost and alone, just not able to enter in. If you have experienced great loss and still feel the pain of it, I encourage you to embrace where you are and do what you need to do, regardless of what others are doing. Your tears and grief become an expression of worship. Your tears tell God of the preciousness of the gift now gone. Your empty heart invites God to fill it with himself. Your emotions of sorrow and anguished heart are validated by heaven. You are where you are and God will meet you there. He says in Isaiah 57:15, *"For this is what the high and exalted One says—he who lives forever, whose name is holy: 'I live in a high and holy place, but also with the one who is contrite and lowly in spirit, to revive the spirit of the lowly and to revive the heart of the contrite.'"*

Today's Prayer

Father God, indeed you are with those who are downcast and sorrowful in spirit. Amidst all the celebration, you do not forget those who need you most. We praise you that you accept every form of worship; those who shout out from the mountain top and those who weep in the valley. Thank you for your Holy Spirit who comes alongside of us to help us in our time of need. I pray for those who are suffering loss, depression and anguish of soul. Lord, in your mercy and compassion, minister to them as only you can. In Jesus' name. Amen.

Today's Scriptures

Isaiah 57:15; Matthew 11:28–30; Romans 8:26–27; Hebrews 4:14–16

Today's Thought

Yesterday I wrote especially to those who were and are feeling the devastation of loss and grief during a season that rings of joy and celebration. I want to encourage each of us to remember those who are hurting at this time. Surely there is someone in our spheres of influence who is depressed, lonely and sorrowful of heart. How can we show the love of Christ to them? First, we affirm and validate their feelings. We give them permission to cry and grieve. We come alongside of them with acceptance, grace and kindness. We can all find our own unique way to do that. Perhaps a phone call or a welcomed visit. An invitation to lunch or dinner if they are up to it. A lovely bouquet of flowers always cheers me up. Our goal is not to talk them out of their sadness, but to be there with them in their grief; we weep with those who weep. We let them talk and refrain from talking about our holiday plans and parties. It's their time. With their permission we could read to them from the Psalms with the desire of giving them hope in the darkness. We go to them with no agenda but to love and respect them. If they are cheered by our efforts, we praise God. If nothing changes, we persist in praising God as we continue to pray for them. If I were the hurting one, these are the deeds that I would cherish.

Today's Prayer

Father God, we need wisdom and sensitivity during these days of Christmas celebration. We may be the one in need of encouragement or in a position to lift up another. I pray that we are in tune with your Holy Spirit as you show us those who need to see your love. We know that you are with our hurting friends; may we be there as well. Help us to esteem others more than ourselves as we look to you for guidance and direction. Lead us to those whom you desire to bless. In Jesus' name. Amen.

Today's Scriptures

Romans 12:15; Philippians 2:1–4; 1 Thessalonians 5:11; 1 Peter 4:8–11

Today's Thought

Yesterday as I was finishing up my Christmas shopping, I had quite a serious fall. I tripped over an uneven walkway. I flew hard and landed on my left side. My head was bleeding and I could not move my arm. God in his providence placed a wonderfully kind couple at just the right place at the right time. They lifted me from the ground and proceeded to care for my wounds. The woman went into a store and came back with a first aid kit, cleaned me up and bandaged me. They stayed with me, offered me a ride home and after a while they carried my packages and walked me to my car. This act of kindness is a reminder to me and hopefully to you that in a world that often seems distant and uncaring, there are people who are not afraid to get involved, help a stranger and give of their time to see to the care of another. I am also reminded that God orchestrates all things. When they woke up yesterday, they had no idea that God had a mission planned for them. He saw to it that they completed his purpose by placing them there for me. Let's remember two things as we near Christmas. God is watching out for each of us and will provide whatever we need in our time of helplessness. Secondly, let us be aware of those around us to whom we can extend kindness.

Today's Prayer

Father God, I am so grateful for two strangers who interrupted their day to help me in my time of need. I have been the recipient of an act of kindness that I will never forget. I know that you were acting in the situation, assuring me that in your providence, you provide. Nothing escapes your all-seeing eye, not even the tiniest sparrow that falls to the ground. Of how much more value are we, your beloved children? I pray that we are in tune to your purposes and the mission you have for us each day. Open our eyes and hearts to those to whom we can extend kindness. In Jesus' name. Amen.

Today's Scriptures

Proverbs 11:25; Matthew 7:12; Matthew 10:29; Colossians 3:12

 December 20

Today's Thought

This morning I was deep in conversation with the Lord, thinking about the fall I took. I thought about the scripture in Hebrews where we are assured that we have a Great High Priest who is touched by our weaknesses, as he, in his humanness, felt what we feel. I reminded Jesus that he never lived long enough to go through the aging process. How can he relate to the things I am experiencing now? I often trip over the smallest of things; my balance is not what it used to be. I have aches where I did not know I had muscle and bone. I have to put on my spare glasses to find my glasses. You get the picture. Jesus may not have grown into old age but he knows all about a broken and shattered body. My heart repents of my lack of understanding. Jesus does know all about the pangs of the human body as we age. He empathizes with all we go through on life's journey. He loves the gray head and carries the old one when the body lets one down. God made provision for the elderly parents by commissioning children to look after them. Paul admonishes us not to rebuke an older man and to treat older women gently, as a mother. God knows, God cares and he will uphold us to the end.

Today's Prayer

Father God, we need you more than ever as our bodies begin to disappoint us. We know aging is an important part of your plan. In the vigor of youth, we tend to feel self-sufficient. Aging reminds us that we are not. Your Word assures us that you are the one who carries us from the womb to the grave. We thank you that these bodies were not created to last forever. Now we can look forward to those new glorious bodies you promised us. Your plans and purposes are wonderful and we praise you. In Jesus' name. Amen.

Today's Scriptures

Leviticus 19:32; Psalm 71:17–18; Isaiah 46:3–4; 1 Peter 5:5

Today's Thought

One of the messages of Christmas I am embracing this year is *"slow down."* When I think of that night when Christ came into our world, I imagine *"a silent night, a holy night."* We know that Jesus was born at night because the shepherds were in the fields tending the sheep. What happens at night? We slow down. The activities of the day begin to catch up with us, the weariness settles in and we begin to slow our pace. When I had my fall a few days ago, I was rushing back to my car after shopping. I make the biggest messes in the kitchen when I try to shortcut the process. I miss some of the greatest blessings when I rush past people who God wants to use to encourage me. This world has a way of driving us into busyness and distraction by convincing us we have to do it all and we have to do it now. That is a lie and contrary to what the birth of Christ is all about. After a long journey to Bethlehem, Mary and Joseph settled in. They slowed down and waited for Mary's time to come. It was a silent night out in the fields. The shepherds were settled in with their sheep and were in a position to hear the glorious message of the Savior's birth. Are we in a position to hear that which God wants to speak to us this Christmas? It will only happen if we are willing to slow down.

Today's Prayer

Father God, you speak and work in the silence of our hearts. How often we miss you because we are so busy and distracted by worldly endeavors. Even the good things we do can be out of balance when we don't take the time to slow down and allow you to minister to us. We fly past so many opportunities that are meant to refresh and nourish us. Lord, help us to step out of the trap of "doing" so we can be more of a "being." Being with you and making our time available to you will always be rewarding. I pray we learn to slow down and embrace the moment. In Jesus' name. Amen.

Today's Scriptures

Psalm 46:10; Jeremiah 31:25; Matthew 11:28–30; Luke 10:38–42

December 22

Today's Thought

Do you have a favorite Christmas memory? As I sat this morning listening to my well-loved Christmas carols, I thought about my first Christmas as a believer in Christ. It was 1981 and I woke up with a bad cold accompanied by chills and fever. My plans were to go to my parents for gift exchange and dinner. I had to send my family on ahead without me. As I cozied up in my PJ's and blanket, I tuned the radio into a station that was playing Christmas music all day long. The carols and hymns all had new meaning for me. I now understood the glorious significance of the birth of a Savior. I celebrated with the shepherds as they were given the sign of a baby wrapped in swaddling clothes who was a King at birth and would one day be the Lamb of God who takes away the sins of the world. I sang to Jesus through my sore throat and it was the most blessed Christmas I ever experienced. Just Jesus and me. This is what I learned. I learned that I did not need the presents. I did not need the food or even the company of others. All of that is good and I praise God for Christmas celebrations. But on my first Christmas as a believer, I learned that all I really need is Jesus and his divine presence in my life. Merry Christmas, dear friends.

Today's Prayer

Father God, your presence is truly one of our greatest gifts. All we need is you. When we have you in our lives, we are complete. When I think of everything else you give us, it is more than my heart can hold. Family, gifts, plenty of food, the warmth of friendship, and so much more. Our soul blesses you and praises you for the amazing gift you sent all those years ago. Jesus is the answer to the ills and sins of this world. He fills all things, especially our hearts. As we celebrate your Gift this Christmas, I pray we understand more than ever that Jesus is enough. We bless his holy name today and forever. Amen.

Today's Scriptures

Zephaniah 3:17; John 1:14; Titus 3:4–7; James 1:17

December 23

Today's Thought

Are you at a loss about what to give the one who has everything? Gifts don't always come wrapped in shiny paper tied together with a big satin bow. Jesus was delivered to us through a simple couple who travelled to Bethlehem only to be left out in the cold. The Gift was born in the humblest of circumstances, and wrapped not in shiny Christmas paper, but in swaddling rags. The gift he brought with him was the Father's forgiveness. Today I am thinking about that gift. Is there someone in your past or present who is waiting for your forgiveness. Perhaps there is someone who has been waiting for an apology from you. Now could be the greatest opportunity for you to go to them. Sometimes regrets go way back. Time, nor distance matter as forgiveness has no limitations. I once had a woman come to me years after an offense; her conscience had bothered her for several years. What a blessed relief for both of us to have worked through our feelings and to extend forgiveness to each other. Nothing can hinder the joy of our spiritual lives more than unforgiveness. Let's all diligently search our hearts this Christmas season and see if there is a gift of forgiveness we need to wrap up in love and give to another. What heavy burdens can be lifted through the greatest gift ever given, forgiveness.

Today's Prayer

Father God, when you sent your Son you sent so much more than we could ever know. When we consider Jesus, we understand your heart of forgiveness. The angels cried, *"Peace on earth."* We know that we will not have peace on earth until Christ returns, but we understand that we can have peace in our hearts through Jesus who came to offer us the Father's forgiveness. Lord, I pray that each of us would search our hearts for any manner of gift we can give that is without cost. We may have to lay down our pride, but the results will be priceless. In Jesus' name, Amen.

Today's Scriptures

Romans 5:1; Romans 12:17–18; Ephesians 4:32; Colossians 3:12–13

December 24

Today's Thought

One divine night long ago God invaded our world with the unimaginable. He sent light into our darkness. He scattered lies with his truth. He laid down the glory and riches of heaven to become poor. He left timelessness to bind himself in time. The eternal One joined with the temporal. He exchanged his glory for human flesh. The ageless became a baby. The Lord God placed himself into the hands and care of a young couple named Joseph and Mary. The Mighty God became vulnerable. The Powerful Most High became weak. The Ancient of Days became subject to a calendar. The Lion of Judah became a lamb. He traded a throne for a manger and royal robes for swaddling cloth. He left behind a myriad of heavenly hosts who continually proclaimed his praise only to be rejected and scorned by those he came to save. He sent hope to a hopeless world. Who would do such a thing? No other god would look upon the helpless with such love and compassion. No other god would leave his lofty position to come down to us. There is only One true God who for the sake of even one, would leave all to secure a single soul for eternity. If you or I were the only sinner on earth, God would still have sent Jesus to live and die and rise up for us.

Today's Prayer

Father God, what a grand story unfolds in the gospels. You saw our need and in the fullness of time you met us in our hopelessness in the Person of your Son Jesus. In the stillness and darkness of our weary world mankind waited for a Savior. All of heaven held its breath as the Holy Spirit overshadowed Mary and God incarnate was conceived in the womb of a woman. On the sacred night of his birth, you turned on the lights. By his birth you fulfilled every promise. You always knew the plans you had for our redemption. We have no words by which we can express our eternal gratitude. Amen.

Today's Scriptures

Luke 1:30–35; Luke 2:8–11; 2 Corinthians 8:9; Philippians 2:9–11

December 25

Today's Thought

Christmas morning can go one of two ways. The parents have carefully prepared everything on Christmas Eve while the children lay snuggled in their beds. When morning arrived, the scene was set, tree lit, presents wrapped and labeled and the cinnamon buns brought fresh out of the oven. Each child took his or her turn carefully unwrapping each gift. A big fuss and heartfelt gratitude over each present was heard. Well, that's not the way it went at our house. We tore out of our rooms way before dawn, saw the gifts and began to rip open the carefully wrapped offerings. We barely paused between gifts to examine and appreciate what we were given, anxiously moving onto the next. In the end, the floor littered with paper and ribbon, we grabbed our favorite toy and ran off to our rooms to play. We can do that with Jesus too. He is the indescribable gift that we can so easily bury beneath all the celebration. I have decided this Christmas to keep Jesus in the center, at the heart of all I do, not only during this season, but all year through. I will reflect on the greatest Gift ever given. I will carefully unwrap every aspect of the story of his birth and the powerful significance his life has had on the world. With deep gratitude I will ponder the wonder of the miracle ... God incarnate, Immanuel, God with us.

Today's Prayer

Father God, there are no adequate words in human language that can fully express our gratitude for the greatest gift ever given. You wrapped your only begotten Son in human flesh and the Word came to live among us. He brought us truth and grace, and fully reflected the love of the Father. How can we ever understand the fullness of your gift? Father, I pray we pause this Christmas season and reflect on the true meaning and deep richness of this indescribable gift. Help us to take our time unwrapping all the truths of the Christmas story. In the name of Jesus. Amen.

Today's Scriptures

Isaiah 9:6; Matthew 1:21; John 1:14; 2 Corinthians 9:15

December 26

Today's Thought

What can we do in preventing the train wreck of sin in our lives? May I suggest three safeguards against ending up in a place we do not want to be. First, we must recognize the danger. Paul said, *"I would not have you be ignorant."* We cannot be oblivious to the danger of sin in our lives. We must recognize dangerous thoughts, dangerous actions, dangerous attitudes, and even dangerous companions. This can only happen as we feed on God's Word, his truth. In that way, we can discern darkness from light. Next, when we see danger heading our way, we need wisdom to make the right choice. That also comes through the Word of God and the help of the Holy Spirit. Lastly, we need the courage to act appropriately in every dangerous situation. To sum up: we recognize the danger; we make a wise choice; and, we pray for the courage to take appropriate action in situations that can lead us into disaster. A wise pastor once said, *"Sin will take you further than you want to go, keep you there longer that you want to stay, and cost you more that you ever wanted to pay."* Such an urgent warning!

Today's Prayer

Father God, we are grateful that in understanding our humanity, you have provided all we need to live a godly life. We do not have to be held captive to sin, Jesus, you have set us free from the power of sin over our lives. At times, in our humanity we fall back into the old ways. But thanks be to God we have the victory over sin and death. Lord, help us to live as if this is a living truth in our lives. Help us to live as women who have been brought back from the grave of ruin. You have redeemed our lives from the pit; we want to live under the law of a godly life. When sin is threatening to overtake us, I pray by your Spirit you open our eyes to the danger, help us make wise decisions, and give us courage to respond biblically. In the name of our Conqueror, Jesus. Amen.

Today's Scriptures

Proverb 22:3; Galatians 6:7–8; James 1:5; 2 Peter 1:3–4

December 27

Today's Thought

Let's make this a "thanksgiving" kind of day. How it will bless God if we spend today just thanking him; not asking for anything? I dare to believe that if we start at the crack of dawn and go into the wee hours of the night, we could not even begin to thank God for all he has done for us. The Bible is jam packed with verses that extol the virtues of gratitude. Truly God is blessed when we lift up our hearts to him in praise, but we are blessed as well. Gratitude improves our health, our mental outlook, our relationships and ushers in an emotional sense of well-being. On the contrary, complaining and whining brings us down to the lowest pit of despair. The choice is always ours. Let's find gratitude even in challenging situations. Many blessings are visible, but many are not. We will never know this side of heaven how good God has been to us in the hidden things. How many tragedies were avoided because God interrupted our schedule? How many prayers he did not answer the way we hoped which saved us much grief? Gratitude for the tangible and intangible keeps our hearts full of joy, hope and contentment in times when we don't understand. Come magnify the Lord with me, let us exalt his name together.

Today's Prayer

Father God, we come to you today with no requests on our lips, with only thanksgiving in our hearts. You are worthy of all our praise and gratitude. We brought nothing into this world and we can take nothing out. In light of this truth, we lift up our empty hands, depending on you for everything. Lord, we are blessed beyond measure. If we never receive another thing from you, we know we already have all we need. You inhabit our praises; may we feel and see your pleasure today. Be magnified in our praise and thanksgiving. In the name of the Jesus, the Worthy One. Amen.

Today's Scriptures

Psalm 34:1–3; Psalm 103:1–5; Psalm 113:1–3; Colossians 2:6–7

December 28

Today's Thought

Some ask, *"If God is good, why is there so much evil in the world?"* We ask the wrong question. The real mystery is this, *"With so much evil in the world, why does God remain good?"* When tragedy hits close to home, we tend to resort to the why questions. Why me, Lord? Why my marriage? Why my child? Why my job? Why my health? Indeed, God is big enough to handle any protest we throw at him; but likewise, he desires that we view life through the lens of his goodness. When our focus gets stuck on what is wrong, how we have been hurt, how much we have lost, we lose sight of the bigger picture. God and his ways can certainly be an enigma. Tragedies have a way of throwing our faith off kilter. God's goodness triumphs over our questions and doubts. God cannot deny his goodness. He is the personification of all that is good. When we look for his mercy and grace, we will see it clearly. When we look at all the evil around us, that's all we will see. When the emphasis of our lives is aligned with his kindness toward us, the evil will pale in comparison. We do not deny that the world is a fallen, broken place, and we will be touched by it, but the larger truth is always that God remains good.

Today's Prayer

Father God, when our world is crumbling all around us, help us to remember that you have not changed. When hard times hit close to home, help us remember that you are on our side; you are for our good; not for our harm. We understand that in all circumstances you are working out your perfect will. I pray that every day, in all the situations, our hearts are full with the wonder of mercy that does not give us what we deserve, and grace that gives us what we do not deserve. In all things, in all ways, you remain good. I pray you grant us spiritual eyes to see the length, depth, height and breadth of your goodness and love. In Jesus' name. Amen.

Today's Scriptures

Exodus 33:18–19; Psalm 34:8; Psalm 145:9; Romans 8:28

December 29

Today's Thought

As a child, growing up with three brothers, I often thought they had advantages over me. They got more food on their plates. They got better running shoes than I did and other older brother privileges. When I would complain and compare, my father had a cliché that always silenced me. He said, *"Mind your own table, Mabel."* That may sound harsh to your ears, but my father had a lesson in mind for me. One day Peter was just told that the day would come when he would no longer be a free man. Others would dress him and lead him where he did not want to go, indicating the kind of death by which Peter would glorify God. Now listen to this discourse, *"When Peter saw him, (John), he asked, "Lord, what about him?" Jesus answered, "If I want him to remain alive until I return, what is that to you? You must follow me"* (John 21:21–22). Jesus' answer is as much for us today as it was for Peter then. When we begin to compare the plans God has for our lives with the plans he has for others, we are like quarrelsome children. We will never be content until we understand that God knows what is best for each one of us. My father taught me to tend to my own business rather than question authority.

Today's Prayer

Father God, the plans you have for us are custom-designed for our particular life journey. We will all glorify you in different and unique ways. Lord, help us to be content with our lot in life. I pray we cease from looking around and envying the ministries and callings of others. May we have a laser focus on our own calling and purpose whatever that may be. Father, you tell us that we will all be rewarded for obeying what you call us to. We can know for sure that we are beckoned by Jesus to follow him as he chooses our path. In the name of the God who leads us. Amen

Today's Scripture

Psalm 32:8; Jeremiah 29:11; John 21:18–22; 2 Corinthians 10:12

December 30

Today's Thought

Here we are, coming to the close of another year. God has been so good! I have a few thoughts I would like to leave with you. It's about love. It's about the truth that nothing on earth or in the heavenlies will ever be able *(have the power)* to separate you from the love of God that is in Christ Jesus. I know this to be true, because you see, dear one, it is never about our love for God, it has always been about his love for us. It's not that we loved him, but that he first loved us. It's no longer about what we have done; it's about what he has done. His love transcends the grave. It transcends all power and principalities. It transcends all our sinfulness and backsliding. It's not about where you have been, it's about where he went for you. He came to earth so we could know that he understands humanity. He went to the cross so we could know that he understands suffering. He rose from grave so we could know that he tasted death and defeated the grave. Now we know that we will rise from the grave as well. He is now in heaven interceding on our behalf. This is a love so deep, so wide, so incomprehensible, we cannot grasp it this side of heaven. But we know it exists. We know it is real. Let's spread the good news all around. *For God so loved the world ...* they need to know what we know.

Today's Prayer

Father God, how can we understand a love so great, a power so mighty, a God so loving, that nothing or no one can separate us from you? We cannot hide from it; we cannot run from it. Your love will chase up down and overtake us because you are relentless in pursuing us with your love. Lord, I pray we end this year and begin the new with the reality of the truth that we are loved and we are your beloved, now and forever. I ask that we not be shy in sharing our testimony and our faith. We praise and exalt your holy and righteous name. Amen.

Today's Scriptures

Isaiah 54:10; Romans 8:31–39; Ephesians 3:14–19; 1 John 4:10

Today's Thought

As we close out this year together, let's consider the path our feet have taken. If you are like me, you set out in the new year with some goals, plans and desires to be fulfilled. Perhaps the Lord spoke some dreams into your heart, desires of his heart, now assigned to you. He spoke this women's devotional into my heart and here I am completing it. I must admit, I am a few days late. There are however, some things that have been left undone. Possibly it's the same for you. Some boxes checked off, some not. Even looking back on your life, you can see that God had a plan and specific purposes for your life. Then sin or procrastination, bad choices or plain laziness got in the way and tripped you up. Truth is, none of us get it right all the time. We all fall short in some way. Cheer up, my friend; it's never too late to catch up with God's plan. No matter how far away you have wandered from his will, he can still work it all together for good. Our Lord is patient with us because it's who he is. God does not simply show patience, He is patience personified. How I wish I could be like that. Sometimes we do have to be patient with ourselves, and sometimes we need the nudging of the Holy Spirit to get us going in God's direction. Wherever you find yourself at the end of this year, the new is coming: new goals; new plans; new strength; and new energy to accomplish that which God places in your hands.

Today's Prayer

Father God, we thank you for the plans you helped us accomplish this year. We look forward to the plans you will assign us in the upcoming year. We know that you always have good for us. Forgive us for the times we fall short due to self-will and stubbornness. We understand that your will is good, perfect and pleasing. Lord, we want that. Thank you for your patience and your determination to pursue us and to conform us to your will. In Jesus' name. Amen.

Today's Scriptures

Proverbs 16:3; Romans 12:2; Galatians 6:9; Hebrews 12:1

Daily Questions and Comments to Challenge Us

These questions and comments are designed to help you think more deeply about what you read. I encourage you to use this section of the book in whatever way suits you best.

May I suggest you have a partner while you go through the devotional, someone who is reading along with you and with whom you can discuss what the daily reading has meant to you and how it challenges you.

This section can also be used for a group Bible study discussion.

I love journaling. Perhaps you do too. If so, begin a new journal for this year and it will be a blessing later in life as you go back and reread all the things God did and what he revealed to your heart during this time. If you have never journaled, now would be a good time to discover the wonderful spiritual benefits in recording your thoughts and prayers.

May the Lord of heaven richly bless you as you spend this time in his Word, listening and learning.

To God be the glory for all He has done.

January 1

Think about your needs as you approach this new year, this new beginning. Talk to God today and share your heart with him. He will meet you right where you are; he will meet you, as sure as the dawn.

January 2

What are your spiritual goals for the new year? Talk to God today about this journey and share with him your hopes and dreams.

January 3

Is authenticity a longing of your heart? Allow God to expose any masks of pretenses you have been wearing. You will be set free and able to fully enjoy the true you.

January 4

What value do you place on God's Word? Are there any ways that you can enhance your personal study of God's Word? Are you willing to develop a plan so that can happen?

January 5

Is there someone you know who is struggling today? Why not bring some encouragement to her in the way of a call, text, card, or an invitation to lunch?

January 6

Has the world and its empty promises disappointed you? Take inventory today of your priorities to see if any changes are needed.

January 7

Do you sometimes feel distant, unnoticed by God? Meditate on today's scriptures and assure your heart that you are known, seen and loved by God.

January 8

Are you learning to be still in the worst of circumstances? It is always in our best interest to trust God and remain calm in the storm. It will soon pass, and the lessons learned are priceless.

January 9

Are the troubles and cares of this world weighing you down? Sort through those things over which you have no control. Then, sort through the situations that you can influence. Know the difference and act accordingly.

January 10

How are you occupying? Are you spending the time you have on earth wisely? Are your interests mainly in the greatest investment possible, sowing into the kingdom of God?

January 11

Is it a struggle for you to sit quietly and wait on the Lord? Waiting on God is a learned spiritual discipline. To begin, practice it in small amounts of time. Soon it will feel comfortable for you. The benefits are eternal.

January 12

Do you struggle with understanding God in three persons? This truth is a mystery none of us will fully comprehend this side of heaven. We believe by faith, and faith comes by hearing the Word of God.

January 13

Do you need to understand God's love for you in fuller ways? Take special notice today of all the ways God is extending his love to you. First, look at the cross and know that it was for you that Jesus laid down his life. No greater love than that exists.

January 14

Are you being held captive in the prison of unforgiveness? Today is the day to make the choice to forgive that one who grievously offended you. If you make the decision to forgive, God will lead you to living in the state of forgiveness.

January 15

How aware are we of the pain of others? Make it a habit to notice those around you who are hurting. Be creative in ways in which you can reach out to them with the comfort of Christ.

January 16

When a child is weaned from his mother's milk, he no longer comes to her with an agenda. Are you bringing your concerns to God with an open heart? Do you come to God with nothing except to allow him to hold and comfort you?

January 17

Do you struggle with understanding a God who has no beginning and no end? No one is able to understand this great mystery. But we live by faith. Let's exercise our faith in those things that are beyond our finite minds.

January 18

Is there something in your life that needs the touch of God's light? God is light and he is able to illumine your path. Go to him today and he will meet you with the truth and direction you need.

January 19

We are all brides. When we come to Christ, we become his betrothed, the promise of the Father. We are sealed for Jesus by the Holy Spirit. Are you preparing for him even as he prepares for you?

January 20

Do you struggle with the reality of a literal resurrection? As you study today's scriptures allow the Spirit of God to reach into the deepest place of your beliefs and seal the truth of resurrection once and for all.

January 21

Are there some ways in which you struggle trusting God to meet your daily needs? Look back over your life and count all the ways he has provided for you. Be amazed, grateful and trusting; he is the same God who provided then and will provide for you now and always.

January 22

Would you allow God to shake the things in your life that need to be shaken so he can have his rightful place? When all the dust settles, you will be more like him.

January 23

In what ways are you as a little lamb? Are you convinced that you need a shepherd? Talk to God about any ways you may be feeling self-sufficient and allow his Word to convince you of your constant need for him.

January 24

In what specific ways does God show you his love? Can you believe that every day you are his favored child? Choose someone today and do or say something to make her feel favored and loved.

January 25

Are you struggling with a besetting sin? Read Romans 7:18–25. You will see that the great apostle Paul knew the inner battle between good and evil. In this passage he gives us all hope through Jesus Christ our Lord.

January 26

Like me, do you place certain expectations on those you love? Would you be willing to take a closer look at that behavior? Being honest and releasing can set you free in wonderful ways.

January 27

How aware are you of the words you speak? We choose to speak life or death. How can you better use your words to be life-giving to you and to others?

January 28

As you think about the rest of your day, remember you will face many choices. Pray that the Lord God, by his Spirit will guide you into choosing the good and right way.

January 29

Have you been carrying around old wounds and hurts? Are they affecting your life and your relationships? Will you allow God to expose those strongholds and yield to that healing and freedom he wants for you?

January 30

Are you convinced that God knows everything there is to know about you? Is there something you have been trying to hide? God knows and loves you still. Open your entire life to the Savior today and he will receive you with love and forgiveness.

January 31

You are fully justified before God in heaven. Jesus stood in your place. He took your sin and gave you his righteous perfection. You can walk in the robe of his righteousness today. This truth should cause us to want to be more like him in every way.

February 1

What is it you want Jesus to do for you? Don't hesitate today, make your request known to him and he will meet you. He already knows and his provision is in his hand ready to give.

February 2

Where do you go when the storm brews? To whom do you look when you feel helpless? No other god can save and deliver like the God of heaven and earth. Run to him at all times. He is there to meet you.

February 3

Have you grown weary of waiting on God to move in your situation? Can you believe that he has not forgotten; that he is still working on your behalf? Talk to him about that today.

February 4

Is God asking something of you in this season of your life? Have you been stalled in following through? Today would be a good day to reassess where you are and where you are going. The Holy Spirit can jump start the hope you need to move ahead.

February 5

Don't allow the enemy to bring condemnation over a past transgression that has been confessed and of which you have repented. God's forgiveness is full and free. Enter into his faithfulness with a heart that believes and responds with gratitude.

February 6

How do you measure your worth? Are there some ways in which thoughts about your worth need to change? God's Word is the place to begin.

February 7

Do you see yourself as God's special needs child? Are you willing to let go of self-sufficiency and independence so you can experience more of God's special care in your life?

February 8

Are you content with who God created you to be? Do you have a tendency to compare yourself with others? Talk with God today about this struggle and especially begin to thank him for making you beautifully in his image.

February 9

Are you allowing God's Word to be your spiritual mirror? God's desire is that every time we approach scripture, we see exactly what it is he wants to show us personally; then we obey.

February 10

God may be calling you to rethink that difficult relationship. Can you possibly see it as a gift that will refine you and perhaps change the heart of that challenging one? Pray about that today and let God have his way.

February 11

Are you anticipating the end times and the return of Christ for his church? We followers of Christ have nothing to fear. Whether we live or die, we belong to the Lord forever. When you feel overwhelmed with life, take on the eternal perspective.

February 12

We honor God most by accepting the unique person he created us to be. Do you believe you are special and created by God for his unique purposes? Cease from looking around and comparing yourself to someone else. Be aware of when and how you may desire that which was not given to you.

February 13

Learn as much as you can about your elected officials. When elections come around, explore your options and learn about those who are running for office. It really matters who we vote for and what they believe.

February 14

How well are you accepting the maturing process? Do you feel you are growing wiser and more beautiful with time? Are you embracing all that comes with aging? The aging process is another way that God chips away at our vanity.

February 15

How we respond in challenging situations is of utmost concern to God. Today, think about that statement and see if changes need to be made in your perspective on trials.

February 16

Can you recognize any ways you may be living under the old covenant of rules and regulations? Take some time this week to examine this matter. We can all be attempting to live under the law without realizing it.

February 17

As we examine our hearts today, let's allow God's Holy Spirit to expose any areas where we may believe or speak lies. Remember that God hates every lie and loves all truth.

February 18

Are you facing a difficult trial right now? Do you feel as if God placed you in a fiery furnace? Believe that Jesus is in the flames with you. He will not leave you there, he will not forsake you. You shall come forth as gold.

February 19

Make a list of all the things you believe to be true about God. Likewise, make a list of your concerns and doubts. Lift both lists up to God today and allow him to unravel the mysteries of his nature.

February 20

What is that one thing in your life you wish you could do over? Do you believe God can bring good out of your worse mistake? What are some of the ways he has already done that?

February 21

Are you resting in the faithful arms of God; or, are you living a self-sufficient life? The latter life will eventually leave you worn out and disappointed. God wants to be your all-sufficient One. Will you let him?

February 22

Have you ever felt disappointed in God? In what ways? God may not work in the way we would like, but he never disappoints us. Can you move past your own disappointments and accept yourself as God accepts you?

February 23

Is there a situation in your life that God is asking you to release to him? When you are ready to let go, he will be there to meet you and uphold you while he works on your behalf. Is today the day for you to relinquish?

February 24

Forgiveness is not optional. Is there someone you need to go to today and offer forgiveness or ask forgiveness? Don't delay another day. Each day, month or year you procrastinate will cost you much.

February 25

When was the last time you encouraged yourself in the Lord? Are you in a place today where that would be helpful? It begins with praise. Scripture tells us to put on the garment of praise for the spirit of heaviness.

February 26

How closely have you been monitoring your thought life? Today is a good day to be cognitive of where you allow your thoughts to take you. Ask the Holy Spirit to help you bring your thoughts under the Lordship of Christ.

February 27

Do you lack wisdom? Ask God for it and he will generously supply what you need. The key is to act in obedience to what he shows you.

February 28

Are you burdened down with a load of guilt and shame over past sins? Today is the day to cast off those lies that keep you bound to your past. Cast all of it upon the One who paid the price for your full pardon.

March 1

Study Ephesians 6 today and make it your habit to put on the full armor of God daily.

March 2

It's always wise to allow God to expose what is in our hearts. We can never hide our secrets from him; he sees all and loves us still. Will you open your whole heart to him today?

March 3

What changes need to be made in your lifestyle so others will want to know the loving Jesus of the Bible? I challenge you to ask three trusted friends in what ways they see Jesus in you.

March 4

Are you choosing joy? I know life can be tough and challenging, but choosing joy helps us keep that heavenly perspective and it blesses our God.

March 5

I hope you have many goods friends on whom you can count. God calls you friend. What an honor. He will be the most faithful friend you will ever have. Talk to him as you would a dear friend. He is waiting.

March 6

I hope you now can distinguish between being loved by God and being his beloved. Journal a letter today to your beloved in heaven.

March 7

Are you able to clearly identify the season you are in right now? Write about how you are feeling in regard to this time in your life. Change will come sooner or later; we must always be prepared to make the adjustment.

March 8

I challenge us today to evaluate our degree of spiritual focus. What race are we running, where are we headed, and how do we want this to end?

March 9

Are you ready to dive into the deeper waters of God's love today? He invites each of us and calls us by name. Won't you surrender to so great a love today?

March 10

What do you think those closest to you will say at your memorial service? What do you want them to say about you after you are gone? Make a list of those things and evaluate your life by what you wrote.

March 11

When the storms of life threaten to drown you, to whom do you run? Jesus is the Rock that is higher than all our circumstances. If you allow him, he will lift you above the storm and keep you safe.

March 12

People will treat us the way we let them. Evaluate your relationships based on how the Lord wants you to be valued and respected. Sometimes we need to teach those close to us how God sees and values us.

March 13

Be on alert today for that special kiss from heaven. God desires deep intimacy and affection in his relationship with you. He has millions upon millions of ways to show you his love. Don't miss it!

March 14

The greatest question we are faced with in life is this, *"What will you do with Jesus?"* Scorn or embrace? Receive or reject? Accept his grace or walk away? The choice will always be ours to make.

March 15

Sooner or later we each have to admit that we should have been on that cross. We all have a part of Barabbas dwelling in our sinful nature. But praise be to God, the great exchange on the cross brought righteousness to us, a righteousness we could never attain on our own.

March 16

Do you continue to carry guilt or shame from past sins? It is crucial that we understand the full forgiveness of God through Christ Jesus. What Jesus did on the cross was enough. We cannot add anything to it that makes it any more effective.

March 17

Have you experienced an empty heart? Have you tried to fill it with things that did not satisfy? Let's stand outside the empty tomb of Jesus for a while today and consider that he is not there, he has risen. Then turn from the empty tomb as Mary did and encounter your glorious living Lord.

March 18

Do you sometimes have a tendency to move away from God when you know you are not at your best? Where are you right now? I hope you are as close as you can be. If not, draw near to him today and he will surely draw near to you.

March 19

Are you plagued by fear? What action steps can you take in overcoming this debilitating emotion? Talk to God about it and he will give you the wisdom that brings freedom and peace.

March 20

What are your doubts? Journal about them today. Tell God about the level of your trust and faith. Lift it up to him as a confession of weakness and he will lift you up into a higher place of trust.

March 21

How often do you rely on your Bible for wisdom in navigating this unstable world? How much time do you devote in seeking the answers for today's uncertain times? God wants his people to discern the times so we can enter into the abundant life.

March 22

We have full and free access to God through Jesus, the Lamb of God. His death and resurrection secured for us a way into the very presence of the Holy One. If you have doubts, you need only to believe.

March 23

Are you facing a fiery trial right now? Rejoice, because God is working in you so he can work through you. The perfecting of your faith is precious and of great value to you and will benefit those around you.

March 24

Do you consider yourself a good listener? If yes, I applaud you. If you need help in that area, learn from Jesus who was always ready to listen and also ready with appropriate answers. Honestly evaluate your listening skills today.

March 25

If you are having difficulty making good daily choices, now is the time to talk to God about living healthier, both physically and spiritually. Every choice we make contributes to our destiny.

March 26

Are your words building up or tearing down? Are your thoughts wholesome and inspiring? Let's all work together on being women whose speech is seasoned with grace and goodness.

March 27

I hope you have dreams and ambitions. The only way to succeed in realizing those goals is to be consistent in every area of your life. If you need to develop consistency, the faithful, constant God will be overjoyed to help you.

March 28

Do you know the call that is on your life? If not, why not ask God today to draw out of you those things he can most use in the lives of others.

March 29

Are you a seeker of God? He rewards the one who is diligent in wanting to know him. Look for him in all ways today. He reveals himself to those who seek.

March 30

Have you accepted Jesus Christ as the only Savior of the world? It is not our sin that keeps us from eternal life; it is rejection of the One who paid our sin debt. Call on him today and you will be saved.

March 31

Do you have regrets over the times you walked away rather than persevered? God is not finished and it's not over till it's over. Trust that his heart is toward you and he does work all things for your good, even when you think it's hopeless.

April 1

Have you learned to trust God in the silence? He does some of his best work while we wait on him. Learn to wait; and, learn to trust the silence.

April 2

If you see yourself caught in the vicious trap of perfectionism, I urge you to get before the Lord and ask him to break this bondage in your life.

April 3

Are you feeling overwhelmed and weary? Have you overcommitted? Perhaps today is the day to think about priorities. Sort through those activities that are of the Lord and the ones you have placed upon yourself.

April 4

Do you know the Bible well enough to distinguish between truth and error? Do you know the God of the Bible in such a way that you would recognize a false teacher? In these last days we must be guarded and armed with the belt of truth.

April 5

We all desire to walk as Jesus walked. Let's pray continually for that mysterious virtue of humility. Let's chase it down.

April 6

We must be sure of what we believe. Lies take us captive to sin, and death is the result. Study the Word of God diligently and take heed to all that Jesus teaches.

April 7

Do you get distracted during church service or during prayer time? We really need to be intentional in worship and prayer, careful not to fall into mindless fantasy. Be aware of those times when distractions want to steal your intimate time with God.

April 8

We need to ask the Lord if there are any ways in us that are not sincere, ways that are not honest, ways that are more for our benefit than that of others. May any hypocrisy be exposed by the genuine light of God's truth.

April 9

Have you suffered loss recently? God is a redeeming God and he is able to bring recovery and restoration. Talk to him about your losses today. He knows and understands; let him comfort you.

April 10

Can you discern any compromise in your lifestyle? In this day God is calling each of us to spiritual maturity and that begins with obedience to his golden rule of love.

April 11

Are you shining your light all around so others may see Jesus? He says we are the light of the world, just as he was. Light your candle and go light your world.

April 12

Do you sometimes think that you have to pull yourself up and get your act together? Take heart, you need not do any such thing. Simply cooperate with the Holy Spirit, the one who works God's good pleasure in you.

April 13

Does your outside walk match up with how you walk within your home? David spent time praying about that. Let's follow his example today.

April 14

When we are offended, God is especially interested in how we respond. These offenses come as tests. He is always looking into the condition of our hearts. Will you choose to please him?

April 15

How are you running your race? My hope is that you are running well. God is laying up for you the victor's crown.

April 16

God sees you through the eyes of love. If you have been unsure about how God sees you, meditate on today's scriptures.

April 17

Are you often feeling disappointed? Perhaps it's a symptom of something deeper. Determine now where you are going to place your expectations and hope.

April 18

Is your light shining? We are not of those who live in dread and fear. We are of the household of faith. Be a faithful witness today.

April 19

Right now, Jesus is calling you to come away with him and dine on the Bread of Heaven. How will you respond?

April 20

If you often feel overwhelmed and disappointed in friendships, it could be that you are attempting to please people. Examine that today and make any necessary adjustments.

April 21

Are you eagerly awaiting the Lord's return when he will make all things new and right? Be strong and courageous, your redemption indeed draws near.

April 22

Who among friends and family knows you best? Do any of them know everything there is to know? Of course not. It is both fearful and wonderful that God knows every intimate detail about your life. Rejoice in that today; you have nothing to hide from him.

April 23

Is there an unlovable person in your life with whom you struggle? First pray for yourself, that God would cause his love to flow in and through you. Then pray for the one who needs your prayers. You will like the results.

April 24

How do you determine your value? Who defines your worth? Do you perhaps need to make adjustments in the way you evaluate yourself? Talk to the Lord about that today.

April 25

I ask that you join me in blessing the Lord's heart through a concert of thanksgiving today. We have so much to be grateful for.

April 26

What battle are you facing today? Are you willing to allow the Lord to fight that battle as you go forth today, singing his praises?

April 27

If your heart had a joy meter, what would you be registering? I hope it would be a perfect 10. If not, begin somewhere in raising your joy level. The Holy Spirit waits to help you by sowing the fruit of joy in your life.

April 28

As we continue to look at the ways we are told to guard our hearts, each of us needs to take inward inventory of the areas where we are growing and those areas where we need help.

April 29

Does the culture of our day have a grip on you? God calls us to swim against the tide of ungodliness. Perhaps today is the day for you to turn and swim against a culture that rejects a godly lifestyle.

April 30

Take note throughout this week what you are allowing in through your eyes. Are the things you gaze at drawing you closer to Jesus and promoting spiritual growth or are they bringing darkness to your soul?

May 1

I want to have ears to hear; how about you? Let's pray today for greater understanding in regard to what we allow into our ears and how we respond.

May 2

Do you stop and think before you speak? This is a good habit for all of us to develop. We will spare ourselves and others much grief if we carefully weigh our words.

May 3

Watch your lifestyle because you can be sure others are watching. Think about how you want others to evaluate your life then go about living that way.

May 4

Let's take inventory of our emotions today. Are they under the control of the Holy Spirit? If not, God by His Spirit can help you bring them under His power.

May 5

How well do you guard your mind? God has made us stewards over our bodies and minds. Let's steward well and become pure in all our thoughts.

May 6

We are bought with a high price, the blood of Christ. Let's determine to live as those who belong to a holy Father. Let's imitate him with our bodies and our minds as we daily guard our hearts.

May 7

I hope you have friends who make you laugh and bring you joy. If so, why not let them know how they bless you. Perhaps you need to seek out friends who lift you up. Do that today.

May 8

What distracts you? Pay close attention this week and take note of what would pull you away from the most important things.

May 9

Are you weary today? Consider it a gift from God. Perhaps he is calling you to himself so he can give you the promised rest.

May 10

Are there any ways in which you desire to be more childlike? Talk to Jesus about that today. He has the help you need.

May 11

Have you somehow jumped off the Potter's wheel? If you desire God to fulfill His eternal purposes in your life, you will need to surrender once again to the wheel.

May 12

Today may be a good day to let someone know how much of an impact they have made on your life.

May 13

Even as Jesus was willing to expose his scars to us, are we willing to allow him access to ours? Are we keeping our painful past locked up for fear of exposure? Give Jesus all your pain today.

May 14

You have just come out of a trial; are currently experiencing a trial; or, there a trial coming. There is no escaping God's testing if you are his child. Rejoice today that He loves you so much He desires to bring you forth as gold.

May 15

As the days of our lives continue to slip by, we need to regularly evaluate where our lives have been and where we are headed. Pray for balance in all things. A wise woman avoids extremes of all kinds.

May 16

Endeavor to be more and more heavenly-minded as you await the appearing of your Savior from heaven.

May 17

What do you value in this life? Where do your priorities lie? We need to keep in mind that the kingdoms of this world are fleeting and will all pass away.

May 18

We all have regrets about taking a shortcut when God's way would have been better. Examine your life today for any shortcuts you may be taking. Make a turn in God's direction that it may be well with you.

May 19

Let's make it a daily habit to ask God to examine our hearts.

May 20

I dare say we can all do better in the area of generosity. It's our human nature to hold back, thinking we won't have enough for ourselves. We need to remember that we can never out give our generous God.

May 21

Are your needs being met today? Can you trust they will be met tomorrow, next week, next year, even for the rest of your life? Today I encourage you to judge between your wants and your needs.

May 22

Are there any ways in which you are seeking your approval from people? Do you look to others for validation? Have you been disappointed in the results? Look to God and him alone and He will not disappoint you.

May 23

Are there circumstances in your life where you would like to see justice? Leave room for God to work on your behalf. Forsake wrath and trust God.

May 24

Imagine your time has come to be present with the Lord. What would you like those left behind to say about your walk of faith? What are you willing to change in order to leave behind a good reputation?

May 25

Consider your life's journey. Think back on all the times you grew weary. Was God faithful in bringing you through? Thank him today as He continues to walk alongside of you all the way.

May 26

Is there a relationship that you walked away from because of how you "felt"? Consider today that God may want to revive and restore that friendship.

May 27

What does it mean to you that Christ lives in you and you live in him? How can this truth change your perspective on life and its struggles?

May 28

What does it mean to you that God rested? What would it look like for you to work from your rest? How do you think this could impact your everyday living?

May 29

Which generation do you belong to? How were you shaped by the generation before you? How can you better understand the generation coming behind you? What are some ways you can help them?

May 30

Do those around you perceive that you know and love Jesus? Are you prepared to speak of your faith in him when appropriate?

May 31

In Romans 7:15–20, Paul isn't saying that as a Christian he still habitually sins. The verses surrounding this passage tell us he was speaking of his life *before* he became a Christian. How has your life changed since you decided to follow Christ? Is there a marked difference?

June 1

Are your daily spiritual disciplines stirring your desire for more of God? Are there some ways you could foster greater delight in the Lord and His Word?

June 2

Do you have a plan for when crisis situations hit? Think about the qualities of the person you could depend on. Would you like to be someone's go-to person when a storm hits his or her life?

June 3

We all need to ask ourselves; am I a hearer of the word only, or a hearer and doer of the word? Only by hearing and doing are we blessed.

June 4

What are your plans for this day? Have you sought the Lord's direction? Our ways are not always his ways, but his ways are always best.

June 5

When we feel distant from God we need to consider the "why" question. The answer will always fall on us. It could be sin, apathy, or any number of emotions. The distance is never God's doing. If you are feeling distant from God, He waits for you to talk to him about it.

June 6

Have you settled it in your heart that you will never deny Jesus, no matter the cost to you personally? We must always be ready to confess Christ in every circumstance.

June 7

What are your unanswered questions? Are you willing to stand before the empty tomb and trust that he who rose from the dead has the answers and believe that he is the answer?

June 8

Together, let's make today a day of high praise to our amazing God. As we lift our voices and hearts up to him in joyful praise, he draws near to us and delights in us.

June 9

Today let's make a check on our words and attitudes. We need to be ever aware of the negativity that comes from a heart that has lost its joy. Take back your joy and spread it to others.

June 10

Do you need to shake off a sleepy spirit? Don't be found wanting at Jesus' return. Call upon God today. He raised Jesus; He can certainly revive your spirit.

June 11

How are you doing in the arena of love? Are you willing to make loving well a priority in your life? What can you work on that will directly impact your ability to love?

June 12

Did your parents discipline you as a child? Can you see any benefits in your life that resulted from that discipline? So it is with the Lord. It may not feel good now, but later you will be glad for it.

June 13

Is it possible that self-control is the one fruit of the Spirit with which you struggle? Find as many scriptures as you can that relate to self-control and meditate on them daily. Soon you will find change happening from the inside out.

June 14

When you are feeling lost, abandoned and unloved, turn to Psalm 136 and read it once again. Remember the times when God showed you his faithful love.

June 15

Examine your heart attitude today. Are there any ways in which you feel you have certain rights? In the exercising of these rights, is someone else being hurt or overlooked?

June 16

Pay close attention to what sort of words come out of your mouth. God calls us to build up, not tear down.

June 17

What is your tendency, to run ahead of the Lord or to lag behind? The best posture is to always wait on the Lord's timing. It will make all the difference.

June 18

Do you ever feel as if you want to throw in the towel and just leave this world behind? You are not alone. It takes courage to live when you would rather die. We are called to courage, not cowardice. Trust in God's Word; a reward is waiting for those who overcome.

June 19

Are you by nature a rule-keeper or rule-breaker? Some like to push the envelope, but God's Word stands true. If we obey it brings life and contentment. If we disobey it yields death and darkness. The choice is ours.

June 20

I hope you have a special place where you meet with the Lord daily. God will meet with you anywhere and at any time. He is as close as your next breath.

June 21

Do you have a plan for your day? Make it a habit to make a plan, lift it to the Lord, then, be flexible and open to allow him to make changes when needed.

June 22

Think about the women in your life. Are they acting as a spiritual safety net for you? Do you need to ask God to make this important provision for you?

June 23

Have you discovered the way to God's holy hill? Let's thank him today that it is not about our perfection; it's Jesus' perfection in us that God accepts.

June 24

Have you experienced a season of complacency in your life's journey? Is your dependence on God or in yourself? We need to be ever watchful so that apathy doesn't set in. Fight it as if your life depends on it.

June 25

To what or to whom is your soul anchored? We all anchor to something or someone. If you have misplaced your trust, begin to talk to God about that today. Find you assurance in Jesus alone.

June 26

As you serve the Lord today remember that he sees the big picture of your life and He is pleased. We still must be realistic about our faults. He can be trusted to continue to work on those rough edges.

June 27

Are you allowing yourself to be stretched through hardship and trials? If yes, then you are one that God is able to mature into the faithful disciple He created you to be.

June 28

Keep your spiritual disciplines close to your heart. Those who need to see will notice. Most importantly, God sees. He is pleased and he richly rewards.

June 29

Study Ephesians 6 today. Make a list of the ways God has equipped you to fight the good fight of faith. Put on the armor of God and never take it off.

June 30

Today my dear friends, I challenge you to address the lies you believe and find God's truth and record it in your journal. Choose you this day whom you will believe and whom you will serve.

July 1

Are you facing an important decision right now? The sweetest place is in God's will. Don't miss what God has for you. Pray, then wait on his wise counsel.

July 2

My challenge today is that each of us write our own unique love song to God, then sing it to him. Listen expectantly for his voice singing back to you.

July 3

Have you been carrying around a load of guilt and shame over past sins? Dear one, release them to God today and walk in the freedom Christ secured for you on the cross. Believing you are forgiven is one of the highest ways you can honor God.

July 4

Are you trying to fight your battles on your own? You will never win. The Lord is your Champion and he longs to be invited into your challenges.

July 5

What are the last words you would want to say before you leave earth? What kind of impact do you want to leave behind? How would you want your obituary to read?

July 6

Do you have a good handle on recognizing your weaknesses? Do you understand what your strengths are? What steps will you take in building up those weak areas?

July 7

Can you talk about an event where you had a choice to do right or wrong? Which did you choose? Pray about developing a more sensitive conscience when it comes to righteousness.

July 8

Do you believe that most frustrations in life involve issues of the heart? Take some time today to think about those issues. Are there ways in which you need to place boundaries around your heart?

July 9

What are the things you know are absolutely true about you? About God? About heaven? What feelings wash over you when you think about standing in the presence of God?

July10

What are some of the ways God speaks to you? Are there some ways in which you feel dull of hearing? Talk to God about that, then, wait hopefully and expectantly.

July 11

How is your spiritual race progressing? Have you recognized any obstacles that may be hindering you? What can you do in order to clear your path?

July 12

Are you able to discern how the culture of our day may be influencing you? Have you identified any areas where you could be holding onto something that God is asking you to surrender? Relinquishing is a process. Will you begin the process today?

July 13

Are there any ways in which you are feeling overwhelmed today? Do you need to learn how to say "No"? Find a trusted friend who will help you distinguish between the urgent and the important when making commitments.

July 14

How are you walking these days? Does your faith-walk fit you well and do others see how comfortable you are in your relationship and walk with Christ? Are there any ways in which your walk can improve?

July 15

What is your well of need today? No need is too great for the Lord to provide. Talk to Jesus about that need and share with him that for which you are thirsting.

July 16

Do you feel old or young? Think about your answer. Are you ready to embrace aging as a gift that leads to eternal life? Are you feeling renewed in your spirit day-by-day?

July 17

At this point in your life, can you perceive that God is up to something? Are you willing to let go of your self-imposed notions so God can stretch and grow you? Are you open to believing God is doing a new thing?

July 18

What role does hope play in your life? To what do you resort when life gets you down? Do you need to look to heaven today with expectant hope?

July 19

Are there things in your life you are trying to keep from God? Attempting to hide can be such a burden. Would you be willing to go to him today with open hands and a trusting heart?

July 20

How diligent are you in feeding on the Word of God? Is there some way you could be helped in being more consistent? Why not come up with a plan today.

July 21

Do you feel forgotten by God? Today go over the scriptures listed and pray that God gives you his reassurance that he cares and is working on your behalf. Share your insights with someone.

July 22

Is there someone with whom you are at odds? Knowing this breaks the Father's heart, are you willing to make a plan to attempt reconciliation. Are you willing to take the first step and leave the results with God?

July 23

Are you walking as a new creation in Christ Jesus? Make a list of some characteristics that make up your new identity. The first two chapters of Ephesians is a great place to start.

July 24

What rules in your daily walk with Christ? When the old nature rears its ugly head, are you prepared to do the 180 degree turn toward the Spirit- life? What's your plan?

July 25

I challenge us today to practice being in the presence of God. Talk to him throughout the day. Invite his presence into every activity and decision. I pray you sense his amazing presence in a multitude of ways.

July 26

I encourage you to join me today in praying for your pastor and your church leaders. Let us pray God's holy conviction upon them to preach, practice and to always hold to the truth of his Word without compromise.

July 27

Are there any ways in which you do not believe you were born for adventure, beauty and courage? What steps can you take in making that truth a part of your belief system?

July 28

How have you experienced the Light of the world? How has it changed you? Are you willing to shine the light of the gospel into your corner of the world? Will you be intentional in doing that today?

July 29

Are there any steps you need to take in assurance that you are connected to the Branch? Are you abiding or simply visiting? Will you make a commitment to continually remain attached to Jesus, our life-giving source?

July 30

Do you have a good understanding of your weaknesses? If you do, it is a strength for you. Are there some ways in which you need God's strength in overcoming a weakness? Why not tell him about it now.

July 31

What effect does pride have on our lives? Why is pride so offensive to the Lord? Is pride affecting any of your relationships? We are urged to chase after humility. Think of some ways you can turn that pride into humility.

August 1

What holds you back from embracing all that God says about who you are? Is unbelief affecting your daily choices? I challenge you to finish the following statement. Find at least five answers in scripture. I am a child of God, THEREFORE ...

August 2

How do you usually respond when a fellow believer falls into sin? Does your view of yourself change when you mess up? Are there any attitudes of the heart that you need to adjust? What does restoration mean to you personally?

August 3

Do you fear intimacy with God or do you welcome it? Describe your relationship with Christ. Is it about rules, facts and doing everything right? Or is it about openness, honesty and vulnerability? What would you like to see change?

August 4

Can you recognize pivotal moments in your life when you made a bad choice that led to dire consequences? How about those good choices that brought blessings? How will you use God's Word and prayer to help you navigate your way into making good choices?

August 5

What reasons could someone have for not wanting to be healed from past hurts? Why would someone choose to remain in misery and pain? At present, are there any unhealed areas in your life? Do you want to be well? How will you respond to Jesus today?

August 6

What place of importance does obedience to God have in your life? Is your obedience to God out of fear or love? Does today's devotion stir you to desire deeper levels of obedience?

August 7

When you mess up, to whom or what do you turn? Do you keep your mistakes hidden where only you can see them? I challenge you to commit Lamentations 3:19–24 to memory. Are you willing to take it a step further and speak it out loud to the Lord when you awake in the morning?

August 8

Do you believe that God has specific assignments for you and purposes to be accomplished? Are there any ways you have been attempting to fulfill God's purposes in your life in your own human understanding and strength? Today, think of ways that you can create an open door of dialog that will encourage another in their calling, then act on it.

August 9

Coveting is defined as wanting something you don't have. Do you sometimes find yourself pining over something that someone else has? Has coveting affected any of your relationships? Has it affected your priorities?

August 10

Being honest, what are your greatest distractions in life? Are there areas that need to be reevaluated because of the time they consume in your day? What adjustments are you willing to make in order to refocus your attention onto the important?

August 11

Have you experienced a desire to "get even" with someone who hurt you? Did you carry through? How did that end? God is the great avenger. Going forward, are you willing to allow God to secure justice for you?

August 12

Do you have a tendency to carry your burdens alone? What are your reasons for "doing it yourself"? What could be preventing you from casting your burdens and cares on Jesus? Are you willing to begin operating in the new way of the Spirit?

August 13

Do you tend to dwell on the history of the past rather than the dreams of the future? Is there something you are dragging around from your past? Ask God to help you leave the past behind so you can focus on all he has waiting for you in the future.

August 14

In light of today's devotion, I encourage you to do some research on persecuted Christians around the world, then think about how crucial it is that we pray for them.

August 15

Do you sometimes feel invisible and insignificant? How does it feel when someone wants to know you on a deep level? I challenge you to thoughtfully read and meditate on Psalm 139 today. Record in your journal all the ways God's knows you, cares about you and loves you.

August 16

Has your life been heading in a certain direction and within a moment taken on a whole new path? How do you respond to these shifts in your plans? Does today's devotion give you new insights on managing unexpected changes?

August 17

Like me, do you have a tendency to over commit? How consistent are you when it comes to saying "no"? What steps can you begin to take in learning how much you are capable of with the time you are given?

August 18

Have you been relying on your own power and strength to get through your daily tasks? How could things change for you if you began your day by asking God for his strength and power to meet your needs for today?

August 19

Do you have family members who share your love for Christ or do you walk alone? Have you had to deny yourself in some ways in order to fully follow Jesus? Do you believe that to gain Christ and his approval is worth more than the approval of friends and family?

August 20

What level of intimacy do you enjoy with the Lord? If you are honest, would you say that it needs some work? What are you willing to do in order to have deeper communion with God on an ongoing basis?

August 21

When you met Jesus, was your love for him a burning love or did you grow into fervency for him? Perhaps your current relationship with him is one of service and duty. Which type would you prefer? What steps can you take going forward in fanning the flame of love for Jesus?

August 22

What particularly stood out to you in today's devotion? Why do you think it struck you the way it did? Was there any concept that was new to you? Write out one of today's scriptures and meditate on it this week.

August 23

What has been your experience with both believers and non-believers? Which relationships leave you feeling better about yourself and closer to Christ? Are you currently in any unsafe relationships? Are you willing to take necessary steps to bring your close relationships into a spiritually healthy balance?

August 24

Fully embrace the work of the Holy Spirit in your life. If you are saved and sealed, nothing will ever separate you from God's love. Be sensitive to the many ways God is working in you by his Spirit.

August 25

Is there something or someone who competes with your trust in God? If we are placing our trust in mankind, how will that affect our relationships? When we place our trust in God, how will that affect our relationships?

August 26

Is there a verse of scripture you have been holding onto as a promise from God? In view of today's devotion take a closer look at those verses and determine if it truly is a promise or is it a principle?

August 27

How would you define grace? Are there any ways in which you need to take off the robe of self-righteousness and put on the Christ's robe of righteousness?

August 28

Do you think of yourself as an ambassador of the King of heaven? Today, think of how you have been representing the one who sends you to a broken world. Can you think of some new and creative ways to reach out to those in your world?

August 29

Do you have a good understanding of the difference between conviction and condemnation? Has today's devotion helped you in any way? As you move forward in your faith-walk with the Lord, be on the alert for any condemnation the enemy tries to throw at you. What scriptures can you rely on in discerning if you are experiencing conviction or condemnation?

August 30

Are you living each day in expectation of God setting you up for a great adventure? Do you look forward to new things or do you cringe when God calls you to move? Are there any ways you need to bring balance to your days? Rest when you must; move when needed.

August 31

Where are you today? Is there some way in which you need to tell God that "even though," you will trust him in your circumstances? Do you believe he is doing something in your life that will surprise and delight you?   Why not express your trust in him right now.

September 1

Is there some area of giving with which you struggle? It could be time, resources, finances or even your authentic self. Joyful generosity does not come naturally to most of us. God is the one who can help us see generosity from his perspective. As our hearts change, so will our attitude in giving.

September 2

Like me, do you sometimes expect to see more godly living from those outside the faith? Do today's scriptures help you understand their lack of capacity to live by God's holy standards? Was there a Christian who drew you to the light of truth? Perhaps you could give them a call or send a card expressing your gratitude for shining the light of Christ into your darkness.

September 3

Are there times when you doubt God's love for you? Do you sometimes feel he loves others more than he loves you? These are lies that can only be replaced by the truth of God's Word. Personize the scriptures that speak of God's love. For example, *"For God so loves (insert your name) that he gave his only Son, so that (you) would not perish but have everlasting life."*

September 4

Did you receive some clarity today between being in Christ and Christ being in you? This is an important truth that must be shared. I challenge each of us to take this truth deeper into our souls by sharing it with someone today.

September 5

Do you live under the cloud of fear of rejection? Are there any behaviors you exhibit that would encourage others to treat you badly? What changes and adjustments can you make in those relationships? Why not journal about it now and develop some action steps that will help you come out of those debilitating cycles?

September 6

Have you given much thought to the future awaiting you as the bride of Christ? Have you been impacted with the truth that preparation for that event begins in the here and now? As a spiritual bride, what steps have you been taking to prepare for that day?

September 7

This is a good time to remind ourselves and our loved ones of the most wonderful gift ever offered ... Jesus Christ, his love, his forgiveness and his promise to never hold our confessed sin against us.

September 8

Do you believe that you were born for such a time as this? It is no mistake that you are of this generation. God has assigned you a mission in your home, neighborhood, community and work place. Pray for the courage and boldness to hold out the words of life to those who are perishing.

September 9

Do you tend to run ahead of God or lag behind? When plans don't go as you had hoped, how do you respond? How tight is your grip and attempt to control outcomes? These are good questions to think about and make any needed adjustments.

September10

Are there things in your life that you crave excessively; love, money, food? What fills your emotional tank? Are these things bringing satisfaction? Are you willing to take a closer look at what fills your thoughts, your time and your heart?

September 11

Does today's thought give you a new perspective on idolatry? Search your heart before God and allow him to expose any areas of your life that need a closer look in regard to people, places and things having too high of a place in your heart.

September 12

What do you need from the Lord today? Be specific when making your request known. He loves to hear from you in the good times and the bad. Let him be the glory and lifter of your head and heart today. He is your greatest encourager.

September 13

Do you think your concept of love is accurate or does it need some adjustments? Can you easily express love to others as well as receive? If you have been damaged by love experiences, God can heal you. He can teach you what true and genuine love looks like. Talk to him about it today.

September 14

Today I encourage you to follow through on my suggestion to go back in time, remember, and honor those who have had great impact and influence on your life.

September 15

Do you have a good understanding of where we are in human history? Do you understand the times in which we are living? How is God asking you to respond?

September 16

We must be challenged to think about our thought life and where it takes us. Have you been diligent in managing your thoughts? When we allow the Holy Spirit to stand guard over our minds, we avoid all kinds of disaster.

September 17

When circumstances lay you out flat to whom or what do you turn? You have probably heard the adage, *"Run to the throne, not the phone."* I find that to be a wise piece of advice. When in distress, always have the million-dollar question on your lips, *"God, what is it you are trying to teach me?"*

September 18

Have you invited the Lord into every aspect of your life? Are there things you withhold? Do you believe he knows all about those closed doors of your heart? Since you are fully known and fully loved by him, why not open up and let him in?

September 19

In our times God has appointed pastors, ministers and priests to preside over his church. I hope you have a shepherd who is faithful to the Lord and his people. If you are blessed with a godly man or woman leading you and his church, why not tell him so. Write, text or call him with appreciation and Christian love. They will be pleased and so will God.

September 20

Think about a past trial that eventually turned into a blessing. What are you going through right now? Would you be willing to express gratitude to God for the blessing he has in store for you at the end of this trial? Open your heart and watch for it.

September 21

Do you enjoy planning for the future? When you devise those plans do you submit them to the Lord? The Word tells us that man makes his plans but the Lord guides his steps. I challenge us to always take our plans to God and to hold them loosely, allowing room for him to make adjustments.

September 22

Do thoughts of a heavenly future spur you on to be an overcomer? Jesus has already secured our victory. We need only to walk in it. We overcome by his power and his victory. Think about that area of your life where you are stumbling, rise up, victorious one. God will help you.

September 23

God wants you to know that you are a favored child. When storms assail us, we have not lost his love. It is often in those storms where he can prove himself the faithful and loving Father that we need.

September 24

Are you feeling forgotten, overlooked, neglected? Those are common to the human experience. But God, in his great love and concern for you, never misses even one of your heartbeats. He knows you through and through and all that concerns you concerns him.

September 25

How are you stewarding your freedom in Christ? Are you giving those around you the freedom to be who they are? Let's evaluate our choices today to see if they are benefiting both ourselves and others.

September 26

Are you sometimes brought down by living day-to-day? Do you feel insignificant and small at times? Cheer up. God has great purpose in every moment of your life. Enjoy every moment of this day to the fullest. That pleases God.

September 27

Judging another can be so subtle. Let's begin to be more aware of those times when we are passing judgment, but call it by different name. Being honest, I need to practice this awareness and so do you.

September 28

Are the women who surround you growing in grace and becoming more Christ-like? Do they draw you to Jesus? All women are not safe for us; some can bring us down. Let's evaluate our relationships to see if we need to make some changes. We will become like the people with whom we associate.

September 29

Are you married, divorced, single or widowed? Are you content in your current state? If not, what would you like to change? Pray about that today as you carefully read 1 Corinthians 7 and allow God to speak to you. He loves you and has wonderful plans for you.

September 30

Pray for a hurting friend today. After praying for her, put feet on your compassion. An unexpected gift, phone call or visit can do wonders in helping your friend feel seen and heard. Above all else, leave her with a sense of hope. Be creative today as God shows you who he wants you to bless.

October 1

You have been promised a kingdom, an everlasting kingdom. Do some comparison today between the earthly kingdom that we now know and the kingdom of heaven to come.

October 2

If you were asked to put a label on your heart, how would it read? Is it fearful, suspicious, or wounded? Today, spend time with the Lord and allow him to reveal the condition of your heart. He desires a heart at rest and filled with peace. Begin the journey.

October 3

Let's be honest, it's hard to be still. If you struggle with waiting on God in quietness and stillness, don't be overwhelmed. Begin with small manageable steps. I think as you practice His presence, it will be so rewarding. He just wants to be with you.

October 4

Are you suffering under the consequences of past sin? Do you believe you are forgiven? Do you recognize that living with consequences does not mean you are not forgiven? Sort through some of those feelings today and allow God to comfort you as you work through this rough place.

October 5

Is there a brother or sister in Christ who is hurting at this time? Are you able to lessen their burden in any way? Is so; do it today. If all you can do is pray, don't underestimate the power of a heartfelt prayer.

October 6

Are you willing to take a serious look at your inner expectations? Will they truly fill and satisfy you once attained? Are there any ways in which you need to take a closer look at your heart's desires? Are you willing to allow God to meet your every expectation in him?

October 7

Think about the people you know who are sitting in darkness, without Christ. You and I are called to be ambassadors in this world, representing our King. Let's do it well. Perhaps one lost sheep will see the light of truth we hold out before her.

October 8

The hand that created you also holds all of your days. When we commit our plans to the Lord's will, they will succeed. Is there any area of your life you are withholding from the hands of a trustworthy God? Are you willing to open them and commit all to him?

October 9

Do you sometimes feel that your bucket is empty? What do you think it will take to fill it? Jesus offers the only cure for sin and condemnation. He offers it in the person of himself. Take a good long drink of that Living Water today.

October 10

What season of life are you in right now? If you are resting or shouting from the mountain top, I am glad for you. If you are in the valley of hard places and struggle, you are also in a good place. This is where you can be stretched and where your faith can grow.

October 11

Who is the person in your life who knows you better than anyone else? What emotions rise up in you when you think about the Lord knowing you through and through? We can rest in that truth because the One who knows us best loves us most.

October 12

Do you feel healthy spiritually? Of the disciplines mentioned in today's devotion, is there an area where you feel you could move up a step? Challenge yourself today for a healthier spirit tomorrow.

October 13

How do you define "feelings"? How have you been defining faith? Do you rely more on your feelings than on God's Word? What changes need to be made?

October 14

How do you respond to today's reading? Like me, I hope you are awestruck at the revelation that God did for you what you could have never done for yourself. He raised you from the dead!

October 15

How much thought do you give to the influence you have in your world? Do you believe that your influence is basically good? If so, that's commendable; keep striving for even greater influence.

October 16

Where are you in life? Can you see the Lord's hand at work in your circumstances? Find scripture that supports the truth of how God's faithful hand is on you and meditate on those realities.

October 17

Today is a good day to evaluate our thoughts, places we go and the people with whom we go. What are we watching, reading and listening to? All of these activities will determine our destiny.

October 18

Does today's reading stir up a hunger for the sweetness of God's Word? Today go above and beyond the scriptures listed and read an entire chapter.

October 19

Let's each evaluate our Christian walk using the standards Paul gives to Titus. Look at those attributes and see if there are any that stand out to you. Are you willing to work on at least one this week?

October 20

I sincerely hope you have a friend who is doing life with you. Why not call her or write her a note expressing your appreciation for her loyal friendship. If you do not have that special friend, ask God to send someone special into your life.

October 21

You are either coming out of a storm, in a storm or heading toward one. Be sure of this beloved, God is in every storm with you. He goes before you to prepare for you treasures in the darkness. He walks beside you and holds you along the way.

October 22

Think about the scariest situation you ever encountered. If you were to tell the story today, how did it end? Are you able to say that you now can see how the Lord's hand was with you and upon you to bring you out?

October 23

Think about how diligent you are over your physical well-being. Can you honestly say you are as diligent in spiritual discipline? If you are not as consistent as you would like, consider asking a trusted friend to help you remain faithful in your spiritual journey.

October 24

What struck you most about today's devotion? Are there some ways in your thinking which may need an adjustment? Do you believe God is good and is able to guide you into the future he has planned for you? Are you willing to let go of the reins and give him control?

October 25

Do world events cause you discomfort? As we see Jesus' prophesies coming to pass, what kind of people ought we to be? More than ever, let us be about the Lord's business in our corner of the world, praying and being his faithful witnesses.

October 26

Have you been growing in the grace and knowledge of the Lord Jesus? Do you see the importance of doing that in the light of where our world is headed? Take some steps today to determine where you may need to shore up those spiritual deficits in your life.

October 27

Like me, you have been praying for your unsaved loved ones. Has today's reading impacted the way you will pray for them? It sure has affected my prayers. Together let's trust God for those loved ones who need him.

October 28

Today is a good day for us to think about what we treasure is and where it lies. Relationship over possessions is Jesus' constant theme. Are we placing more value on people than we are on things? Along with me, I hope you are honest about your earthly sand castles.

October 29

Let's be all that God calls us to be in these last days. Let's bring comfort and hope to those who are fearful and without hope in this world. As we ask God, he will show us who needs our encouragement and who needs to see our unswerving faith.

October 30

I challenge us to read Psalm 23 in light of today's reading. Read slowly through the Psalm, thinking of Jesus and how much he loves you. Personalize the Psalm and make it your loving response to God.

October 31

As we approach these important words of Jesus in Matthew 5, let's open our hearts to any correction, exhortation or encouragement the Lord may have for us.

November 1

I hope you have a better understanding of what Jesus meant by being poor in spirit. Are there any ways in which you need to evaluate any pride that may be lurking in your heart?

November 2

Is there something in your life that needs to be laid before the Lord. He waits on us to bring all the mess to him. He alone is able to forgive and cleanse. Let him comfort you today in your grief and repentance.

November 3

How do you define meekness? Has your perspective changed after reading today's devotion? I love that God always clarifies his spoken Word. Let's pray for the biblical meekness that Jesus portrays.

November 4

Is there anything that you can do to be more righteous before God? The answer is "no." That's right; you and I are perfectly righteous before God because of what Christ did on the cross. However, let's think about those areas where we may not be walking out righteous living. Hand-in-hand with the Lord we can be overcomers in every way.

November 5

Has someone hurt you? Do you desire to get even or have your revenge? Perhaps you just cancelled them out of your life. Are you willing to take another look at Matthew 5:7 and ask the Lord for a fresh look at any situations in your life that call for mercy?

November 6

Do you seek after purity? A pure heart is a lifelong endeavor. If you have never prayed for a pure heart, today would be a good day to begin that journey. If you have been pursuing a pure heart, be encouraged, God is faithful to finish the work he began in you.

November 7

How has your heart responded to today's reading? Is there someone in your life who needs to know the peace that only Christ can give? Share the good news of peace with her. Is there someone with whom you need to make peace? Go to her today and be a true daughter of God.

November 8

Do you pray for the persecuted church around the world? If you need help understanding what our fellow Christians are suffering in other countries, check out one of the ministries that report on the persecuted church around the world. We cannot afford to pretend severe persecution does not exist.

November 9

When was the last time you were reviled or ridiculed for your faith in Christ? It is not a matter of if you will be, but when. We must be prepared to respond as Jesus calls us to respond, in love and gentleness.

November 10

As we come to the conclusion of the Lord's teaching on the beautiful attitudes, let's move forward in our endeavor to please the One who saved us by his grace and mercy.

November 11

My hope is that we have a healthy understanding of conviction, condemnation and contrition. If you are harboring any condemnation over past sin, take it to the Lord today and receive your freedom in his full forgiveness.

November 12

I challenge each of us to view God's word as a mirror in which we see ourselves as God sees us. Look for the ways in which we need to be corrected; also look for the encouragement he gives.

November 13

Believe that God is using you in wonderful ways, even when you do not perceive it. When you recognize ways that God is using you, record it in your journal as future encouragement.

November 14

We know that God speaks in a myriad of ways. Begin to journal the experiences when you know that God has spoken specifically to you through his word, nature or a message you hear. This will be so encouraging during those times when you feel God is silent.

November 15

Is heaven a reality for you? How often do you think about your forever home? Make it a habit of the heart to indulge in imagining the glorious future God has waiting for you. Jesus is making all the preparations for us.

November 16

God loves to bless us. What are some of your hopes for heaven? Take some time this week to talk to God about your thoughts on eternal life. Thank him now for what he has waiting for you.

November 17

The time has come in the history of the church for God's people to be joyful givers. I challenge us today to put aside a portion of surplus and pray about someone you know who has a need. When you give the gift, let your heart fill up with laughter because God will be singing over you.

November 18

Today is a good day to do an honest evaluation of the depth of our relationship with Jesus Christ. Rate your relationship with him on a scale of 1 to 10. Now think of some ways you can deepen your knowledge and understanding of God.

November 19

We all believe things that are not true. Let's look closely at things we believe about ourselves and see if they line up with what God says. If you need help with this, do a search for verses that tell you who you are in Christ.

November 20

Let's be a grateful people today and every day. We have much to be thankful for, beginning with the grace of God that saved us. We also thank him for the gift of eternal life, and everything in between salvation and redemption.

November 21

Does doubt have a place in your life? Thomas, Jesus' doubting disciple, received grace from Jesus in his questioning. He has the same grace for us today in our uncertainties. Take all your misgivings to the One who can open your understanding.

November 22

Take time to think about your unique temperament and personality. How would that look when sharing your faith with others? Talk to the Lord about this and he will be faithful to open doors for you that will feel comfortable and fit you well.

November 23

Crowns were created for royalty. In God's kingdom we are all sons and daughters of the King. Let's walk worthy of that calling, not in pride, but in everlasting gratitude to the One who crowns us with life and honor.

November 24

Are you plagued by strongholds from your past? God has given you a brand new start and a brand new identity. Seek out scripture that tells you who you are in Christ Jesus. A daughter of God need never live under her old identity.

November 25

Can you relate to unfaithful Gomer? Is there something in your life that needs God's restorative touch? When we are unfaithful, God remains faithful. Embrace the truth of his faithful unfailing love and believe that it is for you and it is for now.

November 26

As you read God's Word for the next week, seek out those verses of encouragement and allow the Lord to applaud your successes. Balance encouragement with the correction God gives.

November 27

My challenge today is to commit Psalm 139 to heart. This very intimate Psalm is extremely personal and it is true for each one of us. What a beautiful reminder that we are the beautiful creation of the great Creator.

November 28

What place do money and possessions have in your life? When you pray, what do you ask for most? Our prayers are good indicators of what is going on in our hearts. Are there any adjustments that need to be made in your priorities?

November 29

Discerning the Lord's guidance is not always easy. I find that as I seek him early every morning, I am much more apt to be in the right place at the right time as my day progresses. Are you looking to the Lord at the start of each day so you can give him room to guide your steps? If not, why not start today?

November 30

Do you recognize the conviction of the Holy Spirit when it comes? How are you responding to conviction in your life? If you need help in this arena, God is more than pleased to help you cultivate a willing heart and listening ears.

December 1

Are you aware of God's correction in your life? How does it make you feel when you are rebuked? I urge you not to shy away from the Lord's discipline. Let's accept correction as another aspect of a Father's love.

December 2

I hope you have someone in your life who affirms and encourages you. If not, God will provide if only you ask. Has a dear friend of yours passed on to be with the Lord? Think about her today and thank God for the important part she played in your life.

December 3

Today I challenge you to sit in the presence of the Lord and allow the full weight of your concerns to rest on him. You need not speak a word; he knows what troubles you. Be still; be quiet in the place where only two can be. He will meet you there. That's a promise!

December 4

Think about the season of life you are currently enjoying. Do you have goals for the current year, the next five years or the next ten? Is your heart willing to believe that as long as you have breath God will give you the strength to serve him in some way? Why not sit with him today and map out some future goals.

December 5

The Word exhorts us to exam whether we are in the faith. We need to be sure we will be counted among the sheep when Jesus begins to separate. Let's check our motives in all we do and say in the name of the Lord.

December 6

Are you aware of your weaknesses? If so, this is a strength. Jesus is drawn to the fragile and lowly; he is put off by the proud and self-sufficient. Let's examine our lives today to determine if there are any ways we are building our own castles.

December 7

Let's examine our desire to be in "the know." Think about the times this behavior caused you grief or anxiety. God wants us to lead a quiet and peaceful life. I challenge you to trust that God will let you in on all that pertains to you and your loved ones.

December 8

Think carefully about every word you speak today. Weigh your words carefully before you launch them into the ears of others. Meditate on today's scriptures and make good choices with your words.

December 9

Have you been trying to obey God in every area only to fall flat? I hope you are seeing that God instructs us one step at a time. In what areas do you struggle most with obedience? God is right there to help you.

December 10

How do you respond to those who oppose you? I challenge you today to ask a trusted friend how he or she views the way we handle conflict. We also need to think about how we react in an escalated situation when only God sees.

December 11

Are you sometimes ashamed of your weaknesses? Jesus is never ashamed of you and if you will allow him, he will turn your weaknesses into your greatest strengths.

December 12

Call upon a few good friends who know how to laugh and have fun. Get together for a joke telling session, a funny movie or just to reminisce about the fun adventures you have had together. It will do your body good.

December 13

Is there something or someone in your life who needs to be surrendered to the Lord? Let's have the same mind as Christ when he prayed to the Father, *"Not my will, but your will be done."*

December 14

What's the cup of cold water you hold in your hand today? Are you willing to pour it out as an offering to the Lord? Remember, all you do today in his name matters.

December 15

Have you ever felt frightened and alone? Think about some past experiences when you felt God's presence and protection over you. Do you believe he can do it again?

December 16

Every prophecy in scripture has been fulfilled or will be fulfilled sometime in the future. God means all that he says and he says what he means. How does this speak to you today as you wait for God to work on your behalf?

December 17

I hope this Christmas season finds you doing well and that your soul is prospering. For some however, this may not be the case. I encourage all of us to focus on Jesus, God's indescribable gift. Wherever we may be emotionally, God sees and he cares.

December 18

Today I want to encourage each of us to remember those who are hurting at this time. Surely there is someone in our spheres of influence who is depressed, lonely and sorrowful of heart. How can we show the love of Christ to someone who needs him?

December 19

It's always the right time to perform an act of kindness. Be on high alert today for opportunities to do something good for someone. Then carry that kindness and generosity with you every day, everywhere you go.

December 20

No matter where you are in the stages of life, the body is perishing. Are you experiencing health issues that are out of your control? These are times of opportunity to be more reliant on the Lord. He will carry and sustain you through all circumstances. Trust him for that today.

December 21

What would *"slow down"* look like in your world? Do you practice quiet time on a daily basis? How could it benefit you if you built a *"slow down"* into your day? Do you need to make some changes for that to happen?

December 22

Do you have a favorite Christmas memory? Why not share it with someone today and ask her to share hers. It's good to remember the special times when God did something amazing.

December 23

Is there someone who is waiting for your forgiveness? Why not celebrate the gift of Jesus by imitating him in the act of forgiveness.

December 24

Jesus' death and resurrection was the greatest exchange ever offered to mankind … his righteousness for every sin we ever committed. If you have never considered receiving Christ as Lord and Savior, today can be your day to be born into the family of God. The choice is yours. I pray you choose life.

December 25

What were your Christmases like growing up? Now as a grown up, does Christmas morning look different for you? Think about some ways you and your family can make Christmas an even more meaningful celebration. From me to you today, may your Christmas be most blessed.

December 26

Is there a sin that is holding you captive? Go to a trusted friend today and confess. We are to confess our sins to one another that we may be healed.

December 27

God truly inhabits the praises of his children. Let's exalt his name all through this day and bring to him the praise he deserves.

December 28

Do you lean more toward seeing what is wrong in your world, or focus more on the things that are going well? Now is a good time to evaluate our attitudes and how we view evil in our world verses God's goodness.

December 29

Do you tend to compare your lot in life with that of others? Contentment is essential to a Christian's sense of well-being. Comparison will always leave you feeling discontented. Evaluate your level of contentment to see if any adjustments need to be made.

December 30

Dwell on today's scriptures and receive the Lord's abiding love. Believe that you can never be separated from his loving care.

December 31

Are you excited about a new beginning? Are you willing to leave last year's mistakes and failures behind? Reach out today toward God and He will amaze you as you continue your spiritual race. Set some goals today, commit them to the Lord and He will meet you on the journey.

Notes

All scripture is from the *New International Version* unless otherwise stated.

February 3

Song *I Don't Mind Waiting* by Juanita Bynum 2006; Flow Records

February 19

Quote by Soren Kierkegaad; 1813–1855

March 9

Song *Sea of Love* written by John Philip Baptiste; released 1959

March 11

Quote by Charles Haddon Spurgeon; 1834–1892

March 30

Quote by G.K. Chesterton; 1874–1936

March 31

Definition, Merriam-Webster.

April 2

Quote by Brene' Brown

April 4

Article A Polygamist Cult's Last Stand: The Rise and Fall of Warren Jeffs, By Jesse Hyde; February 2016.

April 8

Definition from Oxford Languages.

April 15

Stats from the Bureau of Labor Statistics.

Stats from American Bible Society.

April 21

Quote from the book *A Tale of Two Cities*, March 1859
written by Charles Dickens; 1812–1870

May 1

Song *Be Careful What You See*, Zondervan Music Publishers, 1956

May 4

Movie *Inside Out*, 2015 by Peter Docter.

May 23

Stats; Cold Case Homicide Stats Project.

June 5

Song *From a Distance*, written in 1985 by Julie Gold; recorded by Bette
Midler; 1990.

June 10

Movie *Snow White and the Seven Dwarfs,* 1937, by Walt Disney
Productions and released by RKO Radio Pictures.

June 15

Quote from *The Declaration of Independence*; originally written by
Thomas Jefferson. Benjamin Franklin and John Adams. The final draft
of the Declaration of Independence was adopted on July 4, 1776, but the
actual signing of the final document was on August 2, 1776.

June 16

Song *That'll Be the Day* Buddy Holly and Jerry Addison for the 1957
That'll Be the Day (album).

July 17

Quote by William Faulkner 1897–1962.

July 20

Definition *"taste"* and *"good"* from Oxford Languages.

August 12

Poem *Footprints in the Sand*; Margaret Fishback Powers, and Owen & Williamson; 1963; Ltd., Brooks & Bentley.

August 15

Poem *Loneliness* by Margaret Slabach.
Quote *Loneliness* by Princess Diana; 1961–1997.

August 16

Song *Detour* written by Paul Westmoreland 1945.

August 19

Book *Though None go with Me* Jerry Jenkins; 2009 Zondervan.

August 27

Cartoonist Hank Ketcham; 1920–2001; *Dennis the Menace* 1951.

September 26

Definition *"common"* from Oxford Languages.
Song *His Eye Is on the Sparrow*; written in 1905 by lyricist Civilla D. Martin and composer Charles H. Gabriel.

October 2

Quote by Aurelius Augustinas Hippomenes; 354–430.

November 23

Quote by William Shakespeare; 1564–1616.

December 2

Song *I Can Only Imagine*; Bart Millard, 1999; released on October 12, 2001; Label: INO/Curb.

CPSIA information can be obtained
at www.ICGtesting.com
Printed in the USA
JSHW020803050223
37135JS00007B/1

9 781664 273023